Diasozo!

The Ministry of Controversy, and the Great Healing

D1525992

Dave Fiedler

Also by Dave Fiedler
Hindsight (Lessons from Seventh-day Adventist Church History)
d'Sozo (The rise and essential role of Adventist medical missionary work)
Tremble (Kellogg's apostasy and its contemporary echoes)
Tactics (Lucifer's rebellion and the Lord's response)

© 2024 by Dave Fiedler
dfiedler@AdventistCityMissions.org

To all who are tired of kneeling to drink and punching at the air.

About the Cover: They say a picture's worth a thousand words. In this case, it's more like it might take a thousand words to explain it. It seems like I've spent that many hours on it, too.

Illustrating "the great healing" isn't as simple as it might look. I started off with a single woman in Biblical dress, reaching to touch the hem of Christ's garment. Naturally, everyone thought of *the* woman who did that as Jesus was walking to the home of Jairus, the ruler of the Capernaum synagogue. The only problem is, that's the wrong story. The word *diasozo* isn't used in that account. And when it is used, it's describing the actions of many people. Besides, the focus of the book isn't ancient history; it's more focused on coming events.

So... more creative (and generally unproductive) AI image generation prompts. *Hundreds* more. (I'll tell you, those things aren't as smart as the advertising makes them sound.) And along the way, I decided to switch to modern clothes, since that's more in keeping with the book.

But, how to illustrate "the ministry of controversy"? The old inquisition torture pictures were just a turn-off, and most everything connected to the whole 666 branding looked kind of kitsch (*thank you, Hollywood*). I finally settled on the "Chaos Star," with its eight arrows representing freedom to head in any direction one might wish. The symbol is barely sixty years old, but it has been adopted by a wide range of movements and organizations advocating for unrestrained freedom. These include groups that focus on magic, politics, role playing games, punk rock, and many more reservoirs of rebellion. Basically, it is a graphical representation of Alistair Crowley's famous summation of occult teaching, "Do what thou wilt."

Diasozo:

1) to preserve through danger, to bring safely through
   1a) to save, i.e. cure one who is sick, bring him through
2) to save, keep from perishing
3) to save out of danger, rescue

When the men of Gennesaret recognized Jesus, they sent out into all that surrounding region, brought to Him all who were sick, and begged Him that they might only touch the hem of His garment. And as many as touched it were _made perfectly well_. Matthew 14:34–36

The Roman commander called for two centurions, saying, "Prepare two hundred soldiers, seventy horsemen, and two hundred spearmen to go to Caesarea at the third hour of the night; and provide mounts to set Paul on, and _bring him safely_ to Felix the governor." Acts 23:23–24

Table of Contents

Yes, this is an Introduction...

but the couple of minutes you can save by skipping it are not worth the risk of being hopelessly confused, so slow down and get oriented before diving into the book!

ELLEN White once used an illustration that I've always liked. She said that, "Some minds are more like an old curiosity shop than anything else." I resonate with that description, since I'm a bit of an information junkie who can imagine practical value in just about any scrap of knowledge available.

But this comparison wasn't written as a compliment. She goes on to say that "many odd bits and ends of truth have been picked up and stored away there; but they know not how to present them in a clear, connected manner." And that's a problem. Clarity is a wonderful trait, built to a degree on precision, but even more so on what she identifies next:

> It is the relation that these ideas have to one another that gives them value. Every idea and statement should be as closely united as the links in a chain. When a minister throws out a mass of matter before the people for them to pick up and arrange in order, his labors are lost; for there are few who will do it.[1]

I've never been "a minister," but I am a teacher and an author, and much the same happens in the classroom as in the church. Connections matter; relationships matter. Giving a long lecture on some profound idea, without actually tying the parts and pieces together, is a waste of everybody's time. It's even more true when you switch over to words on a page. At least the student can try to put things together from the teacher's body language and tone of voice. The reader doesn't have those clues, so expository writing without well connected ideas is virtually guaranteed to land him in a swamp pretty quickly.

---

1. *Review and Herald*, April 6, 1886

That's no insignificant concern with this present volume. There are a lot of details that fit together to make a single surprisingly simple picture. It's a good balance, because too much detail would make the whole business seem contrived, and too much "simplicity" would make it all seem like wishful thinking with no basis in fact.

But we've got a big topic. To cover any single detail to the utmost degree, and then move on to do the same with the next point, and the next, would be tedious. Besides, it would take forever to get across enough of a picture to keep the reader interested. Uninterested readers soon become unimpressed ex-readers, and there's nothing quite so futile as writing a book that no one will read.

For all these reasons, you will find that this volume is more than a little recursive. That just means that one view of an important point from some particular angle, will be followed by a view of the same from another angle. The goal is to keep the interest up with new material, while keeping sight of what has been covered before, so as to maintain those all-important connections intact. If there is any detriment from this, it would be the repetition of some aspects which must naturally occur. So, please keep this in mind, and look for the new elements in each chapter until the full picture comes into view.

Before we go charging down that road, however, a quick look in the rear view mirror will be helpful to some readers. This volume's title is admittedly a possible source of confusion, due to its similarity to *d'Sozo*, a book I wrote about a dozen years ago.

Think of them as "companion volumes." Both titles are related to a Greek root, *sozo*. The first, *d'Sozo*, is a "portmanteau"[2] of the Latin prefix "de," meaning "from" or "of," and the Greek root. The word came to life first as the name of a vegan restaurant that was the "center of influence" for a city mission program.

Diasozo, on the other hand is a "real" Greek word, the definition of which you may have already seen just before the table of contents.

For those wondering about the relationship between the two books, the primary distinction is that *d'Sozo* focuses on the playing out of *sozo* principles within Seventh-day Adventist history, whereas this volume embraces the larger picture of the great controversy as a whole.

I sincerely hope that any time you spend with either will be a blessing.

—*Dave Fiedler*
April 2024

---

2. "A word made by combining the spellings and meanings of two or more other words or word parts." merriam-webster.com/dictionary/portmanteau
   To the millennial generation, it would be known as a "mash-up."

CHAPTER 1

After the Pattern

GOD told Moses—four times—that every detail of the wilderness sanctuary was to be constructed after the pattern he had been shown when they met together on Mount Sinai. We find these verses in Exodus 25, 26, and 27:

According to all that I show you, that is, the pattern of the tabernacle and the pattern of all its furnishings, just so you shall make it.[1]

And see to it that you make them according to the pattern which was shown you on the mountain.[2]

And you shall raise up the tabernacle according to its pattern which you were shown on the mountain.[3]

You shall make it hollow with boards; as it was shown you on the mountain, so shall they make it.[4]

Twice—in Exodus 36 and 38—we are told that God had given special wisdom to the artisans of Israel to make all that the Lord had commanded.[5] In chapter 39, they went to work, making every item and every detail "as the Lord had commanded Moses." In fact, this phrase is repeated ten times in that one chapter![6] Chapter 40 tells the story of putting all the parts and pieces together. Again, everything was to be done "as the Lord had commanded Moses"—and just so we don't miss the point, we are told so eight

---

1. Exodus 25:9
2. Exodus 25:40
3. Exodus 26:30
4. Exodus 27:8
5. Exodus 36:1; 38:22
6. Exodus 39:1, 5, 7, 21, 26, 29, 31, 32, 42, 43

more times![7] That's the last chapter in the book, but when we get to Leviticus 7–9, the same idea is repeated another fourteen times.[8] It's almost like God was trying to make a point.

This book aims to make a similar point. Put bluntly, that would be something along the lines of: "Ellen White's book, *The Ministry of Healing,* is the pattern we need to follow in order to successfully finish the work of taking the three angels' messages to 'every nation, tribe, tongue, and people' and meet the challenges outlined in her more famous book, *The Great Controversy.*"

Remember, that's the blunt version of the claim, and just like in daily life, speaking bluntly can be both good and bad. Sometimes it helps people grasp an idea quickly, but it can also leave a lot of questions and misunderstandings. In this case, there is one obvious issue that we should look at right away. The main source of this confusion is the idea that *The Ministry of Healing* is a book for just doctors and nurses. Since *The Great Controversy* is a book for the whole church, most of whom work in fields other than health care, how could the one be the pattern for the other?

Many have read the title and concluded that *Ministry of Healing* has little or no relevance for them because they are not health care professionals. I did exactly that when it was first brought to my attention.

Even more dangerous is the risk that some people who are—or would like to become—health care professionals, will think that "health care" as defined and practiced by the world is the long-sought key to finishing "God's work on earth."

As a general rule, these misunderstandings come from an incomplete concept of medical missionary work, the great controversy, or both. This book aims to address this confusion by exploring and expanding the way we look at the message of *Ministry of Healing* and *Great Controversy;* by putting medical missionary work into the context of the whole great controversy; and by bringing that controversy back down to earth enough so that we can see its most basic issues in the setting of our daily lives.

In all this, the goal is to see the importance and breadth of the three angels' messages. They are, after all, the primary focus of God's work at this time.

> This is the message of present truth. The first, second, and third angels' messages are to be proclaimed at this time. These messages are not to be eclipsed by any other fancied specialties. Their force and efficiency are to continue as long as time is given for repentance.[9]

That issue of breadth is significant, since progress in this area has been called for:

---

7. Exodus 40:16, 19, 21, 23, 25, 27, 29, 32
8. Leviticus 7:38; 8:4, 5, 9, 13, 17, 21, 29, 36; 9:5–7, 10, 21
9. E.G. White, "Diary: I thank my heavenly Father," March 3, 1901; Manuscript 22, 1901

In these last days it is our duty to ascertain the full meaning of the first, second, and third angels' messages.[10]

That's the balance that's needed. We want the "full meaning," without any "fancied specialties" to distract. Striking that balance is where the guidance of *Ministry of Healing* and *Great Controversy* need to be combined. That will be more clearly seen as we work through the "full meaning," but first, let's swat away those misconceptions about the role of church members, and the worldly concept of medicine:

We have come to a time when every member of the church should take hold of medical missionary work.[11]

The medical missionary work is work that all who will may undertake.... The prosperity of our churches in every locality depends on the co operation of the members with Jesus Christ.... He is only waiting for channels through whom He can work.[12]

When the Lord specified that there should be a health and temperance institution at Battle Creek, He also specified what should be its object. It was not to be fashioned after the character of any other institution in the world.[13]

Medical missionary work is included in the work of the gospel ministry. This is God's plan. No medical fraternity is complete without the gospel ministry.[14]

If the recommendation goes forth from our people that our workers are to seek for success by acknowledging as essential the education which the world gives, we are virtually saying that the influence the world gives is superior to that which God gives. God will be dishonored by such a course.[15]

I ask you to study the 40th to the 42nd chapters of Isaiah. If you will do this prayerfully and carefully, you will receive instruction that will teach you that you need not dishonor God by putting into the minds of students a desire for a worldly education. Men and women bring reproach upon God when they place human instructors before the teachings of the God of heaven. Oh that our people would come to their senses and follow the instruction of their Maker![16]

In place of the world's approach to medicine, the Lord has a pattern, a plan, a method, that He intends to use to wrap up the great controversy.

The whole universe of heaven is looking upon this earth while the great conflict is being carried on between Christ, the Prince of life, and Satan, the prince of the world. And the same conflict was taken up by His disciples when Christ left our world, so

---

10. E.G. White, "Revelation," April 27, 1896; Manuscript 15, 1896

11. *Testimonies*, vol. 7, 62

12. E.G. White, "Notes of the Work During the Week of Prayer," June 16, 1898; Manuscript 77, 1898

13. E.G. White, "Revelation," April 27, 1896; Manuscript 15,1896

14. E.G. White, Letter to J.H. Kellogg, September 23, 1904; Letter 289, 1904

15. E.G. White, Letter to J.A. Burden, November 5, 1909; Letter 140, 1909

16. E.G. White, Letter to J.E. and Emma White, June 16, 1909; Letter 98, 1909

that we are to work and carry the plan of the battle and the contest after Christ's devising, after the pattern.[17]

The principles and outline of this pattern are found in many places, the Bible chief among them. But we are blessed with one exceptionally clear presentation of the principles and practices He is calling for. It's called *The Ministry of Healing*. And, amazingly, it focuses on the central issue of the whole great controversy. That may not be clearly evident just yet, but it will come.

In the meantime, let's establish another perspective on this idea of a "pattern." There's an interesting expression, one that appears more than fifty times in Ellen White's writings, that will be useful to us in this regard: "As in the natural, so in the spiritual."

This was not an entirely new thought with her, of course. After all, Jesus used sheep, and wheat, and fish, and flowers to make His teaching clear. But we tend to think of all those as simply "illustrations." The sheep or wheat or fish or flowers aren't particularly important; they just serve as props for His teaching on the big theological issues.

Or do they? What if there were more to those "illustrations" than we've given them credit for?

This sort of question comes up more pointedly in Ellen White's case, perhaps, than in Jesus' use of nature. In Jesus' case, He simply used the things of nature to make His point. Ellen White, on the other hand, seems to have been given the task of helping our dull minds grasp the significance of Christ's approach. The direct statement of "as in the natural, so in the spiritual" is repeated more than fifty times, but it's her broader discussion of the principle embodied there that solidifies its importance. A quick review of her use of that "as in the natural, so in the spiritual" concept shows why:

The same principles run through the spiritual and the natural world.[18]

As in the natural world, so in the spiritual; God always honors the use of the means He has ordained to do His work.[19]

The Lord has closely connected the spiritual life of man with the plant life, which symbolizes the spiritual experience of all who are seeking to become members of the heavenly family, plants in the Lord's garden.[20]

In the natural world, God has placed in the hands of the children of men the key to unlock the treasure house of His word. The unseen is illustrated by the seen; divine wisdom, eternal truth, infinite grace, are understood by the things that God has

17. E.G. White, "Sermon: The Vine and the Branches," October 27, 1894; Manuscript 43, 1894
18. E.G. White, Letter to Brother and Sister W.W. Prescott, January 18, 1894; Letter 67, 1894
19. *Ellen G. White 1888 Materials*, 111
20. E.G. White, Letter to Brother and Sister G.C. Tenney, January 4, 1900; Letter 6, 1900

made. Then let the children and youth become acquainted with nature and nature's laws. Let the mind be developed to its utmost capacity and the physical powers trained for the practical duties of life.[21]

The parables uttered by our Lord have a significance which but few discern. Leading from the natural kingdom to the spiritual kingdom, they are links in the chain of truth that connects man with God and earth with heaven. Christ.... illustrated truth by natural things, that He might lead up to the high and eternal. He used humble representations, that He might place before the eyes of men the precious gems of truth. By this form of presenting truth, He was educating His disciples in regard to God's processes in the natural world....

All the similitudes presented by our Saviour from nature are God-given lessons. By the natural world God teaches the principles of His working in the spiritual kingdom. He who becomes a student of God's work in nature will soon learn the most precious lessons in regard to the spiritual kingdom.[22]

In short, those "props" that we've mostly ignored in the past, are important! The things and processes of nature depict the "same principles" as work in spiritual matters. They depict "the means [God] has ordained to do His work." While only "few discern" their significance, they are God's chosen means of teaching us about the "principles of His working in the spiritual kingdom."

Simply put, the way things get done in nature is the way things get done in spiritual matters as well.

We'll have cause to remember that, by and by.

---

21. *Counsels to Parents, Teachers, and Students*, 187
22. E.G. White, "Seed-Sowing," March 9, 1898; Manuscript 34, 1898

CHAPTER 2

The Ministry of Controversy

W HAT is the "ministry of controversy"? For our purposes just now, that phrase will refer to the impetus, the motivational power, of conflict. It has a fascination for us. It makes for gripping accounts of the bravery of that "cloud of witnesses" Paul spoke of. And the prospect of that conflict coming to our doors is sometimes the only thing that even comes close to waking us up to the realities of the overall drama of the war which began in heaven and now surrounds us all.

Here are a few notable descriptions of what seems likely to occur in the not-so-distant future:

> While appearing to the children of men as a great physician who can heal all their maladies, [Satan] will bring disease and disaster, until populous cities are reduced to ruin and desolation.[1]

> The ungodly cities of our world are to be swept away by the besom[2] of destruction. In the calamities that are now befalling immense buildings and large portions of cities God is showing us what will come upon the whole earth.[3]

> In the last scenes of this earth's history, war will rage. There will be pestilence, plague, and famine. The waters of the deep will overflow their boundaries. Property and life will be destroyed by fire and flood.[4]

Of course, some will observe that war, pestilence, plague, famine, fire, and floods are not new. Admittedly, this is true, but the frequency, the severity, the

---

1. *Great Controversy*, 589
2. A good Olde Englysh word found in the King James' rendition of Isaiah 14:23! It just means "broom," which explains why it's always sweeping things away.
3. *Testimonies*, vol. 7, 83
4. *Review and Herald*, October 19, 1897

sheer body count, and the financial losses are climbing. Just google "insurance payouts" if you're not convinced. On the other hand, some may believe that all this really bad stuff will all be part and parcel with the seven last plagues, so not of practical concern to "the righteous." But let's continue:

> The Lord gives warnings to the inhabitants of the earth, as in the Chicago fire and the fires in Melbourne, London, and the city of New York. When God's restraining hand is removed, the destroyer begins his work. Then in our cities the greatest calamities will come.[5]

The magnitude of the changes predicted can make it all seem like just a bad dream, but it is not wise to bet against inspiration. It's not always clear exactly what could be done to prepare, but God has warned us beforehand, probably for a good reason.

> I have been shown that most of the rising generation will be swept off by death prior to the time of trouble. Some will live, but most children of believing and unbelieving parents will be spared the day of trial for God's people.[6]

> The wrath of God is preparing to come upon all the cities—not all at once but one after another. And if the terrible punishment in one city does not cause the inhabitants of other cities to be afraid and seek repentance, their time will come.... The destruction will begin in certain places, and the destruction of life will be sudden and but few will escape.[7]

Since "seeking repentance" is still an option after this destruction has begun, it's clear that at least some of these disasters will be before the close of probation. In other words, there's still opportunity to win souls! There's another detail in these quotations that we won't take time to pursue right now, but it's worth noting that four of those five quotations used the word "city" or "cities." That's just a thought to be filed away for future reference.

The "ministry of controversy" is not new, of course. While that which is current or yet future holds a particular interest and importance for us, we can also trace its influence and progress through past ages, and on a much larger scale. Let's shift focus for a moment to look at a useful perspective on this universal drama unfolding around Lucifer's introduction of new principles for the consideration of all God's creation.

This thought will be more fully documented and discussed in the next chapter, but for now we can perhaps summarize the contrast between the two sets of principles like this: God said, "Trust Me, I will freely provide all that is truly for your good; I only ask that you make the good of others your first interest."

---

5. E.G. White, "God's Forbearance," November 22, 1897; Manuscript 127, 1897

6. E.G. White, Letter to Brother and Sister Van Horn, 1878; Letter 51a, 1878

7. E.G. White, "Diary: Corruption of the Cities and Unfaithful Shepherds," September 2, 1902; Manuscript 233, 1902

Lucifer's opposing position was: "God has placed other considerations above my best interest; for that, He cannot be trusted, and I must care for myself—at others' expense if need be."

How high were the stakes? Perhaps an illustration will help:

Pretend that one hundred people were stranded on a conveniently uninhabited tropical island. How would the new society structure itself? On one end of the spectrum is something like this: "Listen up, everyone! We've got to stick together for safety. Never leave camp without telling others, and never leave camp with less than a group of three. As long as we take care of each other, we'll all be OK."

On the other end of the spectrum is this: "This is bad. Who knows what sort of situation we're up against? And what do I know about all these people? I better get a club, maybe make a knife from some scrap metal. Need to be looking out for Number One."

Both scenarios are easy to imagine, and both approaches might actually work to keep someone alive....

Unless there is only enough food on the island to support twenty people. Then what? Simple human reason tells us that generosity becomes suicide for eighty people.

And so the question comes down to this: "Can I follow the Golden Rule in dealing with others and trust God to supply what I need for my best good, or am I better off reserving the right to take care of myself?"

To see this controversy playing out, let's start when Jesus was talking to the seventy disciples who had just come back from their missionary tour. They said, "Lord, even the demons are subject to us in Your name."

And Jesus said something a little strange. According to Luke, His first response was:

"I saw Satan fall like lightning from heaven."[8]

When did this happen? When did Satan fall like lightning from heaven? When he sinned and got kicked out, obviously. And any good Seventh-day Adventist would likely think of this passage:

And war broke out in heaven: Michael and His angels fought with the dragon; and the dragon and his angels fought, but they did not prevail, nor was a place found for them in heaven any longer. So the great dragon was cast out, that serpent of old, called the Devil and Satan, who deceives the whole world; he was cast to the earth, and his angels were cast out with him.[9]

8. Luke 10:18
9. Revelation 12:7–9

For convenience sake, let's call this "Stage One." That makes sense, really, because we're going to move on to "Stage Two" now. Notice this verse:

> Now is the judgment of this world; now the ruler of this world will be cast out.[10]

Again, these are Jesus' words, but on a different occasion. This was said just shortly before the crucifixion, and Jesus set it clearly in the future tense. We generally see the near-future "now" that He spoke of as the crucifixion. But that prompts us to ask if "cast out" in this verse is the same as the "cast out" in Revelation 12. If so, would that mean Revelation 12 is in some way speaking of the cross?

Maybe this will help:

> Christ bowed His head and died, but He held fast His faith and His submission to God. "And I heard a loud voice saying in heaven, Now is come salvation, and strength, and the kingdom of our God, and the power of His Christ: for the accuser of our brethren is cast down, which accused them before our God day and night." Rev. 12:10.[11]

Why is Ellen White quoting *that* verse when she's talking about the crucifixion? We just looked at verses 7–9 and saw the fall of Satan from heaven back before the creation of our world. How could the very next verse be talking about the crucifixion?

Don't worry, this next quotation will start to make sense of it.

> After the crucifixion.... Satan saw that his disguise was torn away, that the character he had tried to fasten on Christ was fastened on himself. It was as if he had the second time fallen from heaven.[12]

At the cross? The second time? It's like there is something about these two events—the fall of Satan in heaven and the death of Christ on the cross—that is so similar that inspired writers mix them all together. Fascinating!

Actually, Ellen White sometimes made the linkage even stronger:

> God... looked upon the victim expiring on the cross, and said, "It is finished. The human race shall have another trial." The redemption price was paid, and Satan fell like lightning from heaven.[13]

But he wasn't even *in* heaven then! How could he fall *from* heaven?

Let's move on to Stage Three, and some familiar verses. Indeed, we just read the first one a moment ago. Nevertheless, read them again and think of the big picture:

> Then I heard a loud voice saying in heaven, "Now salvation, and strength, and the kingdom of our God, and the power of His Christ have come, for the accuser of our

---

10. John 12:31
11. *Desire of Ages*, 761
12. E.G. White, "Our Substitute and Surety," October 7, 1897; Manuscript 111, 1897
13. *Youth's Instructor*, June 21, 1900

brethren, who accused them before our God day and night, has been cast down. And they overcame him by the blood of the Lamb and by the word of their testimony, and they did not love their lives to the death. Therefore rejoice, O heavens, and you who dwell in them! Woe to the inhabitants of the earth and the sea! For the devil has come down to you, having great wrath, because he knows that he has a short time."[14]

Notice the details:

1. The "accuser of our brethren" has been cast down.
2. A group of people have beaten the devil, but they put their lives at risk in the process.
3. Because they overcame, everyone in "the heavens" rejoices.
4. But everyone on "earth" and in the "sea" is in trouble because the devil is running out of time, and he's really mad about it.

Now just step back mentally, look at that sequence, and ask yourself, "What does this sound like? When is all this supposed to happen?"

Yes. You're right. It does sound like the time of the end. That's the way Ellen White used it here:

The apostle John in vision heard a loud voice in heaven exclaiming: "Woe to the inhabiters of the earth and of the sea! for the devil is come down unto you, having great wrath, because he knoweth that he hath but a short time." Revelation 12:12. Fearful are the scenes which call forth this exclamation from the heavenly voice. The wrath of Satan increases as his time grows short, and his work of deceit and destruction will reach its culmination in the time of trouble.[15]

So now we've got three separate historical episodes portrayed in Revelation chapter twelve. It may seem confusing, but hold on; it gets better!

Notice that group of people who will conquer the devil in the last days. For general purposes at least, we might call them the 144,000. Here's a statement that fits in with them right at this point. We don't have all the pieces in place yet to get this one locked into the puzzle properly, but it's worth a moment's thought anyway:

Satan... is an accuser of the brethren, and his accusing power is employed against those who work righteousness. The Lord desires through His people to answer Satan's charges by showing the results of obedience to right principles.[16]

The accusations of Satan are a big deal, as is the role of God's people; they will both come up again. And the "right principles" spoken of here are important, too. But let's just note that this process is accomplished through "show-

14. Revelation 12:10–12
15. *Great Controversy*, 623
16. *Christ's Object Lessons*, 296

ing" more than through "telling." And now we're circling around on our trail, to right where we started. But this time it's Stage Four!

> Like the apostles, the seventy had received supernatural endowments as a seal of their mission. When their work was completed, they returned with joy, saying, "Lord, even the devils are subject unto us through Thy name." Jesus answered, "I beheld Satan as lightning fall from heaven."

This is familiar, but notice what Ellen White sees in this occasion that we might not have:

> The scenes of the past and the future were presented to the mind of Jesus. He beheld Lucifer as he was first cast out from the heavenly places. He looked forward to the scenes of His own agony, when before all the worlds the character of the deceiver should be unveiled. He heard the cry, "It is finished" (John 19:30), announcing that the redemption of the lost race was forever made certain, that heaven was made eternally secure against the accusations, the deceptions, the pretensions, that Satan would instigate.
>
> Beyond the cross of Calvary, with its agony and shame, Jesus looked forward to the great final day, when the prince of the power of the air will meet his destruction in the earth so long marred by his rebellion. Jesus beheld the work of evil forever ended, and the peace of God filling heaven and earth.
>
> Henceforward Christ's followers were to look upon Satan as a conquered foe. Upon the cross, Jesus was to gain the victory for them; that victory He desired them to accept as their own. "Behold," He said, "I give unto you power to tread on serpents and scorpions, and over all the power of the enemy: and nothing shall by any means hurt you."[17]

Do you see all four stages of the process? The scenes of past and future? The order is jumbled a bit so they show up as 1, 2, 4, 3, but they're all there in a single place. Here's a chronological list:

1. 6,000 years ago—The members of the Godhead understood Satan's plans and arguments, and rejected them because Omniscience knew from all eternity the evil of sin.
2. 2,000 years ago—Angels and the inhabitants of the unfallen worlds understood Satan's plans and arguments, and rejected them because they saw the murderous character of Satan revealed at the cross.
3. Near future (hopefully)—The 144,000 will understand Satan's plans and arguments, and will reject them because "obedience to right principles" has prepared them to understand—and successfully resist—the fiercest temptations ever brought to mortal man.
4. 1,000 years later—The wicked will understand Satan's plans and arguments after seeing the course of Satan throughout the conflict with heaven, and they, too, will reject them.

---

17. *Desire of Ages*, 490

Because the need for this whole process is not understood, people often misunderstand the crucifixion and thus cause themselves a lot of confusion. This is where the whole "it's all done at the Cross" problem gets its start. We have plenty of reasons to be thankful for the understanding of the great controversy that has been entrusted to Adventism!

Controversy, conflict, catastrophe—it's potent stuff. It grabs our attention. But there is something annoying about presenting a problem... and stopping there without offering a solution! Fortunately, God doesn't do that to us. It would be wise to give some serious thought to His advice here.

> As religious aggression subverts the liberties of our nation, those who would stand for freedom of conscience will be placed in unfavorable positions. For their own sake, they should, while they have opportunity, become intelligent in regard to disease, its causes, prevention and cure. And those who do this will find a field of labor anywhere. There will be suffering ones, plenty of them, who will need help, not only among those of our own faith, but largely among those who know not the truth....
>
> In almost every church there are young men and women who might receive education either as nurses or physicians. They will never have a more favorable opportunity than now. I would urge that this subject be considered prayerfully, that special effort be made to select those youth who give promise of usefulness and moral strength. Let these receive an education at our sanitarium at Battle Creek, to go out as missionaries wherever the Lord may call them to labor. It should ever be kept before them that their work is not only to relieve physical suffering, but to minister to souls that are ready to perish.
>
> It is important that every one who is to act as a medical missionary be skilled in ministering to the soul as well as to the body. He is to be an imitator of Christ, presenting to the sick and suffering the preciousness of pure and undefiled religion. While doing all in his power to relieve physical distress and to preserve this mortal life, he should point to the mercy and the love of Jesus, the Great Physician.[18]

And that, right there, is the ministry of healing. What's more, that exact ministry is perfectly calculated to end the whole great controversy.

Well, that's easy to say... but if we're going to talk about "the whole great controversy," we need to go back to its beginning and understand what it's really all about.

---

18. E.G. White, Letter to Brother and Sister J.H. Kellogg, September 16, 1892; Letter 34, 1892

CHAPTER 3

In the Beginning...

L ET'S be clear on our starting point: the "beginning" we're talking about here is not the time when "God created the heavens and the earth."[1] Nor is it the time when "the Word was with God, and the Word was God."[2] Unfortunately, sandwiched in between those two "beginnings" is another one, the beginning of sin. This is the one Jesus was talking about when He said the devil "was a murderer from the beginning."[3]

This beginning is when the "mystery of lawlessness" got started.[4] Paul calls sin a mystery for a good reason: no one can explain it. Where did it come from? How did sin originate in a perfect universe? What could possibly lead the highest of all created beings to jump the rails? We don't know. We can't say. And we get ourselves into trouble every time we try to explain it. So let's not do that.

> We need not puzzle our minds for a reason why Satan acted as he did. Could a reason be found, there would be excuse for sin. But there is no excuse.[5]

But there's a difference between "the origin of sin" and "sin." The first is an event that we'll never understand. The second is a thing, and unfortunately we are all going to eventually understand every despicable detail of it. That wasn't God's plan, of course, but Adam and Eve made the mistake of signing up the whole human race—and, indirectly, the whole universe—for a very long, very sad, master's level class on the knowledge of good and evil.

---

1. Genesis 1:1
2. John 1:1
3. John 8:44
4. 2 Thessalonians 2:7
5. E.G. White, "Sin and Its Result," September 24, 1901; Manuscript 97, 1901

That's one aspect of what we call the great controversy. And as Seventh-day Adventists we are privileged far beyond all the patriarchs, prophets, church "fathers," and reformers of any previous age, to have not just a book by that title, but a vast range of knowledge explaining its whole history, both past and future. If you've read through the "Conflict of the Ages Series," you know what I'm talking about. If you haven't... please, get started!

If reading isn't your thing, listen to the audio versions, or hire someone else to read it to you. (There's a missionary opportunity for you! It might be a bit expensive, but getting anyone to read those books is a great idea, even if you have to pay them to do it!)

But, sadly, in processing the mass of information on that topic that we've been blessed to have, there has been a tendency to lose sight of the practical reality of the whole business. Since spiritual matters include an obvious element of the supernatural (God, angels, miracles, etc.), it becomes really easy to think of anything that we don't understand quickly, as "miraculous." The Bible does tell lots of stories about amazing events that are clearly beyond our ability to explain. Creation, the parting of the Red Sea, the feeding of the five thousand—these are all straight up miracles, at least as far as humanity is concerned. And it's not just the big ones. We can't even explain a bush that burns without burning up.

The downside to all this is that it's common for people to think of *all* religious matters in ways that defy any cause-to-effect analysis. We can easily end up thinking that spiritual things *just happen,* with no real connection to anything. In other words, *everything* that's "spiritual" moves into the realm of "superstition."

Don't react too negatively to that word. The root idea is just the belief that one event produces another event, even though there is no connection between the two. While a lot of superstitions are laughably dumb (think, bad luck from a black cat, and good luck from a rabbit's foot[6]), we can easily apply the same sort of "logic" to other, more important issues.

The point here is really simple, but tremendously important: spiritual results may be "miraculous," but they still work from cause-to-effect. The Bible changes lives (miracle enough!), but it does it by putting facts, ideas, and principles into the minds of those who read it. That's why Protestants reject infant baptism. That's the difference between Catholic "sacraments" like the "mass" or "last rites" and real conversion in which the Holy Spirit actually brings about a change of heart (usually, though not always[7]) through the influence of the story of Jesus' love.

---

6. That rabbit presumably started off with four feet, and look how much good that did him!

7. Some people will come up in the first resurrection without ever having heard the least bit about the God of the Bible. How does that work? The Holy Spirit managed to reach them through the influence of nature, and they responded to His leading, living out the principles of God's law.

\ The work of the Holy Spirit is both mysterious and miraculous; we can't explain it (and those who insist on trying, always get themselves into trouble). But we can see the connection, the channel, that the Spirit uses to produce the "new creature." Jesus outlines this in John 16 where He promises that the Holy Spirit will guide us "into all truth."

Could the Holy Spirit do His work without truth? No, because it is the truth that will set God's people free. There is a cause-and-effect working relationship that's important to understand. It goes like this: the Holy Spirit brings truth to the mind; the truth affects the mind; the mind controls the will and changes the life. Anything else is superstition, spiritual fairy dust; just sprinkle some on and everything is wonderful!

Hey! Wait a minute! Moses threw a bush into the water, and it was miraculously made sweet. Elisha tossed some salt into the stew, and it was miraculously made non-poisonous. Jesus put clay on blind eyes, and they were miraculously made whole. Are you saying that was all "fairy dust"?

No. Those were all physical examples—enacted parables if you wish—meant to teach deeper spiritual lessons of the power of God and our need to trust Him. It's at that deeper level—the one that we have such a hard time understanding—where the cause-and-effect nature of God's working is never violated. If it seems confusing for God to use undeniable miracles (events that happen with no discernible connection between cause and effect) to illustrate natural processes that *always* flow from cause to effect, consider the famous saying that "any sufficiently advanced technology is indistinguishable from magic."

The idea is that, when the cause-and-effect relationship of something is totally beyond a person's understanding, it will certainly look like pure magic. Imagine the impression a cell phone would make on a tribesman who has lived his whole life within the confines of stone-age technology. Without at least some basic familiarity with radio waves, CMOS sensors, printed circuit boards, electricity, batteries, plastic, and a few hundred other topics, that cell phone is going to appear magical. But it still works through cause-and-effect.

The plan of salvation is like that, too.

> The Lord Jesus is making experiments on human hearts through the exhibition of His mercy and abundant grace. He is effecting transformations so amazing that Satan with all his triumphant boasting, with all his confederacy of evil united against God and the laws of his government, stands viewing them as a fortress impregnable to his sophistries and delusions. They are to him an incomprehensible mystery. The angels of God, seraphim and cherubim, the powers commissioned to co-operate with human agencies, look on with astonishment and joy, that fallen men, once children of wrath, are through

the training of Christ developing characters after the divine similitude, to be sons and daughters of God, to act an important part in the occupations and pleasures of heaven.[8]

Notice that Satan finds salvation "incomprehensible." Even the good angels consider it "astonishing." The process of salvation is "sufficiently advanced" that understanding the details is still beyond their grasp. We're talking about a pretty amazing thing here!

And yet, despite all the amazement, there is a process, there is a cause which produces the effect. It is "through the exhibition of His mercy and abundant grace" (let's call this, "truth displayed for human viewing") that the "training of Christ" (the influence of truth on the mind) turns "the children of wrath" into the "sons and daughters of God" (by changing the choices made by the mind). In this realm, there is no fairy dust, because it is here that human beings come face to face with the perfect, immutable, unchangeable, eternal law of God.

And with that much understanding, we can get back to "the beginning," the part of the story that we're focused on just now.

> From the very beginning of the great controversy in heaven it has been Satan's purpose to overthrow the law of God.[9]

So, this obviously raises a question. What is the "law of God"? And the saints all respond, "The Ten Commandments." Of course. That's obvious. And yet, there are a few details that raise some questions. For starters, the fifth, seventh, and tenth commandments dealing with parents, non-spouses, and neighbors' spouses seem odd for a heavenly population of angels that "neither marry nor are given in marriage."

And then there's the Sabbath... which didn't even exist until earth's creation week. Hmm....

About now, you might begin to wonder how all of this qualifies as "perfect, immutable, unchangeable, and eternal." After all, why add a whole new requirement (Sabbath observance) to a law that's perfect? Wouldn't that be changing the law? How can that make sense with an unchangeable law?

Fair questions. But there's a difference between "changing" and "adapting." In fact, part of what makes the law perfect is that it can be adapted to anyone, anywhere, anytime—all without changing the law in the least! That may sound like some sort of word-game propaganda double-speak, but it's not. In the terminology the Spirit of Prophecy employs, to "change" is to eliminate or contradict a principle of the law; to "adapt" is to arrange for an appropriate application of the principle.

An illustration may help. In the Olympics, they have "hurdles" races; they have the same at your local junior high, but the hurdles aren't as tall. Why? Because the kids aren't Olympic athletes! They're just kids!

---

8. *General Conference Daily Bulletin*, February 27, 1893
9. *Great Controversy*, 582

The principle of the race is the same; the application of that principle is adapted appropriately for the setting. All of which sounds good, but points out the necessity of understanding the principle involved. Someone who isn't particularly observant might think that the central principle of the hurdles is that all the runners start at the same time, and the prize goes to the one who crosses the finish line first. All true. But that's not the unique nature of the hurdles. That's the same idea as for any race.

So... what *is* the law of God? For us, to be sure, it's the ten commandments. But Jesus made an important clarifying comment on this point once, when a lawyer asked Him which was the greatest commandment:

> You shall love the LORD your God with all your heart, with all your soul, and with all your mind. This is the first and great commandment. And the second is like it: You shall love your neighbor as yourself.[10]

The odd thing is that neither of *those* commandments is found in the Ten Commandments. But Jesus clarifies the situation in the next verse:

> On these two commandments hang all the Law and the Prophets.[11]

Paul said the same thing in different words in his comment that "love is the fulfillment of the law."[12] But how can that be? What's going on with the "unchangeable" law of God? Nothing bad, that's for sure! It's just that we tend to focus on the version of the law that God personalized for sinful human beings. That makes sense, since we are, in fact, sinful human beings. We know that adaptation of the divine law as the Ten Commandments, but we don't always stop to remember that they are specially designed and adapted to help us humans know how to obey the underlying principles of the eternal law of love, the ones that "all the law and the prophets" hang on.

This idea of "adapting" the law may be new to some readers, so let's nail it down a bit more with some inspired authority.

> The law of God existed before man was created. It was adapted to the condition of holy beings; even angels were governed by it. After the fall, the principles of righteousness were unchanged. Nothing was taken from the law; not one of its holy precepts could be improved. And as it has existed from the beginning, so will it continue to exist throughout the ceaseless ages of eternity.[13]

> The Sabbath was hallowed at the creation. As ordained for man, it had its origin when "the morning stars sang together, and all the sons of God shouted for joy."[14]

---

10. Matthew 22:37 39
11. Matthew 22:40
12. Romans 13:10
13. *Signs of the Times*, April 15, 1886
14. *Desire of Ages*, 281

\The Sabbath of the fourth commandment was instituted in Eden. The principles embodied in the Decalogue existed before the fall, and were suited to the condition of holy beings. After the fall, these principles were not changed, nothing was taken from the law of God, but additional precepts were given to meet man in his fallen state.[15]

So the law is eternal; it was adapted for "holy beings" and "even angels were governed by it." At the creation of earth, God gave *us* the Sabbath, especially "ordained for man."[16] And then, after the fall, the principles that had existed from all eternity were "not changed," and certainly "nothing was taken from the law of God," but those principles were further clarified in "additional precepts… to meet man in his fallen state." Presumably, that's when the more specific details of the fifth, seventh, and tenth commandments came in.

Ellen White rarely wrote about these more obscure technicalities, but that doesn't mean she was unaware of them. In perhaps the most striking example of this awareness, she would write it all out, actually using the jargon of the philosophers who spent probably way too much time and effort mapping out things that most people never need trouble their minds about. It's tempting to just skip over this matter, but for the sake of being thorough, consider Ellen White's distinction between "moral law" and "positive law."[17]

> Moral law is universal; positive law is not necessarily universal, but may be restricted or extended according to the will of the law-giver. Moral law must be immutable, while positive law may be changed or abolished, as the law-giver may choose.[18]

As is common in matters of "philosophy," things can get complicated when people try to work out all the right definitions to keep everything straight. The issue that comes up here is the "double use" of the word "moral." It turns out that even "positive law" is "moral" if it perfectly applies the principle of the universal, immutable, moral law.

This is why the ten commandments are "moral law" even though they all "hang" on the two great commandments, which are inherently universal and immutable. Incidentally, the ceremonial law of Old Testament times carried moral accountability, too, until God abolished it. This underscores the problem with anyone who wants to "change times and law"[19] on their own authority!

---

15. *Signs of the Times*, June 10, 1880

16. As Jesus put it, "The Sabbath was made for man, and not man for the Sabbath." Mark 2:27

17. When applied to laws, "positive" does not mean the opposite of "negative." It means that the law was "posited." When a person "posits" a theory, they take a "position" on the subject. "Posit" is defined as: "to set firmly; to affirm." merriam-webster.com/dictionary/posit

18. *Signs of the Times*, June 5, 1901. This same comment appears in Manuscript 79, 1896, with one additional word: "positive law may be *enacted*, changed, or abolished…." The Sabbath is an example of exactly that.

19. Daniel 7:25

OK, with all that clear in our thinking, let's get back to "the beginning"! When Lucifer rebelled against God's law, which "adaptation" of the law was he rebelling against? The one for "holy beings" and "even angels," of course, but what did that look like? These thoughts from the Spirit of Prophecy portray a rather simple view of the law of heaven as it was known at that time:

> To give is to live.[20]

> The great law of life is a law of service.[21]

> Self-sacrifice is the law of self-preservation.[22]

> Self-renunciation is the great law of self-preservation, and self-preservation is the law of self-destruction.[23]

Were there "additional precepts" especially adapted for the angels? Maybe... but it's likely that the law of heaven at that time was pretty simple.

> When Satan rebelled against the law of Jehovah, the thought that there was a law came to the angels almost as an awakening to something unthought of.[24]

Unfallen angels, unlike fallen human beings, didn't need every detail spelled out for them. Perhaps the simple injunction to love God and love others was enough.

> On these two commandments the whole interest and duty of moral beings hang.[25]

If the formal statement of the law was left without a lot of details, it's easy to see how Lucifer could have begun his rebellion without appearing to violate any particular statutes. And Ellen White describes his actions in just that way, with the focus of attention being, not on a detailed "thou shalt" or "thou shalt not," but upon an extremely broad issue. What bothered him, Lucifer claimed, was that God required something from the created beings that He Himself didn't practice:

> Satan... had accused God of seeking merely the exaltation of Himself in requiring submission and obedience from His creatures, and had declared that while the Creator exacted self-denial from all others, He Himself practiced no self-denial, and made no sacrifice.[26]

> Satan had accused God of requiring self-denial of the angels, when He knew nothing of what it meant Himself, and when He would not Himself make any self-sacrifice for others. This was the accusation that Satan made against God in heaven; and after the evil one was expelled from heaven, he continually charged the Lord with exacting service which He would not render Himself.[27]

---

20. *Desire of Ages*, 623
21. *Education*, 103
22. *Education*, 110
23. *Signs of the Times*, July 1, 1897
24. *Mount of Blessing*, 109
25. *Testimonies*, vol. 2, 550
26. *Spirit of Prophecy*, vol. 4, 322
27. *Review and Herald*, February 18, 1890

Satan had declared that God knew nothing of self-denial, of mercy and love, but that He was stern, exacting, and unforgiving.[28]

Lucifer didn't like self-denial... which is kind of a trick, since he claimed that it didn't even exist!

> Unselfishness, the principle of God's kingdom, is the principle that Satan hates; its very existence he denies. From the beginning of the great controversy, he has endeavored to prove God's principles of action to be selfish, and he deals in the same way with all who serve God. To disprove Satan's claim is the work of Christ and of all who bear His name.[29]

This unselfishness that Lucifer didn't like was included in both of the two great commandments. That's what love does: it always puts others' legitimate needs and wishes first. Love is inherently self-denying. Anything trying to pass as "love," that isn't self-denying, is a fraud.[30]

But love also requires wisdom! There is a huge difference between a true need or beneficial desire, and a misguided desire. If a baby wants to pet a rattlesnake, all the love in a wise parent's heart wouldn't be enough to let it happen! Arguing otherwise—as Lucifer did—makes a person look really foolish... but only if those looking on can see the difference! And that was God's problem: the angels and unfallen worlds just couldn't see the outcome of Lucifer's ideas. They couldn't imagine the depth of evil that would come from not putting others first.

In fact, for a time, Lucifer was looking pretty good!

> How shall the universe know that Lucifer is not a safe and just leader? To their eyes he appears right. They cannot see, as God sees, beneath the outward covering. They cannot know as God knows. Then to work to unmask him... would create a state of things which must be avoided.[31]

Since the point of contention was the law of God, and specifically the requirement for unselfishness, I like to illustrate the difference between Christ and Satan like this:

Lucifer says: "I know what I want, and if I have to, I'll kill you in order to get it. I have to do that, since I can't trust God or anyone else to look after me."

Christ says: "I know what's best for you, and if I have to, I'll die so you can have the chance to get it. I don't want to do that, but my Father thinks it's best, and I trust His love and judgment."

---

28. *Review and Herald*, March 9, 1897
29. *Education*, 154
30. This explains why, when the books of record were opened, "Under the general heading of selfishness came every other sin." *Testimonies*, vol. 4, 384
31. E.G. White, Letter to Brother and Sister C.H. Jones, July 4, 1892; Letter 16a, 1892

How God chose to meet this challenge is fascinating in any number of ways, one of them being the obvious difference in His response to Lucifer and the angels as compared to Adam and Eve:

> [Lucifer] was not immediately dethroned when he first ventured to indulge the spirit of discontent and insubordination, nor even when he began to present his false claim and lying representations before the loyal angels. Long was he retained in Heaven. Again and again was he offered pardon on condition of repentance and submission.... Had Lucifer been willing to return to his allegiance, humble and obedient, he would have been re-established in his office as covering cherub.[32]

This has confused many students of the Spirit of Prophecy. It sounds much like, "Neither do I condemn you; go and sin no more,"[33] but very far removed from "without shedding of blood there is no remission."[34] There's a good explanation for this, and many pages from now, it will be duly considered, but just notice for now that at the time of Lucifer's rebellion, "the universe" (including the angels) couldn't see clearly! Even God couldn't show them the truth in a way they could understand!

> Satan's position in heaven had been next to the Son of God. He was first among the angels. His power had been debasing, but God could not reveal it in its true light and carry all heaven in harmony with Him in removing him with his evil influences. His power was increasing, but the evil was yet unrecognized. It was a deadly power to the universe, but for the security of the worlds and the government of heaven, it was necessary that it should develop and be revealed in its true light.[35]

> God desired that a change take place, and that the work of Satan be brought out in its genuine aspect. But the exalted angel standing next to Christ was opposed to the Son of God. The underworking was so subtle that it could not be made to appear before the heavenly host as the thing that it really was.[36]

> Satan could not be presented to the universe at once in his real character. His crooked course must be allowed to continue until he should reveal himself as an accuser, a deceiver, a liar, and a murderer.[37]

If the angels didn't know if Lucifer was right or wrong... how could they decide whose "side" to be on? Lucifer was the highest of the angels! He had been closer to the inner workings of heaven's government than any of the rest of them... what if he was right?

---

32. *Spirit of Prophecy*, vol. 4, 319
33. John 8:11
34. Hebrews 9:22
35. E.G. White, "Christ Our High Priest," March 28, 1900; Manuscript 50, 1900
36. E.G. White, Letter to Brother and Sister D.H. Kress, May 29, 1906; Letter 162, 1906
37. E.G. White, Letter to Brother and Sister C. H. Jones, July 4, 1892; Letter 16a, 1892

But God said he was wrong, and it was impossible to bring the two positions together. It couldn't be both ways... and all the angels had to make a choice. It seems kind of like reaching blindly into a bag and pulling out a rock—white rock, you live; black rock, you die. That's a big deal!

It was a terrible situation to be in, but not hopeless. There was one thing— and *only* one thing—that could save them. Note this point well, because what saved angels is the only thing that can save you.

You're not as smart as the angels. You haven't seen nearly as much evidence as the angels. But you can walk safely, just as two-thirds of the angels did, by faith in God. When full evidence is lacking, faith is all you've got. This is something you need to get used to, because full evidence is going to be lack-ing for some while yet.

CHAPTER 4

The Slipperiest Slope

THIS idea of faith takes us back, one more time, to "the beginning." We need to take a look at the flow of Lucifer's thinking as he swerved into the ditch. This is a fine line, just one step removed from the question of how sin arose. That's the mystery; that one has no answer, so we'll leave it alone. But there's a lot to be learned from looking at Satan's slide down the slippery slope once that first terrible step was taken.

Once upon a time, God said, "Lucifer, please do *this*." No doubt, God had said that to Lucifer many times. But this time, for the first time in his life—the first time in anyone's life—Lucifer thought, "No, *that* is better."

We don't know the details of what might have been involved. Was it a big issue? Or perhaps just a little one? We know that Lucifer was the director of the heavenly choir... what if the whole history of sin began with something as insignificant as God asking for a particular Opening Song when Lucifer had been planning on a different one? (Don't laugh: a few pieces of fruit doesn't look like much, either.)

In any case, in order to get to the point of finding fault with God's expressed will, at least one of two things had to have happened:

1. Either Lucifer believed that God had made a mistake, or
2. He believed that God had deliberately commanded something that was not in his best interest.

It might have played out like this—"Oh wow! I can't believe it! I mean, God has been really smart in everything I've ever seen Him do before, but... look at that! He made a mistake this time!" But even if God had just made a "simple mistake," that was a serious concern. After all, God was in charge of running the universe! Astrophysics is not the place for rounding errors!

Who could trust His wisdom if it had been proven faulty?

And if God *hadn't* made a mental mistake, some sort of a computational error, it was even worse, because that could only mean that He was *intentionally* harming His subjects! Who could trust His love if it had been proven false?

All of which means that the moment the covering cherub could say or think, "No, my idea is better than what God wants," he had lost faith in God's wisdom, and probably His love as well. But that's not all!

If Lucifer was smart enough to spot God's mistake, that meant Lucifer was *smarter than God!* What's more, if God *had* tried to trick Lucifer into doing something that wasn't for his best good, then the mere fact that God had failed to fool him meant that Lucifer was *smarter than God!*

That's the stuff that pride is made of. Now it would be easy for Lucifer to simply do what he was sure was the best thing—after all, *He was smarter than God!*

And that—the blatant act of doing something other than what God has asked—is what we normally call disobedience. But that's not all!

Even if Lucifer never said a word about his disobedience, the influence of his actions told all the other angels, "You can't depend on God to take care of you! You need to take charge of your own life!" This is a lie, of course, but we clearly see Lucifer's determination on this point in the description given by Isaiah:

> You have said in your heart: "I will ascend into heaven, I will exalt my throne above the stars of God; I will also sit on the mount of the congregation on the farthest sides of the north; I will ascend above the heights of the clouds."[1]

But that's not all!

Once Lucifer took the responsibility of caring for himself, it meant he had to do whatever it took to provide for himself. If necessary, that meant stealing. If necessary, that meant murder.

Like Jesus said, Lucifer was "a liar... and a murderer from the beginning."[2]

But, worst of all, was his closing claim that—when he had exalted himself above all others—he would "be like the Most High." That little claim is double-headed. We most often take it to mean, "When I'm exalted, I'll be great and important like God is." But just as surely, it also means, "When I have exalted myself, I'll be like God because *He exalted Himself.*"

That's a serious claim! One which God denies, of course, since "God is love" simply doesn't mesh with self-exaltation.[3]

---

1. Isaiah 14:13–14
2. John 8:44
3. Second Thessalonians chapter two speaks of Lucifer as well, working through his earthly representative, "the lawless one." Notice the end result for those he deceives:

   "The coming of the lawless one is according to the working of Satan, with all power, signs, and lying wonders, and with all unrighteous deception among those who perish, because they did not receive the love of the truth,

This cascade of sinful dominoes is the natural result of losing faith in God. It's important to catch the significance of this. The whole ugly history of sin began when Lucifer lost faith in God because of some unmet desire. Lucifer *wanted* something, and when he didn't get what he wanted, he concluded that God wasn't doing the right thing. Whether he attributed that to an intellectual mistake or an intentional desire to limit or harm, doesn't really matter. In short order, Lucifer lost his confidence in God's love and wisdom.

Incidentally, that's all faith is.

> Faith is a very simple matter; it is confidence in God.[4]

That may not be the most profound theological definition for the word, but functional simplicity is pretty profound, and you'll find that that definition *just works*.

What's more, understanding the *loss* of faith is just as simple.

> What is it to be in an unsaved condition? Is it not to be living without that full confidence in God which is born of love, which leads us to take Him at His word?[5]

This gives us: "Unsaved = No Confidence," but we can do a little Algebra on this. Do you remember how you can take any equation and multiply both sides by negative one, and the equation will still be valid? When we do that to this second quotation, we get "Saved = Confidence in God." Good so far... but now let's do a little Geometry.

Our first statement gave us "Faith = Confidence in God." The right side of that equation just happens to be the same as the right side of our second equation, and that brings up the axiom, "Things which are equal to the same thing are equal to one another." In other words, "Faith = Saved." Or, as Paul put it, "by grace you have been saved through faith."[6]

Long story short: faith is important! And Lucifer had lost it.

_____

that they might be saved. And for this reason God will send them strong delusion, that they should believe the lie, that they all may be condemned who did not believe the truth but had pleasure in unrighteousness."

If you are more used to the King James Version, you may have noticed that the New King James renders it "the lie" instead of "a lie." The Greek supports the use of the definite article here. In other words, the lie these people believe is not just any lie; it's a specific, identifiable lie. As the most basic of all Lucifer's falsehoods, this claim that God exalts Himself at others' expense is a strong contender for that distinction.

4. *Youth's Instructor*, August 30, 1894
5. *Bible Training School*, November 1, 1911
6. Ephesians 2:8

CHAPTER 5

What's this All About?

B EFORE we move on from the "beginning," we need to consider Lucifer's formal accusations against God and His government. It's hard to have a war without something to fight about, so Lucifer had to offer some rationale for his rebellion. The following accusations are compiled from the many different accounts of those long ago events that have been given in the Spirit of Prophecy. Of course, the wording varies from one account to the next, but all the major points fit quite well into the following nine categories. They are listed here, as nearly as I can determine, in the order in which Lucifer brought them up.

1. Angels are holy by nature and wise enough to govern themselves, so they don't need God's law.
2. God was unfair when He exalted Jesus above Lucifer.
3. The plan to create human beings was a mistake.
4. God is selfish, unforgiving, and revengeful.
5. God's law is defective, and needs to be changed.
6. It is impossible to obey God's law.
7. God's law is arbitrary.
8. God's law makes forgiveness impossible.
9. God is lying about all the above.

Let's take a quick spin through the development of these charges, because understanding some of the events that happened along the way will help us later on. Keep one finger here so you can look back at the list.

As we go through these, remember that these are the "public" issues. Long before any of these claims were spread openly among the angels, Lucifer himself had begun to cherish the inexplicable desire for self exaltation. That was the smoldering issue that God addressed by calling for a general assembly of the heavenly population, and clarifying the position of Jesus as His Son, One equal with Himself. This was done discreetly, with no rebuke or condemnation or even any exposure of Lucifer's pride. Still, it didn't sit well.

The first accusation—if you knew nothing else about the case—might look benign, logical, almost inarguable. Experience ought to count for something! *"We're grown up. We've got this now."*

> Satan... boldly contended [that] in struggling to carry out his purposes and have his own way, [he] was only imitating the example of God. If God followed His own will perfectly and continually, why should not the first sons created in His image do so?[1]

All appearances aside, this error   that *anyone* might live securely apart from the guidance of God—was enough to set the entire history of sin into motion.

There is an interesting detail, though, brought to light by the need to give any sort of announcement about Jesus' status. Though not solidly "provable," it seems likely that Jesus had previously been perceived as an exalted angel. Whatever obscurity was involved, something made it necessary for His status to be clarified. One possible explanation for this was that Jesus was providing a "model" for angels, much as He later provided a model for human beings.

Ellen White seems to hint at something of this sort, but I've never found any solid categorical assertions. The following quotation, for instance, includes a phrase which clearly sets Christ apart from the angels, and then in the next sentence another phrase which might easily be taken to mean He was one of the angels.

> [Christ] is the eternal, self-existent Son, on whom no yoke had come. When God asked, "Whom shall I send, and who will go for Us?" Christ alone of the angelic host could reply, "Here am I; send Me."[2]

Another example of Jesus' close identification with the angels is of interest not only on that account, but for its similarity to statements indicating what Christ's life as a man proved:

> Jesus, the Son of God, was not deceived by Lucifer's sophistry. He stood true to principle and resisted every line of reasoning of Lucifer and all the angels who had taken sides with him, thus evidencing that as He stood, *every* angel might have stood.[3]

Plans for earth were definitely under way prior to any open rebellion. What's not as clear is when Lucifer first heard of those plans. Was it, perhaps, not until the general assembly?

---

1. *Spirit of Prophecy*, vol. 3, 77
2. E.G. White. "The True High Priest," September 26, 1897; Manuscript 101, 1897
3. E.G. White, "Diary: Creation and the Sabbath," July 4, 1891; Manuscript 43b, 1891

The great Creator assembled the heavenly host, that He might in the presence of all the angels confer special honor upon His Son.... Especially was His Son to work in union with Himself in the anticipated creation of the earth and every living thing that should exist upon the earth....

Christ had been taken into the special counsel of God in regard to His plans, while Satan was unacquainted with them. He did not understand, neither was he permitted to know, the purposes of God.[4]

Before the fall of Satan, the Father consulted His Son in regard to the formation of man. They purposed to make this world, and create beasts and living things upon it, and to make man in the image of God, to reign as a ruling monarch over every living thing which God should create. When Satan learned the purpose of God, he was envious at Christ, and jealous because the Father had not consulted him in regard to the creation of man.[5]

There were now multiple issues which conflicted with Lucifer's growing acceptance of the "principles of selfishness."[6] First, there was the fact that Jesus had been "exalted" above him. (In reality, of course, it was simply the revelation of His actual status of equality with the Father,[7] though that's probably easier for us to see than for angels at that time.) But the second issue agitating Lucifer's mind was God's plan for a "new and distinct order"[8] of created being. How much he knew of this plan is hard to say, but Lucifer was clearly not impressed.

Satan... opposed the creation of man.[9]

The creation of our world was brought into the councils of heaven. There the covering cherub prepared his request that he should be made prince to govern the world then in prospect. This was not accorded him. Jesus Christ was to rule the earthly kingdom; under God He engaged to take the world with all its probabilities. The law of heaven should be the standard law for this new world, for human intelligences. Lucifer was jealous of Christ and this jealousy worked into rebellion and he carried with him a large number of the holy angels.[10]

These last two quotations are obviously related, but the order of occurrence is debatable. If Lucifer objected first, he could conceivably maintain some dignity later by saying, "Well, if You are determined to create them, at least let me

---

4. *Spirit of Prophecy*, vol. 1, 17

5. *Spiritual Gifts*, vol. 3, 36

6. *Testimonies*, vol. 7, 176. People sometimes think "Lucifer" become "Satan" all at once, but it took longer, and happened in a way that is much like, if not identical to, the way human beings descend to the level of the demonic: "Little by little, Lucifer came to indulge the desire of self-exaltation." *Great Controversy*, 494

7. "Christ is declared in the Scriptures to be the Son of God. From all eternity He has sustained this relation to Jehovah." E.G. White, "Christ Our Only Hope," March 7, 1904; Manuscript 22, 1905

8. *Review and Herald*, February 11, 1902

9. E.G. White, "Diary: January 1890," January 26, 1890; Manuscript 38, 1890

10. E.G. White, "Diary: Creation and the Sabbath," July 4, 1891; Manuscript 43b, 1891

help you keep things under control by serving as Prince." On the other hand, if his request was denied and *then* he began to oppose the idea, it would have looked a lot like a case of "sour grapes." No matter how it appeared while he was still in heaven, by the time the creation actually took place—after he and his angels had been expelled—he was not a happy camper.

> The loyal angels took a deep, rejoicing interest in the creation of our world, and in the creation of man; but Satan took no pleasure in the creation of Adam and Eve.[11]

Lucifer's desire to be the "prince" of this earth clearly falls into the "denied desire" category, and is certainly one issue about which he concluded that God had made a mistake, or—worse—that He just wasn't doing right by him. But there is another aspect to the story just here that deserves consideration.

Why did Lucifer "oppose the creation of man"? Ellen White doesn't elaborate on this explicitly, but the most likely motive for his (selfish) concern comes from the nature of these new creatures, and God's plan for them:

> God has made man capable of constant progress in mental and moral worth. No other creature of His hand is capable of such advancement.[12]

> No other creature that God has made is capable of such improvement, such refinement, such nobility as man.... Man cannot conceive what he may be and what he may become. Through the grace of Christ he is capable of constant mental progress.[13]

> Those who in the strength of Christ overcome the great enemy of God and man, will occupy a position in the heavenly courts above angels who have never fallen.[14]

> The work of redemption involved consequences of which it is difficult for man to have any conception. There was to be imparted to the human being striving for conformity to the divine image an outlay of heaven's treasures, an excellency of power, which would place him higher than the angels who had not fallen.[15]

These last two statements both speak of the status of people *after* they've been saved from sin, which raises the awkward question: "Do human beings end up with some benefit for having once been sinners?" Fortunately, the Spirit of Prophecy eliminates that quandary with a simple answer: No. Human beings are saved—healed—from sin, but not "improved" or "elevated" by it. In fact, the redeemed end up right where God intended people to be from the very beginning. Why change a perfect plan?

---

11. E.G. White, Letter to Brother and Sister Haysmer, January 20, 1900; Letter 78, 1900
12. *Signs of the Times*, January 30, 1901
13. E.G. White, Letter to Brother Covert and those who hold responsible positions in the Indiana Conference, September 27, 1887; Letter 26d, 1887
14. *General Conference Bulletin*, April 1, 1899
15. *General Conference Bulletin*, October 1, 1899

Through the imparted life of Christ, man has been given opportunity to win back again the lost gift of life, and to stand in his original position before God, a partaker of the divine nature.[16]

[Christ] reinstated fallen man on condition of obedience to God's commandments, in the position from which he had fallen in consequence of disobedience.[17]

Satan in his efforts to deceive and tempt our race had thought to frustrate the divine plan in man's creation; but Christ now asks that this plan be carried into effect as if man had never fallen. He asks for His people not only pardon and justification, full and complete, but a share in His glory and a seat upon His throne.[18]

But that's when the great controversy has ended, when God has fought the battle and won. We aren't there, yet, and Lucifer still maintains that making human beings who were capable of rising higher than he could was a very bad idea.

It was the tempter's purpose to thwart the divine plan in man's creation, and fill the earth with woe and desolation. And he would point to all this evil as the result of God's work in creating man.[19]

There is one more detail in regard to Lucifer's "concern" over the creation of human beings that came from the inherent contrast between angels (Lucifer, in particular) and humans. First, notice the archangel's job description:

God was a light so effulgent,[20] that Lucifer occupied the position of covering cherub, so that the universe could at all times look upon His glory.[21]

He who was once the covering cherub, whose work it was to hide from the heavenly intelligences the glory of God, perverted his intellect, and divorced himself from God.[22]

This had been Lucifer's role since his creation, but this "new and distinct order" of created beings didn't fit well, for they were to be "granted communion with their Maker, with no obscuring veil between."[23] Where any rational mind would see a new and higher display of God's wisdom and creative power—resulting in previously unknown and unimagined blessings for all in the universe—Lucifer saw only a threat to his personal prestige.

All the variations of accusation number four seem to have originated from Lucifer simply not getting his way in regard to earth and human beings. Of course, the charge that God was selfish, unforgiving, revengeful, and a whole

---

16. *Signs of the Times*, June 17, 1897
17. E.G. White, "Visit to Paris and Versailles, France," October 1886; Manuscript 75, 1886
18. *Great Controversy*, 483
19. *Steps to Christ*, 17
20. "Effulgent" isn't exactly a common word these days, but in normal use it just means "really, really bright." What additional dimensions of brightness might be involved in divine glory is beyond me.
21. E.G. White, "Before Pilate and Herod," October 1897; Manuscript 112, 1897
22. E.G. White, Letter to Brother and Sister Haskell, September 29, 1901; Letter 197, 1901
23. *Patriarchs and Prophets*, 50

thesaurus full of synonyms proved to be quite adaptable to many contexts, so Satan has continued to use it in many forms. But there is traditionally a weakness in *ad hominem* attacks: they're very personal, but often weak on substance.

It's easy to read between the lines (which is not the same as having a direct inspired statement, it must be pointed out) and see how Lucifer could have felt the need for something more solid than these personal attacks.

That's where the fifth accusation comes into play. What's more solid than the Law of Heaven? Unless, of course, that law is defective and needs revision. This charge moves from the realm of personal criticism, to a clear "policy issue."

Incidentally, if the reader should begin to see similarities between the great controversy and earthly politics, it is not without reason! The similarities are legion, and like many politicians, Lucifer was concerned about appearances. No one wants to look like a troublemaker!

> While claiming for himself perfect loyalty to God, he urged that changes in the order and laws of heaven were necessary for the stability of the divine government. Thus while working to excite opposition to the law of God and to instill his own discontent into the minds of the angels under him, he was ostensibly seeking to remove dissatisfaction and to reconcile disaffected angels to the order of heaven. While secretly fomenting discord and rebellion, he with consummate craft caused it to appear as his sole purpose to promote loyalty and to preserve harmony and peace.[24]

Appearances aside, Lucifer had a definite legislative agenda:

> Satan sought to correct the law of God in heaven, and to supply an amendment of his own. He exalted his own judgment above that of his Creator, and placed his will above the will of Jehovah, and in this way virtually declared God to be fallible.[25]

> The warfare against God's law commenced in heaven. Satan was determined to bring God to his ideas, his way, to force Him to change the law of His government.[26]

God did not remain silent when it came to the defense of His law,[27] but His response may have been a surprise to Lucifer. In Ellen White's telling of the story, God never said, "I don't want to change My law." He never said, "I don't think I ought to change My law." He never even said, "I'm not going to change My law."

Instead, He always said, "The law is perfect and immutable; it cannot be changed." Ellen White puts it like this:

> If ever a change was to have been made, it would have been accomplished when rebellion revealed itself in heaven, and so have prevented the great apostasy of the an-

---

24. *Patriarchs and Prophets*, 38
25. E.G. White, "A Perpetual Memorial," 1894; Manuscript 91, 1894
26. E.G. White, Letter to Sister Eckman, May 19, 1895; Letter 24, 1895
27. Apparently this has always been a "red line" that sinners cross to their peril: "It is time for You to act, O LORD, for they have regarded Your law as void." Psalms 119:126. We will have cause to remember this verse in the context of end time events.

gels. The fact that no change was made in God's administration, even when the most exalted of the angels drew away from allegiance to God's law, is evidence enough to reasonable minds that the law, the foundation of God's government, will not relax its claims to save the willful transgressor.[28]

✎ The law of God is the expression of His character. God possesses absolute, invariable, and immutable independence, and His law is without variableness, unalterable, eternal, because it is the transcript of his character. No event can take place that will in any sense make it necessary to declare a law of a contrary nature. "The law of the Lord is perfect, converting the soul." Any change in the law would mar its perfection. The slightest variance in its precepts would give reason to the hosts of heaven and to unfallen worlds to think that God's counsels and declarations are not to be relied upon, but need to be remodeled, because they are of a faulty character. Should any change be made in the law of God, Satan would gain that for which he had instituted controversy.[29]

If Lucifer had thought he was going to be able to bargain with God over the details of the law, he was badly mistaken! But he wasn't one to give up, so his next claim doubled down on the issue. This one seems to have been designed for the angelic "citizens" of heaven, rather than for God. After he had claimed that the law was defective, you have to think that at least some of the angels would be asking, "What's wrong with it?" and in response, Lucifer craftily chose a lie that could not be "fact checked" by the angels.

"What's *wrong* with it? Nobody can obey it, that's what's wrong with it!"

Satan declared that he would prove to the worlds which God has created, and to the heavenly intelligences, that it was an impossibility to keep the law of God.[30]

This would have been surprising to the angels, none of whom had ever been accused of breaking God's law, but Lucifer had the advantage of rank and reputation.

Lucifer had been the covering cherub. He had stood in the light of God's presence. He had been the highest of all created beings, and had been foremost in revealing God's purposes to the universe. After he had sinned, his power to deceive was the more deceptive, and the unveiling of his character was the more difficult, because of the exalted position he had held with the Father.[31]

Since none of the other angels had been so closely connected with the heavenly government, who were they to say how God had judged their behavior? And if, as Lucifer implied, God had been noting their "transgressions" without so much as a word of warning,[32] who could tell what He would do if He ever decided to impose a day of reckoning? Maybe God really *was* unforgiving and revengeful, after all.

---

28. *Signs of the Times*, April 28, 1890
29. *Signs of the Times*, March 12, 1896
30. E.G. White, "Sanctification and Repentance," October 10, 1894; Manuscript 40, 1894. Of course, this same claim has been applied to human beings as well.
31. *Desire of Ages*, 758

And if Lucifer was right, that the penalty for any transgression, no matter how small, was *death*... well, that could seem like an over-reaction!

Of course, God denied the claim, affirming that obedience was both essential and possible.

The law having now taken center role in the conflict, Lucifer's seventh accusation was presented as a "reasonable" plea for "moderation." The claim that the law is "arbitrary" is at its heart an assertion that the law is what it is, just because God said that's what it was going to be. Like a speed limit, that someone in city hall set at 40.

And, like a speed limit, any arbitrary law can be changed. Politicians do it all the time! Just make it 50. Or 45... or 35.

In claiming that the law was arbitrary, Lucifer was simply supporting his claim that the law needed to be changed—and denying God's statement that it could not be changed. "It's easy, God. Just say something new."

God was not persuaded. The law was still perfect, immutable, unchangeable, and eternal. And, no, it was not arbitrary. But... if the law isn't arbitrary, if it isn't based on God defining, "This is right, and this is wrong," then what *is* it based on?

> Right and wrong are not based upon God's moral government; God's moral government is based upon a distinction between right and wrong. The erroneous view which many have of this subject causes them to rebel against God's law of government as arbitrary.[33]

This is an interesting distinction. We've got "right and wrong," and "God's moral government." Does it really matter which one was based on the other? As long as no one is saying God's government is wrong, how much does it matter? Is this like the old "chicken and the egg" debate?[34]

Apparently not, since the "erroneous view" of "many" makes them end up thinking God's government is "arbitrary." And, apparently, that error at least

---

32. I should make clear that I haven't found explicit inspired testimony that spells out the exact method in which Lucifer capitalized on his high position. So please understand that this scenario is a bit of an extrapolation from the basic accusations. I think it's highly plausible, but fleshing out the details as I have —especially in this footnote—contains a bit of speculation.

    Let me illustrate the idea of God "noting their 'transgressions' without so much as a word of warning." Suppose it came out on the local news broadcast that the government had been running secret traffic cameras on all major roads and highways for the last three years... and now they were going to start reviewing that footage and mailing out tickets. You, of course, would probably have nothing to worry about, but *some* people would likely be a little concerned.

33. E.G. White, "The Moral Law," February 1, 1896; Manuscript 79, 1896

34. Every detail of the law seems to be important. For one thing, God's law is not just some sort of decorative measure; it has a specific job to do, and we better hope it's up to the job!

    "The law of God is the foundation of His government, and is exactly what is needed to preserve life and righteousness." *Signs of the Times*, February 26, 1894

contributes to their decisions to rebel against God. Keep this issue in mind, because that "the law is arbitrary" argument hasn't gone away!

Perhaps the easiest way to see the danger of this error is to look at the connection and relationship between that claim, and where Lucifer went next. The relationship is so "convenient," that you have to ask, "Was number seven an intentional trap? A setup? Or did its relation to the eighth only occur to him after God's denial that the law was arbitrary?" The record isn't clear. What *is* clear, is that Lucifer tried to use accusations seven and eight as a "left jab, right cross" knockout series.

> Satan.... declared that the principles of God's government make forgiveness impossible.[35]

> Lucifer had declared that if the law of God was changeless, and its penalty could not be remitted, every transgressor must be forever debarred from the Creator's favor. He had claimed that the sinful race were placed beyond redemption.[36]

> The condemning power of Satan would lead him to institute a theory of justice inconsistent with mercy. He claims to be officiating as the voice and power of God, claims that his decisions are justice, are pure, and without fault. Thus he takes his position on the judgment seat, and declares that his counsels are infallible. Here his merciless justice comes in, a counterfeit of justice, abhorrent to God.[37]

The idea of telling someone that they can't forgive someone else even if they want to... just seems foolish. But Satan isn't trying to convince God, so much as he is arguing every angle of his claims to persuade everyone but God. To the unfallen universe, he says, "God's law is faulty, it's too harsh; it needs to be changed." But building off the same basic claim, he takes a different approach toward sinners: "Satan declared that there is no forgiveness with God; that if God should forgive sin, he would make his law of no effect. He says to the sinner, 'You are lost.'"[38]

It's easy to read over this claim and just ignore it, but that would be a serious mistake! It's never a good idea to ignore the attack of someone who is trying to kill you. But... how can Fred tell Marvin that it's impossible for him to forgive Sam? The whole idea just sounds stupid.

Until you put the seventh and eighth accusations together. Then it makes sense. Lucifer said that if God couldn't change His law—as He had claimed —then naturally He couldn't do anything to change the punishment. If God can't control His own law, there's no way to stop the natural "punishment" from landing in full force. Hence, no forgiveness.

---

35. *Desire of Ages*, 37
36. *Great Controversy*, 502
37. E.G. White, Letter to Brother and Sister C.H. Jones, July 4, 1892; Letter 16, 1892
38. *Review and Herald*, January 19, 1911

As previously noted, the eighth charge is a metaphorical right cross to the left jab of the seventh. Satan has bet his very existence on the idea that when God tries to evade the seventh accusation, He will leave Himself open to defeat by means of the eighth. In other words, an arbitrary law is easy to change, but God claims His law isn't arbitrary, thus placing it beyond His own control. So then, if God can't control His own law, forgiveness is impossible.

Let's illustrate this on a human level with the most obvious of non-arbitrary laws, gravity: Suppose they hold a town hall meeting to hear the concerns of the locals. Two issues come up: people have been getting hurt in car accidents, and kids have been getting hurt at the skate park. Straight forward problems, so let's solve them. First, we lower the speed limit from 45 to 35 on the streets that have been having the accidents; then we cut the force of gravity by 15%. Problems solved! Everybody's happy. It's been a good day's work.

Ahhh... that it should be so simple. In the human sphere of things, there's just no way to tweak the power of gravity, and that's a lot like what God says about His moral law. It's not arbitrary; it cannot be "tweaked"[39] because it's based on the unchanging distinction between right and wrong.

Lucifer says, "If the law is arbitrary, just change it and cut down on car wrecks (but admit that You lied when You said it couldn't be changed), or stick with Your claim that You can't change the law, and give up on stopping those kids from breaking their arms. Admit it, God! If You can change the law, You've been lying to the universe, and if You made a law that can't be changed, You can't do a thing to help a single 'sinner'!"

Now do you see the point of Paul's claim?

That He might be just and the justifier of the one who has faith in Jesus.[40]

Lucifer didn't know it... yet... but he was in way over his head.

This problem, How could God be just and yet the justifier of sinners? baffled all finite intelligence.[41]

Either one is relatively easy; doing both is incredibly difficult. Satan says it can't be done; God says it can. And for us to not even understand that there's an issue here is like strolling into the middle of a firefight without a clue what all those little "pop, pop, pop" noises might be.

---

39. None of this is to say that God can't overrule gravity if He wants to, but city hall can't. Gravity is just an illustration of the kind of law that can't be changed because it comes from something other than an arbitrary decision—for human beings, anyway.

40. Romans 3:26

41. *Youth's Instructor*, August 31, 1887

CHAPTER 6

Question Period

READERS not familiar with a parliamentary form of government may need a little help on that chapter title. Though the precise wording varies from one country to another,[1] the general idea is a daily time period set aside for questions from opposition parties, directed to the sitting government. In many countries, it's one of the more entertaining aspects of the political landscape. Even the normally staid Wikipedia notes that "Question Period has a reputation for being quite chaotic due to the commonplace cat-calling and jeering from non-participating MPs, but notwithstanding the heckling, Question Period is actually tightly regulated."

Given the confrontational nature of politics, you can imagine the "Gotcha!" value of asking your opponent a pointed question for which he has no good answer.

It's difficult to piece together any exact procedural formula and claim that this is the pattern followed in heaven, but drawing from a number of Spirit of Prophecy statements, it looks like God has sometimes chosen to defer answers to important questions for centuries and even millennia!

From the last chapter, we might be forgiven for thinking that "the angel formerly known as Lucifer," now Satan, has been completely outgeneraled in this whole conflict of his own making. And that's true. But as long as valid questions remain unanswered, Satan still has a chance—theoretically, at least —of coming out on top! Clearly, it's hard for God to claim victory when the war isn't over! Sin still rages with seeming impunity across the globe. If God

---

1. "Question Period" is the common term in Canada (though the official name is "Oral Questions"); many other Commonwealth countries have similar proceedings, often referred to as "Question Time."

is winning, shouldn't it be more obvious? One might think there would be questions on this.

After all, there has been a *lot* of rebellion. It has gone on for what seems like a very long time. It's been ugly. And no one really seems to understand the exact plan to deal with it.

Surprisingly, we aren't the only ones who are more than a little uncertain as to the details of God's dealings with rebellion. Even the angels who remained loyal to the heavenly government had questions.

Apparently, that's OK as far as God is concerned. It's clear, for instance, that angels had serious questions following Satan's expulsion from heaven, but all who chose—despite their questions—to trust God, were welcome still in the heavenly courts.

God apparently didn't offer much of a preview of His plan of action. Even the loyal angels were left wondering! It seems He recognized that proclaiming His own righteousness was never going to do what needed to be done, so He mostly just let the universe watch!

> In this controversy much was to be involved. Vast interests were at stake. Before the inhabitants of the heavenly universe were to be answered the questions: "Is God's law imperfect, in need of amendment or abrogation, or is it immutable? Is God's government in need of change, or is it stable?"
>
> Before Christ's first advent, the sin of refusing to conform to God's law had become widespread. Apparently Satan's power was growing; his warfare against heaven was becoming more and more determined. A crisis had been reached. With intense interest God's movements were watched by the heavenly angels. Would He come forth from His place to punish the inhabitants of the world for their iniquity? Would He send fire or flood to destroy them? All heaven waited the bidding of their Commander to pour out the vials of wrath upon a rebellious world. One word from Him, one sign, and the world would have been destroyed. The worlds unfallen would have said, "Amen. Thou art righteous, O God, because Thou hast exterminated rebellion."
>
> But "God so loved the world, that He gave His only-begotten Son, that whosoever believeth in Him should not perish, but have everlasting life." God might have sent His Son to condemn, but He sent Him to save. Christ came as a Redeemer. No words can describe the effect of this movement on the heavenly angels. With wonder and admiration they could only exclaim, "Herein is love!"[2]

Question Period had lasted a long time, but God was ready to supply some eagerly-awaited answers, and the chance to understand was open to all the universe. It was time to hear from Someone who understood all the issues!

---

2. *Signs of the Times*, August 27, 1902

CHAPTER 7

Expert Testimony

LUCIFER says God can't forgive anyone unless He changes His law. And since God says that can't happen, Lucifer says forgiveness can't happen, either. There's a certain logic to his claim... but is he right?

Well, no. Instinctively we want to resist saying the devil is right, and that's good... but *how* is he wrong? And what will it take to demonstrate his error? That's why the whole universe—and our little messed up world, especially—needed an expert witness.

Being an "expert" hinges on two things: you have to be special enough to deserve the title; and you have to be able to convince others that you're normal enough to know what's important to the jury. If you're just *normal*, why would anyone listen to you rather than the next guy? And if you're *too* special, too far removed from the daily life of "real people," why would anyone listen to you at all?

And so the Son of God came to provide His testimony in human flesh. The universe was watching, a check-list of Lucifer's accusations in hand. True, they had all (except one-third of the angels) chosen to trust God, but, still, there's nothing like putting a nagging perplexity permanently to rest. Could Jesus do that? And, if so, exactly *how* could it be done?

> Christ.... was a perfect representation of the Father, and in His character and practices was a refutation of Satan's misrepresentations of the character of God[1]

> [Christ's] life of sinlessness, lived on this earth in human nature, is a complete refutation of Satan's charge against the character of God.[2]

---

1. E.G. White, "Christ's Mission to Earth," December 9, 1897; Manuscript 143, 1897
2. E.G. White, Letter to Brother and Sister S.N. Haskell, January 18, 1902; Letter 1, 1902

It's important to understand that Jesus' coming to earth was directly related to the issues we've been looking at. Painted broadly, His mission was to refute Satan's accusations, but we'll see that this rebuttal was designed as a two-stage plan. The first objective was to refute the more personal accusations "against the character of God." And, according to Ellen White, He did so, and He did so "completely."

A quick look back at the list on page 26 shows that accusations two and four fall most directly into this category. Lucifer claimed God was unfair, selfish, unforgiving, and revengeful.

His fifth and sixth arguments—the law is defective and needs to be changed because no one can obey it—painted God in an unattractive light as well, albeit less directly. After all, if God made a bad law, He sure isn't as smart as has been claimed! Unless, of course, He *intentionally* made a bad law... which throws doubt on His love.

Ellen White put it like this:

> To admit that God made a law so imperfect that it needed to be changed would be to stamp God as changeable and imperfect.[3]

We skipped over the first claim—that angels were smart and righteous all on their own. Since it's a claim about angels, rather than about God or His law, its application to God is even less direct, but if God had imposed His law on angels unnecessarily, it would make His judgment look suspect, at the very least.

And then, of course, there's that third accusation, the one about human beings. While the focus is on us, Lucifer's charge certainly reflects back on God. Making dangerous new organisms and turning them loose on the universe could easily be seen as a very bad idea.

These are the potentially government-toppling challenges God had to deal with. Great. What was He going to do?

First off, as we've seen, He gave the issue a little time. About four thousand years, to be more precise. But that was four thousand years of human suffering. What's the point? How—exactly—is that a loving thing to do? Especially from the perspective of a suffering human?

This point is not trivial, and refuting Lucifer's claim here was going to be a time consuming task. Even documenting that process will take some time, and require a fair amount of "foundation building" before we tackle it directly, so patience is encouraged. For now, let's start with this:

> Satan determined to sit upon the throne of God in the earth, to sit in the temple of God, showing himself to be God. For ages he seemed to rule as though the world was en-

---

3. *Signs of the Times*, June 5, 1901

tirely his own, and his assumption to supreme authority seemed undisputed. The powers of hell seemed to hold men under their control, and Satan revealed his hellish principles in taking possession of the human body, and plunging his subjects into misery and crime. To all appearances the world had become his subjects, with the exception of a small minority who dared to withstand his power and to dispute his authority.[4]

Praise the Lord for small minorities! But the situation was very bleak. What was God going to do about Lucifer's accusations? And why was it taking so long?

Well, consider Lucifer's first claim, that angels were wise and righteous, and didn't need God's law to guide them. Nothing but a demonstration was going to resolve that argument. In fact, nothing but a demonstration was going to resolve *any* of Lucifer's criticisms.

> God's purpose [was] to place things upon an eternal basis of security. Time must be given for Satan to develop the principles which were the foundation of his government. The heavenly universe must see worked out the principles which Satan declared were superior to God's principles. God's order must be contrasted with Satan's order. The corrupting principles of Satan's rule must be revealed. The principles of righteousness expressed in God's law must be demonstrated as unchangeable, perfect, eternal.[5]

Take a moment and notice the five uses of the word "must." Every one of them involves a manifestation of reality, some disclosing of information. This is important, because if producing factual evidence is God's approach to solving this problem, it behooves us to be familiar with that evidence if we want to be a part of the solution.

God's choice to let Satan proceed relatively unchecked[6] for four millennia may seem excessive. Suffering makes time expensive, not only for those dealing with every form of pain that Satan can dream up, but also for God. To overlook this divine dimension displays an embarrassingly shallow emotional commitment to the first great commandment!

> Few give thought to the suffering that sin has caused our Creator. All heaven suffered in Christ's agony; but that suffering did not begin or end with His manifestation in humanity. The cross is a revelation to our dull senses of the pain that, from its very inception, sin has brought to the heart of God.[7]

By overlooking more than 99.999% of God's suffering due to sin, we leave ourselves open to the devil's suggestion that God is not nearly as loving as He tries to appear! The stark reality is that for just six hours human beings were permitted to view God living out the "unchangeable, perfect, eternal" "princi-

---

4. *Signs of the Times*, June 13, 1895

5. *Review and Herald*, September 7, 1897. Emphasis supplied.

6. The flood was a major exception to this, but we haven't the space necessary to look at it in depth. The Bible assures us that it was deep enough to do what God needed done.

7. *Education*, 263

ples of righteousness" expressed in His law. This is what God must demonstrate to the universe in order to "place things upon an eternal basis of security." This pain to the heart of God has gone on, uninterrupted, since the "very inception" of sin, but for six hours it was demonstrated in a form that was visible and—to a greater but still limited degree—understandable to human beings.[8]

Why do we have such a hard time understanding? For the same reason that children often doubt the "this hurts me more than it hurts you" line. Lacking the mental capacity to feel the empathy of a parent for a child, the child sees only the whip, and that whip isn't hitting Mom or Dad. We are similarly blind.

Abraham's experience with the call to sacrifice his son, his only son, gives us some insight into the magnitude of God's sacrifice.[9] But when it comes to God's pain on behalf of sinners, we might also consider the kind of daily suffering that comes from watching a "slow motion train wreck."

Think of a parent, watching a child with a stubborn streak. As a toddler, it might sometimes almost be cute. But time passes. Stubbornness turns into a resistance to authority, which becomes belligerence. Education suffers. Employment goes from short and difficult, to basically impossible. Homelessness follows, with long hours of nothing to do but self-medicate with one substance or another. And then, one day, the news arrives; the dosage was just too high that last time.

God sees it all, and feels it as we can perhaps never understand.

Ellen White tries to turn our focus to this greater suffering, but has to do so in a way which doesn't detract from the physical horror because there are still sinners who may be reached only through that more understandable portrayal. But Jesus was certainly dealing with a reality beyond physical pain.

> [On the cross, Christ could not] see the Father's reconciling face. The withdrawal of the divine countenance from the Saviour in this hour of supreme anguish pierced His heart with a sorrow that can never be fully understood by man. So great was this agony that His physical pain was hardly felt.[10]

Was this greater pain *exactly* the same as that which "from its very inception, sin has brought to the heart of God"? No. Similar in nature, but not exactly the same. Here's why:

---

8. In recognizing this "suffering that sin has caused our Creator," we need go no further than inspiration in order to understand it. This suffering is what sin "brought to the heart of God," not some weirdly conceived "eternal crucifixion" or continually bleeding "immaculate heart." Such concepts are just one more way in which Satan seeks to distance Christ's sacrifice from simple reality.

9. This is discussed in more detail further on in this book. If you *must* look ahead, you could read reference 12 on page 77. Still, that sort of willy-nilly hopping around through the text is not encouraged.

10. *Desire of Ages*, 753

It was necessary for the awful darkness to gather about [Jesus'] soul because of the withdrawal of the Father's love and favor, for He was standing in the sinner's place, and this darkness every sinner must experience. The righteous One must suffer the condemnation and wrath of God, not in vindictiveness; for the heart of God yearned with greatest sorrow when His Son, the Guiltless, was suffering the penalty of sin. This sundering of the divine powers will never again occur throughout the eternal ages.[11]

¶The pain spoken of in the statement from *Education*, 263, "did not begin or end with His manifestation in humanity." But the "sundering of the divine powers will never again occur throughout the eternal ages." The pain of sin goes on; the pain of the "sundering" has ended.

The pain of sin is God's sense of His children's pain caused by their own separation from Him. The sundering was a personal experience. I'm not qualified to speak authoritatively on God's sense of suffering, but if you asked Abraham, or any "good" parent, whether they would rather die or watch their child die, it might help put the two kinds of suffering in perspective.

The demonstration of the cross was necessary for the simple reason that God's willingness to die in order to bless others, could never be established without actually dying to bless others! Oh sure, He could have told everyone who would listen that He loved all His created beings so much that He would die to help any one of them. But hearing that from the One seated upon the throne of the universe, surrounded by "ten thousand times ten thousand, and thousands of thousands"[12] of adoring angels, might not be persuasive to someone living out a wretched existence in poverty and political oppression here on earth.

Besides, every time God said anything, Satan was right there with his ninth accusation—God is lying. And until the proof was in, who could say? Maybe he was right?

No verbal description could reveal God to the world. Through a life of purity, a life of perfect trust and submission to the will of God, a life of humiliation such as even the highest seraph in heaven would have shrunk from, God himself must be revealed to humanity.[13]

Words alone couldn't do the job. The only avenue God had out of the mess that Satan had caused was this path of actual demonstration. That's a little odd, really, since we are assured that "Our heavenly Father has a thousand ways to provide for us of which we know nothing."[14] And yet—

---

11. E.G. White, "Words of Instruction from the Apostle Paul," July 13, 1899; Manuscript 93, 1899
12. Revelation 5:11
13. *Review and Herald*, June 25, 1895
14. *Ministry of Healing*, 481

There was no other way by which man could be brought into harmony with His unchangeable law, save by the death of Christ.[15]

The only plan that could be devised to save the human race was that which called for the incarnation, humiliation, and crucifixion of the Son of God, the Majesty of heaven.[16]

This was the only way by which the law could be maintained, and pronounced holy, just, and good, by which sin could appear exceeding sinful and the honor and majesty of Divine Authority be maintained.[17]

Only by the humiliation of the Prince of heaven could the dishonor be removed, justice satisfied, and man restored to that which he had forfeited by disobedience. There was no other way.[18]

If human beings are going to be a part of that eternally secure universe God is working towards, the rest of its inhabitants are going to be looking to see that we actually comprehend this demonstration. It is, after all, the only plan that could clear God's government of wrong doing, and give us a chance at forgiveness and eternal life.

It's no surprise, then, that Satan is happy to foster a shallow, one-sided, view of the central event of the whole plan of salvation. To this end, he happily promotes those six hours—the "sufferings of Christ on the cross"—as the sole payment of an arbitrarily imposed penalty for sin. Experience has shown that such a belief works nicely as a way to deflect inquiry and prevent any more accurate understanding.

He has little need to worry about distorting or counterfeiting the idea of defending God's government, since it's entirely foreign to most of Christendom, anyway. And the specific charges of an arbitrary law and the impossibility of forgiveness are so far off the radar map that one could almost believe the devil had little to worry about.

Almost....

---

15. *Signs of the Times*, September 2, 1889
16. *Signs of the Times*, January 20, 1890
17. E.G. White, "I Am the Resurrection and the Life," 1897; Manuscript 131, 1897
18. E.G. White, Letter to Dr. E.R. Caro, January 4, 1903; Letter 6, 1903

CHAPTER 8

The Only Path

THE first four thousand years of earth's history were a sad revelation of human selfishness and corruption. But it was Satan's attacks on Christ during His life on earth, culminating in the crucifixion, that filled out the picture of angelic "wisdom" and "righteousness" when not guided by God's law. Still, simply discrediting Satan wasn't the full answer. Much more evidence was needed to dispel the doubts of God's wisdom and love which had been planted in the minds of the universe.

As Ellen White said, a "crisis had been reached"[1] just prior to Christ's first advent. It was "the fullness of the time," and the Son of God was ready to make this world a stage where the attributes of His Father—as well as those of Satan —would be seen by all the universe.[2]

> The great object that brought Christ to the earth was to reveal the Father.[3]

> "God is love." This was the great truth that Christ came to the world to reveal.... The object of Christ's mission to the world was to reveal the Father.[4]

> Christ came to this world for no other purpose than to display the glory of God, that man might be uplifted by its restoring power.[5]

Ellen White says this so often, that it's easy to take it for granted. Fortunately, Jesus did not let any carelessness slip into His execution of this task.

---

1. *Signs of the Times*, June 5, 1901, quoted previously on page 39.
2. For those who wouldn't object to an illustration drawn from the world of gambling, we might say that the cards were about to be laid on the table.
3. *Signs of the Times*, June 27, 1895
4. *Signs of the Times*, April 11, 1895
5. E.G. White, Letter to O.A. Olsen, August 25, 1896; Letter 87, 1896

❧ God... sent His Son into the world to reveal, so far as could be endured by human sight, the nature and the attributes of the invisible God.[6]

Christ revealed all of God that sinful human beings could bear without being destroyed.[7]

Some jobs require close attention to detail!

Christ exalted the character of God, attributing to Him the praise, and giving to Him the credit, of the whole purpose of His own mission on earth—to set men right through the revelation of God.... When the object of His mission was attained—the revelation of God to the world—the Son of God announced that His work was accomplished, and that the character of the Father was made manifest to men.[8]

This last paragraph has a lot to digest. For starters, notice that she describes "the revelation of God to the world" as "the *whole purpose*" of Christ's mission on earth. In other words, this is not some side issue, some inconsequential matter—this is the "whole purpose."[9]

What's interesting is that we often highlight the salvation of human beings as the preeminent purpose of His coming. And Jesus Himself said that "the Son of Man has come to seek and to save that which was lost."[10] So which is it?

You might expect the answer to be "Both," but that would leave the issue confused. The "two goals" are not in any sense separate. Notice the phrase, "to set men right through the revelation of God." That "setting men right" part is human salvation. It's just that human salvation requires that those humans have an accurate perception of God.

Satan's work since his fall is to misinterpret our heavenly Father.... that He shall be regarded as severe, revengeful, arbitrary, and not exercising forgiveness. Without the correct knowledge of God, the human family would be divested[11] of all divine strength. With false attributes kept before the mind as belonging to God, the human family would be the dupes[12] of satanic lies and the subjects of satanic agencies, and he could practice upon their credulity with success.[13]

This may be starting to sound a little odd. After all, we more commonly talk about salvation being dependent on the sacrifice of Christ on the cross... and

---

6. E.G. White, Letter to J.E. White, November 16, 1903; Letter 250, 1903
7. E.G. White, "A Personal God," October 14, 1903; Manuscript 124, 1903
8. *Signs of the Times*, January 20, 1890
9. To be honest, it's not that easy to decide whether "the whole purpose" or "no other purpose" is the stronger expression of the idea.
10. Luke 19:10
11. This paragraph has some great vocab words! For starters, "divested" means to be "deprived of property, authority, or title." When applied to "all divine strength," that's a major problem!
12. Vocab word #2: A "dupe" is "one that is easily deceived or cheated." For background, the word comes from "duplicitous" ("deceptive in words or actions"), which itself comes from "duplicity" ("doubleness of thought, especially in saying one thing to one group, and something else to another group").
13. E.G. White, "Diary: December 1890," December 10, 1890; Manuscript 51, 1890

this emphasis on a "correct knowledge of God" just sounds a little different. But the cross is here, too. Two statements back, we saw that, "When the object of His mission was attained—the revelation of God to the world—the Son of God announced that His work was accomplished, and that the character of the Father was made manifest to men."[14]

That announcement... that was Jesus saying, "It is finished!" That's where the cross fits in. It was an absolute necessity, since the "character of the Father" is a willingness to make any sacrifice for others' good. The cross just shows that more clearly than any other event, because that's when Jesus took the idea to its absolute logical—and highly visible—conclusion. Anything less would not have done the job.[15]

Here's the same idea of what was accomplished by the cross, phrased even more concisely:

> God's government was secure. His law was proved faultless. The Father, the Son, and Lucifer were revealed in their real relation to each other.[16]

Here, too, we see the precision of the need. There was, indeed, only one path for Christ to follow:

> The great sacrifice of the Son of God was neither too great nor too small to accomplish the work. In the wisdom of God it was complete.[17]

> God could not do more for man than He has done in giving His beloved Son, nor could He do less and yet secure the redemption of man and maintain the dignity of the divine law.[18]

> That the abundance of His grace should be revealed, He could not give less than the fullness, nor was it possible for Him to give more.[19]

Closely related to this idea is another common thought—the recognition that it was only the sacrifice of Christ that would suffice to save mankind. We often phrase this concept in terms of "worth" or "value," pointing out that the

---

14. Incidentally, this statement employs two "em dashes," those really long hyphen things before and after "the revelation of God to the world." The name em dash comes from its width, traditionally the same as the capital "M" character in the font. They are commonly used to set off nonrestrictive clauses—words that provide additional information without changing, or "restricting," the meaning of the sentence. That last sentence is an example, with the words after the em dash adding a definition of the term "nonrestrictive clause." If the sentence read simply, "They are used to set off nonrestrictive clauses," it would mean exactly the same, but the reader wouldn't have the definition so conveniently supplied.

    In Ellen White's case, she is actually defining "the revelation of God to the world" as "the whole purpose" of Christ's mission to earth. It's a big deal.

15. The question has sometimes been asked if Christ could have saved sinners by dying in heaven to "pay their debt." As a simple "payment" we could imagine that that approach would have worked, but as a "revelation" it would literally have been a "no-show" forfeiture of the entire contest.

16. E.G. White, "God's Justice," January 6, 1902; Manuscript 1, 1902

17. *Signs of the Times*, December 30, 1889

18. *Testimonies*, vol. 4, 418

19. E.G. White, "Christ's Manner of Instruction," January 9, 1890; Manuscript 25, 1890

life of Christ is worth more than the life of an angel, thus explaining that no angel could have worked out our salvation. The thought is certainly valid, but it is just as certainly not the only explanation offered for the requirement of Christ's sacrifice. Consider this, for instance:

> He alone, the Creator of man, could be his Saviour. No angel of heaven could reveal the Father to the sinner, and win him back to allegiance to God. But Christ could manifest the Father's love; for God was in Christ, reconciling the world unto himself.[20]

Understood in this light, the cross fits seamlessly into the larger picture of the great controversy. Understood solely as a "payment for sin," it actually poses some problems.

Problems? From the cross?

No, not from the cross. From a misunderstanding of the cross. You see, our understanding of the cross is based on our understanding of forgiveness. And our understanding of forgiveness is determined by our understanding of the law which was broken. All of which goes right back to Lucifer's claim that the law of heaven is something that God says it isn't. Consider:

> The penalty of transgressing the law has fallen upon our Substitute and Surety, and for a time has been suspended, so that the guilty do not feel its weight; but the object of this suspension is not to teach us that its claims are over, its exactions set aside, but to attract us to holiness, to obedience. Nothing is changed except the manner of bringing men to obey the law. Obey its claims we must.[21]

We're not done with that issue just yet, but right now we want to pick up another important thread of thought from Jesus' life. We've already seen that the "whole purpose" of His "mission on earth" was to reveal His Father; now let's take a look at *how* He went about doing that.

> Jesus could not express in words to the understanding of man the love of the Father.... But He did express the love of God in His actions.[22]

We've seen the insufficiency of words before. "Actions" can be seen. They speak more loudly than words. That's not to say that words are necessarily bad. It's just that words alone "could not express... to the understanding of man the love of the Father." Simply put, that means that words—preaching and teaching—were an adjunct to the more central work of Christ's revelation. In that light, this makes perfect sense:

> The Saviour of the world devoted more time and labor to healing the afflicted of their maladies than to preaching.[23]

---

20. *Signs of the Times*, February 13, 1893
21. *Signs of the Times*, August 13, 1894
22. *Signs of the Times*, November 28, 1892
23. *Testimonies*, vol. 4, 225

Jesus knew how to get the most bang for His buck. He did preach, of course. The sermon on the mount, the parables... they were all good. It's just that He could accomplish more in other ways. His words, then, served to deepen the primary impression of His actions. Speaking specifically of the sermon on the mount, Ellen White said this:

> Christ lived every phase of that sermon before He gave it to His hearers. The Beatitudes represent His deeds.[24]

> Christ's sermon on the mount contains lessons which Jesus Himself had lived and acted before He commenced His instruction to the people.[25]

So let's not give up on words. They have their place, but only if they can truthfully point back to the greater revelation of godly actions.

What we've seen in our look at the life of Christ may be boiled down to a very simple formula: He came to reveal the Father,[26] and this necessitated more than words. This revelation required that He "express the love of God in His actions," culminating in His death on the cross. Only then could He claim that His mission was finished. Ellen White sums this all up nicely:

> In all His ministry, all His self-denial and self-sacrifice, Christ's object was to reveal God to the world.[27]

But there are many different kinds of "actions" which might reveal the character of God. No doubt Christ used many—maybe all—of them, but there was one approach which He chose more than any other. There's a reason for that, and it's built right into the vocabulary of the New Testament.

---

24. E.G. White, Letter to J.E. and Emma White, November 16, 1894; Letter 81, 1894
25. E.G. White, "The Avondale School Farm," September 14, 1898; Manuscript 115, 1898
26. We are far from the first to notice this focus: "Here is Satan, who has been seeking with all his power to shut out the true character of God so that the world could not understand it, and under a garb of righteousness he works upon many who profess to be Christians, but they represent the character of Satan instead of the character of Jesus Christ. And if he works on the children of disobedience and they claim to be Christians, don't you see that they misrepresent my Lord? They misrepresent the character of Jesus every time that they lack mercy, every time that they lack humility." E.G. White, "Sermon: Advancing in Christian Experience," October 20, 1888; Manuscript 8, 1888
27. E.G. White, Letter to J. Washburn, W.W. Prescott, A.G. Daniells, W.A. Colcord, January 16, 1906; Letter 58, 1906

CHAPTER 9

A Little Greek

READ the following verses from Matthew, Luke, and Paul, and notice especially the underlined words:

> She will bring forth a Son, and you shall call His name JESUS, for He will <u>save</u> His people from their sins.[1]

> [The Pharisees] began to say to themselves, "Who is this who even forgives sins?" Then He said to the woman, "Your faith has <u>saved</u> you. Go in peace."[2]

> For by grace you have been <u>saved</u> through faith, and that not of yourselves; it is the gift of God.[3]

In each case, the subject is salvation. We have quite a few names for this, everything from "conversion," to "the new birth," to "righteousness by faith." It is a major theme (some would say, "the only theme," but it's really not) of the whole Bible.

"Salvation" is a big topic, but right now we don't need to get all technical about it. All we need to note is that in each of those verses, the underlined word is the translation of the same Greek root word, *sozo*. It's fairly common in the New Testament, showing up with that idea of spiritual salvation about seventy times. But let's move on.

> Jesus turned around, and when He saw her He said, "Be of good cheer, daughter; your faith has <u>made you well</u>." And the woman was <u>made well</u> from that hour.[4]

---

1. Matthew 1:21
2. Luke 7:49–50
3. Ephesians 2:8
4. Matthew 9:22

Jesus said to him, "Go your way; your faith has <u>made you well</u>." And immediately he received his sight and followed Jesus on the road.[5]

[Jesus] said to [the one leper], "Arise, go your way. Your faith has <u>made you well</u>."[6]

You've probably already guessed that the underlined words come from a common Greek root, and that's right. But what makes all this of interest is that the root word in this second set of verses is *sozo*, just the same as the first set. The same word means *both* salvation and healing. These two ideas are not that different. In fact, when Peter cried out, "Lord, save me!" he used *sozo*. It's translated "save," but it's obviously got a more immediate focus than the first resurrection! In this more mundane sense of immediate bodily well-being, *sozo* shows up about thirty times.[7]

And this overlapping of ideas is far from coincidental. There's good reason to see God's hand in all this, because there is a divinely inspired connection between the two concepts.

> The Holy Spirit never has and never will in the future divorce the medical missionary work from the gospel ministry. They cannot be divorced. Bound up with Jesus Christ, the ministry of the Word and the healing of the sick are one.[8]

"Are one." It's almost as if Ellen White knew about the Greek....

But the point of all this *sozo* discussion is simply that when Jesus healed the sick, He not only demonstrated the character of His Father, He also illustrated the process of forgiveness. That's really important, more so than we tend to realize.

> The gospel which He taught was a message of spiritual life and of physical restoration. Deliverance from sin and the healing of disease were linked together.[9]

> The work of Christ in cleansing the leper from his terrible disease is an illustration of His work in cleansing the soul from sin....

> In the healing of the paralytic at Capernaum, Christ again taught the same truth. It was to manifest His power to forgive sins that the miracle was performed.[10]

Ellen White speaks of "healing" sin literally hundreds of times. What's easy to miss in this regard, though, is that healing is never based on someone's "say-so." A judge can throw a case out of court, but doctors don't have that kind of

---

5. Mark 10:52

6. Luke 17:19

7. While we will be focusing on *sozo*, it's worth noting that Greek also offers us a near synonym, *iaomai*, which is defined as "to cure, heal; to make whole; to free from errors and sins, to bring about one's salvation."

    It's a good word, too, but *sozo* is a lot easier when it comes to the phonics! Curiously, of the twenty-eight times *iaomai* appears in the New Testament, seventeen of them (60%) come from Luke. Leave it to a doctor to use a word I can't pronounce!

8. E.G. White, "Come Out and Be Separate," November 1905; Manuscript 21, 1906

9. *Ministry of Healing*, 111

10. *Desire of Ages*, 266–267

luxury. The first is an arbitrary enactment, the second is encumbered with the reality of cells, biology, and chemistry. For Jesus to "forgive" someone of leprosy took more than kind thoughts in His own mind. It took actual power to change the condition and function of someone else's body, and the end result had to pass the inspection of the priests before the leper was allowed to rejoin his family. There are lessons here, for the final healing of sinners—the "great healing" of this volume's subtitle—will be scrutinized infinitely more closely by the watching universe than any leper ever was.

This is perhaps the most important place to remember "as in the natural, so in the spiritual," because forgiveness is not accomplished through spiritual fairy dust! Like all the healings that Jesus used to illustrate it, it is the result of an identifiable process, not an arbitrary decree. So let's learn an important point from the role of a health care provider:

> The first thing to be done is to ascertain the true character of the sickness and then go to work intelligently to remove the cause.[11]

If you're going to study a "process," there's no better place to start than "the first thing to be done." That makes a lot of sense when we're talking about diabetes, but what about "salvation"? How strong are the parallels? How far does this "natural" and "spiritual" thing go?

Let's put a few pieces together. We know that an "unsaved condition" is the result of "living without... full confidence in God."[12] So notice: this "unsaved condition" is the result of a *lack*, the result of *something missing*. The doctors have a name for that sort of problem. Think of scurvy; think of beriberi, rickets, and goiters.

OK, that may not work if you don't have a little medical background, but those are *deficiency diseases*. No vitamin C? You get scurvy.[13] Beriberi is a lack of vitamin B1; rickets is not enough vitamin D; and goiters come from a lack of iodine.

If you were trying to help someone with scurvy, what's the first thing you should do?

"Ascertain the true character of the sickness," of course, and then "go to work intelligently to remove the cause." The "cause" of scurvy is not having enough vitamin C, and "removing" the deficiency is done with limes! Or lemons, or any other source of vitamin C.

---

11. *Ministry of Healing*, 235
12. *Bible Training School*, November 1, 1911. Quoted more fully on page 25.
13. An estimated two million sailors died of scurvy from the 16th to the 18th centuries because ships didn't have fresh produce. In 1747, James Lind, a British naval surgeon, found that he could prevent and cure the disease with fresh citrus fruit. About forty years later—a year after Lind died—the British Admiralty acted on his report, and fatalities began to decline.

That's the way it works in the natural world; what about the spiritual? What about *sozo*?

On the spiritual side of all this, the key is realizing that we've already been told "the true character of the sickness." Being "unsaved" is a deficiency disease! And the cause is exactly what Ellen White said it was. Not just a lack of "God" (Satan knows God in far greater detail than any of us), it's caused by a lack of "full confidence in God."

That loss of confidence, that loss of faith, is the cause that produces the unsaved condition. That's what turned Lucifer into Satan. That's what caused the fall of Adam and Eve. So how would God "go to work intelligently to remove" a lack of "full confidence in God"?

More than likely, He would send Jesus to reveal the character of the Father. To show—not just tell—that God is love, all the way up to and including dying to help someone else. If that doesn't inspire faith, nothing will.

Literally. Nothing. At that point, there's nothing more even God can do.

CHAPTER 10

Apples and Oranges

THE ability to tell the difference between an apple and an orange is generally considered a good thing. Technically, it might be described as "discrimination," which used to be a positive word, but has picked up some serious negative overtones, not because the ability to discriminate is actually bad, but because of the unrighteous actions which too often follow.

Sometimes, it doesn't matter much if one is not discriminating. Both apples and oranges contain vitamin C, for instance, so as long as you eat enough of either, you shouldn't get scurvy.

But sometimes the ability to discriminate is a big deal. We'll be looking now at perhaps the most important distinction that matters to every member of the human race. It's a big deal. So let's get the setting:

Even after the cross, God's victory is not yet complete. That matches well with the observable data, but why not? Because this contest involves every issue Lucifer raised, and some of them haven't been dealt with yet. Most notable on that account is Satan's combo-package claim that *either* the law of heaven is arbitrary, *or* God can't forgive sinners.

God disagrees, of course, but that's not enough to silence the devil. And the idea that God is working to save some sinners, but not all sinners, to offer forgiveness to sinful humans but not to sinful angels, is especially irksome. All of which puts Satan in the position of claiming that nothing of the sort is even the least bit fair!

If we drew a comparison to any other favorable treatment granted on the basis of race or ethnicity, it would be *very* hard to beat a charge of unjust discrimination. If that's not fair in earthly matters, how could God provide forgiveness and eternal life for the sinners He liked, but rule it out for others?

It may seem next thing to heresy to ask if Satan is right, but it's not. God is far more interested in every intelligent being understanding truth, than He is in any amount of uncomprehending loyalty. Faith in the face of uncertainty is a great thing, but God's goal is to move beyond uncertainty. Even if it takes a long time....

Remember those angels who chose faith in God instead of trusting the unproven charges of Lucifer? That was a fantastic choice, but it didn't resolve Satan's charges and the questions he raised. Ellen White acknowledges this in a classic use of understatement: "It was difficult to uproot Satan from the affection of the angels in heaven."[1] So God gave them time to watch, time to think, time to learn. And it payed off—after four thousand years!

> [After the crucifixion] Satan saw that his disguise was torn away. His administration was laid open before the unfallen angels and before the heavenly universe. He had revealed himself as a murderer. By shedding the blood of the Son of God, he had uprooted himself from the sympathies of the heavenly beings.... The last link of sympathy between Satan and the heavenly world was broken.[2]

God's plan is based on "understanding," and He knows that it can take a long time to get people up to speed. Actually, it's safe to say that the only decisive weapon God uses in the whole great controversy is this revelation of the "contrast between the Prince of light and the prince of darkness." Or, as Ellen White put it on another occasion—

> The whole gospel is a continuous explanation of misunderstandings and clearing up of difficulties which Satan manages to create to perplex minds.[3]

But Satan claims that God can't forgive? Does he have a point?

The answer hinges on how we think the process of "forgiveness" *works*. Ultimately, there are two ways to look at the issue: God's way, and Satan's., and we really ought to have this clear in our thinking! But the challenge is not trivial, for just as the earthly sanctuary service included both a "daily" procedure for forgiveness and a "once-at-the-end-of-the-year" procedure for forgiveness, so the full plan of salvation (which, after all, is what the sanctuary illustrated) includes a two-stage model of forgiveness which finds its full development only at the end of time.

It is the evidence provided by this antitypical day of atonement that refutes Satan's last accusations. In fact, to say that this demonstration comes "at the

---

1. E.G. White, "Sermon: Christ's Controversy With the Devil," July 25, 1886; Manuscript 11, 1886

2. *Desire of Ages*, 761. This quotation raises an obvious question: Didn't Cain's murder of Abel reveal Lucifer as a murderer? How could that not have been clear after 4,000 blood-soaked years? The answer would seem to be that there was a categorical distinction between the death of millions of sinful human beings and the single sinless human/divine being. For all the former, Lucifer could merely point out that, after all, it was *God's* law that said sinners must die.

3. E.G. White, "Diary: Love Thy Neighbor as Thyself," 1890; Manuscript 66, 1890

end of time" is like saying "the heart stops beating at the end of life." It's not a coincidence! "No heartbeat" is generally considered a strong indicator of death, not something that "just happens" about the same time.[4] And so the devil's plan is fairly simple: exalt and extend an eviscerated[5] version of the "old" system, and use it to prevent the development of the "new."

It's not a new idea. That's what he did with the Jews. Just keep everyone doing what they've always done, believing what they've always believed, despite the fact that all the teachings of the Old Testament and the whole purpose of the temple that they loved so much were all intended to prepare the way for the coming of something new—the Son of God!

> The ordinances which God Himself had appointed were made the means of blinding the mind and hardening the heart. God could do no more for man through these channels. The whole system must be swept away.[6]

There's a warning in all this.

> Satan... won his great triumph in perverting the faith of Israel.... The principle that man can save himself by his own works lay at the foundation of every heathen religion; it had now become the principle of the Jewish religion. Satan had implanted this principle. Wherever it is held, men have no barrier against sin.[7]

The problem, of course, is that this "legalism," this "works righteousness," just happened to look a whole lot like the divinely specified religious services of the Old Testament. Sacrificial lambs died in the temple every day—until A.D. 70 when Titus and the Roman legions put an end to it all. But is it relevant to us? After all, none of *that* history happened in the antitypical day of atonement. But a few paragraphs back we noticed that the sanctuary service foreshadows a "two-stage model of forgiveness which finds its full development only at the end of time." What are the odds that Satan has a parallel attack for the parallel time in which we live?

For now, let's deal with an easier question: What could possibly make it fair for God to offer forgiveness to sinful humans, but not to sinful angels? Hint—it isn't an arbitrary distinction!

> In the opening of the great controversy, Satan had declared that the law of God could not be obeyed, that justice was inconsistent with mercy, and that, should the law be broken, it would be impossible for the sinner to be pardoned. Every sin must

---

4. Note for medical folks: For the sake of the illustration, let's just not worry about "brain death" and all the other technical variables and alternatives.

5. This Latin term means to remove the viscera, the "internal organs in the main cavities of the body, especially those in the abdomen." Modern readers may relate more easily to the equivalent Anglo Saxon word, "gutless."

6. *Desire of Ages*, 36

7. *Desire of Ages*, 35

meet its punishment,[8] urged Satan; and if God should remit the punishment of sin, He would not be a God of truth and justice. When men broke the law of God, and defied His will, Satan exulted. It was proved, he declared, that the law could not be obeyed; man could not be forgiven. Because he, after his rebellion, had been banished from heaven, Satan claimed that the human race must be forever shut out from God's favor. God could not be just, he urged, and yet show mercy to the sinner.

But even as a sinner, man was in a different position from that of Satan. Lucifer in heaven had sinned in the light of God's glory. To him as to no other created being was given a revelation of God's love. Understanding the character of God, knowing His goodness, Satan chose to follow his own selfish, independent will. This choice was final. There was no more that God could do to save him. But man was deceived; his mind was darkened by Satan's sophistry. The height and depth of the love of God he did not know. For him there was hope in a knowledge of God's love. By beholding His character he might be drawn back to God.[9]

Now we can see why "the whole purpose of His own mission on earth" was "to set men right through the revelation of God." That revelation is the only *cause* that has any chance of producing the desired *effect*. We can also see the diabolical logic of Satan's plan of attack, and recognize the magnitude of the problems created by not understanding Jesus' revelation of His Father. We've seen this statement before, but it bears repeating:

> [Satan's] teachings falsify the character of God, that He shall be regarded as severe, revengeful, arbitrary, and not exercising forgiveness. Without the correct knowledge of God, the human family would be divested of all divine strength. With false attributes kept before the mind as belonging to God, the human family would be the dupes of satanic lies and the subjects of satanic agencies, and he could practice upon their credulity with success.[10]

But Jesus *did* come to earth; He *did* reveal the true attributes of His Father's character; He *did* die to prove that there is nothing God would not do to help another. A focus on that revelation of God has the power to draw human sinners back to God, because it represents unknown "good news" to the darkened

---

8. We will see this more clearly on page 60; just note that Lucifer doesn't really want to be punished, himself. This is "brinkmanship diplomacy." Imagine two guys wrestling right next to a cliff (the "brink"). Assuming lethal intent, they both want to toss their opponent over the edge, and they both know that their opponent wants to do the same to them. Consequently, a defensive policy of hanging on to one's opponent naturally develops. It boils down to, "If you think you're going to throw me over, just know that you're going too."

9. *Desire of Ages*, 761. This explains the approach taken toward Lucifer and the angels who rebelled, that we saw on page 21. Since there were no further revelations of God's glory and love to show them, pardon was "offered... on condition of repentance and submission.... Had Lucifer been willing to return to his allegiance, humble and obedient, he would have been re-established in his office as covering cherub." Forgiveness was a much simpler proposition in the case of angels, but there were limits. They had been given so much that there was nothing held in reserve, nothing more God could show them.

Sadly, when they refused to trust on the basis of what they knew, "The knowledge which [Satan], as well as the angels who fell with him, had of the character of God, of His goodness, His mercy, wisdom, and excellent glory, made their guilt unpardonable." *Review and Herald*, February 24, 1874

10. E.G. White, "Diary: December 1890," December 10, 1890; Manuscript 51, 1890

minds of deceived humanity. Not so for Satan and his companions; they had seen it all before, and called it all lies. In the process, they lost not only the willingness, but the *ability* to believe in even the *possibility* of forgiveness.

> Well, there was war in heaven, and all the disaffected ones were overcome and cast down to the earth. I want to tell you that that wonderful Lucifer who wanted the highest place, lost his hold of heaven. He would not repent, and therefore there are two parties in our world. There is one party that is striving that they may be overcomers by the blood of the Lamb and the word of their testimony.... [Satan and his accomplices] had not the power, the connection with God, the power of discernment, to understand that if they repented, they could be brought back again.[11]

The two groups are as different as apples and oranges, and trying to decide whether it's "fair" to forgive those who can believe in forgiveness while not forgiving those who can't even understand the concept is a fool's errand. Is it fair that a little child could walk safely across a frozen lake while a hefty adult would go through the ice? Reality doesn't stoop to that kind of "fair."

But every intelligent being in all of creation cares about reality! They watched it all, from Bethlehem to Nazareth to Golgotha. Nothing they saw helped Satan's case, and so that list of accusations was looking much worse for wear. Claim number one was proven false by none other than Lucifer and his angels—killing the innocent Son of God simply could not be passed off as either holy or wise. And, after the cross, no one who had been watching (as every intelligent being in the universe had) could believe Lucifer should have gotten Jesus' job (#2); or that humanity was a hopelessly flawed creation (#3); or that God was selfish, unforgiving, and revengeful (#4); or that the law of heaven was so faulty (#5) that no one could keep it (#6). That last point is particularly notable, because Jesus proved it wrong in the best (probably the *only*) possible manner. He just did it! In human nature, no less.

Six of Lucifer's claims had gone down in flames. The universe had learned a great deal... but apparently not all that's needed.

> Yet Satan was not then destroyed. The angels did not even then understand all that was involved in the great controversy. The principles at stake were to be more fully revealed. And for the sake of man, Satan's existence must be continued. Man as well as angels must see the contrast between the Prince of light and the prince of darkness. He must choose whom he will serve.[12]

That's why we're still here two thousand years later. Lucifer made nine accusations against heaven's government, and God is nothing if not thorough. Seven, eight, and nine are still on the table.

---

11. Ellen White, "Thoughts on Revelation 19," April 7, 1910; Manuscript 80, 1910
12. *Desire of Ages*, 761

CHAPTER 11

Fighting Dirty

WE can see how fundamental this argument over the very core nature of heaven's law is to Satan's strategy, from an event long ago. Shortly after the creation of our earth—

> [Satan laid] plans to wrest from God the noble Adam and his companion Eve. If he could, in any way, beguile them to disobedience, God would make some provision whereby they might be pardoned, and then himself and all the fallen angels would be in a fair way to share with them of God's mercy.[1]

This is way up there on the "amazing scale." Satan was so convinced that God's love for Adam and Eve would lead to some means of forgiveness, that he figured his own best chance was to ride their coattails! That makes human beings sound a little special, doesn't it? And he was right! But only up to a point.

God *did* love Adam and Eve to an unfathomable degree. He *did* come up with a plan to forgive them. But Satan's operative theory was based on the assumption that "forgiveness" would have to include changing—or maybe even *abolishing!*—the law. That, however, was not in God's plan. Those details, however, were part of the "mystery kept secret since the world began,"[2] so Satan was in the dark. He couldn't imagine any way for God to squirm out of his two-pronged trap of accusations seven and eight.

Now, lest anyone start to feel uncomfortable with this picture of God and Lucifer going head-to-head in a contest of strategic cleverness... well, let's just say that that's exactly what was going on, and we probably ought to get used to it! That's pretty much the way Ellen White paints it:

---

1. *Spirit of Prophecy*, vol. 1, 29–30
2. Romans 16:25

God had a knowledge of the events of the future, even before the creation of the world.... The plan that should be carried out upon the defection of any of the high intelligences of heaven—this is the secret, the mystery which has been hid from ages.

It's almost enough to make you feel sorry for Lucifer! He picked a fight he could never win! Before we get all weepy-eyed for him, though, it's worth noting that he had every opportunity he needed just by staying *out* of the fight. And, "No, God didn't set him up to lose." Do you see those "dots" in that last quote? In the world of grammar and typesetting, that's an "ellipsis," and it means something has been left out. So let's see what else Ellen White had to say there:

[God] did not make His purposes to fit circumstances, but He allowed matters to develop and work out. He did not work to bring about a certain condition of things, but He knew that such a condition would exist.[3]

It's a classic "divine foreknowledge vs. free will" conundrum. God knew Lucifer was going to rebel, but He didn't do anything to take away his free choice and *make* him rebel. In fact, God did everything He could to *keep* him from destroying himself and countless others. About the only thing God wouldn't do is turn the Archangel into a robot. God's commitment to freedom is so strong, some people try to make it a fault instead of a virtue! But God has that base covered, too, so complaining on that front is not a plan I'd recommend!

Before we move on from Satan's decision to tempt Adam and Eve, note his approach. See if you can spot the key details:

Evil never seeks entrance to the heart as evil, but as goodness and truth.[4]

Satan's work has been the same since the days of Adam to the present, and he has pursued it with great success, tempting men to distrust God's love and to doubt his wisdom.[5]

Satan came to Eve as an angel of light, and persuaded her that this particular prohibition was of arbitrary authority.[6]

Satan had been quite successful in deceiving angels, so he naturally tended to stick with a winning strategy. And the best way to make God's love and wisdom look suspect was to paint it as arbitrary. Same song, second verse.

What difference would that make to Eve? Well, arbitrary laws all share a certain set of characteristics, one of which is that they always require someone to enforce them. Think of a long, straight, smooth stretch of empty highway with an annoyingly low speed limit. Now, just imagine that Joe Hotrod happens to know there aren't any police officers or traffic cameras around.... No enforcer; no penalty! Let 'er rip! As long as he keeps his car on the road, all that happens

---

3. *Signs of the Times*, March 25, 1897
4. E.G. White, Letter to J.H. Kellogg, May 8, 1903; Letter 107, 1903
5. *Review and Herald*, September 30, 1909
6. E.G. White, "Christ Our Strength," 1893; Manuscript 104, 1893

is that he gets where he's going sooner! No bills get magically removed from his wallet; there's no suspension of his driver's license. It seems like a "No harm, no foul" situation all the way around.[7]

"God's busy elsewhere, Eve, and there's no way He'll miss a couple pieces of fruit. Might as well give it a try. And even if He does find out, we can probably get Him to overlook it."

Satan, of course, was thinking far beyond the fruit!

> It was Satan's design that the state of man should be the same with that of the fallen angels in rebellion against God, uncheered by a gleam of hope. He reasoned that if God pardoned sinful man whom He had created, He would also pardon and receive into favor him and his angels. But he was disappointed.[8]

"Disappointed" is classic understatement. It would be no exaggeration to bump that up to "driven completely past the brink of sanity into a permanent state of homicidal mania."

It played out like this: Satan saw how much God loved human beings. He "just knew" that if he could get them to sin, God would find a way to forgive them. Thus far, he was right. But he assumed that "forgiveness" would require a change in the law. As he saw it, God was stuck: change the law to save Adam and Eve, *or* admit that forgiveness was impossible. Either way, Satan wins, because God had denied both claims! Brilliant!

But God didn't follow that script.

It's important for us to understand how vital these claims are to Satan. They are all that stand between him and eternal death. Given the sort of reciprocal relationship between the seventh and eighth accusations, it should be no surprise to find that as soon as he begins to lose ground on seven, he will jump to number eight. And that's exactly the way Ellen White describes the crucial point at the end of time:

> "Will God banish me and my angels from His presence, and yet reward those who have been guilty of the same sins? Thou canst not do this, O Lord, in justice. Thy throne will not stand in righteousness and judgment. Justice demands that sentence be pronounced against them."[9]

Does Satan really want all sinners destroyed? Not likely! He's number one on that list... but he's willing to argue any angle to try and prove God wrong.

---

7. Ignoring a speed limit is one thing. You could perhaps go twice as fast, maybe even three times as fast, and as long as you didn't do something dumb like go off the road or mow down a little child, there would be no natural detriment. Contrast that with one of those yellow road signs with a right-angled arrow. The "punishment" for coming into that kind of a corner at three times the speed isn't really dependent on the presence of a police officer.

8. *Review and Herald*, February 24, 1874

9. *Testimonies*, vol. 5, 474

CHAPTER 12

Details...

I T'S usually the devil who gets credit for being in the details, but don't fool yourself; the One who balanced out the fundamental forces of nature[1] is very much aware of every issue yet pending in the great controversy. Astute readers may have noticed the suggestion back on page 54 that the developments of the antitypical day of atonement may be of importance in laying Satan's final arguments to rest. This is far from a novel idea, since the difference between the "every-day" and the "yearly" services of the sanctuary have long been seen as paralleling the classic theological distinction between "justification" (often defined as "declared righteous") and "sanctification" (often defined as "made righteous").

These definitions tie into our discussion in an obvious manner, since the distinction between the two hinges on their "manner of origin."

A "made" status is the result of some cause-and-effect process that produced a particular result—a result that can be confirmed by some sort of test or observation.

A "declared" status, on the other hand, is exactly that: someone says something or someone is "such-and-such." "This tree is alive," is an example of a declared status, and if that's all the information you've got, and assuming you place some confidence in the judgment of the "declarer," you'll consider that particular tree capable of growth and whatever else a living tree might do. But

---

1. These "bungee cords" that hold together everything in the universe are currently said to be four in number (but don't hold your breath). They are gravity, the weak nuclear force, electromagnetism, and the strong nuclear force. "Balancing" these is no small trick, since the strong force is said to be 6 thousand trillion trillion trillion (that's 6 followed by 39 zeroes) times stronger than the force of gravity. It should also be noted that no human has yet explained how any of these forces actually work, including the magnets on your fridge door.

any "status" that is based on such a declaration is inherently and unavoidably arbitrary, of course, whether the statement is accurate or not. And that's where the theological issues begin.

In Romans chapter four—an extended discussion of righteousness by faith—Paul says that God "calls those things which do not exist as though they did." He sums up Abraham's experience with this by saying "it was accounted to him for righteousness," quickly adds that this was "not written for his sake alone... but also for us," and then labels the whole process as "justification by faith."

Contrast this with the declaration of fact made at the close of time: "he who is righteous, let him be righteous still; he who is holy, let him be holy still."[2] This is not a declaration about anyone other than "he who *is* righteous" and "he who *is* holy." There are no "things which do not exist" in this picture. There is no "accounting." It's just simply, "he who *is*." The person's holiness or righteousness isn't a result of the declaration; the declaration simply acknowledges the reality of the case.

All this is significant, because the whole purpose of the sanctuary, the whole purpose of justification by faith, is to move people from the "sinner" category into the "righteous" category, and as the sanctuary makes clear in all its ceremonies, this process has to start with forgiveness.

This is not some startling realization. Forgiveness is such a basic concept that all Christians acknowledge it as the turning point of the believer's life, the occasion of the "new birth," the basis of all hope for eternity. Jesus taught His disciples to pray, "forgive us our debts." This, as much or more than any other point of Christian belief, should be clear.

And yet, it is the very nature and process of forgiveness that Satan attacks. Just imagine the nerve it takes to tell God He can't forgive anyone, even if He wants to! It all seems ludicrous... until we put that claim together with Lucifer's assertion that the law is arbitrary.

You see, what it takes to "forgive" any infraction is determined by the law that was transgressed. And "forgiveness" works quite differently with an arbitrary law than it does with a law that isn't arbitrary.

How so? Simply put, forgiving the violation of an arbitrary law requires nothing more than a decision on the part of the enforcing authority, someone like a traffic cop who says, "I'm just giving you a warning today, but keep your speed down, OK," or a trial judge attempting to assess the combined significance of hundreds of evidentiary exhibits.

Forgiving the violation of a non-arbitrary law, on the other hand, requires a process, a mechanism, a means to the end.

---

2. Revelation 22:11

Let's try a couple illustrations. Suppose you get an official-looking envelope in the mail one day. You open it up and find that city hall is fining you $500 for driving your car nearly forty miles per hour over the speed limit, and running a red light in the process. Well, you have the option of paying the fine, or contesting the charge in court... so off to court you go.

When the big day comes, you take your place in the courtroom and listen as the Court Clerk reads the charges and the District Attorney presents the government's evidence–a combined radar reading and photograph. When given opportunity to respond, you say, "I plead guilty, Your Honor, with mitigating circumstances."

The judge leans forward, looks you over for a moment, and asks, "You don't contest the evidence?"

"No, Your Honor."

"That's your car? And you were driving it?"

"Yes, and yes, Your Honor."

"So why didn't you just pay the fine? Why waste the court's time?"

"As I said, Your Honor, there are mitigating circumstances which neither the radar nor the camera captured."

"And what might they be?"

"Your Honor, about seven miles west of that traffic light, I came upon a serious automobile accident with obvious multiple fatalities. I immediately called 911, and was told that all Emergency Services units were at a large apartment building fire on the east side of town, and that an ambulance would get to us, at best, in twenty minutes. But, Your Honor, among the bodies in the smaller car was a seven-year-old girl, who—despite an obviously broken leg and heavy bleeding from multiple injuries—was still breathing. Your Honor, she was lying in my passenger seat when I ran that red light. It was nearly midnight, and I could see that there was no traffic on the cross road. I got her to the hospital, Your Honor, and the ER docs managed to pull her through."

The judge thinks a moment, slams his gavel, and says, "Case dismissed."[3]

Isn't that what you'd *want* him to do?

Of course, that privilege given the judge might sometimes be abused. For a sufficient sum of money, even serious crimes might be overlooked entirely... which is *not* what we want, but rumors persist that it occasionally happens. It's just a feature of arbitrary law.

None of which applies to God's law, though, since He says His law isn't arbitrary! Well, none of it applies as long as you believe God, which Satan obviously doesn't! And that's why he claims God can't forgive!

---

3. Easy, right? But that wouldn't work for someone who ignored the yellow sign with the right-angled arrow back on page 60. Gavels can't fix crushed fenders and broken windshields, nor replace lost blood.

Still fuzzy on the logic there? Let's try another illustration:

Imagine that a VIP-type person gets diagnosed with stage four lung cancer. This is obviously going to interfere with plans for his next election cycle, or international concert tour, or blockbuster movie release. It's just inconvenient all the way around, so our VIP goes to talk with the doctor:

"Doc, this is going to make a mess out of my schedule. It's just not a workable thing, so what's it going to cost for you to write me a clean bill of health?" The absurdity of this approach was mentioned briefly back on page 51, but it's important to grasp this aspect of "forgiveness." What it takes to forgive is determined by the law that's been broken. Arbitrary laws, easy-peasy; non-arbitrary laws, not so much.

That's the foundational basis of Satan's claim, and it's been a thorn in the flesh of theologians for a long time.

Well, *some* theologians, but not all. In fact, most of Christendom in the present day quite comfortably embraces the notion of a thoroughly arbitrary moral law. To most people, it has been the least objectionable alternative to the puzzle of Abraham's case. Since Paul assures us that God "calls those things which do not exist as though they did," theologians have been left scrambling for an explanation.

Generally, there have only been two options:

1. When God said Abraham was righteous, He was "calling those things which do not exist as though they did." In other words, Abraham wasn't actually *fully* righteous; God simply modified his "status" (but not his "state"), and then "accounted" him as righteous even though he wasn't completely so.

2. When God said Abraham was righteous, His word had creative power, just as in the creation of physical matter. "He spoke, and it was done; He commanded, and it stood fast."[4] This meant that, at the command of God, an unrighteous Abraham immediately *became* "righteous."

Given these two options—and a notable aversion to any claim of perfect moral purity—most of Christendom is happy to believe option #1, that God arbitrarily pronounces believers "righteous," even if their lives fail to demonstrate any such thing.

But neither option provides a convincing final demonstration. The first theological explanation—saying that something is "X" while it clearly is *and remains* "Y"—seems a lot like lying. Does God get a free pass on that? Lucifer's final accusation comes to mind just now....

---

4. Psalms 33:9

Option #2, on the other hand, implies that righteousness can be imposed on someone by God's "sovereign will," through no choice of their own. To miraculously transform someone from unrighteous to righteous, apart from or possibly even contrary to their own will, seems inviting.

What a convenient way to solve problems!

The drawback, of course, is that free will disappears completely, seemingly at God's sole discretion. But if that approach is acceptable, shouldn't God have used it on Lucifer and preserved the peace and holiness of the whole universe? Portraying God as willing to override Abraham's individuality and freedom is a serious issue, since Paul uses this occasion as a template to explain the righteousness of all believers for all time.

And, once again, we run into a problem with honesty, this time on Abraham's part. He is "accounted righteous" in Genesis 15:6, but in chapter 20 we find him claiming Sarah is his sister. Does Abraham get a free pass on that?

Or, perhaps, God just makes unrighteous Abraham righteous, over and over and over again. If it ends up with Abraham inheriting eternal life, we might say that he wouldn't mind having his personal choices overruled, but then we're left with the question of everyone who *isn't* saved. Why didn't God do the same for them?

The theological answer for that is easy: Predestination![5]

Hold on a minute! That can't be right. This is getting confusing!

Patience, gentle reader. There is yet hope for clarity, because God has more evidence to show.

---

5. Incidentally, if people get mad at you for not believing in predestination, tell them, "Sorry, it's not my choice."

CHAPTER 13

"Exhibit B"

AFTER a 4,000-year wait, Jesus came to earth as "Exhibit A" in the Lord's rebuttal of Lucifer's accusations. The delay for "Exhibit B" was less than half that long, but—sadly—the effort has so far failed to clinch the case.

The little church that Jesus left behind here on earth was a medical missionary establishment. His final commission to the disciples before His ascension concludes with "they will lay hands on the sick, and they will recover."[1] The New Testament records works of miraculous healing by Peter, John, Phillip, and Paul. Luke was known as the beloved physician, and Paul urged Timothy to use a natural remedy. Space constraints require that we largely skip over the historical stories of the early church and her emphasis on healing ministry, but one paragraph from a scholarly journal paints the picture in broad strokes:

> The new Christian ethic of almsgiving, piety and caring for the old, poor and infirm, soon gained a prominence for the church which was out of proportion to the number of Christians in the Roman world. Visiting the sick, elderly and poor was a duty incumbent on all Christians. The modern hospital concept had its origin in the early Christian communities and... their compassion and long term care for suffering was fundamentally different from anything known before. Neither the pagan temples nor the mystery religions created a caring community like that of early Christianity. In time even those Roman emperors who had instituted persecution of Christendom, commented favourably on the Christians' unstinting assistance to all victims of the epidemics (probably small pox) which ravaged the Roman empire during the 2nd, 3rd, and 4th centuries. Christian health ministration was also continued in spite of pa-

---

1. Mark 16:18

tients' poor prognosis for cure—situations in which patients would probably have been abandoned by Hippocratic medicine.[2]

Much the same story may be told of the Waldensian Barbes (many of whom were accomplished physicians)[3], but we must summarize by saying that the health of the church was to a surprisingly large extent linked to her commitment to health ministry.

We must pass over the centuries lightly, stopping only to consider a few events in the later 1800s. We'll begin by noting a frequently overlooked outcome of the famous 1888 General Conference session:

> After the meeting at Minneapolis, Dr. Kellogg was a converted man, and we all knew it. We could see the converting power of God working in his heart and life.[4]

As one might legitimately expect, conversion, the experience of "righteousness by faith," produced predictable results in Dr. Kellogg—he became much nicer, kinder, and more generous. That may not sound like much, but just as it was for first-century believers, it is clearly a marker of the conversion experience:

> [When the believer] is justified because of the merit of Christ, he is not free to work unrighteousness. Faith works by love and purifies the soul. Faith buds and blossoms and bears a harvest of precious fruit. Where faith is, good works appear. The sick are visited, the poor are cared for, the fatherless and the widows are not neglected, the naked are clothed, the destitute are fed.[5]

> Faith in Jesus Christ as our personal Saviour, the One who pardons our sins and transgressions, the One who is able to keep us from sin and lead us in His footsteps, is set forth in the fifty-eighth chapter of Isaiah. Here are presented the fruits of a faith that works by love and purifies the soul from selfishness. Faith and works are here combined.... "Thy righteousness shall go before thee." What does this mean? Christ is our righteousness.[6]

This is what converted people do.

But Dr. Kellogg was something of a special case. Some people just are. Where there are thousands of believers, there are but few Abrahams, Davids, and Pauls. Dr. Kellogg was one of them. Consider a few significant endorsements:

2. Retief, Francois and Cilliers, Louise. (2010). The influence of Christianity on medicine from Graeco-Roman times up to the Renaissance. *Acta Theologica.* 26. 10.4314/actat.v26i2.52579.
3. See pages 127–129 of Demsky, Kathleen M. "Preachers by Night: The Waldensian Barbes (15th to 16th Centuries) [review] / Gabriel Audisio." *Andrews University Seminary Studies* (AUSS) 46.2 (2008): Available at: digitalcommons.andrews.edu/auss/vol46/iss2/8.
4. *General Conference Bulletin*, April 6, 1903
5. *Selected Messages*, Book 1, 398
6. *Review and Herald*, March 17, 1910

Dr. Kellogg has done a work that no man I know of among us has had qualifications to do.[7]

God says of Dr. Kellogg, "He is My physician. Respect him and sustain him."[8]

My dear brother, as I have before written to you, I know that the Lord has placed you in a very responsible position, standing as you do, as the greatest physician in our world.[9]

A particularly interesting compliment was paid the Doctor by Ellen White's son, W.C. White. He wrote to a friend in Battle Creek:

I do not believe there is a person living, not even her own sons, for whom Mother would do more, to help, to encourage, to correct, and to instruct, than Dr. Kellogg. Why is this? Because God has given him great ability, great opportunities, great responsibilities; and as Mother has said to me several times during the last winter; "Dr. Kellogg stands where he can do more to relieve the perplexities of the present situations, than any other living man; and, too, he stands where he can do more to bring confusion, perplexity, and backsliding, than any other man living."[10]

But perhaps the most revealing such comment is one from Ellen White early on in the Doctor's career, three years before we picked up the story:

If Dr. Kellogg will trust himself wholly with God, He will give him tact and perception and skill as a practitioner that has seldom been excelled. Angels of God will stand by his side when human life is in peril, and wisdom from above will be given him. God designs that Dr. Kellogg shall still advance. He has only begun to climb the ladder. The Lord will give him grace that he is now ignorant of, and he will see as he has never seen before. He will realize that there is to be an intelligent discarding of all drugs. Skill and knowledge is to be given him which he is in no case to keep to himself. He is to educate, educate, educate.[11]

Given all this, it's no surprise that he played a larger role than most. Within the calendar year 1892, the Doctor was instrumental in starting three "medical missionary" initiatives: the establishment of an orphanage; the Visiting Nurses program, and the Christian Help Bands. We haven't the space to describe these programs in detail, nor tell the stories that surround each of them,[12] so once again we must suffice with a summary: each of these programs was established

---

7. E.G. White, Letter to G.I. Butler, October 14, 1888; Letter 21, 1888

8. E.G. White, Letter to A.J. Sanderson, October 16, 1901; Letter 139, 1901

9. E.G. White, Letter to J.H. Kellogg, December 12, 1899; Letter 215, 1899

10. W.C. White, Letter to W.S. Sadler, January 20, 1903

11. E.G. White, "Words of Counsel to Young Physicians," July 27, 1885; Manuscript 4b, 1885. It's worth noting that the understanding of how to carry out "an intelligent discarding of all drugs" was promised on condition that "Dr. Kellogg will trust himself wholly with God." Sadly, this condition was clearly not met in the Doctor's later experience: "God cannot give you the knowledge He is prepared to impart, because He sees that you would not make a right use of it, while you view things in a wrong light." E.G. White, Letter to J.H. Kellogg, May 1900; Letter 85, 1900

12. Some of these stories may be found in my previous book, *d'Sozo: Reversing the Worst Evil.*

to carry out principles found in that fifty-eighth chapter of Isaiah that Ellen White mentioned.

And, then, right on the heels of all that—published in the *Review* for all to read—came the unexpected announcement that something big had happened.

> The loud cry of the third angel has already begun in the revelation of the right-eousness of Christ.[13]

That's a major deal. That's the closest God's church has ever come to finishing the task He assigned her, and we would be remiss if we did not try to understand how it came about. The key is in the word "*revelation*," as in "the revelation of the righteousness of Christ." Simply put, a "revelation" is categorically distinct from a "proclamation." The latter consists of words; the former has to have substance, something more tangible, something that can be seen. In a split familiar to the reader by this time, the former is tangible, observable, testable, and the latter is arbitrary.

As it was in Christ's ministry, that tangible element was medical missionary work. Kellogg's personal conversion had led to a still-small but nonetheless growing trend within the church, a trend that followed Jesus' example of bringing healing and salvation together in selfless service. That's what ignited the loud cry. The theology of 1888 was finding its proper sphere in practical service.[14]

Sadly, this development was but little recognized. Many in the church were focused on conflict over "the covenants," personal alienation between various groups of workers, and old animosities against Dr. Kellogg stemming from his advocacy of "health reform."

The record of the next seven years is a sad one, doubly sad because of errors on both "sides" of the divide. By the latter half of the 1890s, Dr. Kellogg became increasingly annoyed with "the ministers" as a class. From his perspective, they had not helped in anything he had tried to do, but he felt they showed a keen interest in assuming the control—and the financial profits—of the Sanitarium.[15]

Not that Kellogg was faultless! His desire to move rapidly forward on a grand scale with no accountability and but little regard for anyone else's interests or concerns was more than enough to make the ministers uneasy.

Sadly, the one group who were in the best position to help the Doctor, "didn't want to get involved." To all such, past and present, belongs the condemnation of

---

13. *Review and Herald*, November 22, 1892

14. Those interested in this "Good Kellogg" aspect can find the story in much more detail in my book *d'Sozo*.

15. Elder W.C. White acknowledged that this had happened, and spoke of a time when "the General Conference Association planned to foster the Medical Missionary work, and then use it as a slave to make money for other work." Little surprise that "this naturally led the leaders of the Medical Missionary work to retaliate." W.C. White, Letter to Brethren W.C. Sisley, C.H. Jones, and A.T. Jones, March 13, 1899; W.C. White Letterbook 13, 22

the cowardly found in Revelation 21:8: "But the cowardly... shall have their part in the lake which burns with fire and brimstone, which is the second death."

But the strangest part of it is that his associates, the physicians right around him seem to act as though they were paralyzed, as though they did not know enough to tell him, "You are on the wrong track." They are afraid to do it... Fastened amid the delusions of these last days are the associates, plastering things all over, just as though he was a saint, when the works have been going on, and they have known it, but they would not put their hand upon it.[16]

If all men had been true and faithful to Dr. Kellogg, he might have been, yes, would have been in a far different position religiously from what he is now in. There was a work to be done under the influence of the Holy Spirit, to arrest a growing un-belief and infidelity, which was making itself felt. But words were not spoken by Dr. Kellogg's associates to arrest and prevent this growing infidelity.[17]

I have a message for you. In many respects you are a weak man. I did think, af-ter the camp-meeting at Fresno, that you would be so imbued with the Spirit of God, that you would move prayerfully and understandingly; but you stand con-demned before God. You are acting the part of Aaron, and the Spirit of God is grieved. Dr. Kellogg has not been helped by you. His associate physicians have done him great harm, but no good.[18]

The presentation given to me of the perils of Dr. J. H. Kellogg—of the subtle, specious workings of the tempter on his mind—is as clear as the daylight. Men who ought to know their duty have upheld him in that which they knew to be wrong. All who thus sus-tain him, bring upon themselves the displeasure of God. Those who should have dis-cerned his dangers and errors have refused light, and therefore they are deceived. I know whereof I speak. I could relate many things, but the time is not yet come.[19]

Our physicians have been warned against the seducing power of satanic agencies. And yet they are sustaining Dr. Kellogg. The enemy seduced the angels, and they thought he was right. We have the result of their choice, and yet the same rebellion against God is going on today.[20]

There's a saying about walking a mile in another's shoes... but those of the cowardly are shoes I would never care to stand in. We'll let Ellen White de-scribe both the good and the bad of what finally ended up as the devil's victory:

The greatest missionary work that can be done in our world is work in ministerial lines combined with medical missionary work. The truth is going forth from the sani-

16. E.G. White, "Remarks of Mrs. E.G. White to the Delegates of the Thirty-sixth session of the General Conference," May 30, 1905; Manuscript 70a, 1905
17. E.G. White, Letter to W.C. White, January 8, 1906; Letter 22, 1906
18. E.G. White, Letter to A.T. Jones, April 9, 1905; Letter 121, 1906
19. E.G. White, Letter to G.C. Tenney, June 29, 1906; Letter 208, 1906
20. E.G. White, "Learning From Past Mistakes," 1907; Manuscript 167, 1907

tarium at Battle Creek as from no other center in our world. Those who have stood up to criticize should instead have participated in the work, showing that they have been enabled by the Holy Spirit to understand that the Lord has used Dr. Kellogg as His man of opportunity to do a great and good work.[21]

Those who refused the warnings of God followed a course of action which brought its sure result. These influences have sometimes made the work of Dr. Kellogg doubly as hard as it should have been. They have led him to stand apart to some degree from the ministry. I desire to present matters as they are presented to me. Such a spirit of criticism and fault-finding has done the work Satan designed should be done. Dr. Kellogg has been led to take the course he deemed it his duty to take. He has not connected with those who were not in sympathy with the work he knew to be of God.[22]

God does not endorse the efforts put forth by different ones to make the work of Dr. Kellogg as hard as possible, in order to build themselves up. God gave the light on health reform, and those who rejected it rejected God. One and another who knew better said that it all came from Dr. Kellogg, and they made war upon him. This had a bad influence on the doctor....

It's not difficult to see how someone "making war upon" you might be a bad influence, and in time it produced an unsurprising result:

This had a bad influence on the doctor. He put on the coat of irritation and retaliation. God did not want him to stand in the position of warfare, and He does not want you to stand there.[23]

The shortcomings of both his detractors and Dr. Kellogg himself simply became too much. The elements of God's work which cannot be "divorced" weren't together![24] That didn't mean that the impossible had been done; it meant that "God's work" had ceased to be "God's work," at least as far as the loud cry was concerned. In a manuscript titled "The Medical Missionary Work" we find heaven's stark assessment:

I have laid out the matter as it has been presented to me. The third angel's message, in the place of swelling into a loud cry, is being smothered.[25]

And the result? It's not pretty:

My brethren, the Lord calls for unity, for oneness. We are to be one in the faith. I want to tell you that when the gospel ministers and the medical mission-

21. E.G. White, Letter to G.A. Irwin, W.W..Prescott, E.J. Waggoner, and A.T. Jones, February 21, 1899; Letter 36, 1899
22. E.G. White, Letter to W.W. Prescott, G.A. Irwin, A.T. Jones, U. Smith, and E.J. Waggoner, February 22, 1899; Letter 38, 1899
23. *General Conference Bulletin*, April 6, 1903
24. E.G. White, "Come Out and Be Separate," November 1905; Manuscript 21, 1906. Quoted more fully on page 50.
25. E.G. White, "The Medical Missionary Work," May 10, 1899; Manuscript 177, 1899

ary workers are not united, there is placed on our churches the worst evil that can be placed there.[26]

Due to his hostile attitude toward the church and his promulgation of pantheism, Kellogg was disfellowshipped in the fall of 1907.[27]

Dr. Kellogg, if not his influence, was gone. As might be expected from One possessing omniscience, the Lord was not caught flat-footed. He had already begun developing a replacement program in Southern California. It was known as the College of Medical Evangelists. Why? Because the object of the school was to train evangelists who knew how to combine the work of healing bodies and healing souls... like Jesus did.

That's a work that still needs to be done. Not that there haven't been some successes over the years since, but that work has never been done fully. "Exhibit B" remains an anticipated but unrealized event. And—disconnected as it may seem—that's why Lucifer's final accusations are still on the heavenly "to do" list.

"Huh? What's all that medical stuff got to do with the great controversy?"

26. E.G. White, "The Foundation of Our Faith," May 18, 1904; Manuscript 46, 1904

27. Those interested in this "Bad Kellogg" aspect can find the story in much more detail in my books *Tremble* and *Tactics*.

CHAPTER 14

Challenging Times

S UPERLATIVES are adjectives with teeth. They describe the last things on the chart. Nothing is bigger than the biggest; nothing is darker than the darkest; nothing costs more than the most expensive. And, notably, nothing is worse than the worst.

When the messenger of the Lord calls something the "worst evil," it ought to catch our attention, especially when it's directed at us. But, sad to say, the warning quoted on page 72 has not yet stirred the church at large to any all-encompassing concerted action. For a century or more now, we have been struggling along under the burden of the worst evil.

To be sure, the picture has not been uniformly bleak. There have been bright spots along the way, but it really can't be said that "the gospel ministers and the medical missionary workers are... united" in any overarching approach to the mission of "taking the gospel to all the world."

It will happen, someday:

I wish to tell you that soon there will be no work done in ministerial lines but medical missionary work.

This may sound like a terrible narrowing down of the work... but it's not. It is, in fact, a picture of God's church getting it right. In this same sermon, Ellen White went on to say:

You will never be ministers after the gospel order till you show a decided interest in medical missionary work, the gospel of healing and blessing and strengthening.[1]

The ministry and the medical missionary work must be combined. Never lose sight of this.[2]

---

1. *General Conference Bulletin*, April 12, 1901
2. E.G. White, Letter to J.H. Kellogg, February 23, 1899; Letter 40, 1899

And though these comments were largely directed toward the ministers of God's church, there's no particular room for throwing stones at them. The lay members aren't exactly sitting pretty in this regard, either:

> We have come to a time when every member of the church should take hold of medical missionary work. The world is a lazar house filled with victims of both physical and spiritual disease. Everywhere people are perishing for lack of a knowledge of the truths that have been committed to us. The members of the church are in need of an awakening, that they may realize their responsibility to impart these truths.[3]

There's nothing much to be gained by pointing fingers here, but there is hope in educating the church as a whole—laymen, ministers, medical workers, and anyone else who will listen—because the biggest hindrance is a profound lack of understanding that there's actually *supposed* to be a connection between the methods of *The Ministry of Healing* and the issues portrayed in *The Great Controversy*. The rhetorical question posed at the end of the last chapter is a fairly accurate depiction of the mindset that prevails across all levels of Adventism (with exceptions, of course), but, as you might have guessed by now, this book hopes to change that.

That may not be a simple task; after all, this "medical missionary stuff" sounds a lot like *Ministry of Healing*, but not much like *Great Controversy*. Do they really go together? Let's see what *Great Controversy* has to say:

> Satan can present a counterfeit so closely resembling the truth that it deceives those who are willing to be deceived,...

Now, *that* sounds like *Great Controversy*. The devil's deception, the need for close discrimination—that's what we're used to from that book. But notice, there's an ellipsis at the end of that quotation. That means there's more to the sentence. In fact, in this case it means there is a nonrestrictive clause that defines what it means to be "willing to be deceived." Which is good, because no one in their right mind would be "willing to be deceived." Let's read on. Let's find out what it takes to be that gullible.

> Satan can present a counterfeit so closely resembling the truth that it deceives those who are willing to be deceived, who desire to shun the self-denial and sacrifice demanded by the truth.[4]

Oh.... That's all it takes to be "willing to be deceived." But don't jump to a mistaken conclusion! This isn't saying that only martyrs will be saved. Self-denial comes in many forms, and if we focus on some great sacrificial act that we

3. *Testimonies*, vol. 7, 62
4. *Great Controversy*, 528

are never called to, we'll miss all the little things that are the main focus of God's interest.

I have been shown that those who are trying to purify their souls through obedience to the truth, yet who have had no opportunity of making special efforts and sacrifices for Christ and His cause, should find consolation in the thought that it is not necessarily the self-surrender of the martyr that is the most acceptable to God; it may not be the missionary whose life has been one of trial and endurance that stands highest in heaven's record, but that of the Christian who is such in his private life, in his daily struggle with himself, in the control of his passions, in cleanness of purpose, in purity of thought, in patience, meekness, and longsuffering under the test of provocation, in piety, in devotion, in his holy faith and trust in God, in his faithfulness in little things, in the management of his family, who keeps the mark of the prize of his high calling ever before him, looking unto Jesus, the Author and Finisher of his faith, keeping it ever in view that he is living for the future, immortal life, and in his home life representing the character of Jesus—that such a one may be more precious in the sight of God than the man who goes as a missionary to heathen lands, or ascends the scaffold to die for his faith.[5]

Far more than commonly thought, it is these daily matters that form the battle ground of faith and self-sacrifice. So let's consider this:

Every eye in the unfallen universe is bent upon those who profess to be Christ's followers. Here, in this atom of a world, an earnest warfare is going on—a battle in which Christ, our Substitute and Surety, has engaged in our behalf, and conquered.

At this point in Ellen White's thought, it's worth noting that there's something odd going on. She just referred to the work of Christ in conquering Satan, but the first sentence says the universe is watching us. Why would they watch *us*? If I were condemned to watch TV, I'm pretty sure I'd rather watch reruns of a good program rather than insultingly terrible new stuff!

But the paragraph goes on....

Now we, Christ's purchased possession, must become soldiers of His cross, and conquer in our own behalf, on our own account, through the power and wisdom given us from above. The influence of the cross of Calvary is to vanquish every earthly and spiritual evil power; and we need to know the plan of the battle, that we may work in harmony with Christ.[6]

What do you suppose the "influence of the cross" would be? Exactly what it was a few pages back! A revelation of the character of God. And the divine plan is to use that influence to finish off Satan and his arguments... as soon as

---

5. E.G. White, Letter to Brother and Sister Irwin, June 29, 1891; Letter 18, 1891. As a matter of trivia, that quotation is a single perfectly grammatical sentence.
6. *Review and Herald*, September 29, 1891

we get on the same page, understand "the plan of the battle," and "work in har‑
mony with Christ." Remember the need for "Exhibit B"?

*Yeah... "Exhibit B." But if "Exhibit B" is somehow built on the "influence of the
cross" doesn't it seem just a little odd that that "influence" hasn't gotten the job done?
It's been a couple thousand years already....*

Indeed. An "influence" that doesn't produce a "result" is questionable. And
since that "influence" is the effect of a "revelation," it's easy to think it should
be most strongly felt by those who were actually there to see the revelation.

But "seeing," as God uses the term, takes in a lot more than simply watching
something happen. Combined with the similarly used term "hearing" to repre‑
sent the whole range of perception, we find that human beings are all too fre‑
quently described as blind and deaf!

> Therefore I speak to them in parables, because seeing they do not see, and hearing
> they do not hear, nor do they understand. And in them the prophecy of Isaiah is ful‑
> filled, which says: "Hearing you will hear and shall not understand, and seeing you
> will see and not perceive."[7]

> Do you not yet perceive nor understand? Is your heart still hardened? Having eyes,
> do you not see? And having ears, do you not hear?[8]

> He has blinded their eyes and hardened their hearts, lest they should see with their
> eyes, lest they should understand with their hearts and turn, so that I should heal them.[9]

> Go to this people and say: "Hearing you will hear, and shall not understand; And
> seeing you will see, and not perceive. For the hearts of this people have grown dull.
> Their ears are hard of hearing, and their eyes they have closed."[10]

> Israel has not obtained what it seeks; but the elect have obtained it, and the rest
> were blinded. Just as it is written: "God has given them a spirit of stupor, eyes that
> they should not see and ears that they should not hear, to this very day."[11]

None of this sounds good. If Israel, God's chosen people, ended up blind and
deaf, what are the odds that we could repeat their failure? Something seems to
be missing in all this, but what?

In a word, "participation." To actually "see" the revelation of the Father's
character takes more than eyes; it takes a heart, surrendered to the point of
breaking. Consider the experience of Abraham:

> Abraham saw Christ. A supernatural light was given him, and he acknowledged
> Christ's divine character.... But Abraham was tested. The command came for him to

---

7. Matthew 13:13–14
8. Mark 8:17–18
9. John 12:40
10. Acts 28:26
11. Romans 11:8

take his son, his only son, Isaac, and offer him as a sacrifice.... This terrible ordeal was imposed upon Abraham that he might see the day of Christ....

Abraham learned of God the greatest lesson ever given to mortal. His prayer that he might see Christ before he should die, was answered. He saw Christ; he saw all that mortal can see and live. By making an entire surrender, he was able to understand the vision of Christ, which had been given him.[12]

It was "by faith" that Abraham, "when he was tested, offered up Isaac."[13] This faith, the kind that leads the believer to live out the law of heaven, to trust God when it's impossible to see a reason for trust, is inspired by "the influence of the cross," but that influence can only be fully understood by one who has—like Abraham—made an "entire surrender." That's what's needed today.

"Hmm... but, uh... what would that even look like... today?"

Well, simply put, it looks like *sozo*. It looks like a divine Physician guiding His patient back to health. It looks like forgiveness, but not the arbitrary kind that would hand the victory to Satan. It's the kind of forgiveness that heals patients, actually turning sinners into saints through—not spiritual fairy dust—but purely non-arbitrary "transformations so amazing that Satan with all his triumphant boasting, with all his confederacy of evil united against God and the laws of his government, stands viewing them as a fortress impregnable to his sophistries and delusions."[14]

Perhaps most importantly, it looks like faith, the kind of faith that Lucifer lost when he doubted God's love and wisdom. That's what the "influence of the cross" restores: "confidence in God."

And one more thing: in our day it looks like medical missionary work. Not "medical work" by itself; not "missionary work" by itself; but the full blown "Gospel Medical Missionary Evangelism" that the Spirit of Prophecy called for a century ago.

Medical missionary work is yet in its infancy. The meaning of genuine medical missionary work is known by but few. Why?—Because the Saviour's plan of work has not been followed.[15]

The most skillful practitioner cannot be called a medical missionary, unless he calls the attention of his patients to Jesus. The Lord calls for a manifestation of the gospel principles of truth and righteousness.[16]

---

12. *Signs of the Times*, May 3, 1899
13. Hebrews 11:17
14. *General Conference Daily Bulletin*, February 27, 1893; quoted previously on page 16.
15. E.G. White, Letter to Teachers in Emmanuel Missionary College, September 21, 1903; Letter 210, 1903
16. E.G. White, Letter to Medical Missionary Workers, April 1902; Letter 208a, 1902

It is God's plan that Loma Linda shall be not only a sanitarium, but a special center for the training of gospel medical missionary evangelists.[17]

Let our ministers who have gained an experience in preaching the Word learn how to give simple treatments and then go forth as medical missionary evangelists.

Workers—gospel medical missionaries—are needed now. We cannot afford to spend years in preparation. Soon doors now open to the truth will be forever closed. Carry the message now. Do not wait, allowing the enemy to take possession of fields now open before you. Let little companies go forth to do the work to which Christ appointed His disciples. Let them labor as evangelists, scattering our publications, talking of the truth to those they meet, praying for the sick, and, if need be, treating them, not with drugs, but with nature's remedies. Let the workers remember always that they are dependent on God. Let them not trust in human beings for wisdom.[18]

This is the plan of the battle. Notice that 120 years ago, Ellen White's concern was "doors... that will forever be closed." We might think of "closed countries" in the 10/40 window, and they surely fit the description. But there's more. To a large degree, she was talking about *cities*. Cities, it turns out, are a major focus of the battle. For one thing, that's where most of the people live, but they are also the key to shaking things up!

The work in the cities is the essential work for this time and is now to be taken hold of in faith. When the cities are worked as God would have them, the result will be the setting in operation of a mighty movement such as we have not yet witnessed.[19]

That "mighty movement" is a good thing, but it sets off some "unintended consequences" that we can't take lightly:

As Lucifer sees that we are making efforts to work the cities as if we meant to give the last message, his wrath will be aroused, and he will employ every device in his power to hinder the work.[20]

What's the deal with cities? Satan seems kind of anxious about them, like he's afraid of what would happen if the stressed out, discontented, overworked slaves he has there ever wake up and realize there's a better way to live.

Another detail: in that last quote, Ellen White speaks of working the cities "as if we meant to give the last message." It's subtle, but don't you detect just a

---

17. E.G. White, Letter to H.W. Cottrell, January 27, 1910; Letter 12a, 1910
18. E.G. White, "A Warning Against Colonization," August 17, 1903; Manuscript 141, 1903
19. E.G. White, "Go, Preach the Gospel," 1910; Manuscript 15, 1910
20. E.G. White, Letter to G.W. Amadon, September 12, 1910; Letter 74, 1910. In connection with this statement, it's worth noting that after a series of highly successful "Your Best Pathway to Health" free medical missionary mega clinics in San Francisco, Oakland, San Antonio, Spokane, Los Angeles, Phoenix, Beckley, and Dallas-Fort Worth—all of which are "cities"—after all that came more than two years of "two weeks to flatten the curve" and the effectual splintering of the Adventist medical community over the question of mandated treatments. Where did *that* come from?

touch of sarcasm there? It's kind of like she's saying, "C'mon, guys! Get serious!" And that raises an interesting question. What would "working the cities" look like if we ever did get serious about it? Well, if getting serious can be taken to mean, "Let's try following directions this time," then it's going to look like—you guessed it!—medical missionary work.

> Henceforth medical missionary work is to be carried forward with an earnestness with which it has never yet been carried. This work is the door through which the truth is to find entrance to the large cities.[21]

---

21. *Testimonies*, vol. 9, 167

CHAPTER 15

Why So Fussy?

W E just closed Chapter 14 with the idea that medical missionary work is God's chosen tool to finish the job of taking the gospel to all the world. It seems like a great idea to have some tool that's up to the task... but what's so special about medical missionary work? This whole "you've got to do it this way" requirement is starting to sound like its own brand of fairy dust! It's kind of like, "Nothing's going to work until you use the magic sauce."

That's not far off, actually, except for one thing: there's no magic involved. It's all cause and effect. Non-arbitrary. Here's how:

> God desires everyone to understand the hateful character of selfishness and to co-operate with Him in guarding His human family against its terrible, deceptive power. The first result of the entrance of sin into the world was the birth of principles of selfishness. The design of the gospel is, by means of remedial missionary work, to confront this evil of selfishness and destroy its destructive power by establishing enterprises of benevolence.[1]

Notice, this is *remedial* missionary work. Now, who do you suppose might have a selfishness problem that needs to be remedied? As the first sentence of the quote implies, *everyone* needs help here, but this remedy is intended primarily for the church. Perhaps things have gotten better in the last century or so, but even if that were the case, the same issues and principles are still involved.

> The gospel will triumph; it will not sustain a final defeat. But for years it has been evident that selfishness under the form of godliness has been entering the church. The perverse ways of Satan have taken the place of love.... By bigotry and narrowness, professing Christians have violated the principles which should ever be sacredly cherished.[2]

---

1. E.G. White, Letter to Brethren and Sisters of the Iowa Conference, November 6, 1901; Letter 165, 1901
2. E.G. White, "Then opened He their understanding...," June 12, 1901; Manuscript 47, 1901

God's purpose in committing to men and women the mission that He committed to Christ is to disentangle His followers from all worldly policy and to give them a work identical with the work that Christ did.[3]

There is some serious "disentangling" that needs to be done, and those "enterprises of benevolence" are the training grounds where we learn to confront the worldly policy of selfishness in our own hearts. This is good for us, and for the world.

As those unhappy people in the cities see Christians working unselfishly—and being a lot happier than they are—the idea comes into their heads that, maybe, just maybe, it really is more blessed to give than to receive. Eventually, they may want to try a little unselfishness and self-denial and self-sacrifice themselves! That's part of God's plan for all His children. And though we might have read right over it in the past, it's a very common motif in the writings of Ellen White. (By the way, the next seven quotations all come from *Ministry of Healing.*)

Individual responsibility, individual effort, personal sacrifice, is the requirement of the gospel.[4]

No one can practice real benevolence without self-denial. Only by a life of simplicity, self-denial, and close economy is it possible for us to accomplish the work appointed us as Christ's representatives.[5]

Consider the life of Christ. Study His character, and be partakers with Him in His self-denial.[6]

His whole life was an example of self-denial.[7]

Teach your children from the cradle to practice self-denial.[8]

We need to follow more closely His example of self-renunciation and self-sacrifice.[9]

The strongest argument in favor of the gospel is a loving and lovable Christian. [But] to live such a life, to exert such an influence, costs at every step effort, self-sacrifice.[10]

But there's a second aspect to this remedy, because those who take unselfishness seriously (as in, anywhere near the same degree that Jesus took it seriously), can quickly run into logistical problems. They're broke; they're out of food; they don't have enough time to do what needs to be done. The obvious so-

3. E.G. White, "Christ Our Example in Every Line of Work," October 27, 1902; Manuscript 130, 1902
4. *Ministry of Healing,* 147
5. *Ministry of Healing,* 206
6. *Ministry of Healing,* 287
7. *Ministry of Healing,* 333
8. *Ministry of Healing,* 386
9. *Ministry of Healing,* 457
10. *Ministry of Healing,* 470

lution is to be a little more "reasonable." To not spend so much money; not give away so much food; not use up so much time helping others that people start to think you're insane.

Jesus had the same problem:

> [Jesus' brothers, the sons of Joseph] heard that He devoted entire nights to prayer, that through the day He was thronged by great companies of people, and did not give Himself time so much as to eat. His friends felt that He was wearing Himself out by His incessant labor... and there were some who feared that His reason was becoming unsettled.[11]

The key here is not the problem, but the solution. The devil always tries to "solve" such challenges in a way that "proves" unselfishness does not exist; God's solution, while it includes the principle of "come... rest awhile," aims to maximize the impact of selfless service.

"Uh-huh. But what if I'm still broke?"

Jesus answered that question, once, when Philip observed that it would take a lot of money to feed a crowd of thousands. In effect, He said, "Let Me handle it."

> As the Son of God lived by faith in the Father, so are we to live by faith in Christ.[12]

And now we're back to faith. It's self-sacrifice that makes faith a necessity, and it's faith that makes self-sacrifice seem reasonable. And without that package you can never love the Lord supremely and your neighbor as yourself —which gets us back to the perfect, immutable, unchangeable, and eternal law of God.

It would be great if that were the end of it all, but even after the life, ministry, death, and resurrection of Christ, there were three accusations left to deal with. And now, a couple thousand years later... there are *still* three accusations left. Is there a plan for dealing with this?

---

11. *Desire of Ages,* 321
12. *Desire of Ages,* 389

CHAPTER 16

The Plan of the Battle

JONATHAN Edwards' famous "Sinners in the Hands of an Angry God" sermon has gotten a lot of bad press for the last century or so. The idea of "scaring people into heaven" does seem like a poor approach, but maybe the original presentation was better than we might think. Another minister, one Stephen Williams, was in the Enfield church when Edwards first preached that sermon. Williams' diary entry for the day recounts that "the power [of] God was seen and several souls were hopefully wrought upon that night, and oh the cheerfulness and pleasantness of their countenances that received comfort."

Neither the propriety nor the success of Edwards' pastoral methods is our interest, though. All the above serves only as introduction to one of the more memorable mental images in the sermon:

> O sinner! Consider the fearful danger you are in: it is a great furnace of wrath, a wide and bottomless pit, full of the fire of wrath, that you are held over in the hand of that God, whose wrath is provoked and incensed as much against you, as against many of the damned in hell. You hang by a slender thread, with the flames of divine wrath flashing about it, and ready every moment to singe it, and burn it asunder.[1]

The point of citing all this unfashionably vivid "hellfire and brimstone" preaching is simply this: For Satan, this is as real as it gets, and that "slender thread" is nothing more nor less than his remaining three accusations against the government of heaven. He will live or die, depending on the failure or success of the Lord to prove them wrong.

---

1. enfieldhistoricalsociety.org/old-town-hall/jonathan-edwards-and-sinners-in-the-hands-of-an-angry-god/ That's the original source, but the quotation above uses the modernized spelling for Williams' words as found in Wikipedia.

Let's just say, he's strongly motivated.

For a refresher, here are his final three claims:

7.   God's law is arbitrary.

8.   God's law makes forgiveness impossible.

9.   God is lying about all the above.

We can find some good news by recognizing that the last of these is simply a conditional recap of the first eight. Satan claimed that he was right on each of the disputed points, and that God was not only wrong, but dishonestly so. To date, though, nothing has gone his way. God has already been proven correct on the first six issues; when He's proven correct on the seventh and eighth, number nine just sort of evaporates. That means we've only got two accusations to focus on! And, as we've seen, those two are inseparably twisted together into a single composite dealing with the salvation/healing (*sozo*) of God's people. If only we knew how to tackle *that* issue....

More good news! We do have the battle plan! It's been given to us in black and white. And—amazingly enough—it just happens to nail down those last two issues!

> In the character of God's people a living testimony will be borne that will contradict the fallacy of Satan, who has declared that the law of Jehovah is arbitrary, and holds its subjects under a cruel bondage.[2]

> The Lord desires through His people to answer Satan's charges by showing the results of obedience to right principles.[3]

Results! That's cause-and-effect. Just like "obedience to right principles" in lifestyle produces health, "obedience to right principles" in spiritual matters produces spiritual health. And those right principles? Of course! They're just supreme love to God and unselfish love for our neighbors. "Right principles" *are* the law of heaven! God is going to end the controversy by showing that the "great healing" is accomplished through non-arbitrary means.

This whole procedure is *sozo!* Healing, salvation—same word, same process! And since sin is a deficiency disease, the obvious way to "work intelligently to remove the cause" is to develop in God's people the faith they lack, the same faith that Lucifer lost. We've seen some of this already, but there's another side to the matter, one that we may not have seen clearly yet, that we need to consider, too, because it's a major component of "the plan of the battle."

> The followers of Christ know little of the plots which Satan and his hosts are forming against them.... The Lord permits His people to be subjected to the fiery ordeal of

---

2. *Review and Herald*, August 13, 1895

3. *Christ's Object Lessons*, 296

temptation, not because He takes pleasure in their distress and affliction, but because this process is essential to their final victory. He could not, consistently with His own glory, shield them from temptation; for the very object of the trial is to prepare them to resist all the allurements of evil.[4]

What? God is not going to shield His people from temptation? *We've got a promise for that!* He can't just dump us, can He? Look at the Bible verse!

> God is faithful, who will not allow you to be tempted beyond what you are able, but with the temptation will also make the way of escape, that you may be able to bear it.[5]

So? Is God going to keep His promise or not?

Of course He will. And more. Not only will He keep them from being tempted too strongly (He's been doing that since Adam's day), but He will use those temptations like a divinely administered exercise plan to strengthen His people. But every time God tells Satan that he has to step back and leave us alone, the devil cries foul. "You're interfering with the test! You can't say they've chosen Your government, when You won't even let me give them my best sales pitch!"

This is the same argument we see, *twice*, in the book of Job.

> Then the LORD said to Satan, "Have you considered My servant Job, that there is none[6] like him on the earth, a blameless and upright man, one who fears God and shuns evil?" So Satan answered the LORD and said, "Does Job fear God for nothing? Have You not made a hedge around him, around his household, and around all that he has on every side? You have blessed the work of his hands, and his possessions have increased in the land. But now, stretch out Your hand and touch all that he has, and he will surely curse You to Your face!"
>
> And the LORD said to Satan, "Behold, all that he has is in your power; only do not lay a hand on his person." So Satan went out from the presence of the LORD.[7]

This first test is terrible, almost beyond imagination. Job's oxen, donkeys, and camels were stolen, and his sheep, servants, and children were killed. Worst of all, the "fire of God from heaven" which killed the sheep and some of the servants, and the sudden "great wind from across the wilderness" which destroyed the eldest brother's house and killed all Job's children and more of his servants had the appearance of divine origin. After all, the servant plainly said it was the "fire of God."

In response, "Job arose, tore his robe, and shaved his head; and he fell to the ground." Understandable enough. But the verse has two more words; it concludes by saying that Job "fell to the ground *and worshiped.*"[8]

---

4. *Great Controversy*, 528
5. 1 Corinthians 10:13
6. This admission on God's part that there was no one else like Job on the earth gives us some idea of the "score" at this point in the contest!
7. Job 1:8–12
8. Job 1:20

And he said: "Naked I came from my mother's womb, and naked shall I return there. The LORD gave, and the LORD has taken away; Blessed be the name of the LORD." In all this Job did not sin nor charge God with wrong.[9]

Satan was not happy with this result, so Moses' account of the drama moves directly to the next act:

Again there was a day when the sons of God came to present themselves before the LORD, and Satan came also among them to present himself before the LORD. And the LORD said to Satan, "From where do you come?", So Satan answered the LORD and said, "From going to and fro on the earth, and from walking back and forth on it." Then the LORD said to Satan, "Have you considered My servant Job, that there is none like him on the earth, a blameless and upright man, one who fears God and shuns evil? And still he holds fast to his integrity, although you incited Me against him, to destroy him without cause."

So Satan answered the LORD and said, "Skin for skin! Yes, all that a man has he will give for his life. But stretch out Your hand now, and touch his bone and his flesh, and he will surely curse You to Your face!"

And the LORD said to Satan, "Behold, he is in your hand, but spare his life."[10]

Both times, Satan's complaint was that God's protection invalidated the test of Job's loyalty. If Job did what God required merely for the hope of gain, the true motive was greed, not love for God nor acceptance of the principles of heaven's government. And Satan was right. That kind of interference all but nullified any claim of Job's devotion to God. Stronger evidence—a different kind of evidence—was needed.

Job—probably the second book of the Bible to be written[11]—is an obvious type of God's people at the end of time. The test Job faced was, pure and simple, a proving of his faith in God. You know he had to be asking, "Would a loving God torture me like this?"

Remember, Job knew nothing about the goings on in heaven. Satan's involvement in the whole matter was hidden from him, and everyone was telling him that all this trouble came from God's hand. Even God said to Satan, "you incited Me against him" (though Job knew nothing of this).

For reasons of divine wisdom, God is often willing to have His "permissive will" described as if it were His "active will." Ellen White describes this matter of attribution like this:

From those who have no sense of the goodness and mercy of God, who refuse His merciful warnings, who reject His counsels to reach the highest standard of Bible requirements, who do despite to the Spirit of grace, the Lord would remove His protect-

9. Job 1:21–22
10. Job 2:1–6
11. Genesis was the other book written by Moses during his forty years in Midian, prior to the Exodus. See *Signs of the Times*, February 19, 1880. Chiastic structure would argue that Genesis was written first.

ing power. I was shown that Satan would entangle and then destroy if he could, the souls he had tempted. God will bear long, but there is a bound to His mercy, a line which marks His mercy and His justice.

I was shown that the judgments of God would not come directly out from the Lord upon them, but rather in this way: they place themselves beyond His protection. He warns, corrects, reproves, and points out the only path of safety; then, if those who have been the objects of His special care will follow their own course independent of the Spirit of God after repeated warnings, if they choose their own way, then He does not commission His angels to prevent Satan's decided attacks upon them. It is Satan's power that is at work at sea and on land bringing calamity and distress, sweeping off multitudes to make sure of his prey. Storm and tempest both by sea and land will be, for Satan has come down in great wrath. He is at work. He knows his time is short, and if he is not restrained we shall see more terrible manifestations of his power than we have ever dreamed of.[12]

Trials are permitted to come upon the chosen people of God. The expression is used, "God tempted Abraham;" "God tempted the children of Israel." This means that the Lord permitted Satan to tempt them in order that their faith might be found unto honor and glory when the judgment shall sit, and when every man shall be judged according to the deeds done in the body. God knows every heart, every motive, every thought in the heart of man; but He permits Satan to try, and tempt, and test His believing ones in order that their trust and confidence in God may be revealed. In the trial, if true to God, they reveal the fact that they render obedience to His written Word.[13]

Temptation is a complex issue. God certainly has promised to protect us from excessive temptation, but there's a reason—and a goal—in that. Perhaps an illustration will help.

Suppose I am determined to bench press 200 kilograms. That is far more than I weigh, and many would look at me and say, "Impossible."[14] But determination can produce strange results....

For those who know even less than I do about this sport, it is important to understand that the "bench" involved is used to support the weight lifter as he is lying on his back, staring up at the ceiling—and a bar full of weights. One of the side effects of this position is the very real danger that, should the effort to lift the bar not be successful, it could come down on the weight lifter. A quick Google search readily yields this helpful gem from an obviously authoritative source:

---

12. E.G. White, Letter to Brother and Sister Uriah Smith, August 8, 1883; Letter 14, 1883
13. E.G. White, "Dear Brethren in the Seventh-day Adventist Faith," June 7, 1894; Manuscript 27, 1894
14. Full disclosure: For all I know, it may be impossible. I know so little about weight lifting that there may well be some physiological ratio between body mass and what can be lifted of which I am completely ignorant. But this is an illustration, not a body building magazine.

A barbell on your chest can roll down on your neck and strangle you. Or it can roll down your belly, mashing your soft internal organs and possibly tearing an artery, resulting in you bleeding out. **Because the bench press can potentially kill you**, it's highly recommended that you perform the bench press with a spotter.[15]

But determination can produce strange results.... So I get a spotter and begin the process of building muscles. Fifty kilos is too easy, so I add weight. But one hundred and fifty is too much for me to lift. I can't even get it back on the support stand, so my spotter saves me. More exercise. My spotter is there, watching carefully, and occasionally saving my neck, soft internal organs, and arteries as I gain strength. 160, 170, 180, 190, 195, 198, 199. My spotter has spared my life countless times by now, but I'm getting close! And finally, one beautiful day when the sun is shining and the bluebirds are singing, I bench press 200 kilograms. Mission accomplished, and the evidence is right there in plain sight. All the doubters are put to shame, and I, according to the web site, have notched a new level of true manliness.

Ludicrous as that story is, it illustrates a vital truth. God *has* promised to shield us from *excessive* temptation... and He will be absolutely faithful to do that. But the best way to shield from excessive temptation is to make sure there *are* no excessive temptations by strengthening His people to the point that they can handle the worst that can be thrown at them. (Keen readers will recognize that the 200 kilogram goal in the story falls short of the greatest possible weight... but the important point is the spotter part, and no illustration gets everything right.)

If we choose faith, God can use temptation to strengthen faith, preparing us for greater obedience. But we must cooperate with His treatment plan like a patient under the skillful care of a physiotherapist. It hurts to stretch, it hurts to lift... but done properly it strengthens and heals muscles.

Now, let's go back and revisit the statement that started this discussion:

> The Lord permits His people to be subjected to the fiery ordeal of temptation, not because He takes pleasure in their distress and affliction, but because this process is essential to their final victory. He could not, consistently with His own glory, shield them from temptation; for the very object of the trial is to prepare them to resist all the allurements of evil.[16]

And one more as review:

> ⟩ Every eye in the unfallen universe is bent upon those who profess to be Christ's followers. Here, in this atom of a world, an earnest warfare is going on—a battle in

---

15. artofmanliness.com/health-fitness/fitness/the-4-rules-of-bench-pressing-without-a-spotter/ Emphasis in the original! Don't kill yourself!

16. *Great Controversy*, 528

which Christ, our Substitute and Surety, has engaged in our behalf, and conquered. Now we, Christ's purchased possession, must become soldiers of His cross, and conquer in our own behalf, on our own account, through the power and wisdom given us from above. The influence of the cross of Calvary is to vanquish every earthly and spiritual evil power; and we need to know the plan of the battle, that we may work in harmony with Christ.[17]

When God's people are indeed able to "resist all the allurements of evil," it will only be through faith in His love, wisdom, and power. Eternally secured by the demonstration of the cross, their faith *in* Him holds them faithful *to* Him, just like the faith of the angels who never fell held them. And when their faith is strong enough to "resist all the allurements of evil," Jesus can step back and say, "Satan, your witness." (Remember the book of Job?)

Why? Because the whole business has gone full circle. The faith in God's love and wisdom that Lucifer lost, and then stole from Adam and Eve, God's people have finally regained. They have been "forgiven" just like a patient who's foolishly damaged his body, but listened to the Doctor, changed his habits, did the exercises, and found his way back to health. It's called *sozo*. And in this earth's final days—just in time for the "complete fulfillment of the new-covenant promise: 'I will forgive their iniquity, and I will remember their sin no more.'"[18]—God's treatment plan includes the prognosis of *diasozo*,[19] the *complete* restoration of our faith.

One of the more striking ways in which this is portrayed in the writings of Ellen White is her use of the phrase "Substitute and Surety." She repeats this hundreds of times, so often that one might assume she is quoting a Bible verse, but not so. This is her own construction, her own effort to describe the reality of Christ's work.[20] "Substitute" is clear enough, but what does "Surety" mean? Dictionary definitions point in two directions: a surety may be either something that helps correct an undesirable situation (say a company's failure to deliver a product on time, or an unforeseen disaster such as fire or flood), or it may be something that assures a desirable outcome without failure. The first case is like insurance, that steps in to minimize or restore some sort of loss. The second case is more nearly a guarantee.

So, when Ellen White writes of Christ as our "Substitute and Surety," what does she mean? The most helpful approach to this question is to look for her

---

17. *Review and Herald*, September 29, 1891
18. *Great Controversy*, 485. Quoted more fully on page 89.
19. We've seen *sozo*. Now it's time to meet his big brother! The prefix adds the idea of a completed healing or salvation. In Matthew 14:36 it is translated "made perfectly well"!
20. In fact, a Google search for "substitute and surety" yields little but incidental use of the phrase from non-Adventist sources.

uses of "surety" other than in the combined phrase. See if you can tell which of the two meanings she is using:

"God with us" is the Surety of our deliverance from sin, the assurance of our power to obey the law of heaven.[21]

Through Christ, man's Substitute and Surety, man may keep the commandments of God. He may return to his allegiance, and God will accept him.[22]

The Lord in His great mercy sent a most precious message to His people through Elders Waggoner and Jones. This message was to bring more prominently before the world the uplifted Saviour, the sacrifice for the sins of the whole world. It presented justification through faith in the Surety; it invited the people to receive the righteousness of Christ, which is made manifest in obedience to all the commandments of God.[23]

We see there is nothing in law to save us, but Christ has become man's Substitute and Surety. He has worked out man's redemption. Then what must man do? He must repent, because he has broken God's holy law. It is just as necessary that we should keep that law now as it was for Adam and Eve to keep that law in Eden.[24]

Jesus is our Surety and Mediator, and has placed at our command every resource, that we may have a perfect character.[25]

The Redeemer of the world in the wilderness of temptation fought the battle upon the point of appetite in our behalf. As our Surety He overcame, thus making it possible for man to overcome in his name.[26]

Jesus... became the sinners' Substitute and Surety. He Himself bore the penalty of the law which the sinner deserved, in order that the sinner might have another trial, another chance to prove his loyalty to God and His commandments.[27]

Christ came to our world as man's Surety, preparing the way for him to gain the victory by giving him moral power.[28]

As the divine Substitute and Surety, He elevates the fallen race in character, and brings their minds into healthful sympathy with the divine mind. Those who are partakers of the divine nature see that true greatness means continual humiliation, self-denial, self-sacrifice. Those who have spiritual eyesight will discern that God does not honor those who are honored by the world, but those who are true to principle.[29]

---

21. *Desire of Ages*, 24

22. E.G. White, "The Ladder to Heaven," 1884; Manuscript 13, 1884

23. *Testimonies to Ministers*, 91

24. E.G. White, "Sermon: At Grimsby, England," September 21, 1886; Manuscript 80, 1886

25. *In Heavenly Places*, 18

26. *Review and Herald*, April 19, 1887

27. E.G. White, Letter to Henry D. Wessels," October 8, 1895; Letter 97, 1895

28. *Signs of the Times*, May 27, 1897

29. E.G. White, Letter to Brother Shannan, December 26, 1896; Letter 97, 1896

He came to be their Surety, to overcome in their behalf, to live for them a sinless life, that through His power they might obtain the victory over evil.[30]

Christ came to our world to be man's Surety, to overcome in his behalf, to live for him a sinless life, that in His power they might obtain the victory over sin.[31]

When man sinned, Christ offered to stand as his Substitute and Surety, in order to provide a way whereby the guilty race might return to loyalty. He took humanity and passed over the ground where Adam stumbled and fell. Without swerving from His allegiance, He met the temptations wherewith man is beset, and resisted every plausible representation of hope that sinners can be saved in their sins. Christ's righteousness is distinctly made apparent in overcoming every temptation.[32]

Christ has consented to become man's Substitute and Surety.... and through His perfect obedience to God's law give man an opportunity to return to his allegiance to God. He will give him moral power that he may have strength to gain the victory over sin.[33]

Jesus is our Surety and Mediator, and has placed at our command every resource, that we may have a perfect character.[34]

Christ ventured a great deal when He came here to stand upon the battle field, when He came here clothed with humanity, standing as our Surety, as our Substitute, that He would overcome in our behalf, that we might be overcomers in His strength and by His merits.[35]

And, finally, to show that all this has something to do with our main line of thought concerning Satan's accusations:

[Christ] showed in the great controversy with Satan that He was fully able to remove the stigma and discount the degradation of sin which Satan had placed upon the human family. By taking humanity and combining it with divinity, He was able to meet every demand of the law of God, to overcome every objection which Satan had made prominent as standing in the way of man's obedience to God's commandments.[36]

What might that look like? Exactly like righteousness by faith. Like Isaiah 58. Like self-denial and self-sacrifice. Exactly like we've been told. But looks can be deceiving; arbitrary announcements can be inaccurate. Much as in Job's case —though more so—there is need of full-on *demonstration*.

In the last great conflict of the controversy with Satan those who are loyal to God will see every earthly support cut off.[37]

---

30. *Signs of the Times*, June 17, 1903
31. *Signs of the Times*, August 26, 1903
32. E.G. White, Letter to Brethren and Sisters in the Southern Union Conference, January 12, 1904; Letter 25, 1904
33. E.G. White, "Sermon: A Peculiar People," July 14, 1887; Manuscript 25, 1887
34. *Youth's Instructor*, September 22, 1892
35. E.G. White, "Sermon: The Great Sacrifice Made for Us," July 24, 1891; Manuscript 8, 1891
36. E.G. White, Letter to Captain Christiansen, January 2, 1894; Letter 11a, 1894
37. *Desire of Ages*, 121

Oh! Can you imagine! How horrible! Every earthly support... gone!

It is safe to let go every earthly support and take the hand of Him who lifted up and saved the sinking disciple on the stormy sea.[38]

Oh... well, at least that's some comfort.

We can never perfect a round, full, Christian experience until every earthly support is removed, and the soul centers its entire affections about God.[39]

Oh....

The point is, faith shines brightest when it's all you've got. It may sound scary, but it's really "the highest and most precious of all human experiences, the constant dependence of the soul upon God."[40]

And losing "every earthly support" is just the warm up. It's like one five-year-old telling another, "I'm not going to be your friend anymore!" And since "friendship with the world is enmity with God,"[41] it's hard to say this is a bad development!

The real demonstration, the proof that the "great healing" has finally been achieved... that's still coming. In fact, that final demonstration comes after the loud cry, the sealing, and the close of probation. Once the seven last plagues have begun to fall, and the death decree is put in place, then comes the greatest test—the greatest demonstration—of them all.

38. *Testimonies*, vol. 4, 558
39. E.G. White, Letter to Fannie Bolton, February 10, 1894; Letter 6, 1894
40. *Testimonies*, vol. 7, 172
41. James 4:4

CHAPTER 17

A Functional Design

WITHIN the Adventist sub-population there exists a fascinating array of unique terms—perfectly familiar to us, but often foreign to the non-Adventist world. But that very familiarity can pose a challenge. While it may not have bred the outright "contempt" of the proverb, there is ample evidence to show that it has bred a kind of careless complacency. Simply put, we use the terms, have a general concept of their meaning, but too often fail to really understand their role or function in God's plan.

At the close of Chapter 16 is a list of events—all yet future—which we associate with the final days of earth as we know it. Here are the items: the loud cry, the sealing, the close of probation, the seven last plagues, and the death decree. Other events might be inserted into this progression,[1] but right now we need not be more specific than this, except to add one more detail: the time of Jacob's trouble. This final item was mentioned as well, but only as the "greatest demonstration."

Like any product of design, whether some mechanical marvel, electronic gadget, or social system, we can look at these events and see the evidence of the Designer's intelligence. But what if some of the parts seem purposeless? What does that imply?

Many stories have been told of home auto mechanics (and perhaps some in professional shops as well) who have re-assembled a car engine, only to find that they have "extra parts." Simple logic says that those parts may actually be needed, in which case they really aren't "extra."

But what does it mean when the car runs fine without them?

---

1. The Latter Rain, the Shaking, the National Sunday Law, and the International Sunday Law for instance.

What if a design calls for six moving parts to accomplish a task that could be done with one? Why is "one click" better than "Right-click > Menu > Sub-menu > Selection"? And what if one whole component of a complex system has no identifiable function at all?

Which brings us to our point: Are the standard features of Adventist eschatology functional? Do they accomplish something? Or are they just sort of decorative elements pinned onto God's overall plan?

After an introduction like that, it should be no surprise that this volume maintains that the items listed above all have specific functions, that each contributes a needed element to the resolution of the great controversy.

Let's start at the beginning of the end: the loud cry. This is convenient because we've already touched on that topic back in Chapter 13. We saw that "the loud cry of the third angel [had] already begun in the revelation of the righteousness of Christ."[2] That revelation of God's character came through faulty human beings (Dr. Kellogg being the most notable) carrying on the only kind of ministry that Jesus Himself could use to reveal His Father: a combined work of teaching, preaching, helping, and healing.

This makes sense, because we are assured that:

> [The] glory of the character of Christ, can never be expressed in words. Human language is inadequate to reveal it. It must be made manifest in the life.[3]

That work was begun by 1892, but was being "smothered" by 1897.[4] Precisely because the loud cry has a critical mission, because it is a needed element, we have remained here ever since. Nonetheless, the Lord's prediction is that, "We shall see the medical missionary work broadening and deepening at every point of its progress, because of the inflowing of hundreds and thousands of streams, until the whole earth is covered as the waters cover the sea."[5] The deficiency is not the plan for the loud cry, it's simply that the "hundreds and thousands of streams" part has yet to be tried.

But this raises a logical question: Why is the loud cry needed? What's the point of a clear "revelation of the righteousness of Christ"? We've done without one for almost 2,000 years, so how can it suddenly be a necessity?

That's a bit like asking why a car needs a fuel pump... it's because the rest of the machine won't work without it! Same with the revelation of God's character at the end of time. It makes the rest of the plan of salvation work. That means that the last-day revelation of God's character has a function that it

---

2. *Review and Herald*, November 22, 1892

3. *(Australasian) Union Conference Record*, June 1, 1900

4. E.G. White, "The Medical Missionary Work," May 10, 1899; Manuscript 177, 1899. Quoted more fully on page 71.

5. E.G. White, "Medical Missionary Work," April 16, 1901; Manuscript 32, 1901

must accomplish. And that's why the task of "taking the gospel to all the world" is more than a quantitative proposition; quality matters, too.

Suppose every person on earth could be forced to listen to an official explanation of "the gospel" straight from the Vatican. Would "then the end will come" be a likely result? No? Welcome to the issue of quality.

When Jesus spoke of the gospel and the end, He was specific:

> This gospel of the kingdom will be preached in all the world as a witness to all the nations, and then the end will come.[6]

It's not just *any* gospel He's talking about; it's *this* gospel. That may sound confusing, but we've already seen a very similar requirement in Ellen White's admonition that "we need to understand the plan of the battle, that we may work in harmony with Christ."[7] And just as looking at a fuel injector can give us a good idea why a car needs a fuel pump, we can learn a few things about the loud cry by looking at the next event on our list, the sealing.

Many view the seal of God as a diploma, a congratulatory indication of attainment. But teachers, principals, and college presidents don't pass out report cards and diplomas before administering the final test. That makes sense, really. And since the final test—the time of Jacob's trouble (more on that soon)—comes well after the sealing, we need to re-evaluate the role of the seal. If it isn't a diploma, what is it? Does it have an essential function? Or is it just decoration?

If it's not essential, then—by definition—it isn't needed. Maybe God will finally decide to just move on without it. Maybe skip the 144,000, too, since it's the seal that really defines that group. All that seems unlikely, but why not?

It's helpful to notice the chronology of these events. The seal comes after the loud cry, but before the close of probation. So... what is it's *purpose*?

When we stop to remember that all God's dealings with human beings at the end of time are wrapped up in His response to Satan's final accusations, it begins to make sense. God's "weapon of choice" in the great controversy is always *demonstration*, so let's ask, What issue might possibly need to be demonstrated to the universe at large shortly before the second coming?

It's easy to be too focused on ourselves here, on our concerns, our issues. But the universe thinks on a rather larger scale than we tend to. The obvious point of concern for everyone in the universe (excluding fallen men and fallen angels) is exactly that! *Fallen men and fallen angels!* That's what the universe is thinking about! For two reasons: First, they all know about the plan to take *some* of those fallen human beings to heaven.

---

6. Matthew 24:14
7. *Review and Herald*, September 29, 1891. Quoted more fully on pages 75 and 89.

Seriously? Does that sound like a good idea? These folks who were "born in sin," who have never known a single day of heavenly perfection in their entire lives, whom Inspiration has described as "the whole head is sick, and the whole heart faint. From the sole of the foot even to the head, there is no soundness in it, but wounds and bruises and putrefying sores,"[8] you want to take them to *heaven?* Is that sensible? Is that safe?

The "war in heaven" back in Lucifer's day was trauma enough; no one is looking for more.

But there's another issue as well. Those "fallen angels" are evil. There's no denying it; after all, they were all party to the crucifixion. But Saul, aka Paul, consented to Stephen's death... and others, too, for whom we have no accurate body count beyond "many of the saints... when they were put to death, I cast my vote against them."[9] How is Paul a candidate for salvation, but Lucifer is so categorically not?

Angels lived for who-knows-how-long in a society where everyone loved everyone. That means Gabriel loved Lucifer. But there's no talk of saving Lucifer. Wouldn't you *want* the angels to at least wonder about the possibility of *their* friends being saved from eternal death?

It's the fate of fallen men and fallen angels that grips the thoughts of the unfallen world, not just for sentimental reasons, but because these issues strike to the very heart of Lucifer's last two accusations. God says He's going to heal human sinners, but not angelic sinners. Is that arbitrary? Is it even possible?

And so, back to the seal of God: what is its purpose? The sealing and the events to follow, provide the perfect opportunity for God to clarify this whole process of forgiveness, and—not inconsequentially—to show that redeemed sinners will be safe in heaven. And, of course, in order to qualify as any sort of a "demonstration," it must be open to the view of the target audience. Notice:

> What is the seal of the living God, which is placed in the foreheads of His people? It is a mark which angels, but not human eyes, can read.[10]

So God directs the "mightiest of angels"[11] to place His own seal on the 144,000. While the task is performed by an angel, it is God Himself who is in charge, for there's a demonstration to be made. Or maybe that should be 144,000 demonstrations to be made. It is here that God establishes beyond all doubt His ability to... ummm... to do... to do *what?*

OK, let's try a simple illustration: "Triathlons," "ultra marathons," and "tough mudders" have become a thing. Running, or swimming, or riding a bike for in-

---

8. Isaiah 1:5–6
9. Acts 26:10
10. E.G. White, Letter to J.H. Kellogg, December 18, 1898; Letter 126, 1898
11. *Testimonies to Ministers*, 444

sane distances through mud, or heat, or cold has come (in some minds) to be the epitome of self-control, determination, and general achievement. It remains to be seen how much of that transfers over to the conflict with sin,[12] but the real value of all this is not our interest at the moment. Let's just pretend that the starter's gun for the most popular of all these competitions is soon to sound.

By "popular," I mean eight million participants.[13] But shortly before that gun goes off, I put little gold stars on the foreheads of one hundred forty-four of the participants. Some with the gold stars look like real contenders in the race, others, not so much. Some on crutches or in wheelchairs get stars. Some who are mere children get stars.

One hundred forty-four out of eight million is not a big percentage, just one out of every 55,000 or so. But using whatever secret algorithmic criteria is controlling this operation, I hand out the gold stars, and—BANG!—off they go!

A few hours (days, weeks, months, or whatever) later, the race is over. Of the original eight million, exactly one hundred forty-four successfully completed the route. Amazingly enough, these winners are all sporting little gold stars on their foreheads! Every one of them! What a coincidence!

In what currently passes for the "real world," I'd have a great future in the "sports betting" branch of legalized theft. In what we need to constantly remind ourselves *really is* the real world of the great controversy, God will use a dignified version of our story to demonstrate to all the universe that He can identify true faith in His children.

What does faith have to do with the seal? Just about everything. In the case of the 144,000, faith is the not-so-secret criteria that God uses to determine whom to seal. Angels can see the seal, but the sealed ones *can't*. Much like Job, they are left in the dark as to the invisible realities of the contest being fought out around them, because faith is neither tested nor demonstrated in the light. But when the dust has settled, there are 144,000 examples of the power of faith to successfully "resist all the allurements of evil."[14]

Just as importantly, there are 144,000 examples of God's ability to identify true faith—*before* the rest of the universe can see it. No false positives; no false negatives; just perfect accuracy. That's what the seal is for. That's what it accomplishes. And that's why it's absolutely essential to the plan of salvation.

---

12. "For bodily exercise profits a little, but godliness is profitable for all things, having promise of the life that now is and of that which is to come." 1 Timothy 4:8

13. That's one one-thousandth (+/– a bit) of the world's current population, for reasons which will soon be obvious. Of course, given a few well-timed pandemics, plagues, food shortages and the like, it may end up being the total world population at some point in the future. Who knows?

14. *Great Controversy*, 528. Quoted more fully on page 85.

CHAPTER 18

Faith, Brother!

SO the whole process of the sealing is to establish God's ability to detect faith. OK. But some may wonder if that ability was ever actually questioned, and—for that matter—what real difference does any of that make? After all, there's a whole chapter in the book of Hebrews that has quite a bit to say about faith. And, in his epistles, Paul deals with faith, actually elevating it to the point of declaring that the righteous are "saved through faith."[1] None of this sounds particularly unique to the end of time.

To a great degree, it's not... but only to a degree. Faith has played a crucial role in the plan of salvation since Adam sinned, but there is an aspect of its power that is yet to be demonstrated. We've spoken of it already: the power of faith to enable believers to "resist all the allurements of evil." But as we've seen before, speaking about something, and showing the truth about something, are two very different things.

We might look at Enoch and Elijah, or maybe even Moses, and think that surely they must have already demonstrated every important feature of faith. After all, they're all in heaven! But, no, as important as their examples have been, it would appear that none of them demonstrated the full picture of faith.[2] Nor did Jesus, for that matter, though without some explanation that sounds more than a little heretical. The explanation for that comment will come in a few pages. Right now, though, we need to set the stage by looking at the role of faith in a more general manner.

---

1. Ephesians 2:8
2. This isn't an assertion worth fighting over. If someone else should prefer to believe that Enoch, Elijah, and Moses *did* demonstrate "the full picture of faith," then it's still possible to believe that the numerical distinction between three cases and 144,000 cases is an adequate explanation of the still-unfinished business of salvation. For me, either explanation works, but I lean toward the categorical distinction rather than the quantity issue.

We saw, back in Chapter 4, that at or near the original inception of sin, Lucifer lost faith in God. It was distrust of God's love and/or wisdom that fueled Lucifer's desire for autonomy and self-sufficiency.

How he thought he could do this is unclear; that he was determined to try is not:

> Satan erected his standard of revolt against God in heaven. He aspired to be like God, and determined to assert a power of independence of God. His after-history has revealed a persevering determination to establish his empire, governed by laws, and replenished with resources, independent of God.[3]

We saw, in Chapter 10, that "even as a sinner, man was in a different position from that of Satan." That all-important difference came from Lucifer sinning "in the light of God's glory," despite "understanding the character of God, [and] knowing His goodness" as "no other created being" had ever been privileged to do. With Adam, it was a different story:

> But man was deceived; his mind was darkened by Satan's sophistry. The height and depth of the love of God he did not know. For him there was hope in a knowledge of God's love. By beholding His character he might be drawn back to God.[4]

Since "an unsaved condition" is just "living without that full confidence in God which is born of love, which leads us to take Him at His word,"[5] it's safe to say that for us to be "drawn back to God" is the same as regaining "confidence in God" which is the same as "faith," and—fortunately—that is "a very simple matter."[6]

All the above is just to support *this*: faith and hope come through a "knowledge of God's love... [and] character." This, too, is a very simple matter. It ain't brain science nor rocket surgery, folks! But we are so used to thinking of salvation (that's what "hope" is focused on, after all) as some sort of undefinable, incomprehensible, magical, and thoroughly arbitrary bestowal of a theological mystery, that it's actually hard to wrap our minds around the reality that there is an understandable cause-and-effect method to redemption.

But without that understanding, we really have no good explanation for one of the most basic elements of Christian life: the recognition that individual believers are called to take "this gospel of the kingdom [to] all the world as a witness to all the nations."

3. *Review and Herald*, June 21, 1898

4. *Desire of Ages*, 761

5. *Bible Training School*, November 1, 1911. Quoted more fully on page 25.

6. *Youth's Instructor*, August 30, 1894. Quoted more fully on page 25.

The key question here is simple: *Why?* What actual need is there for this to happen? It's not a minor matter, for the completion of that task is said to be before "the end will come."[7] But why?

In all likelihood, the majority of human beings who have ever lived—multiple billions of them—have died without ever hearing so much as a whisper of "this gospel." Of "*any* gospel," for that matter. And God is entirely capable of dealing with their cases in the judgment. So the idea that the gospel has to go to all the world "so everyone will have a chance to be saved" falls woefully short of a good explanation.[8]

But, surely, the "Great Commission" has some purpose to it.

For starters, any additional revelation of God's character provides a better opportunity to re-gain faith in Him (and thus come into a "saved condition"), so a simple desire to "love our neighbors as ourselves" is a great motivation for mission. But still, it's that "all the world" part that is harder to explain. Why must "the end" wait for *that?*

This is where an understanding of the relationship between faith and knowledge is essential. We just said that an increase in knowledge of God increases the opportunity for salvation, and that's true... sometimes. But it was the full knowledge of God's character which made Lucifer's case hopeless.

> Lucifer in heaven had sinned in the light of God's glory. To him as to no other created being was given a revelation of God's love. Understanding the character of God, knowing His goodness, Satan chose to follow his own selfish, independent will. This choice was final. There was no more that God could do to save him.[9]

How can a knowledge of God's character save some and condemn others? Simply put, it's a matter of faith. If increased knowledge of God is received in faith, faith grows; if it's received without faith, faith withers. Without faith, the perceptive ability of finite beings is limited. There's only so much they can know of God, and every new revelation uses up some of the remaining possible reserve. After seeing all that I can take in of God's character, I will either respond in faith and trust Him in everything (in which case I am fitted to receive

---

7. Matthew 24:14
8. Does this mean all the "unevangelized heathen" are hopelessly lost? Some Christians would tell you they are. They never "confessed the Lord Jesus Christ with their mouth," (see Romans 10:9–10) so it's off to eternal torment for them. It's interesting that those most strongly of this opinion hold to the most outrageously arbitrary concept of salvation! Not your thoughts, not your actions, not your character determines salvation! It's just the "magic words" that count.

   Unsurprisingly, the Lord disagrees: "How surprised and gladdened will be the lowly among the nations, and among the heathen, to hear from the lips of the Saviour, "Inasmuch as ye have done it unto one of the least of these My brethren, ye have done it unto Me"! How glad will be the heart of Infinite Love as His followers look up with surprise and joy at His words of approval!" *Desire of Ages,* 638
9. *Desire of Ages,* 761

further revelations, a process that can continue for eternity), or I trust Him in nothing. Lucifer was at the "nothing" end of that scale, while Adam and Eve were at the still-more-to-see stage.

Despite 6,000 years (give or take) of God's dealing with human beings, despite the one matchless revelation of the Father's character by Christ Himself, the great majority of us remain in that still-more-to-see category.

> The world needs today what it needed nineteen hundred years ago—a revelation of Christ.[10]

But there's one major difference: Jesus isn't here, and that necessarily requires a shift in the Lord's operational plans. What could God possibly do without Jesus here to do it?

> What the world needs today is the light of Christ's example reflected from the lives of Christlike men and women.[11]

Those "Christlike men and women," it should be noted, weren't born that way! They were all certifiable sinners, which puts the lie to Satan's claim that forgiveness is impossible without changing the law. It is entirely possible, and these people are the demonstration of that truth.[12] Through the revelation of the character of God, through the strengthening of faith (starting with that "measure of faith" that "God has dealt to each one"[13]), "confidence in God" has been restored. Forgiveness has come, not through arbitrary pronouncement, but through the very real cause-and-effect measure of beholding and choosing to *participate*—remember Abraham![14]—in the restoration of the character of God in their own hearts. That's the way healing works. That's *sozo*.

Of course, for many it went the other way. Rejecting the revelation of the righteousness of Christ, turning from the self-denial and self-sacrifice He has called His followers to embrace, they have revealed the principles of Satan's government rather than the law of God.

That's the way a knowledge of God works. It either softens or hardens, but it never leaves the heart the same. And when everyone on earth has seen the revelation of Jesus in the lives of men and women much like themselves, but

10. *Ministry of Healing*, 143
11. *Testimonies*, vol. 9, 135
12. It is this demonstration of restored sinners that Jesus could not provide by Himself. He was never a sinner, and so needed no restoration. This is why it was said (on page 98) that even Christ's example had not displayed every aspect of the power of faith.
13. Romans 12:3
14. "The command came for him to take his son, his only son, Isaac, and offer him as a sacrifice.... This terrible ordeal was imposed upon Abraham that he might see the day of Christ....

"Abraham learned of God the greatest lesson ever given to mortal.... By making an entire surrender, he was able to understand the vision of Christ, which had been given him." *Signs of the Times*, May 3, 1899

now transformed into the likeness of Christ, they will hear the call that they, too, can "fear God and give glory to Him." That they, too, can "come out of Babylon" and reject the mark of the beast, opting instead for the seal of God. And since everyone on earth has seen this revelation, everyone will become either soft or hard (just like being either cold or hot). The "playing field" of knowledge having been leveled out, the spotlight is on the only other significant variable: faith.

Every scientist and auto mechanic knows that too many variables in an experiment make it difficult if not impossible to understand or predict the outcome. Pure water at "standard temperature and pressure" will always boil at 100° Centigrade. But throw in a few unidentified mineral salts... now when does it boil? No one knows.

Same thing with faith, when there are varying amounts of knowledge.

This is why "this gospel" needs to go, not just "to all the world," but "to every creature."[15] Not as a theory, not in words alone, but as a living demonstration for all to see in the "lives of Christlike men and women." When knowledge is standardized, the effect of faith becomes clear.

The "plan of the battle" is to standardize knowledge by flooding the world with "the knowledge of the glory of the LORD, as the waters cover the sea."[16]

How much of the sea is covered by water?[17]

That should do the job.

You don't think it's possible? Well, fortunately, God is still working to build up faith. We'll pray for you.

---

15. Mark 16:15
16. Habakkuk 2:14
17. Disregard pack ice, OK?

CHAPTER 19

Load Up the Bar!

IN Chapter 16 I used an illustration about bench pressing 200 kilos. The main
focus of the story was the role of the "spotter," the one who keeps the weight
lifter from killing himself. But the application of the story was to Ellen White's
comment that—

> The Lord permits His people to be subjected to the fiery ordeal of temptation, not
> because He takes pleasure in their distress and affliction, but because this process is
> essential to their final victory. He could not, consistently with His own glory, shield
> them from temptation; for the very object of the trial is to prepare them to resist all
> the allurements of evil.[1]

This is a portrayal of circumstances quite late in the eschatological account
given in *Great Controversy*. At that time, there will be no shielding, but we can
easily see that the work of the "spotter" goes on steadily today. This may look
like a contradiction, but it is not. There is a difference between "now" and
"then." The key to understanding that difference is to recognize that the work
of shielding goes on with a definite purpose! The "very object" of the whole
process is to prepare God's people "to resist all the allurements of evil."

It's that "all the allurements" part that we need to consider just now. In the
illustration, the totality of the challenge was represented by the 200 kilos.
Heavy enough for most of us, but there are more weights that could go on the
bar. How much weight is "all" the weight?

As commonly happens with illustrations, this one is broken on this part of the
coming reality. With the weights, there's always one more, but God has laid out a
plan to encompass "all the allurements of evil," and cross them all off the list at once.

---

1. *Great Controversy*, 528

Is that even possible? Just like there's always one more weight, isn't there always one more sin? Theologians sometimes talk about the "seven deadly sins," but does anyone really believe that's all there are? How could anyone know that "*all* the allurements" had been resisted?

The answer lies in the common root of all sin. As we saw with Lucifer, the central issue is faith, so a sufficiently strong test of faith actually addresses all the variations. This changes the challenge from "how to cover all the different *kinds* of sin," to "how to construct the hardest possible test of faith."

But, still... couldn't a test of faith always be made just a little bit harder? Humanly speaking, it seems like it could... if the situation looked just a little more hopeless, or the testing circumstances went on just a little while longer, or the pain level (physical or emotional) got ratcheted up just a little bit more. How do you ever get to the end of this? How does God plan to show that the people He wants to take to heaven can resist *all* the allurements of sin?

Our human judgment may not have enough discrimination to actually recognize the answer to that question. Logic seems to fall short, but Inspiration depicts a test that seems to satisfy the universe, a test that does indeed address the central issue of faith in a way that marks it as a superlative sort of test. This test, coming at the end of time, has been foreshadowed in the lives of the "best" of the righteous all down the ages. In short, there is strong circumstantial evidence that this test, what we refer to as the time of Jacob's trouble, provides all the evidence the unfallen universe needs to see.

Of course, some theologies would argue with the entire notion of Christians resisting all temptation at *any* point before glorification. Here's why:

> Those who suppose that they understand philosophy think that their explanations are necessary to unlock the treasure of knowledge, and to prevent heresies from coming into the church. But it is these explanations that have brought in false theories and heresies, causing men to teach for doctrine the commandments of men. Men have made desperate efforts to explain the meaning of what they thought to be intricate Scriptures, but their efforts have only darkened what they thought to make clear.[2]

On the basis of both Scripture and Spirit of Prophecy, it is time for God's people to do what should have been done long ago—recognize such ideas as a ploy of the devil and dismiss them as unworthy of notice.

> If we walk in the light as He is in the light, we have fellowship with one another, and the blood of Jesus Christ His Son cleanses us from all sin.[3]

---

2. E.G. White, Letter to J.E. and Emma White, August 21, 1896; Letter 122, 1896

3. 1 John 1:7. Notice that there is a difference between the "sin" spoken of in this verse, and the "guilt of sin" that is often read *into* this verse.

He will subdue our iniquities.... [and] cast all our sins Into the depths of the sea.[4]

All sin, from the least to the greatest, may be overcome by the Holy Spirit's power.[5]

Who is denying Jesus Christ? Who is it? It is those who are making a profession of godliness, those who are claiming to believe in Jesus Christ and yet are assimilating to the world. They are following another pattern. But Christ is our example in all things; and if we imitate the life of Christ, we shall be separate from all sin.[6]

Obedience to the gospel is the remedy for all sin and selfishness.[7]

In word and deed Christ's followers are to be pure and true. The attention of the world is to be called to Him who takes away all sin. In this world—a world of iniquity and corruption—Christians are to reveal the attributes of Christ. All they do and say is to be free from selfishness, and from covetousness, which is idolatry. Christ desires to present us to God "without spot or wrinkle or any such thing," purified through His grace, bearing His likeness.[8]

God asks us to believe in Him as One able to save from all sin. And He asks us to bring into our lives the grace that will keep us from sin. There is no limit to the measure of grace that Christ is willing to bestow on us. He can give you grace that will enable you to show to the world that Christianity is a divine system which uplifts and ennobles human beings.[9]

When [our brethren in responsible positions] consecrate heart and soul to the service of God, they will find that an experience deeper than any they have yet obtained is essential if they would triumph over all sin.[10]

But in spite of this kind of inspired testimony, we find it hard to believe.[11] The idea that God can deliver sinners from sinning would be doubted far less than it is, if only there were more examples of success! But that's exactly where we have problems with the idea: it doesn't seem to work all that well. Certainly not all that commonly.[12]

Instead, we find it much easier to acknowledge our continual need of forgiveness. And it's true! We have more than enough need for forgiveness. Praise

---

4. Micah 7:19. Again, the parallelism is between "iniquities" and "sins," not the guilt that comes from sin.

5. *Review and Herald*, September 19, 1899

6. E.G. White, "Sermon: At Grimsby, England," September 26, 1886; Manuscript 84, 1886

7. E.G. White, Letter to W. Covell, March 1900; Letter 65, 1900

8. E.G. White, "Christian Ministry," February 4, 1902; Manuscript 11, 1902

9. E.G. White, Letter to Addie S. Watson, April 28, 1903; Letter 72, 1903

10. *Testimonies to Ministers*, 514

11. The claim that no one could obey God's law was number six on Lucifer's list, and Jesus disproved it long ago. It's ironic that so much theological fire power still gets blasted about on this issue. It's a bit like the Allied powers of World War II re-staging the D-Day invasion of Normandy—with live ammunition on both sides—just to see if they can lose this time.

    "Henceforward Christ's followers were to look upon Satan as a conquered foe. Upon the cross, Jesus was to gain the victory for them; that victory He desired them to accept as their own." *Desire of Ages*, 490

12. Despite the assurance that "there are Enochs in this our day." *Christ's Object Lessons*, 332

the Lord for forgiveness... but whatever happened to victory? Where does it fit in our mental map of the Christian life?

We'll come back to that... but it will be helpful to first nail down the circumstances and the nature of the one test that demonstrates the reality of the saints' victory. As already mentioned, the test is administered during the time of Jacob's trouble. That puts it after the close of probation, well into the period of the seven last plagues. This is the period covered in Chapter 39 of *The Great Controversy*. That chapter makes it clear that "mercy no longer pleads for the guilty inhabitants of earth."[13]

> Unsheltered by divine grace, they have no protection from the wicked one. Satan will then plunge the inhabitants of the earth into one great, final trouble. As the angels of God cease to hold in check the fierce winds of human passion, all the elements of strife will be let loose. The whole world will be involved in ruin more terrible than that which came upon Jerusalem of old.[14]

The emphasis is squarely upon the Sabbath, since it "has become the special point of controversy throughout Christendom." Due to "the persistent refusal of a small minority to yield to the popular demand... it will be urged that the few who stand in opposition to an institution of the church and a law of the state ought not to be tolerated." This sentiment will culminate in the death decree, which aims to eliminate the non-conformists.

> The people of God will then be plunged into those scenes of affliction and distress described by the prophet as the time of Jacob's trouble.[15]

This whole chapter is one it would be well to have fresh in our memories, but of particular interest just now is that at that time, after the close of probation, Satan's last ditch argument is a complaint that God is being arbitrary.

> [Satan] numbers the world as his subjects; but the little company who keep the commandments of God are resisting his supremacy. If he could blot them from the earth, his triumph would be complete.[16] He sees that holy angels are guarding them, and he infers that their sins have been pardoned; but he does not know that their cases have been decided in the sanctuary above. He has an accurate knowledge of the sins which he has tempted them to commit, and he presents these before God in the most exaggerated light, representing this people to be just as deserving as himself of exclusion from the favor of God. He declares that the Lord cannot in justice forgive their sins and yet destroy him and his angels. He claims them as his prey and demands that they be given into his hands to destroy.[17]

---

13. *Great Controversy*, 613
14. *Great Controversy*, 614
15. *Great Controversy*, 616
16. The possibility of "complete triumph" for Satan should be more than a little sobering.
17. *Great Controversy*, 618

Satan is still fixated on his remaining three accusations; surely, for us to give them a little thought seems like a prudent thing.

The chapter in *Great Controversy* continues, stressing the central nature of faith in the ordeal of the saints.

> Their confidence in God, their faith and firmness, will be severely tested.... Satan... hopes so to destroy their faith that they will yield to his temptations and turn from their allegiance to God.[18]

It is a fearful ordeal, one which Ellen White assures us will be far more stressful than we can imagine.[19] And yet it is not self-interest that motivates the righteous. Though they do not know every detail of the events and spiritual battle raging around them, they do understand enough to know that they are in a special place, a special time, a special role as priests and kings representing the government of heaven.

> If they could have the assurance of pardon they would not shrink from torture or death; but should they prove unworthy, and lose their lives because of their own defects of character, then God's holy name would be reproached.[20]

It is this long awaited outcome of reproach or vindication that has the entire unfallen universe on the edge of their seats. With the result of this demonstration by the sealed ones of earth, the government of heaven will stand or fall. And it is in this setting that the final test is given. Surprisingly, this test, this agonizing trial, does not come to God's people as a matter of destruction at the hands of the wicked. No, this final proving of their spiritual health comes in relation to God Himself.

Explicitly described only once in all of Ellen White's writings (so far as I've been able to find), this crowning evidence of *diasozo* follows the pattern set in the accounts of Job, Abraham, David, and even Christ Himself. As Job, who could only see divine punishment; as Abraham, who could only see an illogical hypocrisy in the command to kill his son; as David, who would write, "How long, LORD? Will You hide Yourself forever? Will Your wrath burn like fire?";[21] and as Jesus Himself, who quoted the Psalm, "My God, my God, why have You forsaken Me?";[22] in much the same manner, though with greater intensity and immediacy than any previous mortals have been tested, the sealed ones see God as bent on their destruction.

---

18. *Great Controversy*, 618
19. See *Great Controversy*, 622.
20. *Great Controversy*, 619
21. Psalm 89:46
22. Psalm 22:1

The single statement detailing this appeared, not in the *Review and Herald*, the general paper for the church, but rather in the designated "missionary paper" intended for wide distribution to the non-Adventist world, the *Signs of the Times*.[23] The article is entitled, "Jacob and the Angel," and it is in all major features a close parallel to similar passages in other publications like *Patriarchs and Prophets*, and *Great Controversy*.

And then there is that one monumental exception:

> Those who live in the last days must pass through an experience similar to that of Jacob. Foes will be all around them, ready to condemn and destroy. Alarm and despair will seize them, for it appears to them as to Jacob in his distress, that God himself has become an avenging enemy. It is the design of God to arouse the dormant energies of His people to look out of and away from self to One who can bring help and salvation, that the promises given for just such a time may be seen in their preciousness, and relied upon with unwavering trust.

"Those who live in the last days," the subjects of this paragraph, will be real people. Normal people, the kind who have families, and homes, and jobs. But one by one, those jobs, those homes, and—sadly—sometimes even those families will be stripped from them due to their loyalty to God. With "every earthly support" taken from them, they will at last be forced to flee to the mountains, though armed foes intent on taking their lives will find them even there.

Here, in their utmost extremity, they stand faithful to God. God—the One who has promised to care for them, the only One who can save them now, the One for whose honor they would lay down their lives. And then, through whatever means the Lord has at His disposal, "it appears to them... that God Himself has become an avenging enemy."

That "avenging enemy" description is a reference to the "avenger of blood," the one who pursued you as you fled for your life to the city of refuge. The avenger had only one purpose. He was there to kill you. And it's worth noting that he was fully authorized to kill you, even if a later inquiry might find that the death of his relative had been entirely accidental, and that you were entirely innocent

And that's what God Himself will look like to the righteous. You trusted Him when you lost your job. You trusted Him when you lost your house. You even trusted him with your broken heart when you lost your family. But

---

23. Merely as an unquantified, subjective personal observation, I would note that there are more uniquely pointed or startlingly specific statements from Ellen White in the pages of the *Signs* than in any other single source. No idea why.... Several such examples appear in this book. For those who enjoy such projects, a page-by-page skim over the footnotes for *Signs* references would be worth the time and calories involved.

now... now the very One whose promises you thought you could trust, has come to kill you.

Do you trust Him now?

Can you say with Job, "Though He slay me, yet will I trust Him."[24]

Can you look the divine Executioner in the eye and say, "Into Your hands I commit My spirit."[25]

This test is not like being burnt at the stake when the Spirit was there to sustain the martyr through the promises of God's Word. This is the test of trust when God has manifestly proven Himself to be untrustworthy. It's obvious. You can see it, plain as day.

So will you walk by sight, or walk by faith? That's the question that holds the breathless attention of every inhabitant—fallen or unfallen—of the universe.

But there's one more, final sentence to the paragraph from that *Signs* article. It's short, only four words, but it packs a punch.

> Here faith is proved.

Indeed! Faith, that "confidence in God" which is the opposite of an "unsaved condition." The faith that Lucifer lost, that Adam lost, that Christ held firm until death—that faith, that *sola fide* of the Reformation, will in the final examination be shown to be the source of the spiritual health exhibited by the righteous who live through the time of Jacob's trouble. They are *made perfectly well!* They are *saved!*

The law is still as immutable as always and the means of salvation proven to be entirely devoid of any arbitrary element. And, not inconsequentially but almost incidentally by this time, the Lord has been proven honest in all His ways. Lucifer's arguments have all gone down in flames.

The proof of that? Two paragraphs further on in the article, we find this:

> Dangers thicken on every side, and it is difficult to fix the eye of faith upon the promises amidst the certain evidences of immediate destruction. But in the midst of revelry and violence, there falls upon the ear peal upon peal of the loudest thunder. The heavens have gathered blackness and are only illuminated with the blazing light and terrible glory from Heaven. God utters His voice from His holy habitation. The captivity of His people is turned. With sweet and subdued voices they say to one another, "God is our friend."[26]

---

24. Job 13:15
25. Luke 23:46
26. *Signs of the Times*, November 27, 1879

CHAPTER 20

A Second Probation

BEFORE we move on to a full discussion of the "great healing," it will be helpful to give a little more thought to the matter of probation. We commonly speak of individual probation, which closes either at death (most commonly, at which point a person is either saved or lost) or upon the commission of the unpardonable sin (obviously resulting in a lost result).

But at the end of time we have the general close of probation, when all individual cases are closed, even for those still living. Since the majority of those alive at that time will not be among the saved, it's like they all commit the unpardonable sin, *en masse*. But how does that happen?

This general close of probation is a marked deviation from our perception, at least, of the norm. We know it is only a minority of those dying around us day by day (and for millennia past) that will be saved, but all but the worst of sinners are lost through neglect rather than by committing the unpardonable sin in any obvious way. They simply failed to take advantage of the offered salvation.

All of which leads to the thought that there is something unique about the end of time, even within the experience of the lost. How could so many people commit the unpardonable sin at the same time? We'll get to that. But first, back to the issue of probation.

There is a third sense in which Inspiration speaks of probation: that of the probation of the race as a whole. Not as individuals, but the whole package deal of humanity. This is not an irrational concern, nor irrelevant to the overall issue of Lucifer's rebellion, given that "Satan... opposed the creation of man."[1]

---

1. E.G. White, "Diary: January 1890," January 26, 1890; Manuscript 38, 1890

The Spirit of Prophecy refers to individual probation quite commonly, to the general close of probation much less often, and to this whole-race probation least of all. Nevertheless, the concept is clearly a part of the overall picture. We saw an example of this way back on page 9, but our focus at the time was Satan's fall from heaven:

> God... looked upon the victim expiring on the cross, and said, "It is finished. The human race shall have another trial."[2]

Notice that this additional "trial" for the "human race" was definitely not Jesus on the cross, since it is clearly depicted as being a future event following the crucifixion. Here are a few more examples:

> A second probation, purchased by the death of the Son of God, has been granted to the human race.[3]

> The heart will break with emotion as we think of what it has cost heaven to place the sinful race upon probation.[4]

> Adam's sin plunged the race into hopeless misery; but by the sacrifice of the Son of God, a second probation was granted to man.[5]

> All His righteous demands must be fully met; for this second probation granted to the fallen race cost an infinite price, even the life of the Son of God.[6]

> When Adam's sin had forfeited eternal life, at infinite cost God provided for the race a second probation.[7]

> Infinite wisdom devised the plan of redemption, which places the race on a second probation by giving them another trial.[8]

The wording varies a bit, to be sure, but notice that all but the last of those quotations at least implies that the second probation was only guaranteed following the crucifixion. So what about the first four thousand years of humanity's sorry existence? They had only the symbols, and the chance to exercise faith in what had not yet happened.

But perhaps the single most defining difference between individual probation and whole-race probation is the question of what it takes to nullify or violate or cancel or terminate (pick your own term) that status. For the first whole-race probation, it took a single failure with the forbidden fruit.

---

2. *Youth's Instructor*, June 21, 1900
3. E.G. White, "Unfaithful Servants," April 1, 1900; Manuscript 23, 1900
4. E.G. White, Letter to J.E. White and W.O. Palmer, May 11, 1901; Letter 97, 1901
5. *Christian Temperance and Bible Hygiene*, 15
6. *Review and Herald*, September 13, 1898
7. *Signs of the Times*, February 24, 1904
8. *Testimonies*, vol. 3, 484

This is (fortunately!) not the way it works with individuals. If that were the case, it would be quite a claim to say that any of us are currently on our "second probation"! And if not the second, which sequential probation *are* you living in? What? You haven't kept track?

Say it again: fortunately, that's not the way it works with individuals.

But what about the whole human race? The statements above seem to stress that "*second* probation" idea. After six thousand years of sin, it seems like we've surely done worse than steal some fruit! But we're still in our second probation! How does *that* work?

Simply put, it *doesn't* work that way. There is a designated "second probation" for the race, but the determining test hasn't even begun yet. When it does, it will be a winner-takes-all contest pitting the government of God against the claims of Satan. The prize at stake is the earth, the human race, and universal supremacy.

Universal supremacy? That's the way Inspiration presents it. Is there a mechanism for replacing God as the ruler of the universe? Let's be honest: no human being has a clue as to the political workings on that level. Fortunately, we can move forward believing there will never be any such need, but if our sinless-from-birth Savior could have failed in His earthly mission, it seems reasonable to regard the risk of 144,000 previously sinful human beings as a serious matter.

> The temptations to which Christ was subjected were a terrible reality. As a free agent, He was placed on probation, with liberty to yield to Satan's temptations and work at cross-purposes with God. If this were not so, if it had not been possible for Him to fall, He could not have been tempted in all points as the human family is tempted."[9]

This second probation issue is not to be dismissed lightly. Those who understand the plan of the battle will realize the magnitude of the contest. They will recognize that any failure on their part would not only forfeit the opportunity for human acceptance into the sinless universe, but cause "God's holy name... [to] be reproached."[10]

That's what's at stake in the time of Jacob's trouble.

Does that seem kind of melodramatic, perhaps? To anyone not used to viewing the world through the great controversy lens, it may seem a little much, a bit overdrawn. But I don't think it is. Here's why:

> [Satan] considered that to be the god of this world was the next best thing to gaining possession of the throne of God in heaven.... The Lord Jesus Christ came to dispute the usurpation of Satan in the kingdoms of the world. The conflict is not yet ended; and as we draw near the close of time, the battle waxes more intense.[11]

---

9. *Youth's Instructor*, October 26, 1899
10. *Great Controversy*, 619
11. *Review and Herald*, April 14, 1896

Satan knows that his usurped authority will soon be forever at an end. His last opportunity to gain control of the world is now before him, and he will make most decided efforts to accomplish the destruction of the inhabitants of the earth.[12]

From the Jewish age down to the present time, Satan's warfare has been directed against the Son of God and his work; and he still flatters himself that he will obtain the victory.[13]

In the hosts of evil there is jarring and discord, but they are all firm allies in fighting against heaven. Their one aim is to disparage God, and their great numbers lead them to entertain the hope that they will be able to dethrone Omnipotence.[14]

Satan is at work with intense activity to corrupt or sweep from the earth the upholders of piety, and success will attend the workings of Satan unless we arise in the strength of God and resist him.[15]

We must not think that Satan will cease for one moment in his efforts to do to Christ's followers as he did to Christ.[16]

Zechariah's vision of Joshua and the Angel[17] applies with peculiar force to the experience of God's people in the closing scenes of the great day of atonement.... Satan numbers the world as his subjects; he has gained control even of many professing Christians. But here is a little company who are resisting his supremacy. If he could blot them from the earth, his triumph would be complete.[18]

We have a work to do, every one of us, and time is short. We have but a little time now! And we want that Satan shall not take the victory of the whole world. He is at work—the devil and the fallen angels. You remember that.[19]

As noted before, the idea of a "complete triumph" for Satan is a sobering thought. But shouldn't we be thinking sober thoughts? Perhaps we should be doing more to "remember that."

This next quotation goes a thousand years beyond our current focus, but if anyone is inclined to doubt the devil's determination and forward-thinking approach to the great controversy, this should correct that error.

[Satan] has in mind still another battle, when he shall have in his ranks all who are not on the Lord's side, and in that battle take not only the kingdoms of the earth but also the kingdom of heaven.[20]

---

12. *Testimonies to Ministers*, 464
13. *Review and Herald*, March 9, 1886
14. *Special Testimonies*, Series B, No. 2, 6
15. E.G. White, Letter to Brethren and Sisters in California, April 13, 1887; Letter 92, 1887
16. E.G. White, "All That Will Live Godly in Christ Jesus Shall Suffer Persecution," August 19, 1897; Manuscript 87, 1897
17. Another depiction of the time of testing.
18. *Prophets and Kings*, 587
19. E.G. White, "Talk to the Students at Loma Linda," April 5, 1910; Manuscript 79a, 1910
20. E.G. White, "Diary: The Use of Means and Family Responsibilities," October 20, 1903; Manuscript 204, 1903

But back to the idea of a "whole-race probation"....

No matter if you consider the number 144,000 more symbolic than literal, they are a distinct group. They "are the ones who come out of the great tribulation, and washed their robes and made them white in the blood of the Lamb." [21] They are a special sub-set of humanity:

> "No one could learn that song except the hundred and forty-four thousand who were redeemed from the earth." [22]

> As we were about to enter the temple, Jesus raised His lovely voice and said, "Only the 144,000 enter this place," and we shouted, "Alleluia!" [23]

There have been many debates as to whether the number 144,000 is symbolic or literal, but the group is certainly a small proportion of humanity. But, if they are so special, how is it that everyone else on earth is lost? Why are there no "normal" Christians being saved then? It's like the whole population is bifurcated into zeroes and tens, with no numbers between.

There is a logic to the system, though. We've seen the two-edged relationship between a knowledge of God and faith. The more a person knows about the glory of God, the more he will be "drawn back to God." [24] Unless he *isn't* drawn back to God. In that case, the more a person knows about the glory of God, the less God can do to save him.

This knowledge of God is transformative. "By beholding we become changed," whether that be for good or evil. And this knowledge is both needed and promised. Remember?

> What the world needs today is the light of Christ's example reflected from the lives of Christlike men and women. [25]

> We shall see the medical missionary work broadening and deepening at every point of its progress, because of the inflowing of hundreds and thousands of streams, until the whole earth is covered as the waters cover the sea. [26]

The whole earth... covered with WHO doctors, nurses, and mandated public health lockdowns? Surgery ops, ventilators, pharmacies, x-rays, CAT scans, IV drips, and EUA injections all supported by massive PR measures in every form of media? No... not on God's watch.

> The earth shall be full of the knowledge of the LORD as the waters cover the sea. [27]

---

21. Revelation 7:14
22. Revelation 14:3
23. *Testimonies*, vol. 1, 68
24. *Desire of Ages*, 761
25. *Testimonies*, vol. 9, 135
26. E.G. White, "Medical Missionary Work," April 16, 1901; Manuscript 32, 1901
27. Isaiah 11:9

The earth will be filled with the knowledge of the glory of the LORD, as the waters cover the sea.[28]

Indeed. There has always been a difference between "medical work" and "medical missionary work," but the realities of being persecuted for the sake of the truth make it obvious that much of the "machinery" of our current medical system will not be available to God's people as their work expands and the world deteriorates. Circumstances will eventually put the "simple" back into "simple remedies" with the full force of the law.[29] Which is fine, really, because—

God ordinarily works through very simple means.[30]

It's important to never look at the Lord's healing methods solely from a "physical health" point of view. He intends to accomplish more, and doesn't consent to being limited by the findings of even randomized double blind placebo controlled studies. For reasons of His own, God thinks a simple approach should be used.

It is of no use to have seasons of prayer for sick persons, while they refuse to use the simple remedies which God has provided, and which are close by them.[31]

And this idea of having a world-wide impact... uh-huh, that's what it looks like when "this gospel" goes to all the world, to every person on the planet. "This gospel," carried by preaching, teaching, helping, healing—"a work identical with the work that Christ did"[32]—takes the knowledge of the glory of God to every one of them. It's really the only way it could ever be done.

And—unsurprisingly now—each one exposed to "this gospel" will eventually be either "drawn back to God," or choose to follow in the footsteps of Lucifer. It is this that "closes probation"; not some arbitrary "Times up!" ruling from the throne of God. Faced with the glory of the character of God, everyone goes one way or the other.

As we near the close of this earth's history, we advance more and more rapidly in Christian growth, or we retrograde just as decidedly.[33]

As the members of the body of Christ approach the period of their last conflict, "the time of Jacob's trouble," they will grow up into Christ, and will partake largely of His spirit.[34]

---

28. Habakkuk 2:14
29. This doesn't mean all of "modern medicine" is evil; it simply means that even the good of it will be increasingly unavailable. God will be honored as His simple means are contrasted with the increasingly complicated measures that will be needed to sustain "health" in spite of the violation of the laws of health.
30. E.G. White, Letter to Brother Tyszkiewicz, March 3, 1889; Letter 32, 1889
31. E.G. White, Letter to Brother T.A. Chapman, November 29, 1898; Letter 106, 1898
32. E.G. White, "Christ Our Example in Every Line of Work," October 27, 1902; Manuscript 130, 1902. Quoted more fully on page 81.
33. E.G. White, Letter to Brethren in Responsible Positions, November 1890; Letter 1f, 1890
34. *Testimonies*, vol. 1, 353

Those only... who will take a high, noble stand in self-denial and self-sacrifice, will be channels of light to the world. Those who do not advance will retrograde on the very borders of the heavenly Canaan![35]

There will be a general proclamation of truth, the whole earth will be lightened with the glory of God, but those only will recognize the light who have sought to know the difference between holiness and sin.[36]

We've seen this issue before. The most basic claims of the most basic counterfeit the devil has to offer all those "who are willing to be deceived":

Satan had accused God of requiring self-denial of the angels, when He knew nothing of what it meant Himself, and when He would not Himself make any self-sacrifice for others. This was the accusation that Satan made against God in heaven; and after the evil one was expelled from heaven, he continually charged the Lord with exacting service which He would not render Himself. Christ came to the world to meet these false accusations, and to reveal the Father.[37]

Unselfishness, the principle of God's kingdom, is the principle that Satan hates; its very existence he denies. From the beginning of the great controversy, he has endeavored to prove God's principles of action to be selfish, and he deals in the same way with all who serve God. To disprove Satan's claim is the work of Christ and of all who bear His name.[38]

This is the test of humanity's second probation, and it comes when the "avenging enemy" makes it harder than ever to believe that "God is love."[39] The decisive test the universe is waiting to see comes not from Satan, but from God Himself. How ironic, though, that all the cardio and strength training exercises needed to prepare for the event—even the bench pressing!—were made possible courtesy of the devil's temptations.

This will not be a happy day in the kingdom of darkness!

35. E.G. White, Letter to Brethren and Sisters Attending Oakland Meeting, March 1, 1887; Letter 53, 1887
36. E.G. White, Letter to David Paulson, December 17, 1903; Letter 268, 1903
37. *Review and Herald*, February 18, 1890
38. *Education*, 154
39. Even though the hardest test comes from God, Satan is far from blind to the opportunity this gives him to turn everything on its head, so far as appearances go:
    "One effort more, and then Satan's last device is employed. He hears the unceasing cry for Christ to come, for Christ to deliver them. This last strategy is to personate Christ and make them think their prayers are answered. But this answers to the last closing work, the abomination of desolation standing in the holy place." E.G. White, "Satan's Last Deception," 1884; Manuscript 16, 1884
    It seems a safe bet to think that this counterfeit "Christ" will, superficially at least, look a great deal more loving than the "avenging enemy" Christ.

CHAPTER 21

And All These...

THE last chapter discussed the need and manner of a "whole-race" probation. Oddly, though, it didn't have much to say about the vast majority of
the race. That "minor detail" will receive our attention now.

Surprisingly, perhaps, we'll begin that consideration with Paul's desire to
move on to "perfection":

> Therefore, leaving the discussion of the elementary principles of Christ, let us go
> on to perfection, not laying again the foundation of repentance from dead works and
> of faith toward God, of the doctrine of baptisms, of laying on of hands, of resurrection
> of the dead, and of eternal judgment. And this we will do if God permits.[1]

Paul's discussion of what this all means focused largely on Christ's role as
our great High Priest, which he lays out as a decided change from the era of
Levitical priests. The key point is that Jesus became a priest of an entirely different order:

> This hope we have as an anchor of the soul, both sure and steadfast, and which en-
> ters the Presence behind the veil, where the forerunner has entered for us, even Jesus,
> having become High Priest forever according to the order of Melchizedek.[2]

One of the most intriguing aspects of this transition from Levi to
Melchizedek is found in Chapter 7:

> For the priesthood being changed, of necessity there is also a change of the law.[3]

As much as some "believers" might wish, this is not any change in the perfect, immutable, unchangeable, and eternal law of God. It means that the cere-

---

1. Hebrews 6:1–3
2. Hebrews 6:19–20
3. Hebrews 7:12

monial law—one part of the "positive law"—was no longer to be observed, and that the location of intercession had moved to the heavenly sanctuary.

The usefulness of those things had ended. They were over, but many of the Jews "minds were blinded," and they had difficulty recognizing that anything stipulated by God might one day "pass away."[4]

Skipping over chapters 8, 9, and 10 entirely,[5] we come to the more familiar Chapter 11, the "Faith Chapter," which points the reader to the heroic righteousness of those exhibiting true faith down through the ages. Our interest at the moment, though, takes us to the final two verses of the chapter:

> And all these, having obtained a good testimony through faith, did not receive the promise, God having provided something better for us, that they should not be made perfect apart from us.[6]

This seems a little strange, doesn't it? Faith—the one thing of utmost importance—they all had. But none of them received the promise. That is delayed, waiting for "us." All of which naturally raises the question of who "us" might be.

Normally, "us" (first person, plural, objective pronoun) includes the speaker. But this creates a problem, since Paul is now as dead as all the folks he listed off, and there is no evidence that he received "the promise" any more than the rest did. His life ended with an executioner's sword to the back of the neck. Like so many others "of whom the world was not worthy,"[7] he awaits the resurrection.

So who is "us"?

Quite simply, "us" is the class of people Paul was among when he wrote—the living believers. Less simply, "us" have never yet been "made perfect." As a result, the faithful dead of all ages (the "they" of the verse above) have also not yet been "made perfect."

Over time, the membership of "us" keeps changing as people join the group through conversion and leave the group through apostasy or death. Those who die in faith move from "us" (the living believers) to "they" (the righteous dead). When it's all said and done, though, there is only one set of "us" that plays the pivotal role of being made "perfect in regard to the conscience"[8]—and that is the living saints at the end of human probation.

That final "us," is the 144,000, of course, and this is why their performance in the time of Jacob's trouble has significance for the "whole race." But this idea of one group determining the fate of the whole human race may seem a bit

---

4. See Hebrews 3:7–16.

5. There's a whole new book right there, but not right now.

6. Hebrews 11:39–40

7. Hebrews 11:38

8. Hebrews 9:9

sketchy. The claim here is that something special is accomplished through the "complete fulfillment of the new covenant"[9] that makes "the promise" available to those who had "obtained a good testimony through faith" but who had not been "made perfect" themselves.

It sounds like a great idea (for "they"!), but is it fair? Or even reasonable?

It sounds a bit like the neighborhood klutz, the kid with two left feet, saying, "My friend can jump from the three-point line and do a slam dunk, so we both just got $255 million contracts with a pro basketball team."

Is there any line of reasoning that can make sense of that?

Surprisingly enough, there is (at least in the weightier sense of salvation by covenant; making sense out of professional sports contracts is a fairly hopeless proposition), and it has been prefigured all down through sacred history. It is common, in scripture, to find that a covenant with one person, or a limited number of people, ends up affecting vast numbers of others. The first such case is Adam and Eve, who played a uniquely pivotal role! The "bad" side of their effect is easy to see, but it's also true that when God made the covenant with them, the "enmity" was promised not to them alone, but to all the seed of the woman.[10]

When Noah was found faithful, God made a covenant with him (remember the rainbow?) and it extended to "every living creature that is with you, for perpetual generations."[11]

Abraham received the covenant promises four times (the last time in company with Isaac), and the blessing always extended far beyond himself:

> In you all the families of the earth shall be blessed.[12]

> To your descendants I have given this land, from the river of Egypt to the great river, the River Euphrates.[13]

> I will establish My covenant between Me and you and your descendants after you in their generations, for an everlasting covenant, to be God to you and your descendants after you.[14]

> In your seed all the nations of the earth shall be blessed, because you have obeyed My voice.[15]

When Jacob was fleeing Esau's anger and received the dream of the ladder to heaven, the blessing of the covenant was promised him, including:

---

9. *Great Controversy*, 485. Quoted more fully on page 89.
10. Genesis 3:15
11. Genesis 9:12
12. Genesis 12:3
13. Genesis 15:18
14. Genesis 17:7
15. Genesis 22:18

In you and in your seed all the families of the earth shall be blessed.[16]

Years later, on the occasion of the original "time of Jacob's trouble," not only did Jesus—the "Angel of the Covenant" with whom he wrestled—renew the covenant with Jacob (now "Israel"[17]), but his life and the lives of all his extended family were spared.

We could go on, but perhaps that's enough to establish the idea that one individual or one group entering into covenant with God is capable of extending blessings far beyond their number.

But... isn't that kind of *arbitrary?*

No, and it's worth understanding *why* it's not. When "this gospel" goes to all the world, everyone will see the most contextually relevant revelation of God's character that could possibly be given them. Human beings—sinners like themselves—saved from sin, *healed* from sin, serving others unselfishly in every practical way despite persecution, economic boycott, and talk of a death penalty. In the process, the whole world has the chance to see that God *sustains* these people, providing at least their minimal needs, and providing whatever is needed for them to serve others.

God is able to make all grace abound toward you, that you, always having all sufficiency in all things, may have an abundance for every good work.[18]

(Now, if by any chance you have slipped into a sort of shallow, inattentive trance-like state from too much reading, you should stop and go over that last Bible verse again. It's pretty much a blank check, as long as your expense account is only showing "good works." That's a promise worth claiming, and a goal worth working for!)

But back to what the world will see when "this gospel" is spreading like some sort of blessed viral pandemic. Not only are these healed sinners blessing all they can in every way they can, but they are more than willing to explain the simple, cause-and-effect means of their own healing. And it *is* simple; it's just confidence in God... in everything, in every way, at all times, under any circumstance.

With this revelation for all to see, the variable of knowledge is taken off the table and out of the equation. The outcome of "saved or lost" then hinges on a single point. Theologians would call it "faith."

---

16. Genesis 28:14
17. A sign of the change of character is another common element in stories of entering into the covenant. Abram and Sarai became Abraham and Sarah, Jacob became Israel, Saul became Paul, and the church of Pergamos is promised a new name. Similarly, in Zechariah 3, Joshua is given a change of raiment. Of course, the epitome of this is the "new covenant," in which the law is written in the heart, or—as Ezekiel put it—believers are promised a new heart.
18. 2 Corinthians 9:8

And before the crucial test is given, God identifies every person with the genuine article, places His seal on them, gives Satan free access short of murder, and tells the universe, "Watch this! These people are going to flatten every obstacle the devil can put in their way. They don't know it, but I can see that they have true faith, and together with 'this gospel' that's enough to guarantee their success. How certain am I? Certain enough to risk My whole government on the outcome."

> It is impossible to give any idea of the experience of the people of God who shall be alive upon the earth when celestial glory and a repetition of the persecutions of the past are blended. They will walk in the light proceeding from the throne of God. By means of the angels there will be constant communication between heaven and earth. And Satan, surrounded by evil angels, and claiming to be God, will work miracles of all kinds, to deceive, if possible, the very elect....

> Fearful tests and trials await the people of God. The spirit of war is stirring the nations from one end of the earth to the other. But in the midst of the time of trouble that is coming—a time of trouble such as has not been since there was a nation—God's chosen people will stand unmoved. Satan and his host cannot destroy them, for angels that excel in strength will protect them.[19]

Those strong angels aren't an overreaction, by the way:

> No scientific theory can explain the steady march of evil workers under the generalship of Satan. In every mob wicked angels are at work, rousing men to commit deeds of violence.[20]

But the important point just now is that the 100% accuracy of God's sealing is proven by the 100% "pass" rate of those who endure the test of Jacob's trouble, including the "avenging enemy" aspect we looked at in Chapter 19. This proves that God knows how to identify true faith, but it does more than that. It proves that all the knowledge of God any person could benefit from, *without* faith, leaves them in hopeless slavery to sin; but that same knowledge, *with* faith, results in the saints crushing Satan under their feet,[21] *every. single. time.* One hundred forty-four thousand times over.

We didn't talk about the "investigative judgment" in this book, but let's suffice by saying that it focuses on a single, simple question: Did this person have true faith? Jesus was the judge of that, and on that basis He pronounced the ultimate fate of all who have lived on earth. Some passed that critical examination, others did not.

19. *Testimonies*, vol. 9, 16–17
20. E.G. White, Letter to J.E. White, November 16, 1903; Letter 250, 1903
21. See Romans 16:20.

Perhaps none of those whose names were retained in the Book of Life could truthfully be said to have resisted "all the allurements of evil." But neither could it be said that they had seen all of God's character that could benefit them.[22] Other than a few debatable outlying cases (Job, Enoch, Abraham, Elijah, Daniel, etc.), it's hard to believe that any of them had been completely *diasozo'ed*. The teaching of the gospel, the verdict of the judgment had *declared* them righteous, when the reality of their lives—in most cases, anyway—would not have made it appear completely so.

The classic case, of course, is the thief on the cross. Had he gained the experience necessary to "resist all the allurements of evil" for the rest of a normal lifetime? Of course, he didn't have a normal lifetime to deal with, so it has often been argued that he remained sinless for the few hours he had left. Who of us can say? But dying on a cross with Jesus a few feet away and promising you that you'll be with Him in paradise is a far different matter than seeing Him as an avenging enemy out to kill you notwithstanding your sacrifice of all the world has to offer in order to serve Him loyally. Did the thief learn enough to pass *that* test? In less than six hours? That would be... *very* impressive, to put it mildly.

But ever since apostolic days, even the best of Christians have died, confessing their continued need for the imputed righteousness of Christ to cover the defects of their characters. This is classic (little "o") orthodox Christianity. But it doesn't sound much like *diasozo!*

Why not? Because it isn't. It's standard New Testament Christianity, but not "complete fulfillment of the new-covenant promise"[23] Christianity. The heroic example of Christians down through the ages could make a whole new "Faith Chapter" many times over. If you've ever read Foxe's *Book of Martyrs*, or the Anabaptist equivalent, *The Martyrs Mirror,* you know what I mean. It's inspiring material, but "they" "did not receive the promise."[24]

Nonetheless, "they" of all ages *did* have faith! And that's what salvation is based on. Martin Luther had it right! And once the demonstration of the 144,000 is on record for all to see, the Lord can point to the faithful dead of all ages, and say to every interested party in the whole universe, "You've seen that I can identify true faith (144,000 "hits" and zero "misses" is a lot better than random odds), and you know that the investigative judgment found all these to have that true faith. You've seen that true faith combined with a knowledge of 'this gospel' invariably results in the resistance of 'all the allurements of evil.' These are my people; we can teach them the details of 'this gospel' when they

---

22. Looking for an exception? Abraham may be your best option. Consider what was said of him back on page 46.

23. *Great Controversy*, 485. Quoted more fully on page 89.

24. Hebrews 11:39

get here. It's time for the marriage supper of the lamb. I desire that they also...
may be with Me where I am.[25] If anyone here present knows of any reason that
My bride and I should not be joined in holy matrimony, speak now or forever
hold your peace!"

And in all the universe, not an objection will be raised.

That's such an inviting picture... so why would the Lord wait? Why let His
people die off, generation after generation? Why not kill the wicked and get on
with an eternity of joy?

For the same reason God has been willing to suffer from sin ever since its
very beginning.[26] Because there is only one way to defeat sin, and that is to
demonstrate the truth at every step.[27] Until that's done, you can count on those
last three claims never going away by themselves.

To forget this is one of the most perilous mistakes God's people can make!
True, the world is probably more wicked than ever before; the things they put
on TV and the internet, the things that go on *in public*, are more disgusting
than when you grew up; and the idea of someone blowing up the whole world
with a few hundred nuclear weapons is not hard to imagine. But you know
what? *None of that* means that "Jesus just *has* to come soon!"

> When men begin to weave in the human threads to compose the pattern of the
> web, the Lord is in no hurry. He waits until men shall lay down their own human in-
> ventions and will accept the Lord's way and the Lord's will.[28]

Astoundingly, He has left the timing of earth's final events in the hands of
His people to decide. Maybe we should take that seriously, rather than letting
the Lord's enemies set the agenda.

25. John 17:24
26. We looked at this back on page 40: "Few give thought to the suffering that sin has caused our Creator. All heaven suffered in Christ's agony; but that suffering did not begin or end with His manifestation in humanity. The cross is a revelation to our dull senses of the pain that, from its very inception, sin has brought to the heart of God." *Education*, 263
27. We saw this as well, in the same chapter: "Time must be given for Satan to develop the principles which were the foundation of his government. The heavenly universe must see worked out the principles which Satan declared were superior to God's principles. God's order must be contrasted with Satan's order. The corrupting principles of Satan's rule must be revealed. The principles of righteousness expressed in God's law must be demonstrated as unchangeable, perfect, eternal." *Review and Herald*, September 7, 1897
28. E.G. White, Letter to Brother and Sister J.A. Burden, July 29, 1901; Letter 181, 1901

CHAPTER 22

And Angels, Too...

BACK on page 95 it was said that the two big questions on the minds of the unfallen universe were the dual issues concerning fallen men and fallen angels. What's needed to resolve those questions is evidence that God's plan to reward *some* sinful humans with eternal life, while consigning *most* sinful humans and *all* sinful angels to eternal death, is defensible. And by "defensible," we mean that neither the *reasons* for doing this nor the *means* of doing this are arbitrary.

In the test of the avenging enemy, we saw the proof that it is objectively safe to save all who will trust the Lord in everything, in every way, at all times, under any circumstance. Through the demonstration of the sealing and the work of the investigative judgment, we saw the proof that it is safe to save the faithful of all ages, even though they themselves never faced that hardest of all tests of faith. In this way, the blessing of the "complete fulfillment of the new-covenant promise"[1] extends far beyond the 144,000.

That answers the first of the two big questions, and just to get the matter out of the way—despite having to severely disrupt the chronological flow of presentation to do so—we'll look at the issue of the eternal destruction of *most* sinful humans and *all* sinful angels now. The concern is understandable, since the action is said to be irreversible. The sentence of "you shall be no more; though you are sought for, you will never be found again,"[2] carries a heavy load of finality with it.

---

1. *Great Controversy*, 485. Quoted more fully on page 89.
2. Ezekiel 26:21

And the concern is fueled by a good thing—love. Remember, everyone who will ever be subject to the second death was loved. By God, of course, but by others as well. Even Lucifer.... How long did Gabriel and Lucifer work in close companionship and harmony? We have no figure to put on it, of course, but is it hard to think that they might have been "best friends"? And that they might have both believed that they would be "best friends forever"?

If your best friend in grade school, grows up, moves away, and ends up being a mass murderer, does that erase all your fond memories? You may have nothing but contempt for his eventual murderous rampage, but wouldn't you still wish he could somehow be taken back to that former state of innocence and friendliness?

And so, if I may put some hypothetical words into Gabriel's mouth, can't you hear him asking, "Jesus, how come you can save *those* sinners, but not my friends? Isn't there something you can do?"

To push the boundaries further than I think Gabriel would ever go, what possible excuse could God give? After all, He's *God*. He can do anything!

Really? What does "impossible" mean to you?

> Satan had disguised himself in a cloak of falsehood, and for a time it was impossible to tear off the covering, so that the hideous deformity of his character could be seen. He must be left to reveal himself in his cruel, artful, wicked works.[3]

"For a time" (which is now some 6,000-ish years, and counting), even God couldn't fully portray the true nature of sin. All He could do was allow sin to reveal itself. So, that's *one* thing God couldn't do. Any more? Well, yes, actually.

> All heaven knew that God could not change or abolish His law to save man.[4]

> God could not change one iota of his law to meet man in his fallen condition.[5]

That's the immutable law, so no big surprise by now.

> God could not personally communicate with sinful men.[6]

The difficulty here being the consequent death of sinners. A serious problem, to be sure, but God has nonetheless, through the work of Christ, done so much in our behalf that He has actually run into another impossibility:

> God cannot do more for His heritage than He has done to secure their salvation.[7]

Oddly, though, the one path of redemption devised by Omnipotence is not just the "most" that could be done. It is also the least that would work.

---

3. *Spirit of Prophecy*, vol. 4, 319
4. *Spiritual Gifts*, vol. 2, 274
5. *Review and Herald*, February 27, 1900
6. E.G. White, "A Personal God," October 14, 1903; Manuscript 124, 1903.
7. E.G. White, Letter to J.E. White, August 10, 1896; Letter 155, 1896

God could not do more for man than He has done in giving His beloved Son, nor could He do less and yet secure the redemption of man and maintain the dignity of the divine law.[8]

God could not give less than the fullness, nor was it possible for Him to give more.[9]

There are more impossibilities. Hundreds of different phrasings can be found in the Spirit of Prophecy writings, but most of them are derived from this one:

God cannot save man against his will from the power of Satan's artifices.[10]

Free will is clearly the major obstacle standing in the way of God's plans and intentions. You can see it in each of these otherwise scattered pronouncements from Ellen White.

God cannot dwell in your heart or thoughts where self rules supreme.[11]

God cannot use men who, in time of peril, when the strength, courage, and influence of all are needed, are afraid to take a firm stand for the right.[12]

God cannot respond to one soul that does not respond to His grace offered, His love bestowed.[13]

God cannot do great things for His people because of their hardness of heart and sinful unbelief.[14]

God cannot glorify His name through His people while they are leaning upon man and making flesh their arm.[15]

God cannot bless a self-indulgent church.[16]

To end this listing with a slightly more pleasant note....

God cannot be satisfied until the fallen race is redeemed, reclaimed, and reinstated to their holy privileges, having free access to the tree of life.[17]

Lest the reason for all this discussion be lost in the shuffle, just note that it applies full force to my unauthorized scripting of Gabriel's question about fallen men and fallen angels. They have free will, too, and when used in the wrong way, it eventually comes to the point where God can do nothing more to help them. But this presents another problem, since it's one thing to say, "I

---

8. *Testimonies*, vol. 4, 418
9. *Signs of the Times*, January 2, 1901
10. *Testimonies*, vol. 4, 32
11. E.G. White, Letter to Maria Chase, June 12, 1865; Letter 2, 1865
12. *Prophets and Kings*, 142
13. E.G. White, Letter to Edson and Emma White, August 24, 1897; Letter 153a, 1897
14. *Testimonies*, vol. 3, 171
15. *Testimonies*, vol. 5, 729
16. E.G. White, "Faithfulness in the Work of God," March 12, 1899; Manuscript 25, 1899
17. *Signs of the Times*, April 11, 1895

can't do anything more," and it's another thing to show that there really is nothing more that could possibly be done.

Far more than for the rest of us, showing that absolutely no viable options remain is particularly hard for One who is omnipotent! How is God supposed to do that?

Fast forward a thousand years. Specifically, fast forward over *"the* millennium," as in the time between Christ's second coming and His return for final judgment. As Christ, the angels, and the redeemed descend toward the earth, the wicked are raised so they can observe all that happens. Christ's feet touch the Mount of Olives and it splits into a great plain. The Holy City descends, but off to one side of the multitude, not coming down over them so they end up standing in Central Park. How do we know this little detail? Because as soon as the city has landed, Christ leads the righteous through the gates, into the city.[18]

An unspecified period of time is then given the wicked, who use the opportunity to accept a whole new crop of lies that Satan has prepared for the occasion, organize themselves into a fighting force, and arm themselves with whatever weapons may seem appropriate. (I have long pondered the process of bringing ancient warriors up to speed on the use of ICBM's, though I suspect my own understanding of the devil's preferred weapons systems is at least as far removed as their swords are from the missiles.) Finally, the decisive moment has come:

> At last the order to advance is given, and the countless host moves on—an army such as was never summoned by earthly conquerors, such as the combined forces of all ages since war began on earth could never equal. Satan, the mightiest of warriors, leads the van, and his angels unite their forces for this final struggle. Kings and warriors are in his train, and the multitudes follow in vast companies, each under its appointed leader.
>
> With military precision the serried ranks advance over the earth's broken and uneven surface to the City of God. By command of Jesus, the gates of the New Jerusalem are closed, and the armies of Satan surround the city and make ready for the onset.[19]

Did you catch it?

Something absolutely incredible just happened. No, not the army surrounding the city. That's what armies do. The whole purpose of Satan's last ditch effort is to tear God from the throne and take it himself. Nothing unexpected there.

---

18. *Great Controversy*, 662–663
19. *Great Controversy*, 664

The amazing thing is what Jesus did. He closed the gates. That means they had been *open*. With the wicked of all ages outside the city, the gates were left open! And, as if to make sure there was no doubt about what gates are for, almost the first thing the wicked had seen upon their resurrection was Jesus demonstrating how to get huge numbers of people into the city.

In an earlier account of these events, Ellen White mentioned one additional detail of interest: "Just as [Jesus] closed the gates of the city, the curse was pronounced upon the wicked. The gates were shut."[20]

A curse? For all those whose cases were decided at least a thousand years before? Seems a bit late in the game for that. And why would that curse be sandwiched in between two mentions of the closing of the gates? Unless, of course, the closing of the gates marked the end of some significant development. Something like the final, "But you are not willing to come to Me that you may have life"[21] moment, perhaps?

It would be foolish to give anyone the idea that he could find acceptance with the Lord at that late date. And yet... the gates were open....

And that raises a question. Would Jesus, the One who is "the same yesterday, today, and forever,"[22] the One who said "whoever comes to Me I will by no means cast out,"[23] the One who has "no pleasure in the death of the wicked"[24]— would "this same Jesus"[25] let a repentant and trusting sinner into the city?

It's hypothetical, of course, since in all the multitudes of the lost there is not one with enough faith in God's good will to venture anywhere near those open doors. Does Jesus invite them? We are not told, but it would not change the outcome. Just as the 144,000 passed the hardest possible test of faith to answer one question of the unfallen universe, so the wicked have answered the other by failing the easiest of all tests.

There is nothing more that even God can do for them. They just don't trust Him. Destruction is the most merciful option.

---

20. *Early Writings*, 53
21. John 5:40
22. Hebrews 13:8
23. John 6:37
24. Ezekiel 33:11
25. Acts 1:11

CHAPTER 23

Loose Ends

BACK now from our preview of events after the millennium. Our next major point of consideration is to see if it's reasonable to believe in a non-arbitrary method of healing/forgiveness for sinners. Before we go there, however, a couple details deserve a moment's notice.

Let's start in Leviticus 16, the chapter that set the order of events for the day of atonement. Naturally, much of the attention paid to this chapter has focused on the high priest entering into the most holy place to "make atonement for himself, for his household, and for all the assembly of Israel."[1] But we want to look at what happens immediately after that.

> And he shall go out to the altar that is before the LORD, and make atonement for it, and shall take some of the blood of the bull and some of the blood of the goat, and put it on the horns of the altar all around. Then he shall sprinkle some of the blood on it with his finger seven times, cleanse it, and consecrate it from the uncleanness of the children of Israel.[2]

Verse 20 goes on to tell of the scapegoat, upon whom the forgiven sins of all Israel are placed before he is led into the wilderness by a "fit man."[3] The scapegoat represents Satan, and the fit man is the 144,000.

Chronologically, that puts the cleansing of the altar—the altar of sacrifice out in the courtyard—right after the close of probation (the high priest leaving the most holy for the last time), and before the millennium (Satan being bound

---

1. Leviticus 16:17
2. Leviticus 16:18–19
3. "Fit man" is the more literal KJV wording. Other translations use words like "suitable" (NKJV), "appointed" (HCSB), and "a man who is in readiness" (NHEB).

in the wilderness).[4] That's the time of the plagues, the time of Jacob's trouble. And the blood put on the horns just then is an atonement for the altar.

But the altar represents the *cross*... and the cross is the thing that makes atonement for *everything else*. How could an atonement ever be needed for the cross? And why right after the close of probation? This seems odd....

It's one thing for the sanctuary to be defiled; after all, that's where confessed sins went all during the year. But the altar? Sins didn't stay on the altar, they went into the holy place in the blood of the sacrifice, or they were borne by the priest who ate the sacrifice. The altar is the very source of forgiveness... how could the altar ever be defiled?

Think of the use, and the understanding, of the altar (the cross) up until the close of probation. The cross is indeed the reason anyone has hope for forgiveness, but until the demonstration of *diasozo*, until it's seen that God's people have been *healed* from sin, that they have been "brought safely through" the snares of Satan—until then, the hope of forgiveness is based entirely on faith that God will regard a diseased patient who is actually sick, as if he were a healed patient who is actually well.

It's a "declared" righteousness, all the way up until it's demonstrated as a "made" righteousness. And Satan has a lot of complaints on that account because a declared righteousness is as arbitrary as the day is long! Remember his last ditch argument, even after the close of probation?

> "Will God banish me and my angels from His presence, and yet reward those who have been guilty of the same sins? Thou canst not do this, O Lord, in justice. Thy throne will not stand in righteousness and judgment. Justice demands that sentence be pronounced against them."[5]

It's a strong argument. It's served Lucifer well for about six thousand years. But at the very end of the antitypical day of atonement the process of forgiveness itself is cleansed of all the defilement Satan sought to attach to it. God's people, healed of all their diseases, are fit enough to lead the scapegoat away into the wilderness, nevermore to trouble the camp of Israel.

This end result is, and always has been, the goal:

> The atonement of Christ is not a mere skillful way to have our sins pardoned; it is a divine remedy for the cure of transgression and the restoration of spiritual health. It is the heaven-ordained means by which the righteousness of Christ may be not only upon us, but in our hearts and characters.[6]

---

4. *Great Controversy*, 485
5. *Testimonies*, vol. 5, 474
6. E.G. White, Letter to Sister, 1906; Letter 406, 1906

Please notice that last sentence. The atonement is a "means" to an end. It's a process, a method—it's not fairy dust. And the goal of it all has always been that God's people may be cured and restored. A declared righteousness is a great tool to begin the process of healing a sinner's faith. It's a huge step of reconciliation, giving sinners who have been alienated from God a way to even entertain the idea that He actually does love them.

Despite Paul's best efforts to straighten out our thinking on this point, many people still instinctively feel that the sacrifice of Christ served to reconcile God to sinful human beings. It is, of course, the exact opposite! God's love was never withdrawn from sinners; it's the sinners' faith which was withdrawn from God.

> For if when we were enemies we were reconciled to God through the death of His Son, much more, having been reconciled, we shall be saved by His life. And not only that, but we also rejoice in God through our Lord Jesus Christ, through whom we have now received the reconciliation.[7]

> Now all things are of God, who has reconciled us to Himself through Jesus Christ, and has given us the ministry of reconciliation, that is, that God was in Christ reconciling the world to Himself, not imputing their trespasses to them, and has committed to us the word of reconciliation. Now then, we are ambassadors for Christ, as though God were pleading through us: we implore you on Christ's behalf, be reconciled to God.[8]

> The Saviour's sacrifice was not to create in God a love that had not before existed; it was but the expression of a love which had not been appreciated or understood.[9]

OK, new topic; another loose end. From this same period of the time of Jacob's trouble, we find a good explanation for something else that has long perplexed careful readers of *The Great Controversy*. The difficulty comes from this passage:

> Jacob's history is also an assurance that God will not cast off those who have been deceived and tempted and betrayed into sin, but who have returned unto Him with true repentance. While Satan seeks to destroy this class, God will send His angels to comfort and protect them in the time of peril. The assaults of Satan are fierce and determined, his delusions are terrible; but the Lord's eye is upon His people, and His ear listens to their cries. Their affliction is great, the flames of the furnace seem about to consume them; but the Refiner will bring them forth as gold tried in the fire. God's love for His children during the period of their severest trial is as strong and tender as in the days of their sunniest prosperity; but it is needful for them to be placed in the furnace of fire; their earthliness must be consumed, that the image of Christ may be perfectly reflected.[10]

---

7. Romans 5:10–11
8. 2 Corinthians 5:18–20
9. E.G. White, "God's Love For Man," 1892; Manuscript 41, 1892
10. *Great Controversy*, 621

This is from the chapter on "The Time of Trouble," so the setting is definitely after the close of probation. Many have questioned the comment at the end of the paragraph about the "earthliness" of the righteous. If it is something that needs to be "consumed," doesn't that make it "sin"? And shouldn't that have been taken care of before the close of probation?

Maybe Ellen White made a mistake. Maybe she didn't really mean "earthliness." But she probably did, since she used the same word in a parallel but entirely different passage. When writing about "Joshua and the Angel," the story of Zechariah chapter 3, which is another depiction of the time of Jacob's trouble, she wrote:

> The assaults of Satan are strong, his delusions are subtle; but the Lord's eye is upon His people. Their affliction is great, the flames of the furnace seem about to consume them; but Jesus will bring them forth as gold tried in the fire. Their earthliness will be removed, that through them the image of Christ may be perfectly revealed.[11]

"Earthliness" seems like a real thing, even after the close of probation. But what is it? *Great Controversy* says it is to be consumed; *Patriarchs and Prophets* says it is to be removed. Whatever it is, it can't be good. But is it sin? Is there anything that's not good, but not sin?

Recognizing that the test at that time is focused on the faith of the believers, and remembering that the process involves them having "every earthly support... cut off," gives us a starting point. If every earthly support is gone, all that could be left is the desire for that support. And that takes us to another parallel experience: the Garden of Gethsemane.

Obviously this is not the saints at the end of time. This is Christ Himself, but His experience explains the "earthliness" question.

When Jesus prayed, "not My will, but Thine be done," it was a prayer of submission. But it also pointed to another reality: Jesus didn't *want* to do what His Father wanted Him to do. The circumstances and the magnitude of the ordeal created a desire in Jesus that was not in harmony with His Father's will. It wasn't good, but it *wasn't sin!* Why not? Because Jesus had enough faith in His Father to remain submitted.

In response to Jesus' triple-repeated prayer, the Father made no change whatsoever in "the cup" Jesus was asked to drink. Instead, Gabriel was sent to strengthen Him to drink it. Notice, though, how Gabriel went about his task. He didn't lecture Jesus about His moral responsibility to fulfill the promise He made before the earth was created. Gabriel didn't discuss the logistical difficulties it would create if Jesus decided not to carry out the plan. Instead, he "pointed Him to the open heavens, telling Him of the souls that would be saved

---

11. *Prophets and Kings*, 589

as the result of His sufferings."[12] It was, in fact, "for the joy that was set before Him [that He] endured the cross, despising the shame."[13]

In a very real sense, the work of sanctification is largely re-educating our sense of desire to actually *want* the good things God wants for us. This, too, is a part of the at-one-ment process. We see this addressed in the last verse of Isaiah 58—quite notably following all the conditions of benevolence and Sabbath observance: "Then you shall delight yourself in the LORD."[14]

This is a whole different sermon, but when you break down human choices, they are always decided by one or more of three factors: moral imperative (conscience), logical value assessment (common sense), and desire.[15] Those three are listed in descending order of authority and severity of damage caused by ignoring them, but experience shows that, in the end, desire always wins. This is why it's critical to have not just our behavior changed, but to have the change of heart which leads us to love God's will.

> "All true obedience comes from the heart. It was heart work with Christ. And if we consent, He will so identify Himself with our thoughts and aims, so blend our hearts and minds into conformity to His will, that when obeying Him we shall be but carrying out our own impulses. The will, refined and sanctified, will find its highest delight in doing His service. When we know God as it is our privilege to know Him, our life will be a life of continual obedience. Through an appreciation of the character of Christ, through communion with God, sin will become hateful to us."[16]

Temptation is not sin; it doesn't produce guilt. But the righteous at the end of time have spent their whole lives depending in varying degrees upon the support of earthly organizations, paychecks, powers, procedures, processes, people, and who knows what all else. This desire for earthly support—the natural result of a lifetime of experience—needs to go! And perhaps there is nothing so calculated to separate one's trust and dependence from an unworthy person or organization as having them try to kill you for no good reason!

"Earthliness consumed" is essentially just the flip-side of the "avenging enemy" issue. "No servant can serve two masters; for either he will hate the one and love the other, or else he will be loyal to the one and despise the other. You cannot serve God and mammon."[17]

---

12. *Desire of Ages*, 693

13. Hebrews 12:2.

14. Isaiah 58:14

15. Thanks to Lois Eggers for this observation. Her book, *Common Sense Psychology*, based on Ellen White's *Mind, Character, and Personality* volumes is recommended reading.

16. *Desire of Ages*, 668

17. Luke 16:13

CHAPTER 24

Change Is Hard

THE Bible is divided in two for a reason, and the book of Hebrews is the Apostle Paul's effort to make sure that division was recognized, and understood. Of those two goals, he was undoubtedly more successful on the first, but opportunity remains on number two, so let's take a look at his core position.

> For the law, having a shadow of the good things to come, and not the very image of the things, can never with these same sacrifices, which they offer continually year by year, make those who approach perfect. For then would they not have ceased to be offered? For the worshipers, once purified, would have had no more consciousness of sins.

This seems like a simple logical relationship. If there's a problem, and some system or mechanism or process is put in place that solves the problem, then that system or mechanism or process can stop. It's about as self-evident as the maxim that you always find the missing item in the last place you look.

Let's hope so! Continuing to look after you've found the lost coin, or sheep, or whatever, doesn't make any sense. But as long as the goal is unattained, the work goes on. And that's the picture Paul paints of the Old Testament sacrificial system:

> But in those sacrifices there is a reminder of sins every year. For it is not possible that the blood of bulls and goats could take away sins.

The solution to all this was something (technically, Someone) different:

> Therefore, when He came into the world, He said: "Sacrifice and offering You did not desire, but a body You have prepared for Me. In burnt offerings and sacrifices for sin You had no pleasure.

"Then I said, 'Behold, I have come—in the volume of the book it is written of Me—to do Your will, O God.'"

This is apparently an important point in Paul's mind, because he goes right back and says it all again, in only slightly different words:

> Previously saying, "Sacrifice and offering, burnt offerings, and offerings for sin You did not desire, nor had pleasure in them" (which are offered according to the law), then He said, "Behold, I have come to do Your will, O God."[1]

This seems to be the climax of all this reasoning, and Paul makes it about as plain as plain can be: "He takes away the first that He may establish the second."[2] It's kind of like every commercial that's ever been made for a new version of an existing product. "Our first model was good, but this one is fantastic!"

Paul continues with his contrast between old and new:

> By that will we have been sanctified through the offering of the body of Jesus Christ once for all. And every priest stands ministering daily and offering repeatedly the same sacrifices, which can never take away sins. But this Man, after He had offered one sacrifice for sins forever, sat down at the right hand of God, from that time waiting till His enemies are made His footstool. For by one offering He has perfected forever those who are being sanctified. But the Holy Spirit also witnesses to us; for after He had said before, "This is the covenant that I will make with them after those days, says the LORD: I will put My laws into their hearts, and in their minds I will write them," then He adds, "Their sins and their lawless deeds I will remember no more."

Paul is quoting Jeremiah 31, of course, the new covenant promise. This is an important point in his letter. In fact, he had already quoted that promise even more completely than he does here, back in Chapter 8. Those verses, just as a point of trivia, comprise the longest direct quotation of the Old Testament to show up anywhere in the New Testament. And now he quotes the key section again. Why all this emphasis and focus? Because it all supports one of the most radical things he would ever write:

> Now where there is remission of these, there is no longer an offering for sin.[3]

You can imagine the shock wave this would send through the Jewish members of the still-young Christian community. After a divinely inspired ritual such as the services in the temple at Jerusalem has been practiced for nearly two thousand years, it's not that easy to convince everyone that, "God's done with that now. Put it away."

---

1. Hebrews 10:1–9a
2. Hebrews 10:9b
3. Hebrews 10:10–18

The proof of that difficulty played out in Paul's own life.[4] The Biblical account shows up in Acts 21, and Ellen White tells the story in her book, *Acts of the Apostles*, Chapter 38.

When Paul and his companions arrived in Jerusalem with the gifts from the Gentile believers, they were met with an "officially" warm greeting. Acts 21:17 says, "when we had come to Jerusalem, the brethren received us gladly." Similarly, when he had recounted "in detail those things which God had done among the Gentiles through his ministry.... they heard it, [and] they glorified the Lord."[5]

But life is seldom so simple. Ellen White provides some background and insight into the complexity of the larger situation:

> In the earlier years of the gospel work among the Gentiles some of the leading brethren at Jerusalem, clinging to former prejudices and habits of thought, had not co-operated heartily with Paul and his associates. In their anxiety to preserve a few meaningless forms and ceremonies, they had lost sight of the blessing that would come to them and to the cause they loved, through an effort to unite in one all parts of the Lord's work. Although desirous of safeguarding the best interests of the Christian church, they had failed to keep step with the advancing providences of God, and in their human wisdom attempted to throw about workers many unnecessary restrictions. Thus there arose a group of men who were unacquainted personally with the changing circumstances and peculiar needs met by laborers in distant fields, yet who insisted that they had the authority to direct their brethren in these fields to follow certain specified methods of labor. They felt as if the work of preaching the gospel should be carried forward in harmony with their opinions.[6]

Fortunately, this problem had been addressed some years earlier at the time of the Jerusalem council, the story of which is found in Acts 15. But that was then, and time had passed....

> [After the council,] when it became apparent that the converts among the Gentiles were increasing rapidly, there were a few of the leading brethren at Jerusalem who began to cherish anew their former prejudices against the methods of Paul and his associates. These prejudices strengthened with the passing of the years, until some of the

---

4. Ellen White repeatedly indicates that Paul wrote Hebrews, but I could not find any indication of *when* it was written. My guess is that these passages were penned after his arrest, in which case he deserves a lot of credit for maintaining a calm manner in his presentation, and not stooping to blame his brethren for the trouble they had caused him.

5. Hebrews 21:19–20

6. *Acts of the Apostles*, 400. This book was published in 1911, and for anyone familiar with the administrative struggles of the Adventist Church during the two decades before, it's hard to overlook the obvious similarity of Ellen White's comments here, to the things she wrote to church administrators who had been inclined to impose "many unnecessary restrictions" on "laborers in distant fields." The introduction of Union Conferences at the 1901 General Conference session helped in this regard, but Ellen White makes it clear that the issue had not gone extinct.

leaders determined that the work of preaching the gospel must henceforth be conducted in accordance with their own ideas. If Paul would conform his methods to certain policies which they advocated they would acknowledge and sustain his work; otherwise they could no longer look upon it with favor or grant it their support.

These men had lost sight of the fact that God is the teacher of His people; that every worker in His cause is to obtain an individual experience in following the divine Leader, not looking to man for direct guidance; that His workers are to be molded and fashioned, not after man's ideas, but after the similitude of the divine.[7]

Back to the time of Paul's arrival in Jerusalem now: After hearing his presentation of the work among the Gentiles, and after the presentation of the generous gift from those far away churches—

The men who, while numbered among those who were in charge of the work at Jerusalem, had urged that arbitrary measures of control be adopted, saw Paul's ministry in a new light and were convinced that their own course had been wrong, that they had been held in bondage by Jewish customs and traditions, and that the work of the gospel had been greatly hindered by their failure to recognize that the wall of partition between Jew and Gentile had been broken down by the death of Christ.

This was the golden opportunity for all the leading brethren to confess frankly that God had wrought through Paul, and that at times they had erred in permitting the reports of his enemies to arouse their jealousy and prejudice. But instead of uniting in an effort to do justice to the one who had been injured, they gave him counsel which showed that they still cherished a feeling that Paul should be held largely responsible for the existing prejudice. They did not stand nobly in his defense, endeavoring to show the disaffected ones where they were wrong, but sought to effect a compromise by counseling him to pursue a course which in their opinion would remove all cause for misapprehension.

"Thou seest, brother," they said, in response to his testimony, "how many thousands of Jews there are which believe; and they are all zealous of the law: and they are informed of thee, that thou teachest all the Jews which are among the Gentiles to forsake Moses, saying that they ought not to circumcise their children, neither to walk after the customs. What is it therefore? the multitude must needs come together: for they will hear that thou art come. Do therefore this that we say to thee: We have four men which have a vow on them; them take, and purify thyself with them, and be at charges with them, that they may shave their heads: and all may know that those things, whereof they were informed concerning thee, are nothing; but that thou thyself also walkest orderly, and keepest the law. As touching the Gentiles which believe, we have written and concluded that they observe no such thing, save only that they keep themselves from things offered to idols, and from blood, and from strangled, and from fornication."[8]

7. *Acts of the Apostles*, 401
8. *Acts of the Apostles*, 403–404

The counsel of the leaders was a reflection of the difficult circumstances in which the Jerusalem believers lived. They meant well, but their comprehension was far too limited to overcome the temptation to seek a "reasonable" co-existence with the Judaism that God had rejected.

> The brethren hoped that Paul, by following the course suggested, might give a decisive contradiction to the false reports concerning him. They assured him that the decision of the former council concerning the Gentile converts and the ceremonial law, still held good. But the advice now given was not consistent with that decision. The Spirit of God did not prompt this instruction; it was the fruit of cowardice. The leaders of the church in Jerusalem knew that by non-conformity to the ceremonial law, Christians would bring upon themselves the hatred of the Jews and expose themselves to persecution. The Sanhedrin was doing its utmost to hinder the progress of the gospel. Men were chosen by this body to follow up the apostles, especially Paul, and in every possible way to oppose their work. Should the believers in Christ be condemned before the Sanhedrin as breakers of the law, they would suffer swift and severe punishment as apostates from the Jewish faith.[9]

Nobody likes punishment, especially not when it is "swift and severe," but this raises some questions. How many years had it been since the crucifixion? How many years since Stephen's death marked the "close of probation" for the Jewish people as a group at the end of the 490 years of Daniel 9?

And "Christians" were still seeking to tick off all the boxes so they could pass as loyal Jews (and—coincidentally—avoid persecution)?

Hello?

Ellen White's account continues:

> Many of the Jews who had accepted the gospel still cherished a regard for the ceremonial law and were only too willing to make unwise concessions, hoping thus to gain the confidence of their countrymen, to remove their prejudice, and to win them to faith in Christ as the world's Redeemer. Paul realized that so long as many of the leading members of the church at Jerusalem should continue to cherish prejudice against him, they would work constantly to counteract his influence. He felt that if by any reasonable concession he could win them to the truth he would remove a great obstacle to the success of the gospel in other places. But he was not authorized of God to concede as much as they asked.

It's a sad day when the one who wrote twenty-five percent of the New Testament has to "win... to the truth" "many of the leading members of the church," but sad days sometimes come. Unfortunately, this effort—though well intended—led Paul to overshoot the mark.

---

9. *Acts of the Apostles*, 404

When we think of Paul's great desire to be in harmony with his brethren, his tenderness toward the weak in the faith, his reverence for the apostles who had been with Christ, and for James, the brother of the Lord, and his purpose to become all things to all men so far as he could without sacrificing principle—when we think of all this, it is less surprising that he was constrained to deviate from the firm, decided course that he had hitherto followed. But instead of accomplishing the desired object, his efforts for conciliation only precipitated the crisis, hastened his predicted sufferings, and resulted in separating him from his brethren, depriving the church of one of its strongest pillars, and bringing sorrow to Christian hearts in every land.[10]

If, indeed, this all happened before Paul wrote Hebrews, you can see why he might spend a little extra time clarifying the increased understanding of the covenant that came in New Testament times, as compared to the understanding of Old Testament times. It's a shame he ended up going to prison, but we are the beneficiaries of his clarity.

---

10. *Acts of the Apostles*, 405

CHAPTER 25

Unveiled

PAUL'S epistle to the Hebrews was a shocking book in the first century. When taken seriously, it's still radical a couple millennia later. In Paul's day, perhaps the most revolutionary element was the teaching that God's people were to move on from the practice of the old system of sacrifices and ceremonies:

> Now where there is remission of these, there is no longer an offering for sin.[1]

And the reason was simple: the old system didn't solve the problem. Despite a faithful following of the divine specifications, sin continued:

> Every priest stands ministering daily and offering repeatedly the same sacrifices, which can never take away sins.[2]

It wasn't that the life of a sheep was suddenly devalued in A.D. 31; it was that the recognition of God's people was called to a higher goal, and that goal was not obtainable through the old system. Some believers, of course, had come to this same conclusion on their own long before Paul ever taught it:

> From the crucifixion to the resurrection many sleepless eyes were constantly searching the prophecies, some to learn the full meaning of the feast they were then celebrating, some to find evidence that Jesus was not what He claimed to be; and others with sorrowful hearts were searching for proofs that He was the true Messiah. Though searching with different objects in view, all were convicted of the same truth—that prophecy had been fulfilled in the events of the past few days, and that the Crucified One was the world's Redeemer. Many who at that time united in the service never again took part in the paschal rites. Many even of

---

1. Hebrews 10:18
2. Hebrews 10:11

the priests were convicted of the true character of Jesus. Their searching of the prophecies had not been in vain, and after His resurrection they acknowledged Him as the Son of God.[3]

But not all could see so clearly. In 1 Corinthians 3, Paul wades into what was probably the most fundamental theological minefield of his day. Developing the contrast between the work of God before Christ, and the work of God after Christ, he speaks "boldly":

> For if what is passing away was glorious, what remains is much more glorious. Therefore, since we have such hope, we use great boldness of speech—unlike Moses, who put a veil over his face so that the children of Israel could not look steadily at the end of what was passing away.[4]

What made this such a bold move? Well, it immediately put Paul into conflict with his countrymen. And lest that seem like old news from centuries ago, just remember that the same issue gets plenty of "present tense" treatment in the Spirit of Prophecy:

> The cross of Calvary is given that man may have correct views and hold theories that are not perverted. If his senses were not bewitched with Satan's philosophy, he could see to the end of that which was to be abolished.[5]

What is this that was "to be abolished"? The simple answer is, "all the ceremonial and sacrificial services of Old Testament times." That much seems clear enough, but it's not only the Jews who can be short sighted here:

> The Jews turned from the Lord Jesus, whom the prophets foretold as the coming Messiah, and they had not been able to see to the end of that which was abolished. In making void the law of God, in turning from the truth with aversion, the Christian world have turned from Christ, and have made manifest the fact that they were not accustomed to looking upon truth of heavenly origin.[6]

> Many in the Christian world also have a veil before their eyes and heart. They do not see to the end of that which was done away. They do not see that it was only the ceremonial law which was abrogated at the death of Christ. They claim that the moral law was nailed to the cross. Heavy is the veil that darkens their understanding.[7]

But as with so many Biblical topics, "there's more than meets the eye" here. It's the matter of "looking steadily at" or "seeing" "the end of what was passing away" that seems as hard for us to grasp as it was for the Jews. Paul's rather di-

---

3. *Desire of Ages*, 775
4. 2 Corinthians 3:11–13
5. E.G. White, "The Truth As It Is In Jesus," June 21, 1897; Manuscript 58, 1897
6. E.G. White, Letter to J.E. White, October 22, 1895; Letter 84, 1895
7. *Review and Herald*, April 22, 1902

rect assessment more than likely applies to us as well: "blindness in part has happened to Israel."[8]

To see the end of the ceremonial law is not simply to note its termination. God intends that we also understand the purpose for which it was instituted. Even more, He intends that we embrace and implement that purpose. Just knowing that the ceremonial law is done away, and the moral law is still in force, doesn't meet the need.

> Over the spiritual eyes of altogether too many there has been hanging a veil. Many have been teaching the binding claims of God's law, but have not been able to see to the end of that which was abolished.[9]

This may sound like a whole new topic of consideration, but it is in reality very closely tied to something we've seen before: "the whole purpose of [Christ's] mission on earth."

> Christ came to reveal to the world the knowledge of the character of God, of which the world was destitute. This knowledge was the chief treasure which He committed to His disciples to be communicated to men.... They were blinded by pride and prejudice so that they could not see to the end of that which was abolished. Jesus came to change the order of things that then existed, and reveal to them the character of the Father.[10]

It was the revelation of the Father's character that was to change "the order of things" that had prevented men from "seeing to the end of that which was abolished." That sounds like a good thing, but what does it mean? What is this "end" that we're supposed to see?

> [At Pentecost] the veil which had prevented them from seeing the end of that which was abolished was now removed, and the object of Christ's mission and the nature of His kingdom were comprehended with perfect clearness.[11]

> The wonderful plan of redemption must be discerned in the death of Christ. There is to be a seeing to the end of that which was to be abolished, that the complete restoration may be understood.[12]

Don't overlook the wording here: "complete restoration" is the language of healing, the language of reality.

> The order and working efficiency of the church are to far exceed those of the Jewish church, inasmuch as their light—the glory of the reality—is the advanced light, for the character and wonderful work of their redemption is laid out in clear lines.[13]

8. Romans 11:25
9. E.G. White, "Diary: Christ Our Righteousness," February 27, 1891; Manuscript 21, 1891
10. *Review and Herald*, November 1, 1892
11. *Spirit of Prophecy*, vol. 3, 266
12. E.G. White, "The Truth As It Is In Jesus," June 21, 1897; Manuscript 58, 1897
13. E.G. White, "Diary: December 1890," December 13, 1890; Manuscript 51, 1890

"Seeing to the end of that which was abolished" is just seeing the full meaning, the reality beyond the symbol, of the ceremonial law. And since the ceremonial law—including the sanctuary with all its services and offerings—just happens to be a depiction of the whole plan of salvation, this kind of "seeing" is not a small matter!

> The Son of God did not die that man might always remain a transgressor; for Christ is not a minister of sin. He died that by that act man might no longer remain a rebel against God's law. He died to point men to the way of faith and obedience, that they might see to the end of that which is abolished. When sinners have a view of the plan of salvation, there is no more disposition to cavil concerning the law; for the way of truth and light is open to their understanding.[14]

"Seeing to the end of that which is abolished" doesn't leave us at the end of animal sacrifices. It leaves us at the end of the whole process of sacrifice and forgiveness:

> "This is the covenant that I will make with them after those days, says the LORD: I will put My laws into their hearts, and in their minds I will write them," then He adds, "Their sins and their lawless deeds I will remember no more." Now where there is remission of these, there is no longer an offering for sin.[15]

"Seeing to the end of that which is abolished" takes us to the end of all "offering for sin" at the "complete fulfillment of the new-covenant promise."[16]

Well, that was a bit of a diversion, but let's get back to the trials and tribulations of the Apostle Paul. It turns out that people who couldn't (or, possibly, *wouldn't*) see to the end of things were a major problem for him.

> The greatest difficulty Paul had to meet arose from the influence of Judaizing teachers. These made him much trouble by causing dissension in the church at Corinth. They were continually presenting the virtues of the ceremonies of the law, exalting these ceremonies above the gospel of Christ, and condemning Paul because he did not urge them upon the new converts.[17]

The continuation of the old at the expense of the new is a tried-and-true trap of the devil. Incredibly, we still hear calls today for a return to the ceremonies of Old Testament times, but God has moved on.

> Christ has taken His people into His church. He has swept away every ceremony of the ancient type. He has given no liberty to restore these rites, or to substitute anything that will recall the old literal sacrifices.[18]

---

14. *Signs of the Times*, July 14, 1890
15. Hebrews 10:16–18
16. *Great Controversy*, 485. Quoted more fully on page 89.
17. *Review and Herald*, April 22, 1902
18. *Review and Herald*, February 25, 1896

This was the point of transition between two economies and their two great festivals. The one was to close forever; the other, which He had just established, was to take its place, and to continue through all time as the memorial of His death.[19]

In this ordinance, Christ discharged His disciples from the cares and burdens of the ancient Jewish obligations in rites and ceremonies. These no longer possessed any virtue.[20]

The ceremonial law was to have no force after Christ died as a sin-offering.[21]

The ordinances which God Himself had appointed were made the means of blinding the mind and hardening the heart. God could do no more for man through these channels. The whole system must be swept away.[22]

The old system was the same as it had always been. The temple still stood (until A.D. 70, anyway), the priests still served in imposing ceremonial garb, the animals still shed red blood and died as impressively as always. But there was no longer any virtue in the system.

The opposite temptation, of course, is for us to look back from our "enlightened era" and think there never had been any virtue in the old system. After all, it's obvious now that "it is not possible that the blood of bulls and goats could take away sins."[23] And it's true; animal sacrifice never could solve the problem of sin. Indeed, as Paul put it, "in those sacrifices there is a reminder of sins every year."[24]

At its heart, the insufficiency of the old system was that it didn't accomplish the one thing that mattered most: for "the law, having a shadow of the good things to come, and not the very image of the things, can never with these same sacrifices, which they offer continually year by year, make those who approach perfect."[25] So why did God ever establish that whole system of things in the first place?

It "was symbolic for the present time in which both gifts and sacrifices are offered which cannot make him who performed the service perfect in regard to the conscience."[26] The symbol *did* have value as a symbol. It represented the greater reality, but it was only a representation, and never capable of "finishing the job." It did, however, provide a mechanism—a *divinely appointed* mechanism—which gave the believer something on which to rest his faith. In this way, the

19. *Review and Herald*, May 31, 1898
20. *Review and Herald*, June 14, 1898
21. E.G. White, "The Law and the Gospel," August 14, 1900; Manuscript 58, 1900
22. *Desire of Ages*, 36
23. Hebrews 10:4
24. Hebrews 10:3
25. Hebrews 10:1
26. Hebrews 9:9

sacrificial system "worked" for the believer, since what God desired first was faith, and the Old Testament system could foster faith.

Did it occur to them that a dead animal wasn't going to be sufficient to deal with a matter of spiritual condition? Sure... some believers, some times, to some degree. Abraham, Moses, David... but the majority of even "the righteous in Israel" did not see far beyond the sacrifice, and since it was, in fact, divinely appointed, it would have appeared well nigh unto blasphemy to imply that God's own means of dealing with sin was insufficient.

Don't miss the challenge here. The idea of animal sacrifice was firmly entrenched in the Jewish mind. But not only was it an animal, it was *their* animal. True, God did "provide for Himself the lamb for a burnt offering" instead of having Abraham carry through with the sacrifice of Isaac.[27] But for the next 2,000 years, the animals for sacrifice came from the individual sinner or from the nation as a whole. More than ninety times, the Bible refers to *"his"* or *"their"* sacrifice or offering. Whether it was a sin offering, a trespass offering, a heave offering, a burnt offering, a grain offering, or a drink offering, it was what the sinner presented to the Lord. We may think it should have been obvious that all the sacrifices they gave represented "the Lamb of God" *from God*, but it's not easy to show how it would have been so.

The change of perspective from "I give to God," to "God gives to me" was just one part of seeing to the end of that which was passing away. Truly, the ability to see the fuller meaning of the symbol and move into the new covenant was a blessing that came only if our "Father who is in heaven... revealed this to you." The alternative was to remain stuck in the blindness of "flesh and blood" which could never see the truth.[28]

After the crucifixion, the old system was passing away; a new system was becoming clear to the minds of God's people. Paul was insistent (likely because he knew the dullness of human comprehension made it a necessity): Jesus "takes away the first that He may establish the second."[29] And the goal was clear:

> For if the blood of bulls and goats and the ashes of a heifer, sprinkling the unclean, sanctifies for the purifying of the flesh, how much more shall the blood of Christ, who through the eternal Spirit offered Himself without spot to God, cleanse your conscience from dead works to serve the living God?[30]

> Therefore, brethren,... let us draw near with a true heart in full assurance of faith, having our hearts sprinkled from an evil conscience.[31]

---

27. Genesis 22:8
28. Matthew 16:17
29. Hebrews 10:9
30. Hebrews 9:13–14
31. Hebrews 10:19, 21

Not quite two thousand years later, though, a difficulty seems obvious. The goal that Paul sought throughout his writing of this epistle remains elusive. Perfection seems beyond our grasp. And yet, that was the apostle's repeated emphasis throughout the book:

> Therefore, leaving the discussion of the elementary principles of Christ, let us go on to perfection, not laying again the foundation of repentance from dead works and of faith toward God, of the doctrine of baptisms, of laying on of hands, of resurrection of the dead, and of eternal judgment. And this we will do if God permits.[32]

> Therefore, if perfection were through the Levitical priesthood (for under it the people received the law), what further need was there that another priest should rise according to the order of Melchizedek, and not be called according to the order of Aaron?[33]

> For the law made nothing perfect; on the other hand, there is the bringing in of a better hope, through which we draw near to God.[34]

We've already looked at Hebrews 9:9 and 10:1, both of which very specifically point to the old system's inability to produce perfection in the believer, but when it comes to faith in Christ, we find Paul saying this:

> For by one offering He has perfected forever those who are being sanctified.[35]

This is speaking of Jesus, of course, and the one offering is clearly His death on the cross. And yet, in the next chapter, Paul confirms the perfection of believers, but frankly admits a continued delay. There is a marker, though, perhaps a trigger to the process. We've seen it before:

> And all these, having obtained a good testimony through faith, did not receive the promise, God having provided something better for us, that they should not be made perfect apart from us.[36]

But, pray tell, what does it take to make *that* happen?

---

32. Hebrews 6:1–3. It's worth reflecting for a moment on how much time and effort is still spent trying to ensure that every believer has precisely the same view of repentance, faith, baptism, ordination, resurrection, and judgment.

33. Hebrews 7:11

34. Hebrews 7:19. It seems obvious that if one system's defect was the lack of perfection, then the better option would be a system that provided it.

35. Hebrews 10:14

36. Hebrews 11:39–40

CHAPTER 26

What's the Holdup?

OR, in a more classically Adventist phrasing, "What will it take to finish the work?" The desire to do all that needs to be done to bring about the fulfillment of "the Blessed Hope" is about as basic as it gets within Adventism. Even the name implies the desire. But "hope deferred makes the heart sick,"[1] and it's been a while now. What's the holdup?

Approaching the question from the ground of "they should not be made perfect apart from us" has been... challenging, shall we say. Even those who believe in "character perfection," don't claim that they have achieved the desirable goal.[2] Of course, those who assert that there is no perfection this side of glorification have added their influence to the challenge of even believing in the goal, let alone attaining it.[3]

But, for those willing to at least entertain the thought that something special marks God's church at the end of time, Paul's comment about being made perfect—no matter the exact form this perfection is understood to take—cannot be lightly overlooked. Being "made perfect" has got to be a good thing, and "us" seem to be delaying it. We ought to look into this!

In the book of Hebrews, Paul is focused on perfection. We noted his desire to "go on to perfection,"[4] in our last chapter, and the idea keeps coming up as

---

1. Proverbs 13:12
2. Those who have made the claim—and I've met a few—have rather quickly, and sometimes dramatically enough to end up in prison, demonstrated that something was amiss.
3. And, yes, I've met these folks, too. While they tend to track more "liberal" in many ways that may shock some Adventist sensibilities, it must be admitted that they generally keep their drama to a sub-criminal level, at least in the sight of local law enforcement.
4. Hebrews 6:1

we read through the epistle. "Therefore, if perfection were through the Levitical priesthood," he asks, what need is there for "another priest... according to the order of Melchizedek."[5]

When he says that "the law made nothing perfect" but that through Christ "there is the bringing in of a better hope,"[6] it's hard to think he's aiming for anything less than the perfection he's been writing about.

He dismisses the "gifts and sacrifices... offered" in the earthly sanctuary as insufficient because they "cannot make him who performed the service perfect in regard to the conscience."[7] In contrast he extols the ability of "the blood of Christ" to "cleanse your conscience from dead works to serve the living God."[8] But the most challenging of his statements about the perfecting of God's people comes in a single, common sense question:

> For the law, having a shadow of the good things to come, and not the very image of the things, can never with these same sacrifices, which they offer continually year by year, make those who approach perfect. For then would they not have ceased to be offered? For the worshipers, once purified, would have had no more consciousness of sins.[9]

The logic is simple: if the goal of the sanctuary services is perfecting the believers, doesn't it make sense to end the services when the believers are actually perfect? Of course it does! And that's exactly what Paul says Jesus has done:

> But this Man, after He had offered one sacrifice for sins forever, sat down at the right hand of God, from that time waiting till His enemies are made His footstool. For by one offering He has perfected forever those who are being sanctified. But the Holy Spirit also witnesses to us; for after He had said before, "This is the covenant that I will make with them after those days, says the LORD: I will put My laws into their hearts, and in their minds I will write them," then He adds, "Their sins and their lawless deeds I will remember no more." Now where there is remission of these, there is no longer an offering for sin.[10]

We touched on this "no longer an offering" idea back on page 145, but at that point the issue was considered as it appeared to the people of the first century, addressing the end of the sacrificial system at the temple in Jerusalem. That was the "issue of the day," back then, but it's settled history now. And yet there are other elements in the passage that imply that more than history is involved.

---

5. Hebrews 7:11
6. Hebrews 7:19
7. Hebrews 9:9
8. Hebrews 9:14
9. Hebrews 10:1–2. Incidentally, the Greek for the word "consciousness" in verse 2, is the same word as is translated "conscience" in Hebrews 9:9.
10. Hebrews 10:12–18

Questions arise on the "perfected forever" part. Especially since those thus perfected are then described as *"being* sanctified." The pairing of the clearly past tense "perfected" with the on-going "being sanctified," seems... odd. At the beginning of the passage is another question mark: how long does it take "till His enemies are made His footstool"?

And yet all this has been standard theology for a long time now. Believers are declared "perfect in Christ," and are "enrolled," if you wish, in an on-going (but seldom completed) program of sanctification. To call this "odd," is quite mild. Satan calls it dishonest, arbitrary, unjust, and a disgrace to God's boasted holiness. It is, he claims, cause enough for the universe to reject the current Administration of heaven and to install him as the rightful sovereign.

> When Christ steps in between the tempted souls and Satan, the adversary is angry and opens up with a tirade of abuse and accusation, declaring that Christ is unfair in protecting these souls, and in lifting up a standard against him. But the Lord says unto him, "The Lord rebuke thee, O Satan; even the Lord that hath chosen Jerusalem rebuke thee: is not this a brand plucked out of the fire?"[11]

That "rebuke," as we've seen, is to finally come through the demonstration of human faith, developed in the hearts and minds of healed sinners.[12] That faith, stronger than the test of the "avenging enemy," marks their entrance into the "complete fulfillment of the new-covenant promise."[13] And, like their father, Abraham, all who enter the covenant exert an influence that extends blessing far beyond themselves.[14] On the basis of that demonstration by the living saints, the sleeping saints are proven safe to save because they had faith, even if they didn't always know the ideal way to manifest it.[15]

We've seen this picture from multiple angles, in various ways; what we haven't seen, is how to get it done. How do we move from the "here and now" (a true but often trembling faith and a declared but often faulty righteousness), to the "there and then" (an invincible faith and a tested, proven, and demonstrated righteousness)? What is the treatment plan for the disease of sin?

Exactly what it's always been!

Oh... so every patient is going to die?

No. Every patient is going to live.

I don't see that happening... are you sure you don't mean "be resurrected"?

---

11. E.G. White, "Dear Brethren in the Seventh-day Adventist Faith," June 7, 1894; Manuscript 27, 1894

12. See discussion of this point beginning on page 108.

13. *Great Controversy*, 485. Quoted more fully on page 89.

14. See discussion of this point beginning on page 119.

15. This is tricky ground, which is why it is undoubtedly a good thing that "the Father... has committed all judgment to the Son." (John 5:22) That trickiness is also why it's necessary that the perfect accuracy of Christ's judgment be demonstrated through the sealing and testing process.

True, the resurrection is vital—for "they" will be raised only when "us" are proven to be healed—but don't miss the more important point. Every patient who completes the prescribed therapy is going to live. It's the natural end result.

Unfortunately, thus far the patients' precarious spiritual/physical health has made it impossible to complete the treatment in the majority of cases. The smaller portion of the patient population—the "Enochs"[16]—seem to have completed the course of treatment, but full demonstration is lacking since world circumstances didn't provide opportunity for the gold standard, single variable, controlled experiment of the time of Jacob's trouble. Through no fault of their own, the "Enochs" of earth have also passed from the ranks of the living "us" and are now numbered among the sleeping "they." Well... all the "Enochs" except Enoch and Elijah, that is! In similar but not identical circumstances is one other group—those raised to life at the time of Christ's resurrection (plus Moses) are not "among the sleeping," but nor will they ever be "among the translated."

Treating sin is kind of like treating cancer. Radiation can kill cancer; chemo can kill cancer; surgery can kill cancer. Totally guaranteed. Take your pick—any of the three will work. It's just that in serious cases, when the patient lacks the vitality to endure the treatment, or there are just too many cancer cells in too many places, all three treatments will kill the patient before the cancer's gone.

But since we've described sin as a deficiency disease, let's use that kind of health issue as an illustration. With an unfavorable set of contributing circumstances, patients may become deficient in many nutrients, such as calcium, iodine, iron, niacin, and vitamin D. The obvious means of prevention is an adequate amount of the nutrient on a normal basis, but for a serious case of deficiency where one might be inclined to resort to some sort of mega-dosage, it should be noted that too much of any of those nutrients can cause illness as well.

With sin, we've pointed to the loss of faith as the root issue. This goes all the way back to Lucifer, and remains true for anyone in "an unsaved condition."[17] Faith is simply "confidence in God," which comes from knowing Him well enough to trust His wisdom, power, and love. Which is why Jesus "came to this world for no other purpose than to display the glory of God, that man might be uplifted by its restoring power."[18]

---

16. Remember, "there are Enochs in this our day." *Christ's Object Lessons*, 332
    For those who have "died in the faith," the treatment of understanding the character of God will continue as soon as it can be arranged. The result in those cases will be exactly the kind of full restoration that the demonstration of the sealing has proven as the outcome.
17. Both cases are covered in Chapter 4.
18. E.G. White, Letter to O.A. Olsen, August 25, 1896; Letter 87, 1896

It was, in fact, "the whole purpose of His own mission on earth."[19]

When Adam sinned, he didn't need a "Take two aspirin and call me in the morning" prescription. It was more like, "Stop the bleeding! Get his heart going!"

> After the fall, Christ became Adam's instructor. He acted in God's stead toward humanity, saving the race from immediate death.[20]

> As soon as Adam sinned, the Son of God presented himself as surety for the human race, with just as much power to avert the doom pronounced upon the guilty as when He died upon the cross of Calvary.[21]

But what was actually done then? Certainly not the crucifixion. We generally look at Christ's role as a promise that appropriate payment would be made at some future date. That such a pledge was made is certain. That Christ's sacrifice was the *only* way Heaven "could reveal the Father to the sinner, and win him back to allegiance to God"[22] is also certain. But what kept Adam from dying *right then?* The idea of a "divine IOU" nicely explains the prevention of an *arbitrary* execution of the sinner, but it doesn't fit well with a non-arbitrary law that operates in real time. A promise of some future action doesn't help the kid at the skate park who is falling toward the cement. A real time crisis requires a real time intervention.

Adam and Eve lacked the faith to believe that God could still love them when it was self-evident that they had eaten the forbidden fruit. The very real—and very obvious!—loss of their garments of light[23] showed that Satan had lied when he told Eve that "this particular prohibition was of arbitrary authority."[24] They felt their nakedness and the sting of guilt long before God came to meet with them in the cool of the day.

> Sin is the only nakedness, the only degradation, the only dishonor, that we can know; it is the only thing that will make us afraid to meet God.[25]

Even worse, His coming to visit did nothing to reassure them! They assumed that God would resent their disobedience, so His presence only aggravated their

19. *Signs of the Times*, January 20, 1890. Quoted more fully on page 45.
20. E.G. White, Letter to Brethren, June 24, 1900; Letter 91, 1900
21. *Review and Herald*, March 12, 1901
22. *Signs of the Times*, February 13, 1893. Quoted more fully page 47.
23. "As soon as the holy pair transgressed the law of the Most High, the brightness from the face of God departed from the face of nature." E.G. White, "God in Nature," May 20, 1896; Manuscript 74, 1896
   "After Adam and Eve had sinned, they became conscious that their garments of purity and brightness, the covering given them by God, had fallen away from them. They saw that they were naked, and, ashamed to respond to God's call, they hid themselves among the trees of the garden.... Deprived of the divine covering of light and innocence, they are afraid to meet their God." E.G. White, Letter to Peter Wessels, June 26, 1896; Letter 106, 1896
24. E.G. White, "Christ Our Strength," 1893; Manuscript 104, 1893; quoted more fully on page 59.
25. *Review and Herald*, January 26, 1897

guilt, leading them to hide. That's what sin does. The entire human population of the planet was now in "an unsaved condition."[26] Their lack of faith was complete, with no reason to expect any improvement. Their spiritual hearts were not beating, and death was knocking at the door. What would God do?

He had Adam kill a lamb, and told them that they were forgiven. He told them that He still loved them.

The promise of a Redeemer, and the offering of a sacrifice, both worked to restore their confidence that God might actually treat them with something other than outraged justice. Though details and understanding were lacking— and much of even that picture of God would be further obscured over time— this was a revelation of the character of God. He *is* love, and this gave them hope, and confidence in Him ("faith"), once again.

But Satan continues to paint "God... as severe, exacting, revengeful, and arbitrary,... One who could take pleasure in the sufferings of His creatures."[27] and he generally succeeds in convincing the masses that that's what God is like. It's far too easy for us to believe his claim that God is revengeful, since that's the way we naturally are, ourselves.

There was much about the plan of salvation that Adam and Eve didn't grasp.[28] But they had God's promise that He loved them, and that He would accept a sacrifice as a token of faith in the Redeemer to come. What was done just outside the gate to Eden was "first aid," sufficient to stabilize the patients and keep them from dying. But the full treatment of the disease of sin was a much longer process than anyone but God could imagine.

When Jesus came to earth, the treatment plan called for His death on the cross as an indispensable necessity to reveal "all of God that sinful human beings could bear without being destroyed."[29] We needed a mega-dose, just not *too* mega:

> [Had Jesus] appeared with the glory that was His with the Father before the world was, we could not have endured the light of His presence. That we might behold it and not be destroyed, the manifestation of His glory was shrouded. His divinity was veiled with humanity—the invisible glory in the visible human form.[30]

And that, right there, seems to be the problem: God doesn't want to kill us, but we're not cured yet. What to do?

---

26. *Bible Training School*, November 1, 1911. Quoted more fully on page 25.
27. *Signs of the Times*, January 20, 1890
28. The long years of the great controversy were mercifully hidden from their understanding, for instance. "When Adam and Eve first heard the promise [of a Savior], they looked for its speedy fulfillment. They joyfully welcomed their first-born son, hoping that he might be the Deliverer." *Desire of Ages*, 31.
29. E.G. White, "A Personal God," October 14, 1903; Manuscript 124, 1903
30. *Desire of Ages*, 23

Continue the treatment!

But how? He's already shown us all we can endure. That was two thousand years ago, and the umpteenth generation of patients is on life support now.[31] How could we ever see more of the glory of God? And, besides, Jesus isn't here now. Yes, we looked at the need for "the light of Christ's example reflected from the lives of Christlike men and women,"[32] but isn't that kind of like asking terminal patients to take charge of the hospice ward? None of this is making sense! The pandemic is raging. The virus is resistant to every antibiotic[33] God has thrown at it; does He have anything more?

Well, fortunately, yes He does. We've seen it before, on pages 108 and 132—the loss of every earthly support. But that phase of treatment requires an even greater level of pre-procedure preparation.

> It is God's design to manifest through His people the principles of His kingdom. That in life and character they may reveal these principles, He desires to separate them from the customs, habits, and practices of the world. He seeks to bring them near to Himself, that He may make known to them His will.[34]

The problem is that to a great extent the "customs, habits, and practices of the world" are *our* customs, habits, and practices as well! To separate from these can seem like death itself, especially when our minds have been steeped in the unquestioning "affirmation" of every conceivable "identity" to which we—or anyone else—may lay claim. How does God propose to prepare us for this wholesale denial of so much that we have seen ourselves to be?

---

31. Somewhat discouragingly, all previous generations are currently dead.
32. *Testimonies*, vol. 9, 135. Quoted more fully on pages 101 and 114.
33. Yes, I know I'm mixing my metaphors, maladies, and medicines. Deficiency diseases aren't caused by viruses, and it's unlikely such a disease or a virus would respond to antibiotics, but just play along with it for now. The subject deserves more drama than we usually give it.
34. E.G. White, "God's Design in Establishing Sanitariums," December 22, 1899; Manuscript 166, 1899

CHAPTER 27

Little Things

THE last chapter closed with a question, the central point of which is whether or not God has a workable plan to prepare His people for the loss of "every earthly support." The question may sound doubtful, but there's plenty of reason for optimism. For one thing, we've got stories that make it look like a doable thing. How else do you explain the fiery furnace, the lions' den, and all the martyrs down through history?

With that in mind, this is the perfect time to consider one of Ellen White's favorite phrases: "to prepare a people." Its Biblical roots are clear, but she uses these words to describe a work not yet accomplished, whereas Luke 1:17 presents it in completed form, "a people prepared for the Lord."

The obvious question is, what are they being prepared for? It's the answer to that question which makes this phrase so interesting. To be more precise, we should say *answers*, for there are quite a few, among them such terms and phrases as "the judgment," "the day of the Lord," "the second coming," "the final test," and "to meet their God."

Of the more than four hundred times Ellen White uses "to prepare a people," well over half include the words "to stand," as in "to prepare a people to stand in the trying crisis before us."[1]

Common to all these variations, though, is the idea of the end times. That's what the preparation of a people is all about. There is a "great test," a "final test," a "time of test," the "test of Jacob's trouble," coming. It may be in the "day of judgment," or the "day of the Lord," or the "day of Christ's return"—whatever the phrasing, the point is we have something to get ready for. And by this

---

1. *General Conference Bulletin*, April 1, 1898

time, it should be no surprise that all this preparation is intended to fit God's people for the last, decisive test and demonstration of faith.

An obviously strained illustration may make the point. Imagine you are a member of some sort of ultra-secret "special forces" team, training for some sort of ultra-secret mission. You don't know where you'll be called to go or what you'll be called to do—your job is just to be ready to meet whatever challenge presents itself.

You note your commanding officer is putting a lot of emphasis on suspended positions... hmmm... does that mean something? But monkey bars seem kind of juvenile. And what's with the weird variations? Skipping every other bar seems reasonable; you can get done with the exercise in about half the time. Stretching for every third bar even makes a certain amount of sense.

But half-spins on every bar? Half-spins on every other bar? Full spins? Arm hopping? Knee grips? Knee grips from bar to bar? Knee grips to every other bar? Toe holds? Toe holds to every third bar? The whole process is beginning to look like a mockery engineered by a sadistic drill sergeant!

And then one morning at 0217 hours the klaxon in the barracks goes off. Four minutes and thirty-six seconds later you're on the transport plane, donning your gear, headed for the drop zone. A general you've never seen in your life explains the route your unit will take to be the boots on the ground while the enemy is distracted and softened up by the air show overhead. He assures you that there is a high probability of maintaining the element of surprise, since you will be advancing from a quadrant the enemy has not reinforced, there being no possibility of approach from that direction until a specially designed, technology-stretching, never-before-deployed titanium alloy structure is set in place by two CH-53K King Stallion helicopters less than three minutes before your arrival on scene.

And the details? It's a 739-meter-long monkey bars[2] stretching across a 210-meter-deep river gorge.

This development imposes a very real test. How many members of the platoon will make it across? Suddenly a whole range of physical strength and motor-muscle skill, with no two individuals exactly the same, is reduced to two possible outcomes. All the variables of strength, dexterity, experience, and endurance combine to decide the result. Some make it across, some don't. That's the way reality works.

The Spirit of Prophecy describes the infinitely more serious reality like this:

> Those who exercise but little faith now, are in the greatest danger of falling under the power of satanic delusions and the decree to compel the conscience. And even if

---

2. I know, a rational person would have made it a foot bridge, but this is an entirely fictional example made to illustrate a point, not to depict a genuine battle plan! Maybe this design is a weight saving feature. Besides, there is always the possibility that the infamous oxymoron "military intelligence" might have come into play. Remember the forty years of inaction by the British Admiralty back on page 51.

they endure the test they will be plunged into deeper distress and anguish in the time of trouble, because they have never made it a habit to trust in God. The lessons of faith which they have neglected they will be forced to learn under a terrible pressure of discouragement.

Presumably, some will rise to this challenge, but just as truly, some will not. That's the way reality works. In that light, Ellen White's advice in her next sentence makes a lot of sense!

> We should now acquaint ourselves with God by proving His promises.[3]

The final test of God's people reduces the whole possible strength-range of faith down to a starkly binary "triumphant faith" or "no faith" division. It's an amazing thing, really, that the totality of a person's spiritual condition can be distilled down to a single issue. But it's not new; we've seen it ever since the Garden of Eden:

> In every matter God was to be obeyed; but the test of man's obedience in everything was to be found in his faithfulness in carrying out one particular command, in abstaining from taking of the forbidden tree. The result of obedience would be eternal life, and the outworking of disobedience would be death.[4]

Similarly, even the family of Noah may have had some nagging doubts, and people on the outside may have had a strong gut feeling that a flood really was coming, but the difference that expressed their faith was which side of the door they were on. For Lot, the line was "in" or "out" of Sodom. In Revelation, all the world is divided into those with the seal of God, and those with the mark of the beast. The "analog system" gets accurately collapsed into the binary reality. Amazing!

But back to our main focus.... What is God's plan to prepare His people for the testing times depicted in *Great Controversy*?

Little things.

What?

Little things. Faithfulness in little things. You know, those insignificant pesky issues that "reasonable" people find so easy to ignore. Conveniently for us, just about every such issue is dealt with in the pages of *Ministry of Healing*. And the sound bite quotes are classic!

We've all heard them before, but here's a quick refresher selection:[5]

> The Saviour's life on earth was a life of communion with nature and with God. In this communion He revealed for us the secret of a life of power.[6]

---

3. *Great Controversy*, 622
4. *Signs of the Times*, October 8, 1894
5. Are these clubs to beat people with? Or good advice that would actually help us both now and in the face of the coming challenges? Opinions vary quite a lot on that point.
6. *Ministry of Healing*, 51

All who are under the training of God need the quiet hour for communion with their own hearts, with nature, and with God. In them is to be revealed a life that is not in harmony with the world, its customs, or its practices; and they need to have a personal experience in obtaining a knowledge of the will of God. We must individually hear Him speaking to the heart. When every other voice is hushed, and in quietness we wait before Him, the silence of the soul makes more distinct the voice of God.[7]

If we wanted a name tag for this category, we might call it "country living." *Ministry of Healing* has a whole chapter called "Choice and Preparation of the Home" which makes a strong case for getting out of Dodge. Here's another of Ellen White's many such warnings:

The time is come that the warning must be made for removal from the cities in contemplation not of what you will see and hear in the future, but of what you now see and what is developing now—right now—and is increasing in a higher and more determined degree of sin and transgression, resulting in such a state of things that the mountainous regions will be sought for.[8]

Do note that there a quite a few basic skills required for a more rural lifestyle, and it takes a while to master them all. Heating your cute little country cottage with a wood stove sounds like a great idea until you kill yourself felling that first big tree. But back to our survey of *Ministry of Healing* sound bites:

The Saviour ministered to both the soul and the body. The gospel which He taught was a message of spiritual life and of physical restoration. Deliverance from sin and the healing of disease were linked together.[9]

Oh look! That's *sozo!*

Everywhere there is a tendency to substitute the work of organizations for individual effort. Human wisdom tends to consolidation, to centralization, to the building up of great churches and institutions.... [But] Christ commits to His followers an individual work—a work that cannot be done by proxy. Ministry to the sick and the poor, the giving of the gospel to the lost, is not to be left to committees or organized charities. Individual responsibility, individual effort, personal sacrifice, is the requirement of the gospel.[10]

And medical missionary work! Who knew all this was in one handy book?

No one can practice real benevolence without self-denial. Only by a life of simplicity, self-denial, and close economy is it possible for us to accomplish the work appointed us as Christ's representatives.[11]

---

7. *Ministry of Healing*, 58
8. E.G. White, "Diary: Corruption of the Cities and Unfaithful Shepherds," September 2, 1902; Manuscript 233, 1902
9. *Ministry of Healing*, 111
10. *Ministry of Healing*, 147
11. *Ministry of Healing*, 206

Well, that seems self-explanatory. But this next one, from the chapter on "Mind Cure" may not be as obvious. If you replace that chapter title with something like "Mental Therapy," it's easier to see how it fits with about 95% of all "media," and especially the suddenly ubiquitous "internet influencers."

> God desires to bring men into direct relation with Himself.... Satan works to thwart this purpose. He seeks to encourage dependence upon men. When minds are turned away from God, the tempter can bring them under his rule. He can control humanity.

> The theory of mind controlling mind was originated by Satan, to introduce himself as the chief worker, to put human philosophy where divine philosophy should be. Of all the errors that are finding acceptance among professedly Christian people, none is a more dangerous deception, none more certain to separate man from God, than is this.[12]

But who could overlook the traditional stumbling stones of "lifestyle standards"? You know... the "borderline legalistic" issues of clothes and food.

> The Bible teaches modesty in dress.... Any device designed to attract attention to the wearer or to excite admiration, is excluded from the modest apparel which God's word enjoins.... It was the adversary of all good who instigated the invention of the ever-changing fashions.... Another evil which custom fosters is the unequal distribution of the clothing, so that while some parts of the body have more than is required, others are insufficiently clad. The feet and limbs, being remote from the vital organs, should be especially guarded from cold by abundant clothing.

Worth noting: the same chapter says that our clothes—

> should have the grace, the beauty, the appropriateness of natural simplicity. Christ has warned us against the pride of life, but not against its grace and natural beauty. He pointed to the flowers of the field, to the lily unfolding in its purity.... By the things of nature Christ illustrates the beauty that heaven values, the modest grace, the simplicity, the purity, the appropriateness, that would make our attire pleasing to Him.[13]

Enough of that. Let's close with the ever popular matter of dietary advice and the role it has in developing the self-control necessary to deal with the loss of "every earthly support." For a "little thing," it gets surprisingly high ratings from God:

> The light God has given on health reform is for our salvation and the salvation of the world.[14]

> Those foods should be chosen that best supply the elements needed for building up the body. In this choice, appetite is not a safe guide.... Grains, fruits, nuts, and vegetables constitute the diet chosen for us by our Creator.... Persons who have accustomed themselves to a rich, highly stimulating diet have an unnatural taste, and they cannot at once relish food that is plain and simple. It will take time for the taste to become natural and for the stomach to

---

12. *Ministry of Healing*, 243
13. *Ministry of Healing*, 287–293. All from a chapter titled simply, "Dress."
14. *Testimonies*, vol. 7, 136

recover from the abuse it has suffered.... Regularity in eating is of vital importance. There should be a specified time for each meal. At this time let everyone eat what the system requires and then take nothing more until the next meal.... We must individually answer to God for our habits and practices. Therefore the question with us is not, "What is the world's practice?" but, "How shall I as an individual treat the habitation that God has given me?"[15]

Monkey bars may seem juvenile... but that doesn't mean they could never be important. And these little items in *Ministry of Healing* have the power to help us, or—if neglected—the power to hurt us. Those who learn to make principled decisions in their youth, we are told—

are continually learning to think and to act for themselves independent of what others may say and do. They are learning to have true moral courage to do right, and choose the right, although there is a cross in so doing.[16]

But there is a flip side to the issue. Jesus put it this way: "He who is faithful in what is least is faithful also in much; and he who is unjust in what is least is unjust also in much."[17] Ellen White strikes the same note.

The reason why many of us will fall in the time of trouble is because of laxity in temperance and indulgence of appetite.[18]

Perhaps we miss the reality of the issue when we focus on "indulgence of appetite"... perhaps it all goes back to something deeper:

True conversion to the message of present truth embraces conversion to the principles of health reform.[19]

Anyone who shifts their concern to "spiritual matters," thinking to find a convenient way to ignore the kind of nitty gritty counsel in books like *Ministry of Healing,* is playing a high-risk game. But the key question is how can "little things" be so big? Is God just mad at people for eating too much ice cream? Or does it really take a "sound mind and body" to face the end time tests?

Given that the first option is an obviously arbitrary response, and the second is at least plausibly grounded in defensible reality, I'd go with number two.

But why? Why should the 144,000 have to be clear-headed and healthy?

---

15. *Ministry of Healing,* 295–310. This little montage is from the chapter, "Diet and Health." We haven't even touched "Flesh as Food," "Extremes in Diet," "Stimulants and Narcotics," or "Liquor Traffic and Prohibition." That's a lot o column inches for a minor topic, more than enough to raise suspicions of legalism. And yet, somehow God seems to think it's important. Odd....

16. *Testimony to the Church at Battle Creek* (1872), 61

17. Luke 16:10

18. *Review and Herald,* October 21, 1884. This idea has been ridiculed, of course, but even the sarcastic inquirer with his "How many Big Macs does it take to be lost?" jibe, will eventually find his final answer in either a "one" or a "zero."

19. E.G. White, Letter to D.A. Parsons, March 28, 1909; Letter 62, 1909

Because they are the ones to take "this gospel," the "loud cry," the "revelation of the righteousness of Christ" to all the world. Jesus revealed "all of God that sinful human beings could bear without being destroyed,"[20] and changed the world, but didn't end the conflict. God's plan calls for "recovered sinners" to make the final revelation, and that's one thing Jesus is not. The 144,000 are fully qualified as "sinners," but the "recovered" part is still in progress. They clearly can't portray the glory, the character, of God to the world if they don't understand it, and they'll never understand it if their heads are in a continual muddle from "health habits" that land outside the broad parameters of God's counsel.

Even with that, though, there's a challenge we should consider: where are these people going to learn all this? Even the personal example of Christ, extended through the work of His apostles, didn't ring down the curtain. What could possibly be missing? Or, put another way, Does God have anything more to offer? Indeed, He does, and we need to get on the same page He's on with this.

Think of it like this: the goal is for God's people to reveal His character. Jesus revealed all we could bear... but we need more, somehow. That sounds like a good way to overload whatever circuits would burn out first if Jesus were to let a little too much "divinity flash through humanity."[21] But what to do?

Since the full physical manifestation of His glory would overload our sin-degraded perception, His final line of treatment is a much more gradual process directed at our (also sin-degraded) minds. The only thing left that's equal to the task of portraying His glory—His character—is actually just a transcript of it.

We've seen it before: it's the perfect, immutable, unchangeable, and eternal law of God; the point of objection way back when Lucifer started this whole mess.

> [God's] law is a transcript of His own character, and it is the standard of all character. This infinite standard is presented to all that there may be no mistake in regard to the kind of people whom God will have to compose His kingdom.[22]

> The glory of Christ is revealed in the law, which is a transcript of His character, and His transforming efficacy is felt upon the soul until men become changed to His likeness. They are made partakers of the divine nature, and grow more and more like their Saviour, advancing step by step in conformity to the will of God, till they reach perfection.[23]

---

20. E.G. White, "A Personal God," October 14, 1903; Manuscript 124, 1903
21. This "divinity flashing through humanity" construction shows up about one hundred fifty times in Ellen White's writings. When that happened, sinners shrank back in terror, felt as if they were before the final judgment, and generally got a taste of the "horror of great darkness" that comes with a condemning conscience. The point is, there is a limit to what sinners can bear.
22. *Christ's Object Lessons*, 315
23. *Review and Herald*, April 22, 1902

This "the law is a transcript of God's character" phrasing is more than common in Ellen White's writing. If you've read her books or articles or letters or manuscripts... you've run into it. There's no debate to be had as far as that goes. But to pin the success of the whole plan of salvation on the hope that "the law" is going to reveal something more than Jesus Himself revealed in His life on earth.... That seems a bit much. For one thing, this eternal law has been around a long time. Does it make sense to expect it to do what it's never done in the past?

On the face of it, it doesn't look hopeful, but the consistent linkage of the law to Satan's concocted issue of "arbitrary" authority just doesn't go away. Maybe there's something here, after all.

> God desired His people to render obedience to Him, not as a forced, arbitrary exaction, but because they realized that obedience to His law, the transcript of His character, would make them men and women of understanding.[24]

Maybe that "realization," that "understanding," will come yet. Maybe... but it seems like it's going to take a whole new twist on the issue. Is there really anything *new* to see in the eternal law?

---

24. E.G. White, "The Lord's Vineyard," December 15, 1898; Manuscript 166, 1898

CHAPTER 28

The Case for New Light

WHEN Jesus did not return at the "passing of the time" in 1844, it was obvious that there had been a significant error somewhere in the Millerites' expectations. The easiest response would have been to discard the whole package and move on with "real life." Many did exactly that, but some just couldn't shake the conviction that—on the whole—the influence of the Advent movement had been positive. Surely some explanation could be found.

And so began a period of extraordinary Biblical discovery. In the next two decades, the "pioneers" of Adventism hammered out the broad outlines, at least, and sometimes quite a lot of minutiae, on a whole range of topics. Starting with William Miller's contribution, the list of major new understandings includes the link between Daniel 8 and Daniel 9, which led to the establishment of 457 B.C. as the starting date for the 2300-day prophecy; the unconscious state in death (widely advocated by George Storrs, a Millerite preacher); and Samuel Sheffield Snow's "law of the full years" and application of sanctuary typology which refined the termination of the 2300-days right down to October 22, 1844.

Immediately after the "passing of the time" (now more commonly called the "great disappointment") came a recognition of the heavenly sanctuary, followed by the re-emergence of spiritual gifts, (especially the acknowledgment of Ellen White as a chosen messenger of the Lord); the seventh-day Sabbath; the investigative judgment; and an understanding of Revelation's depiction of the United States, including the Sabbath's role in the conflict over the seal of God and the mark of the beast.

That's a lot to process in twenty years! Not to mention a few "second tier" items like church organization, the reinterpretation of the Laodicean message (which painted themselves in a not-so-positive light), and the beginnings of both dress reform and health reform.

One term we use to describe such theological advances is "new light." The Bible verses had been there all along, of course, but getting them pulled together in a way that made sense, that didn't contradict the rest of Scripture, had never been done before. The resulting clarity was "new." And it set Adventism apart from every other denomination.

But for whatever reasons (ranging from divine intent to human negligence, I suspect), there hasn't been a lot of new light since that time. This is important to us just now, because the last chapter closed with a quotation that we should look at again:

> God desired His people to render obedience to Him, not as a forced, arbitrary exaction, but because they realized that obedience to His law, the transcript of His character, would make them men and women of understanding.[1]

She is speaking here of ancient Israel, but immediately moves on to quote Paul: "Now all these things happened to them as examples, and they were written for our admonition, upon whom the ends of the ages have come. Therefore let him who thinks he stands take heed lest he fall."[2]

The implication is strong that we, too, might fail to realize the real significance of "obedience to His law." Which means there's something there we haven't seen yet, and the remedy for that is "new light."

But that's a pretty brash assertion. It's not like we haven't read—maybe even memorized—the ten commandments. As Adventists we've mapped out the distinction between the moral law and the ceremonial law... one was in the ark, the other in the side of the ark. We know all that.

Once upon a time, it was even said that "as a people, we have preached the law until we are as dry as the hills of Gilboa that had neither dew nor rain."[3] What could there be for us to learn about the law?

Well, given that Psalm 119 is all about God's law (aka precepts, statutes, commandments, words, judgments, testimonies, and ordinances), and just happens to be the longest chapter in the Bible... there may be a few details about the law that we've missed.

That's actually a great question, even an obvious question, after looking at Ellen White's comments on the issue of "new light." So let's look at a few of them, shall we? First off, let's see if there's any particular reason to expect new light. After all, maybe we already know everything we need to know.

---

1. E.G. White, "The Lord's Vineyard," December 15, 1898; Manuscript 166, 1898
2. 1 Corinthians 10:11–12
3. *Review and Herald*, March 11, 1890

We have every reason to believe that the Lord will send us increased truth, for a great work is yet to be done. In our knowledge of truth, there is first a beginning in our understanding of it, then a progression, then completion; first the blade, then the ear, and after that the full corn in the ear. Much has been lost because our ministers and people have concluded that we have had all the truth essential for us as a people; but such a conclusion is erroneous and in harmony with the deceptions of Satan; for truth will be constantly unfolding.[4]

Alrighty then... maybe we don't have it all figured out. But, is that *really* what she was saying?

[When asked,] "Sister White, do you think that the Lord has any new and increased light for us as a people?" I answered, "Most assuredly. I do not only think so, but can speak understandingly. I know that there is precious truth to be unfolded to us if we are the people that are to stand in the day of God's preparation."[5]

If ever a people have need of clearer and increased light from heaven, it is the people whom God has made the repository of His law.[6]

We need to search in the lessons of Christ for the true meaning of His words; for it remains to be discovered. As we do this, the new aspect of some truths will be seen; we shall see the far-reaching compass of others, and the connection of some with others. Thus we shall find a harmonious whole. We must put our minds to the task of searching, with humble, holy, determined purpose, and with much prayer. The diligent seeker will receive his reward.[7]

One challenge with new light, though, is that it can be very disruptive. Disruption can be good. And disruption can be very bad. So the challenge is to distinguish between something that contradicts previous truth (a bad disruption), and something that merely contradicts the habits or practices or policies that have been built up on partial truth (a potentially good disruption).

Think of the twelve believers that Paul found in Ephesus. They had been baptized into "John's baptism." That was good! So Paul asks, "Did you receive the Holy Spirit when you believed?" A perfectly legitimate question, but it caught the Ephesians flat-footed, and they frankly confessed, "We have not so much as heard whether there is a Holy Spirit."

"Aww!" says Paul, "Have I got some new light for you!"

So Paul told them that John pointed the people to Jesus as the Messiah. No doubt there was a lot of detailed explaining that didn't get recorded, but in the end they were "baptized in the name of the Lord Jesus. And when Paul had laid

---

4. *Signs of the Times*, May 26, 1890
5. *Selected Messages*, Book 3, 174. This "day of God's preparation" is the same idea as "to prepare a people," by the way. And, do notice that her reply is based on an "if"!
6. E.G. White, "The Discernment of Truth," January 1889; Manuscript 16, 1889
7. E.G. White, "Christian Service in the Living Church," June 10, 1891; Manuscript 7, 1891

hands on them, the Holy Spirit came upon them, and they spoke with tongues and prophesied."[8]

The Bible doesn't tell us exactly what these believers had been doing before, but it seems unlikely that they were speaking with tongues and prophesying! By any reckoning, that had to be disruptive!

And, finally, lest there be any confusion on our need for new light—

> To our brethren who are standing in this self-confident, self-satisfied position, who talk and act as if there was no need of more light, we want to say that the Laodicean message is applicable to you.[9]

You may not see the bearing of all this new light discussion, but bear with me. There is a reason for it. But before jumping into all those details, it will be helpful take a look at the matter of timing as it relates to new light. Sacred history implies that this is an important point, since it's not like the revelation of divine truth proceeded at a constant pace in the past. Between Malachi and Matthew—about four hundred years—there were no recognized Biblical prophets, so it's no surprise that new light wasn't a feature of that time period. Barely a century after Ellen White's death, where do we sit in this regard?

> By the increase of knowledge a people is to be prepared to stand in the latter days.[10]

> The Spirit and power of the coming One will be imparted in large measure to those who are preparing to stand in the day of God, who are hastening the second advent of our Lord and Saviour Jesus Christ. To these faithful ones Christ gives special communications....

> God would not have any one of us think that in these last days there is no more that we need to know. This is a continual snare of Satan. He would not have us meet coming events without that special preparation which is essential to guide us through every difficulty.[11]

> The Lord reveals many things that it is needful for His people to understand in these last days. Many things, which are now dark and mysterious to many, even to Bible students, will as the end draws near be plainly understood by those who are not drawn into Satan's snare.[12]

> I stated that... there was to be special light for God's people as they neared the closing scenes of this earth's history. Another angel was to come from heaven with a message, and the whole earth was to be lightened with his glory. It would be impossible for us to state just how this additional light would come. It might come in a very

---

8. Acts 19:1–6

9. *Review and Herald*, April 1, 1890

10. E.G. White, "Testimony Concerning The Views Of Prophecy Held By Brother John Bell, No. 2," December 6, 1896: Manuscript 32, 1896

11. E.G. White, "Christian Integrity in the Ministry," 1886; Manuscript 15, 1886

12. E.G. White, Letter to G.I. Butler, April 11, 1906; Letter 126, 1906

unexpected manner, in a way that would not agree with the ideas that many have conceived. It is not at all untimely or contrary to the ways and works of God to send light to His people in unexpected ways.[13]

No "time setting" here, but the idea that new light is to play a role in the work of God near the end of time keeps coming up. It just makes sense... unless we deny that any special accomplishment or demonstration of "the manifold wisdom of God" is yet to be "made known by the church to the principalities and powers in the heavenly places."[14]

But now, finally, the big question: where would we go looking, what topics should we consider if we were serious about seeking new light? Let's start with a surprisingly nuanced, "honorable mention" prize for the book of Revelation:

> In these last days it is our duty to ascertain the full meaning of the first, second, and third angels' messages.[15]

> There may be things in the Revelation that we do not understand. But by earnest, prayerful study, especially of those texts that relate particularly to our own time, we may understand the position of Christ and His relation to God and to us, as we cannot understand unless we are familiar with this book.[16]

> It is true that there are prophecies yet to be fulfilled. But very erroneous work has been done again and again, and will continue to be done by those who seek to find new light in the prophecies, and who begin by turning away from the light that God has already given. The messages of Revelation 14 are... to be sounded everywhere. But the Lord does not lay upon those who have not had an experience in His work the burden of making a new exposition of these prophecies, which He has, by His Holy Spirit, moved upon His chosen servants to explain.[17]

It seems natural, when considering the possibility of new light for end times, to jump to apocalyptic prophecy, with Revelation, Daniel, and maybe a "minor prophet" or two coming readily to mind. But these prophecies get scant mention in Ellen White's comments on new light. From the selections above, it seems good to at least pursue the "full meaning" of the three angels' messages.

But not everything is up for revision! "Turning away from the light that God has already given" on those messages, and coming up with a new interpretation of them is clearly out of bounds. This danger was played out on "the big stage" a few decades ago. Here's the background on that:

13. E.G. White, Letter to R.A. Underwood, January 18, 1889; Letter 22, 1889
14. Ephesians 3:10
15. E.G. White, "Revelation," April 27, 1896; Manuscript 15, 1896
16. E.G. White, "Talk at Washington, D.C.," c. April–July 1904; Manuscript 165, 1904
17. E.G. White, "Testimony Concerning The Views Of Prophecy Held By Brother John Bell, No. 2," December 6, 1896: Manuscript 32, 1896

In the 1980s, an Adventist theologian from Australia by the name of Desmond Ford promoted what he called the "apotelesmatic principle."[18] He claimed that this "principle" (in scare quotes because it seemed open ended enough to allow just about anything) pointed to a virtually unlimited number of "fulfillments" of Bible prophecy.

If he could point to a parallel or two where some event was similar to a prophecy, he felt his "principle" meant that the new event was as much a fulfillment of the prophecy as any other event. In practice, this was used to minimize to the point of elimination the whole understanding of the 2300-day prophecy and the work of Christ in the Most Holy Place of the heavenly sanctuary.

Understandably, there was pushback against abandoning the established position on "the scripture which above all others had been both the foundation and the central pillar of the advent faith."[19] Sadly, there was also widespread enthusiasm for Ford's "turning away from the light that God has already given," all the way from laymen to denominational leaders at the General Conference. It was the "theological heavyweight bout" of the day, wasting precious time and resources all through the '80s and '90s. The echoes of those battles can still be heard.

But the devil is shrewd, and although Ford was officially sanctioned,[20] the resulting conservative emphasis on the historicist approach to prophetic interpretation presents an opportunity for Satan to push us towards the ditch of tradition. The dates for the 2300 days of Daniel 8, the 1260 days of Revelation 12, and their related prophecies have been secured.[21] But extending that solidity to the point that any suggestion of broader meaning than has been "historically" seen in prophetic scriptures poses a risk. Caution is good; a baseless knee-jerk denial would be bad.

> To say that a passage means just this and nothing more, that you must not attach any broader meaning to the words of Christ than we have in the past, is saying that which is not actuated by the Spirit of God.... The truth, as it is in Jesus, is capable of constant expansion, of new development.[22]

But if new light isn't to be centered upon apocalyptic prophecy, where *should* we expect it? That's a good question, worth a chapter of its own.

---

18. Falling into the "weird-but-true" category of facts is the little detail that the original meaning of *apotelesmatic* is "of or relating to the casting of horoscopes." In fairness, it must be noted that this is considered an "archaic" meaning, and not what was intended by Dr. Ford.

19. *Great Controversy*, 409

20. His ministerial license, but not his church membership, was taken away. Since the question of church membership is a matter for the local church to decide—as opposed to having demands come down from "on high"—the church at Pacific Union College afforded a dependable safe haven for Dr. Ford.

21. Within mainstream Adventism, anyway, if not the sizable segment of "progressive Adventists" who still revere Dr. Ford as a hero.

22. *Review and Herald*, October 21, 1890

CHAPTER 29

Unto the Perfect Day

WHEN the Bible says that "the path of the just is like the shining sun, that shines ever brighter unto the perfect day,"[1] it seems obvious that "light" will be increasing until then. Ellen White certainly gives us reason to not only expect new light, but to expect it particularly in the context of closing events.

That's good to know, but the catalog of all the things humans don't understand perfectly about Scripture is large. Are they all of equal importance at the end of time? Which ones should we leave for exploration throughout eternity? Which ones should we be focusing on now? See if you can spot the answer:

> The Lord is ready to disclose to His church more and more of His wonderful power and to open new lines of thought in regard to the great plan of redemption.[2]

> I tell you in the fear of God that up to this time the Bible truths connected with the great plan of redemption are but feebly understood. The truth will be continually unfolding, expanding, and developing, for it is divine, like its Author.[3]

> I could give you subjects that would put to the stretch your thoughts and mind, and yet there is a great deal more. The great plan of redemption is not half comprehended. If we could only understand the plan of salvation, we would be the happiest people upon the face of the earth.[4]

Given the dissatisfaction of most of the world, being happy has some real appeal. Seriously, what would you trade for something that has no downside and just makes you happy? But back to the list:

---

1. Proverbs 4:18
2. E.G. White, Letter to J.H. Kellogg, April 15, 1892; Letter 18, 1892
3. E.G. White, "Counsels to Ministers: The Need of a True Concept of Righteousness by Faith," September 13, 1889; Manuscript 27, 1889
4. E.G. White, "Sermon: Having Our Conversation in Heaven," July 24, 1886; Manuscript 9, 1886

The great plan of redemption, as revealed in the closing work of these last days, should receive close examination....

OK, another interruption. So far, the evidence presented points pretty strongly towards the possibility of new light on the "plan of redemption." You probably caught that. But this statement (started above and continued below) is going to branch out a bit now—and following quotations will also—so don't miss the additions.

The scenes connected with the sanctuary above should make such an impression upon the minds and hearts of all that they may be able to impress others. All need to become more intelligent in regard to the work of the atonement, which is going on in the sanctuary above. When this grand truth is seen and understood, those who hold it will work in harmony with Christ to prepare a people to stand in the great day of God, and their efforts will be successful.[5]

The whole world needs to be instructed in the oracles of God, to understand the object of the atonement, the at-one-ment, with God. The object of this atonement was that the divine law and government might be maintained. The sinner is pardoned through repentance toward God and faith in our Lord and Saviour Jesus Christ. There is forgiveness of sin, and yet the law of God stands immutable, eternal as His throne.[6]

Had men been obedient, they would have understood the plan of God's government.... The mystery of redemption, the incarnation of Christ, His atoning sacrifice, would not be, as they are now, vague in our minds. They would have been not only better understood, but altogether more highly appreciated.[7]

There goes the simplicity of that single item focus on the plan of redemption! Oh well, life is rarely that uncomplicated. Our additions so far are: the sanctuary, the atonement, and the incarnation.

But, wait a minute! Isn't it obvious that, if not exactly synonyms, there is a lot of overlap between these items? The incarnation made possible Christ's sacrifice, which was to work out the atonement of sinners to God, which was all foreshadowed in the sanctuary. It kind of all makes sense. But we have another batch of statements that strike even deeper into the shared connection of all this. Let's look:

Said my guide, "There is much light yet to shine forth from the law of God and the gospel of righteousness. This message, understood in its true character and proclaimed in the Spirit, will grow to large importance such as you scarcely dream of, and will lighten the earth with its glory.... His law will be looked upon as the rule of His government."[8]

The principles of God's law are contained in the two precepts, "Thou shalt love the Lord thy God with all thy heart, and with all thy soul, and with all thy strength, and

5. *Testimonies*, vol. 5, 575
6. E.G. White, "The Third Angel's Message," December 17, 1897; Manuscript 163, 1897
7. *Review and Herald*, July 3, 1900
8. E.G. White, "A Call to a Deeper Study of the Word," November 1, 1888; Manuscript 15, 1888

with all thy mind; and thy neighbor as thyself." When we realize this, there will be a searching after truth, a deep conviction of the far-reaching claims of God's law.[9]

We have only glimmering light in regard to the exceeding breadth of the law of God. ... Many who claim to be teachers of the truth have no conception of what they are handling when they are presenting the law to the people, because they have not studied it; they have not put their mental powers to the task of understanding its significance.[10]

We need to study diligently that we may gain a knowledge of the laws of God. How can we be obedient subjects if we fail to understand the laws that govern the kingdom of God? Then open your Bibles, and search for everything that will enlighten you in regard to the precepts of God; and when you discern a "thus saith the Lord," ask not the opinion of men, but, whatever the cost to yourself, obey cheerfully.[11]

A new purpose must possess the mind, for there is a special work to be done in all our churches. Christ has revealed His law in these last days, and this most sacred truth is constantly unfolding and impressing the intellect of youth and the aged.[12]

The law is not only the foundation of God's government, it's the foundation of all those other things listed as topics ripe for new light. The plan of redemption is all about resolving the problem created by breaking the law. As our understanding of the law becomes clearer, our understanding of what is needed to solve the problem becomes clearer. The sanctuary and the atonement are both similarly founded on the law reverently kept in the Ark of the Covenant in the Holy of Holies.

The incarnation of Christ was primarily to provide a revelation of the Father's character. That was "the whole purpose of His own mission on earth," and it required Him to "fulfill" the law[13] for the obvious reason that the law was exactly the same as His Father's character.

To have new light on the law of God is anything but trivial, since it affects pretty much everything else in the universe. It's like redefining the "c" (which describes the speed of light as "constant,"[14] as in "never-supposed-to-be-redefined") in Einstein's famous "$E=mc^2$." The challenge is that "c" shows up in a whole bunch of equations describing all sorts of fun details about physics and the universe in general. Change "c" and all sorts of things look different. That's what new light on the law is like.

You may have seen something in regard to the righteousness of Christ, but there is truth yet to be seen clearly.... You will see the law of God and interpret it to the people

---

9. *Review and Herald*, August 9, 1898

10. *Review and Herald*, February 4, 1890

11. E.G. White, Letter to J.E. White, November 1895; Letter 82, 1895

12. E.G. White, "Work to Be Done at Riverside," 1911; Manuscript 59, 1911

13. Matthew 5:17

14. "Constant" is commonly given as the background thought behind "c," but nothing is ever so simple.... Originally, "c" was taken from the Latin *celeritis*, meaning "swiftly."

in an entirely different light from what you have done in the past, for the law of God will be seen by you as revealing a God of mercy and righteousness. The atonement, made by the stupendous sacrifice of Jesus Christ, will be seen by you in an altogether different light. You will see sin in its heinous character.[15]

New light sounds like a good thing, but like the gospel itself, it sometimes brings more sword than peace.[16] Why? Probably lots of reasons, but perhaps the most significant is that the most basic requirement of "new light" is that it not contradict "old light." Every Adventist knows that line by heart. And it's true!

But the problem comes in when some people can't (or won't) "see to the end" of the old light. Think of the transition from Old Testament to New Testament. The instruction from God was clear in regard to the sacrifices of every kind. What kind of animal, how much salt or flour, what the priest does, what the penitent does, etc., etc. It was all spelled out in messages that came through incontestably divine channels.

So how come some Jews were able to accept Paul's conclusion that "there is no longer an offering for sin," and others thought it was rank heresy? Or how about touching an absolutely raw nerve, by supporting the work of the apostles with your tithe rather than following the command to give it to the Levites?

These were real issues back in the day! And they (along with other matters) created an irreconcilable distinction between post-crucifixion Judaism and the new Christian church. But what decided who went which way? Well, at it's base, it was the issue of faith, and one's acceptance or rejection of the call to serve others. But the more surface issue was one's understanding of the old system. Some "minds were blinded." For them, there was a "veil" which remained "unlifted in the reading of the Old Testament." They couldn't see "the end of what was passing away."[17]

Since this experience of seeing the law clearly is a part of the process that distinguishes the "unjust" and "filthy" from the "righteous" and "holy,"[18] any special treatment in the testing process would be construed by the devil as arbitrary favoritism. Jesus rules this out in the parable of the two houses. He must have stressed the point, since both Matthew and Luke seem to have specifically caught the significance of what He was saying.

In Matthew's telling of the parable, "the rain descended, the floods came, and the winds blew and beat on that house" of the wise man, but it didn't fall. On the other hand, "the rain descended, the floods came, and the winds blew

---

15. *Signs of the Times*, November 13, 1893
16. Matthew 10:34
17. 2 Corinthians 3:13–14
18. Revelation 22:11

and beat on that house" of the foolish man, "and great was its fall." Same description, same challenge, different results.

Luke says the "stream beat vehemently" against both houses, like Matthew, twice using exactly the same phrase to describe the action of the water. In other words, no favoritism.

It makes sense, then, since God's administration doesn't deal in arbitrary measures, that *everyone* is going to see the law in its true light eventually.

> When the judgment shall sit, and every one shall be judged by the things written in the books, the authority of God's law will be looked upon in a light altogether different from that in which it is now regarded by the Christian world.[19]

> In the day of final judgment, when every man shall be judged according to the deeds done in the body, nothing will seem to have existence but character and the law of God.[20]

Just as the character of the Father has been obscured in many minds, so has the *transcript* of His character. Through the mercy of God—and over the loud, persistent, blasphemous and yet unrefuted objections of Satan—salvation has been made provisionally available to billions who never saw nor heard the story of Jesus' revelation of His Father. Their concept of God was faulty, their understanding of the law was partial at best, but they embraced faith with a true heart.

> Up to the time of Christ's first advent, men worshiped cruel, despotic gods. Even the Jewish mind was reached through fear, and not love.

The statement does not say that all such worshipers were lost and it certainly doesn't say that they were all saved. But sometimes, anyway, "the Jewish mind *was reached*." It's true that "fear" is to be cast out by "perfect love,"[21] but if no one can be saved by faith before that task is complete, the number of the redeemed will be small! Fear, it seems, is not a mature motive, but it *is* motive enough to inspire saving faith. "By faith Noah, being divinely warned of things not yet seen, moved with godly fear, prepared an ark for the saving of his household, by which he condemned the world and became heir of the righteousness which is according to faith."[22]

The motive of fear, though, is not what God wants as an eternal condition, so the "reached through fear" quotation continues, "Christ's mission on the earth was to reveal to men that God was not a despot, but a heavenly Father, full of love and mercy for His children."[23]

---

19. *Review and Herald*, May 7, 1901

20. *Review and Herald*, February 12, 1901

21. 1 John 4:18

22. Hebrews 11:7

23. *Signs of the Times*, September 23, 1908

Building upon the in-person revelation of Christ, and as a necessary clarification of "this gospel"; as a necessary part of the demonstration made through the sealed ones of earth; as a necessary preparation for the test of the "avenging enemy"; for all these reasons and more—it is God's plan to equip His last day disciples with a clearer understanding of His law than has been obtained by any previous group of fallen humanity.

> The law is an expression of God's idea. When we receive it in Christ, it becomes our idea. It lifts us above the power of natural desires and tendencies, above temptations that lead to sin.[24]

Armed with that understanding, "us" will finally provide the demonstration that proves God is "just" (He did not change the law in order to forgive these sinners) as well as the "justifier" (the One who "makes just," who heals, forgives, makes perfectly well) both "us" and "they."[25]

Oh, and one more area of new light: medical missionary work.

> Every additional truth which the Holy Spirit has revived and brought to the front is to develop additional principles of the Word and the kingdom of God. It is a fresh air time, increasing light in opening to minds the principles of holiness and fresh elements of virtue. It is the bringing upon the highest platform a power of medical missionary work bound up with the gospel ministry. The pride of physical and medical science will be bound up in the gospel, and the Holy Spirit will be the subduing agency through the gospel ministry in a variety of methods of healing, which leads those who will be on the Lord's side to separate from sin and sinners. It is the power of God unto all who believe. And this power is not in name, neither is it bound up in companies and written vows and pledges and doctoring. It gathers grapes from thorns, and figs from thistles, because of the transforming power of God's grace.[26]

---

24. E.G. White, Letter to Uriah Smith, June 6, 1896; Letter 96, 1896
25. If you jumped into the middle of the book, this isn't going to make a lot of sense. That's why there are chapter numbers! Oh well, I've done it, too, so I'll forgive you. But, at a minimum, you really need to back up to at least Chapter 21.
26. E.G. White, Letter to Frank Belden, 1903; Letter 308, 1903

CHAPTER 30

The Dull Scholars

IF you read Ellen White enough, you begin to recognize that she saw the whole world and every experience in it as a microcosm of the great controversy. Her application of principles to what might seem a small and mundane issue is often shown by her vocabulary to be simply a scaled down version of the same principles as they might be applied on a universal scale. Here's an example that can give us hope!

> Teachers must consider that they are dealing with children, not men and women. They are children who have everything to learn, and it is much more difficult for some to learn than others. The dull scholar needs much more encouragement than he receives. If teachers are placed over these varied minds, who naturally love to order and dictate and magnify themselves in their authority, who will deal with partiality, having favorites to whom they will show preferences, while others are treated with exactitude and severity, it will create a state of confusion and insubordination.[1]

From the perspective of the angels, of the universe at large, we human beings must certainly be the dullest of dull scholars. Through the unrelenting care of God, through the life, ministry, sacrifice, resurrection, and intercession of Christ, we have received a level of "encouragement" which has left all observers incredulous.

"What does He see in them?" is one of those sentences which might legitimately be repeated over and over, with emphasis placed sequentially on each word (go ahead, try it)... and likely no one in the universe could answer any *one* version, let alone all six!

If we could attribute our dullness to lack of opportunity ("Hey, I haven't lived thousands of years like you angels have!") it might not be so bad, but the

---

1. *Fundamentals of Christian Education*, 269

evidence says we tend towards "dull" to such a degree that lack of time just isn't enough of an excuse. If there is any one sphere of "understanding" in which we must seem more pathetically dull than any other, it's likely our inability to even begin to see what a mess we are.

As noted way back on page 40, "God's purpose [was] to place things upon an eternal basis of security."[2] It's a great plan, but the dull scholars keep messing it up. The easiest thing would be to practice a little eugenics and just get rid of them! We seldom think of this as an option, but Ellen White saw it clearly:

> It would be much easier to destroy fallen human beings than to reform them. Satan says, "They shall not be reformed." But Christ came to this earth to uplift and elevate the race.[3]

> God might have cut Himself loose from fallen beings. He might have treated them as sinners deserve to be treated. He might have commanded the angels of heaven to pour out upon our world the vials of His wrath. He might have removed this dark blot from His universe. But He did not do this. Instead of banishing them from His presence, He came still nearer to the fallen race.[4]

> How much easier would it seem to the human mind for God to have destroyed out of the world the creatures He had made, and so put an end to sin! But the Lord chose the costlier plan.[5]

Without trying to make anyone look bad, some of the statements like this make it clear that 1) God doesn't always tell the angels everything He's going to do before He does it and 2) that the extra "encouragement" God has given sinful human beings is truly a mind-stretching revelation for the angels:

> All heaven watched the movements of God with intense interest. Would He once more manifest His wrath? Would He destroy the world by fire? The angels thought that the time had come to strike the blow of justice, when, lo, to their wondering vision was unveiled the plan of salvation. Wonder, O heavens, and be astonished, O earth! God sent His only begotten Son into the world to save the world![6]

Fortunately, God is willing to give us dull scholars "much more encouragement." And, I would think, much more explanation of the lessons we should have mastered long ago. Which makes a perfect lead-in to a chapter on God's "How-to" counsel for getting His church away from the status quo and moving forward with "the plan."

We've looked at "little things" as preparatory for the bigger test of losing earthly support. That's good... but it hasn't been earthshaking (nor churchshak-

2. *Review and Herald*, September 7, 1897
3. E.G. White, Letter to Those Laboring in the Southern States, July 25, 1902; Letter 115, 1902
4. E.G. White, "God's Love Manifested," February 16, 1900; Manuscript 21, 1900
5. *Youth's Instructor*, December 30, 1897
6. E.G. White, "Diary: January to March 1890," January 10–March 1, 1890; Manuscript 22, 1890

ing, for that matter). Though the world arguably keeps getting worse, there's not a whole lot of evidence that the church is getting better. That's a problem, for the simple reason that God is not waiting for the world to get sinful enough to trigger the second coming. He's waiting for a group *to whom* He can reveal His law, and *through whom* He can reveal His character. Remembering that Christ could only reveal His Father's character through a combined ministry of preaching, teaching, helping, and healing, it has been encouraging to see an uptick of interest in medical missionary work in recent years. Ranging from small, individual efforts to increasing interest in various training programs, to the national-headline grabbing impact of large "mega clinics" where Adventist volunteers provided free health care, every such development is a step in the right direction.

But the devil's counterattack in 2020 fragmented the denomination's medical missionary working force, and produced one of those "*X* steps forward, *Y* steps back" situations. It's not clear to me, but I cling to the hope that $X > Y$.

But what should the dull scholars be learning? What do we need to know to continue moving forward? One answer stands out in the Inspired counsel, and it is loaded with significance on both the positive and the negative sides of the issue:

> We need to beware lest we suffer the same fate as did ancient Israel. The disobedience and destruction of the Israelites is recorded for our instruction, that we may avoid doing as they did. These things are written "for our admonition, upon whom the ends of the world are come." If we pass by these inspired cautions and warnings, and develop the wrong traits of character developed by the children of Israel, what excuse can we plead?...

> Our work is presented before us in the fifty-eighth chapter of Isaiah. This chapter marks out a right and a wrong course, and gives assurance that if we follow the right, we shall receive the blessings specified. If we take up the very duties around us, we shall avoid the faults condemned in ancient Israel. God would teach us to exercise calm, unwavering trust in Him who is "the Way, the Truth, and the Life."[7]

When Ellen White says "the fifty-eighth chapter of Isaiah," it's a literary device that means medical missionary work, the kind of work Jesus did, the applied theology of Jones and Waggoner that once upon a time started the loud cry. But if that is to be "our work," why is it such a focus in *Ministry of Healing*, and yet so seemingly foreign to *Great Controversy*?

That's a fair question. Ellen White would be the best one to ask, but since that's not an option now, I'll hazard a guess: "audience and purpose."

Every sermon, every book, is directed toward some particular audience. Similarly, every serious communication has an intended purpose. *Great Controversy* is intended for distribution to the public. It is intended to capture their

---

7. E.G. White, "The Lord's Vineyard," December 15, 1898; Manuscript 166, 1898

interest and inspire the reader with loyalty to God. It is primarily a chronological narrative—a story—that illustrates over and over again the principles that distinguish the work of God from the work of Satan.

And what did your English teacher tell you is the essential central element in any good story? It's true! "Conflict" is what makes a story. Any sort of conflict forces a piece of writing to become stretched out over time, just because it takes time to resolve the issue. It's that progression of events over time that we call a "story," and stories are far more engaging than "position papers." If you're writing for a general audience that isn't already committed to whatever position you prefer, go with a story.

"Conflict," incidentally, happens to be closely related to the word "controversy," the "ministry" of which was mentioned at the very beginning of this book. We'll see more of that shortly.

The obvious first goal of *Great Controversy* is to arrest the reader's attention, to make him take stock of his own relationship to the battle of good versus evil. The book outlines issues and events—some yet future—but does not spend a great deal of ink detailing every method and procedure to be used by those loyal to God. Why not? Because stories are more compelling than "how-to" manuals, and when you're writing for an uncommitted, if not blatantly hostile, audience, your influence ends when they stop reading.

But, surely, if the principles and methods of *Ministry of Healing* are important to success in the conflict at the heart of *Great Controversy*, the book should at least mention them....

And, yes, it does. On page 452, for instance, Ellen White quotes "Cry aloud, spare not..."[8] (Isaiah 58:1–2) but then jumps down to verses 12–14, about the Sabbath. She doesn't quote verses 3–11 (the false fast contrasted with "deal thy bread to the hungry..."), but do you think maybe we should read those verses, too?

Nine pages later, Ellen White comments on converts brought to the truth through revivals "wherever the word of God has been faithfully preached": "These souls," she says, "rose to walk in newness of life... to follow in His steps, to reflect His character, and to purify themselves even as He is pure."

In the next paragraph she specifies just a bit of what that really means: "The fruits of such revivals were seen in souls who shrank not at self-denial and sacrifice."[9]

---

8. Largely because of the "spare not" part, this seems to be the favorite section of the chapter for some folks. Ellen White's advice may help on this point: "Sometimes it becomes necessary for God's messengers to 'cry aloud' and to 'spare not;' but even then the reproof is borne by the truth itself, and not by the human agent. In speaking words of reproof, let us put all the Christlike tenderness and love possible into the voice." E.G. White, "Talk: Words to Ministers," September 16, 1902; Manuscript 127, 1902

9. *Great Controversy*, 462

Two pages further on, we find this prediction: "Before the final visitation of God's judgments upon the earth there will be among the people of the Lord such a revival of primitive godliness as has not been witnessed since apostolic times." That sounds like a real milestone! But it is not to be gained without opposition. She also predicts that—

> The enemy of souls desires to hinder this work; and before the time for such a movement shall come, he will endeavor to prevent it by introducing a counterfeit. In those churches which he can bring under his deceptive power he will make it appear that God's special blessing is poured out; there will be manifest what is thought to be great religious interest. Multitudes will exult that God is working marvelously for them, when the work is that of another spirit. Under a religious guise, Satan will seek to extend his influence over the Christian world.[10]

Now, there's a funny thing about counterfeits. They aren't very effective if they don't look a lot like the real thing. Which raises the question, what does "primitive godliness" actually look like?

That's an important point. The most commonly counterfeited bill in the world is the US $100 note, but if you've never seen a real one before, you'll likely never spot a half decent counterfeit. So, what does "primitive godliness" look like? How much of *that* have you seen?

If we define it as something like "pure doctrine," then we should be looking for false doctrine as a counterfeit. Well, there's certainly more than enough false doctrine running loose in the world, so maybe that's the point she was trying to make. Or, maybe not.

In the next paragraph, she contrasts the true and false revivals she's been talking about:

> Wherever men neglect the testimony of the Bible, turning away from those plain, soul-testing truths which require self-denial and renunciation of the world, there we may be sure that God's blessing is not bestowed.[11]

Her main emphasis is on a very basic level. The problem with "Modern Revivals" (the title of the chapter) is that they ignore the law of God, and so they don't end up doing much reviving!

> [In false revivals] the hope of salvation is accepted without a radical change of heart or reformation of life. Thus superficial conversions abound, and multitudes are joined to the church who have never been united to Christ.[12]

---

10. *Great Controversy*, 464
11. *Great Controversy*, 464
12. *Great Controversy*, 468

That's a problem! For the simple reason that "the followers of Christ are to become like Him—by the grace of God to form characters in harmony with the principles of His holy law. This is Bible sanctification."[13]

What's behind this trend toward "superficial conversions"?

> The desire for an easy religion that requires no striving, no self-denial.[14]

> Human reasoning has ever sought to evade or set aside the simple, direct instructions of the word of God. In every age, a majority of the professed followers of Christ have disregarded those precepts which enjoin self-denial and humility, which require modesty and simplicity of conversation, deportment, and apparel. The result has ever been the same—departure from the teachings of the gospel leads to the adoption of the fashions, customs, and principles of the world. Vital godliness gives place to a dead formalism.[15]

We've seen this before... it's not new... but it's about the easiest thing in the world to overlook. And, unfortunately, it marks us as "willing to be deceived." It says so! In the same book!

> Satan can present a counterfeit so closely resembling the truth that it deceives those who are willing to be deceived, who desire to shun the self-denial and sacrifice demanded by the truth.[16]

Does *Great Controversy* spend a lot of time on "health ministry," or "medical missionary work"? No, not really. It just says that "Bible sanctification" makes "the followers of Christ... like Him."

A bit more on the idea of Satan and his counterfeits: more than any of us, Satan knows what the real $100 bill looks like, so it's no surprise that—

> Satan will come in to deceive if possible the very elect. He claims to be Christ, and he is coming in, pretending to be the great medical missionary.[17]

Incidentally, speaking of counterfeits, imagine the possibilities open for counterfeiting a never-before-seen item. It's like passing a fake US $100 bill to someone who believes such a thing exists, but has never seen one before. And what if you could convince millions of people who didn't know otherwise, that the US $100 bill had a picture of William Henry Harrison on it. (You don't remember Harrison? He *was* president, even if for only thirty-one days.)

But imagine if much of the world had read the line, "Give me a Harrison," and understood it to be a demand for $100. Or heard, "He got away with five of my Harrisons" in a famous movie. Repeat that over and over. Books, movies,

13. *Great Controversy*, 469
14. *Great Controversy*, 472
15. *Review and Herald*, December 6, 1881
16. *Great Controversy*, 528
17. *General Conference Bulletin*, April 6, 1903

podcasts, streaming services, YouTube. Pay the "Independent Fact Checkers" to all agree; have the idea relentlessly pushed by "Science," and every government on earth. Whatever it takes....

Sure, it's hard to imagine, but just imagine it anyway.

Of course, 10% of the population still knows that Ben Franklin belongs on that bill. But if everyone around them says it's Harrison.... What are the odds that a counterfeiter might try a picture of Harrison?

Now, consider this seemingly unrelated idea:

> The Lord would have our perceptions keen to understand that those mighty ones who visit our world have borne an active part in <u>all the work</u> which we have called our own. These heavenly beings are ministering angels, and they <u>frequently</u> disguise themselves in the form of human beings. As strangers they converse with those who are engaged in the work of God. In lonely places they have been the companions of the traveler in peril. In tempest-tossed ships angels in human form have spoken words of encouragement to allay fear and inspire hope in the hour of danger, and the passengers have thought that it was one of their number to whom they had never before spoken.
>
> <u>Many</u>, under different circumstances, have listened to the voices of the inhabitants of other worlds. They have come to act a part in this life. They have <u>spoken in assemblies</u>, and opened before assemblies human histories, and have done works which it was impossible for human agencies to do. <u>Time and again</u> have they been the <u>generals of armies</u>. They have been sent forth to cleanse away the pestilence. They have eaten at the humble board of families. <u>Often</u> they have appeared as weary travelers in need of shelter for the night.[18]

Praise the Lord for the work of angels! But note the underlined words; they seem to paint a picture of far greater angelic assimilation into human society than we're used to thinking of.

Assemblies? Like parliament, or congress? *Generals?* Whoa! Could *you* just stroll into any capitol on earth and say, "Hello, I'd like to say a few words today." Or bark out a command like, "Hold fire!" and expect anyone to listen?

No? God's angels have.

So, given that the devil is sure to demand equal rights for his angels, and given that most of the world has heard the idea that a bunch of people are going to just disappear one day, why *wouldn't* Satan's angels make it happen? How hard is it for an angel to disappear? After all, the devil has spent a few hundred years setting the stage. And books and movies have made even the non-Christian world think the "secret rapture" is what the Bible teaches. It's like Harrison on a C-note. Even if it's *not* true, if everyone believes it....

But I'm not a prophet, and this is clearly just speculation.

---

18. E.G. White, "The Day of Reckoning," March 11, 1898; Manuscript 39, 1898

CHAPTER 31

What Did They Say?

MANY pages back, the question was asked, "How do we move from the 'here and now' (a true but often trembling faith and a declared but often faulty righteousness), to the 'there and then' (an invincible faith and a tested, proven, and demonstrated righteousness)? What is the treatment plan for the disease of sin?"

We've been considering that question ever since, noting the importance of "little things," the value of "new light," highlighting a special emphasis the Lord has placed on basic matters such as the plan of redemption, the gospel, the atonement, and—underlying it all—the law of God.

But what makes it all happen? It's like the old joke about the bowling ball at the top of a hill, boasting that it has "potential."[1] Potential is all well and good... but what accounts for this?

> When the storm of opposition and reproach bursts upon them, some, overwhelmed with consternation, will be ready to exclaim: "Had we foreseen the consequences of our words, we would have held our peace."

This is said of God's people during the "little time of trouble" just before the close of probation. And it makes it sound as though they had somehow found the magic words that finally set "closing events" into motion. To us, that may sound like a good thing; to them, at that time, it doesn't look so obviously good!

> They are hedged in with difficulties. Satan assails them with fierce temptations. The work which they have undertaken seems far beyond their ability to accomplish. They are threatened with destruction. The enthusiasm which animated them is gone;

---

1. For anyone who's not a fan of physics, that's a reference to the "potential energy" stored in the ball by virtue of its elevation.

yet they cannot turn back. Then, feeling their utter helplessness, they flee to the Mighty One for strength. They remember that the words which they have spoken were not theirs, but His who bade them give the warning. God put the truth into their hearts, and they could not forbear to proclaim it.[2]

This is intense. The pressure is on, and the stakes are high, but our interest at the moment is that this whole situation seems to have been triggered by "the words which they have spoken." What did they say?

These quotations are drawn from the chapter entitled "The Final Warning," and the author leaves no doubt that "the warning" that God "bade them give" is the full package of the three angels' messages, combined with the loud cry of the fourth angel depicted in Revelation 18:1. This is classic Adventist eschatology. It's all here: "the announcement of the fall of Babylon," with "additional... corruptions" such as "the teachings of spiritualism," is boldly given as a warning that all should "come out of her" and "receive not of her plagues"[3] which are soon to fall.

> The Sabbath will be the great test of loyalty, for it is the point of truth especially controverted.... While one class, by accepting the sign of submission to earthly powers, receive the mark of the beast, the other choosing the token of allegiance to divine authority, receive the seal of God.[4]

But once again, a wider selection of Ellen White sources adds some details to the picture. As a result—despite our chapter title—the question ends up shifting more towards "What did they say *different* this time?"

The point is, Adventists have been preaching the three angels for quite a long time now, but with far less dramatic results. A markedly different reaction from the world strongly implies that something new has been added to the picture. And *Great Controversy* agrees:

> Heretofore those who presented the truths of the third angel's message have often been regarded as mere alarmists. Their predictions that religious intolerance would gain control in the United States, that church and state would unite to persecute those who keep the commandments of God, have been pronounced groundless and absurd. It has been confidently declared that this land could never become other than what it has been—the defender of religious freedom. But as the question of enforcing Sunday observance is widely agitated, the event so long doubted and disbelieved is seen to be approaching, and the third message will produce an effect which it could not have had before.[5]

---

2. *Great Controversy*, 608
3. *Great Controversy*, 603–604
4. *Great Controversy*, 605
5. *Great Controversy*, 605

That shift in circumstances is an obvious wake up call for at least part of the population, but there is more going on here. Perhaps it's no surprise now, but the loud cry follows the same pattern of all that we've seen important to the communication of God's revelation in past ages.

> All the light of the past, which shines unto the present and reaches forth into the future, as revealed in the word of God, is for every soul who will receive it. But the glory of this light, which is the very glory of the character of Christ, can never be expressed in words. Human language is inadequate to reveal it. It must be made manifest in the life....

As has been said before, words alone aren't enough to portray the divine character, nor the character of "Christlike men and women," for that matter. But what would that actually look like? Find out here!

> The whole of the sixty-second chapter of Isaiah is a representation of the work Christ will do through those who follow His example.[6]

No, that recommendation wasn't just for effect. You really ought to put this book down now and go read Isaiah 62. I'll wait....

OK, now we can go on. Did you catch the second verse? (You probably better look again. I'll wait....)

Now *that's* a revelation! When the Gentiles see their righteousness and all kings see their glory, God's people—those Christlike men and women—are putting on a world class "revelation of the righteousness of Christ."[7] In case you've forgotten, that was the way Ellen White described the beginning of the loud cry.

It seems kind of obvious, really. Just as Christ—who was a perfect reflection of His Father, and whose work was described in Isaiah 61—could not reveal His character by words alone, so those who come to reflect the character of Christ (featured in Isaiah 62) cannot reveal His character by words alone. But just such a revelation is the whole goal:

> The purpose which God seeks to accomplish through His people today is the same that He desired to accomplish through Israel when He brought them forth out of Egypt. By beholding the goodness, the mercy, the justice, and the love of God revealed in the Church, the world is to have a representation of His character. And when the law of God is thus exemplified in the life, even the world will recognize the superiority of those who love and serve God above every other people on the face of the earth.... Not to this world only, but to the universe are we to make manifest the principles of His kingdom.[8]

---

6. E.G. White, Letter to Brethren, June 24, 1900; Letter 91, 1900
7. *Review and Herald*, November 22, 1892. Quoted more fully on page 69.
8. *(Australasian) Union Conference Record*, June 1, 1900

It's worth noting that even though the world "will recognize the superiority of those who love and serve God," that's no guarantee that the world will love that superiority! Hence, the "storm of opposition and reproach" we read about at the beginning of this chapter.

But before the storm, comes the revelation that gives force and substance to the proclamation of the message. It's the methods, the tactical measures of that revelation that we want to look at now. What do God's people do—and say— differently the time their witness actually works? Look for the clues:

> Much of the prejudice that prevents the truth of the third angel's message from reaching the hearts of the people, might be removed if more attention were given to health reform....
>
> This branch of the Lord's work has not received due attention, and through this neglect much has been lost. If the church would manifest a greater interest in the reforms through which God Himself is seeking to fit them for His coming, their influence would be far greater than it now is.... Although the health reform is not the third angel's message, it is closely connected with it. Those who pro- claim the message should teach health reform also. It is a subject that we must understand, in order to be prepared for the events that are close upon us, and it should have a prominent place.[9]
>
> What saith the Lord in the fifty-eighth chapter of Isaiah? The whole chapter is of the highest importance. "Is not this the fast that I have chosen?" God asks, "to loose the bands of wickedness, to undo the burdens, and to let the oppressed go free, and that ye break every yoke? Is it not to deal thy bread to the hungry, and that thou bring the poor that are cast out to thy house?... Then shalt thou call, and the Lord shall answer; thou shalt cry, and He shall say, Here I am."
>
> "If thou turn away thy foot from the Sabbath... I will cause thee to ride upon the high places of the earth, and feed thee with the heritage of Jacob thy father: for the mouth of the Lord hath spoken it." Verses 6–9, 13, 14.
>
> This is our work.... The Lord's command to His servants is: Cry aloud, spare not, lift up thy voice like a trumpet, and show My people their transgression, and the house of Jacob their sins." Verse 1. A message that will arouse the churches is to be proclaimed. Every effort is to be made to give the light, not only to our people, but to the world.[10]
>
> I cannot too strongly urge all our church members, all who are true missionaries, all who believe the third angel's message, all who turn away their feet from the Sab- bath, to consider the message of the fifty-eighth chapter of Isaiah. The work of benef- icence enjoined in this chapter is the work that God requires His people to do at this time. It is a work of His own appointment. We are not left in doubt as to where the message applies, and the time of its marked fulfillment, for we read: "They that shall

---

9. *Christian Temperance and Bible Hygiene*, 121
10. *Testimonies*, vol. 8, 159

be of thee shall build the old waste places: thou shalt raise up the foundations of many generations; and thou shalt be called, The repairer of the breach, The restorer of paths to dwell in." Verse 12....

That ellipsis takes the place of five more sentences about Isaiah 58 and the Sabbath, but then—still in the same paragraph—Ellen White carries on with a conclusion to her logic. The next sentence starts with "thus": "because of this," "as a result or consequence of this," "therefore."

So... what's the logical end result of this connection between Isaiah 58 and the Sabbath? What can we learn from all this?

> Thus genuine medical missionary work is bound up inseparably with the keeping of God's commandments, of which the Sabbath is especially mentioned, since it is the great memorial of God's creative work. Its observance is bound up with the work of restoring the moral image of God in man. This is the ministry which God's people are to carry forward at this time.[11]

If two things are "bound up inseparably" it's kind of like a two-for-the-price-of-one deal. If you have A, you automatically have B as well. Great.

But there's a flip side to this. That same logic also forces the conclusion that if you *don't* have A, you don't have B either. And that is cause for serious concern for all who believe they are "keeping the commandments," but don't have any interest in medical missionary work.

> The union that should exist between the medical missionary work and the ministry is clearly set forth in the fifty-eighth chapter of Isaiah.... If the work of the third angel's message is carried on in right lines, the ministry will not be given an inferior place, nor will the poor and sick be neglected. In His word God has united these two lines of work, and no man should divorce them.[12]

> The work of God is not divided; it is one, and if there is any separation between the medical missionary work and the ministry, it will be because the Holy Spirit is not working upon hearts.[13]

And that is at least *part* of what makes the difference between all the failed attempts to re-start the loud cry, and the work of God's people when it actually happens.

But it's too early for any victory celebrations. It turns out that we're all still pretty dull scholars, and we've got some lessons to learn before we're ready for the big stage. Promises come with conditions, you see.

---

11. *Testimonies*, vol. 6, 265
12. *Testimonies*, vol. 6, 289
13. E.G. White, Letter to J.H. Kellogg, February 23, 1899; Letter 40, 1899

When God's people do personal work as He designs it to be done, the promises of Isaiah fifty-eight will be fulfilled to them. His righteousness will go before them; His glory will be their rereward.[14]

The study of surgery and other medical science receives much attention in the world, but the true science of medical missionary work, carried forward as Christ carried it, is new and strange to the denominational churches and to the world. But it will find its rightful place when as a people who have had great light, Seventh-day Adventists awaken to their responsibilities and improve their opportunities.[15]

Challenge enough, for sure! But promises are more than conditions; promises also show where God wants His work to go, and what He intends to accomplish. Here's one to remember:

The medical missionary work is a most exalted work. It is one of the principal means of preparing a people to stand as God's family in the last days. It is not merely something that will gain for us a round of applause from the world.[16]

But that's all about what God's people will *do*. Medical missionary work, personal work, exalted work... that's the *revelation* that we've seen so often, but there is still a place for *proclamation*. So, what did they *say*?

The chapter title makes it sound like there really ought to be an answer to that question, but I've never found it in any explicit form in the Bible or Spirit of Prophecy. Sorry for the let down.

But I think there are some fairly strong possibilities, so I'll present them merely as possibilities. Reader discretion is advised.

Given the context of the times—the need to "take the gospel to all the world" (this is still before the close of probation), increasing opposition on the Sabbath/Sunday issue, decreasing "earthly support," and the role of medical missionary work (aka, self-denial)—given all that, what verbal message would further God's work and stir things up so much? And, for that matter, to whom would those words be spoken? The church? The world? Both?

It seems to me (and you're free to hold a different opinion) that the words we're looking for might well be primarily addressed to fellow believers. The shaking comes to the church before it comes to the world, and there's clearly something that produces this:

As the storm approaches, a large class who have professed faith in the third angel's message, but have not been sanctified through obedience to the truth, abandon their position and join the ranks of the opposition. By uniting with the world and partaking of its spirit, they have come to view matters in nearly the same light; and when the

14. E.G. White, Letter to Brother and Sister D.H. Kress, April 28, 1902; Letter 68, 1902
15. *Evangelism*, 518
16. E.G. White, "The Work of the St. Helena Sanitarium," July 14, 1902; Manuscript 169, 1902

test is brought, they are prepared to choose the easy, popular side. Men of talent and pleasing address, who once rejoiced in the truth, employ their powers to deceive and mislead souls. They become the most bitter enemies of their former brethren. When Sabbathkeepers are brought before the courts to answer for their faith, these apostates are the most efficient agents of Satan to misrepresent and accuse them, and by false reports and insinuations to stir up the rulers against them.[17]

What might offend these professed believers? What sort of testing duty might be so directly contrasted with "the easy, popular side"?

One of the oldest tricks in the realm of scholarly research is to actually read the next paragraph, and when we do that, who do you think we bump into? You guessed it! The next paragraph is where we find those who are "ready to exclaim: 'Had we foreseen the consequences of our words....'" So, does that give us any idea what they might have said?

Hold that thought; let's look at another piece of evidence before we try to form a conclusion. This one comes from an earlier description of the "little time of trouble." In fact, this is the passage that introduced the whole idea of a "little time of trouble."[18]

> I saw that God had children, who do not see and keep the Sabbath. They had not rejected the light on it. And at the commencement of the time of trouble, we were filled with the Holy Ghost as we went forth and proclaimed the Sabbath more fully. This enraged the churches, and nominal Adventists, as they could not refute the Sabbath truth.[19]

Like many of Ellen White's earlier writings, the language is very simple and direct. That's what makes *Early Writings* fun to read. Aside from the simpler phrasing, though, the account here is similar to her later accounts... with one exception. The phrase, "proclaimed the Sabbath more fully," appears no where else.

Is that important? Does it mean anything special?

I think there's a good chance that that particular detail is the best answer to the question, "What did they say?"

---

17. *Great Controversy*, 608
18. As a trivia question, how many times do you think Ellen White used the phrase "little time of trouble" in the whole of her writings? Answer: zero. I'll admit, I was surprised.

    A small book titled, *A Sketch of the Christian Experience and Views of Ellen G. White,* was published in 1851. It contained an account of a vision Ellen White had received April 3, 1847. Three years later a "Supplement" to *Experiences and Views* was published to provide answers to some questions raised by the book. (Both are now included in *Early Writings.*) In the Supplement, she wrote of "a short period just before [the seven last plagues] are poured out, while Christ is in the sanctuary. At that time, while the work of salvation is closing, trouble will be coming on the earth, and the nations will be angry, yet held in check so as not to prevent the work of the third angel." That comment is quoted on page 143 of *Last Day Events,* beneath a supplied heading that says "The Little Time of Trouble." That's the only place in her writings that that phrase appears, and she didn't write it. Who knew?
19. *A Sketch of the Christian Experience and Views of Ellen G. White,* 17

I think there's a good chance that when God's faithful ones do proclaim the Sabbath more fully, that it will be directed at least as much to the church as to the world. Not well received by the "nominal Adventists," it is this proclamation—united with the living revelation of the saints, of course—which stirs up the "professed believers," exposing them in time as "bitter enemies," "apostates," and "agents of Satan."

But what does "proclaiming the Sabbath more fully" mean. What would that sound like in modern English? I'm happy to share my thought on that—but again I need to stress that it is just my thought, not explicit inspiration. And... I need to wait a few chapters. It would spoil the conceptual flow to go into that right now.

"Here is the patience of the saints."[20]

---

20. Revelation 14:12

CHAPTER 32

Chapter 11

THE reader may be tempted to imagine that the chapter title contains a typo, or that a glitch occurred in some software-controlled numbering scheme. There is nothing of the sort, but readers are to be readily forgiven for their confusion, especially those not familiar with the common name for the United States' legal provisions surrounding bankruptcy. In fact, "Title 11 U.S. Code Chapter 11—Reorganization," commonly known simply as "Chapter 11," will give you all the ins and outs of how an individual or a business (large or small) can admit to their creditors that the day of deep reckoning has come.

Let's just call it a happy coincidence that "Chapter 11" of the book of Hebrews is similarly famous, and arguably more so on a global basis. Oddly enough, the two documents share some characteristics.

The phrase, "at the end of one's rope," comes to mind. Some dictionary entries stress the idea of someone losing patience with some annoying circumstance. I find this unrelated to the imagery of the phrase, so I would argue that a more general definition such as "a state in which one is not able to deal with a problem, difficult situation, etc., any longer,"[1] is more faithful to the meaning.

Still, the mental picture of someone who used an 80-meter rope to rappel down a 120-meter cliff seems to better catch the flavor of both bankruptcy and the sometimes stressful experience of "living by faith." "Dying by faith" is presumably stressful as well.

---

1. merriam-webster.com/dictionary/the end of one's rope

Of the sixteen "heroes" mentioned by name in Hebrews chapter 11,[2] only two died as the direct result of their heroism, but there is still the darker subtext of the unnamed "others" who—

> were tortured, not accepting deliverance, that they might obtain a better resurrection. Still others had trial of mockings and scourgings, yes, and of chains and imprisonment. They were stoned, they were sawn in two, were tempted, were slain with the sword. They wandered about in sheepskins and goatskins, being destitute, afflicted, tormented—of whom the world was not worthy. They wandered in deserts and mountains, in dens and caves of the earth.[3]

True enough, these all "obtained a good testimony through faith," but nonetheless they "did not receive the promise."[4] The idea that those "upon whom the ends of the ages have come"[5] are going to have an easier time of testing seems patently absurd.

True enough, there are those who confidently assert that there is no categorical distinction between the salvation process of all ages past and the salvation process at the end of time, but this position robs God of any "reason" for ending the current stage of the great controversy. If nothing special happens at the end, what makes it "the end"?

More pointedly, if God isn't waiting for some additional demonstration of the superiority of heavenly over devilish principles, then what possible excuse can He offer for the continued sorrows and afflictions of the suffering millions here on earth?

Is the great controversy like a game where the clock keeps running until it just stops because... well, because time's up. "The clock ran out. It's over." Who cares if the winning team got there only through luck? Who cares if the losers might be right when they say, "We didn't get beat; we just ran out of time"? Is that an argument God is going to leave on the table for Satan to pick up and run with? Not likely, and He will prevent it by the simple expediency of testing everyone at once, and then "let the chips fall."

> When the test is over, when men have taken sides for or against the law of Jehovah, the season of mercy and probation is ended. Then God will move in the straight line of justice to give to every man as his works have been. Some will receive the reward of well doing, others the reward of their evil deeds.[6]

---

2. For the record, they are Abel, Enoch, Noah, Abraham, Sarah, Isaac, Jacob, Joseph, Moses, Rahab, Gideon, Barak, Samson, Jephthah, David, and Samuel. Abel and Samson were the fatalities.

3. Hebrews 11:35–38

4. Hebrews 11:39

5. 1 Corinthians 10:11

6. E.G. White, "The Truth As It Is In Jesus," June 21, 1897; Manuscript 58, 1897

But our interest just now is the fate of the poor folks stuck swinging at the end of their too-short rope. We've previously considered the loss of "every earthly support," and in the last chapter we saw the "consternation" of the 144,000 as they see what a hornet's nest has been stirred up by their witness, in both word and deed, to the righteousness of the law and their refusal to break it.

To set the scene with some specificity, we are still considering the "little time of trouble," the period just before the close of probation. This means that there are still souls to be saved, and so those who have learned of Christ return love for hatred, even though it stirs up mostly more hatred. That's unusual.

And yet, our picture of the circumstances in which the righteous find themselves is still perhaps quite inaccurate. If we simply take current conditions and then subtract some or all of the obvious "earthly supports" of employment, equal treatment before the law, housing, and the freedom to get what we need at the local Walmart... well, let's just say that we may have missed a few details.

Way back in Chapter 2, we saw a glimpse of the circumstances around this time. The "ministry of controversy," it was said, would result in "populous cities... reduced to ruin and desolation," if not completely "swept away." The list of predictions includes "pestilence, plague, famine, fire, and flood." And all of this must be navigated by both righteous and wicked.

Our first thought might be the need for immediate trauma care, and there's sure to be lots of that. But it's likely that the disruption of supply chains caused by these disasters will provide a more-than-sufficient supply of "suffering ones, plenty of them, who will need help, not only among those of our own faith, but largely among those who know not the truth."[7]

Supply chains? Like food?

Sure, food will be a big item, but don't overlook what will happen when your local pharmacy has nothing to offer. It varies from country to country, of course, but 66% of the adult population in the United States (55+% in Canada) regularly take prescription medications. Heroin is not the only drug that has withdrawal challenges!

But there's more to the picture, because there's a fair chance that not only will God's people be homeless at that time, they may well be refugees in some unfamiliar location. Why? Because we messed up, much like the Jews:

> Had the Hebrews been true to their trust, they would have been a power in the world.... But they did not keep their covenant with God.... Yet the purpose of God must be accomplished. The knowledge of His will must be spread abroad in the earth. God brought the hand of the oppressor upon His people and scattered them as captives

---

7. E.G. White, Letter to Brother and Sister J.H. Kellogg, September 16, 1892; Letter 34, 1892. Quoted more fully on page 12.

among the nations.... Scattered throughout the countries of the heathen, they spread abroad the knowledge of the true God.... Thus the work which God had given His people to do in prosperity, in their own borders, but which had been neglected through their un-faithfulness, was done by them in captivity, under great trial and embarrassment.[8]

To be fair, this problem wasn't confined to the Jews; even in the days of the apostles, "dull scholars" existed:

> The day of Pentecost came. Great additions were made to the church. In one day five thousand were converted. The disciples began to think that they had a work to do in Jerusalem, in shielding the members of the church from the snares of the enemy. They did not realize that strength to resist temptation is best gained by active service. They did not educate the new church-members to become workers together with God in carrying the gospel to those who had not heard it. Instead, they were in danger of being satisfied with what had been accomplished. To scatter His representatives abroad, where they could work for others, the Lord permitted persecution to come upon His church. Stephen and several others died for their faith; then the members of the church were scattered; and the gospel was proclaimed with power "in all Judea, and in Samaria, and unto the uttermost part of the earth."[9]

It's just plain hard for believers to grasp how serious God is about taking His truth—the same thing as "His character," by the way—"to all the world." The temptation to "settle down" is one of the most pervasive, even in our day.

> Many of the members of our large churches are doing comparatively nothing. They might accomplish a good work if, instead of crowding together, they would scat-ter into places that have not yet been entered by the truth.[10]

> If the church of Christ were fulfilling the purpose of our Lord, light would be shed upon all that sit in darkness and in the region and shadow of death. Instead of congre-gating together and shunning responsibility and cross bearing, the members of the church would scatter into all lands, letting the light of Christ shine out from them, working as He did for the salvation of souls, and this "gospel of the kingdom" would speedily be carried to all the world.[11]

Faced with this same problem again, what are the odds the Lord will come up with a brand new approach? You think? Or maybe, just maybe, He'll do the same thing all over again.

> The time is at hand when believers will be scattered into many lands.[12]

---

8. *Testimonies*, vol. 5, 455

9. *Pacific Union Recorder*, November 20, 1902

10. *Testimonies*, vol. 8, 244

11. *Mount of Blessing*, 42

12. *Review and Herald*, June 2, 1904

We have but a short time in which to work. Why do not those to whom God has committed great light move out into new places? They will have to do this, whether they wish to or not; for God will scatter them into many places.[13]

There will come a time when there will be a great scattering—a scattering that we do not now dream of, and it will be brought about in unexpected ways. Some of you will be taken away to remote regions, but God will have a work for you there.[14]

The time is soon coming when God's people, because of persecution, will be scattered in many countries. Those who have received an all-round education will have the advantage wherever they are.[15]

The reference to "an all-round education" in this last quotation is a hat tip to the Nashville Agricultural and Normal Institute, more commonly known as Madison College. In those early days, the curricula included a heavy emphasis on what we would today call "the trades." This is apparently not a bad idea, since the "advantage" Ellen White spoke of would likely extend to the kind of situations that might be covered in this thought provoking statement:

I have spent one-half hour talking with two of our brethren in regard to their disposing of their property and removing their families to the southern field for the purpose of doing missionary work, having a school, and preparing their children to work in various lines in the missionary work, such as cultivating farms, building humble homes, and teaching the people the art of building and the art of cultivating the soil. The time will come that all who live upon the earth will need to understand the cultivating of the land and the building of houses and varied kinds of business.[16]

Despite the small distraction on the education issue, the point is clear: God doesn't think it's unreasonable for any random believer to uproot himself from the midst of the saints and head off to work for the unreached. Of course, His plans are tailored to each person and situation, and this is not a one-size-fits-all prescription. But the odds are good that it *is* a one-size-fits-a-whole-bunch-of-folks-who-have-never-done-it-yet prescription.

So now, to re-cap the situation: reaching the end of your rope may well include the loss of employment, home, friends, family, public safety, the power to buy or sell, everything you ever considered to be your "roots," and the ability to get back to some part of the world where they speak a language you know.

From the world's point of view, you're bankrupt.

---

13. E.G. White, Letter to A.G. Daniells, June 28, 1901; Letter 61, 1901

14. E.G. White, "The Work in Mountain View," September 10, 1906; Manuscript 73, 1906

15. E.G. White, Letter to Brethren in Positions of Responsibility, January 6, 1908; Letter 32a, 1908

16. E.G. White, "Diary Fragments, January to December 1908," May 8, 1908; Manuscript 126, 1908
   It's the "all who live upon the earth" part that raises the most questions. That doesn't seem to be limited to church members. Despite a coming need to know those things, it's obvious that most people don't know them... which makes it really easy to imagine a fair amount of "societal unrest."

CHAPTER 33

Reorganization

WHAT comes after bankruptcy? What do you do when your best efforts have failed, and there's no way you will ever dig yourself out of the hole you're in? A fairly standard assessment is that the first important step is to get past the stage of denial.[1]

For the Christian, that's good news! That denial of our utter and total helplessness was never a good thing anyway. The idea that, if we try really hard, we just might succeed at managing our own lives, is what God has been targeting all along. After all, that's all Lucifer wanted to do from the very beginning.

This autonomy, this independence from God, seems quite reasonable within the Western world view, especially. Of course, other perspectives can be just as wrong by placing the individual under the control of a more "collectivist" leadership of sinful human beings. Just as the latter is related to the "earthliness" that must be "consumed," the former belongs to the "creature merit" camp of unrighteousness. Truth be told, we have all been infected with both diseases; it's just that we tend to display one or the other set of symptoms more strongly.

The end result of God's purification and proving process produces saints free of all this, and that's a great thing. But the question still on the table for us is not so much the end of the process, but how we even get the process started.

In other words, how does God reorganize church members past bankruptcy, get them off of dead center, explode the status quo, re-start the loud cry, and generally move things forward toward the "finishing of the work"? What does *that* look like?

---

1. But, in case you've forgotten, the process of financial restructuring that comes after bankruptcy is called "reorganization," hence the chapter title.

We've spoken of faithfulness in little things. We've documented the need for a revelation of God's character through a combined ministry of teaching, preaching, helping, and healing. We've considered the probability of "new light," especially in regard to our understanding of the law, since that's the foundation of the gospel, the atonement, the plan of redemption, the sanctuary message, and almost every other topic on which we've been given any reason to expect greater light. We've seen the devil's continued reliance on the as-yet un-refuted accusations of an arbitrary law or an unjust forgiveness ("Either one will be fine, thank you."), and noted Paul's assurance that God is both "just and the justifier of the one who has faith in Jesus."[2] And, of course, we've traced the whole rebellion back to the inexplicable and indefensible loss of that "very sim-ple" commodity of faith (aka, confidence in God).

All this accords well with Jesus' recommendation that we not neglect "the weightier matters of the law: justice and mercy and faith."[3] And, at the base of it all—the very base of "God's moral government"—we have the "distinction be-tween right and wrong." Sadly, confusion on this point has caused many to "rebel against God's law of government as arbitrary."[4]

All this has been true for a long while now, and yet we're still here. The search for the "magic bullet"[5] that will kick end time events into gear has been a lifelong quest for countless lay members and ministers of the church. Indeed, it is this that has been the driving force that has given rise to most every strange development within Adventism for the last century or more.

If you know the history of, say, the Adventist Reform Movement, or the Shepherd's Rod, or the Sanctuary Awakening Fellowship, or even the more re-cent crop of fringe claims like lunar sabbaths, and holy name, and feast keep-ing, and 2520, and anti-trinitarianism... they all gained traction with sincere but unguarded members through their claims that *this* new thing would "finish the work" and bring the second coming.

But none of them did. Many who bought into these ideas, and perhaps even more who simply watched from the sidelines, have realized that the promise was never fulfilled. Sadly, this kind of repeated disillusionment has led many to conclude that the "blessed hope" is just a lie....

The devil, of course, has been more than pleased with all this. Not only has he deluded many, but he has often managed to tie up vast amounts of the

---

2. Romans 3:26
3. Matthew 23:23
4. E.G. White, "The Moral Law," February 1, 1896; Manuscript 79, 1896. Quoted more fully on page 33.
5. Fittingly, this term stems originally from a medical setting, and is defined as "a substance or therapy capable of destroying pathogens (such as bacteria or cancer cells) or providing an effective remedy for a disease or condition without deleterious side effects." merriam-webster.com/dictionary/magic bullet

church's human, intellectual, and financial capital in the work of refuting the misguided claims and attacks from people who began by hoping to help the church complete her God-given mission.

This is not an arena into which any sane person walks lightly. At least as much timidity and trepidation as was shown by Elihu,[6] is appropriate for any small contribution to the discussion. The other thing that's needed is solid inspired support. Wild, weird claims may convince "some of the people, some of the time," but they might also land you in state prison as was the case with Wayne Bent (aka, Michael Travesser; aka, "Messiah") of the "Lord Our Righteousness" offshoot.[7]

The idea of "solid inspired support," is the best safeguard we could ask for, since none of the groups or theories mentioned has anything anywhere near a "clear mandate" from the Bible or Spirit of Prophecy. True believers in any of the above will differ with that assessment, of course, but they can't do so on the basis of a clear, straight-forward, commonly repeated, strongly emphasized, call for action from Inspiration. It's just not there for any of those ideas.

Instead, when we go looking for the clear intent of Bible and Spirit of Prophecy, the closest thing we find to a magic bullet is an amazingly simple idea—just start doing what God has called us to do. That will, of course, require a bit more explanation, but first let's set the stage. This is a good starter:

> Through faith man accepts the world's Redeemer as his Captain, and... in cooperation with God is to act an important part in revealing the glory of God to a world in the darkness of transgression. Unless man shall fully cooperate with Christ in the work of rescuing souls from evil, the plan of salvation can never be carried out.[8]

The operative phrase here is "fully cooperate." This will scare some, since it brings up thoughts of "perfection," which has gotten a lot of bad press in recent decades. But don't listen to those who try to tell you that nothing short of absolute divine perfection is acceptable to God.[9] "Full cooperation" with God is not so complex as they would lead you to believe:

---

6. Elihu was the youngest of Job's four "friends" who showed up to lecture him. Because of his youth, he kept his mouth shut for thirty-two chapters, letting his elders carry the standard of orthodox theology against Job's protest that he was innocent. When the other three ran out of arguments, Elihu stepped in to save the day. Unfortunately, his speech fills six chapters, but contributes nothing new to the discussion. The best we can say for the man is that when the Lord's "wrath [was] aroused against" Eliphaz, Bildad, and Zophar, and they were commanded to offer a sacrifice of seven bulls and seven rams, and get Job to pray for them—at least God chose to ignore Elihu.
7. wikipedia.org/wiki/Lord_Our_Righteousness_Church
8. *Signs of the Times*, October 8, 1894
9. This was the approach taken by Desmond Ford. His argument basically amounted to "since you can't be as perfect as God, there's not much sense in trying to obey at all." He wouldn't have phrased it quite like that, of course, but plenty of his followers got that message anyway.

He has shown you, O man, what is good; and what does the LORD require of you but to do justly, to love mercy, and to walk humbly with your God?[10]

And we may take courage from the Lord's assurance that He is more interested in our success than we are! Remember the bench press? Remember the spotter? You may not be pressing two hundred kilos, but that's no reason to give up.

The sinner may say, "I have sinned, and yet I did love Jesus. I am sorry that I have grieved the heart of infinite love. I have fallen many times, and yet He has reached out His merciful arm to save me.... I love Him, and will serve Him." The sinner's sin will not appear against him if he holds fast his faith and the beginning of his confidence firm unto the end.[11]

As comforting as the message of forgiveness is, and as much as we all need it, still the final, successful refutation of Satan's accusations takes more than love and happy sentiment. In fact, it takes a direct frontal attack on the most dangerous stronghold of Satan's principles.

No... that's not the Vatican. It's the hearts of God's own people, and the most daunting obstacle that delays or prevents professed believers from standing for God in time of crisis is a dislike for self-sacrifice.

Wait a minute... I've seen this before!

Indeed, you have... but here it is again:

Satan can present a counterfeit so closely resembling the truth that it deceives those who are willing to be deceived, who desire to shun the self-denial and sacrifice demanded by the truth.[12]

The devil knows all this, of course, so he designs every attack to leverage the natural tendencies of human hearts. But he's a better multi-tasker than any human being, so look how much he mixes together when he wants to kill you:

Wonderful scenes, with which Satan will be closely connected, will soon take place. God's Word declares that Satan will work miracles. He will make people sick and then will suddenly remove from them his satanic power. They will then be regarded as healed. These works of apparent healing will bring Seventh-day Adventists to the test. Many who have had great light will fail to walk in the light, because they have not become one with Christ. His instruction is not palatable to them.[13]

What all is going on here? Well, probably the first thing to notice is that this is aimed specifically at Adventists. And then (unlike Elijah on Mt. Carmel) we've got satanic miracles to deal with... and not just any miracles, these are miracles of healing.

---

10. Micah 6:8
11. E.G. White, Letter to My Ministering Brethren, December 19, 1897; Letter 21, 1897
12. *Great Controversy*, 528
13. E.G. White, Letter to Brethren Laboring in Battle Creek, November 1903; Letter 275, 1903

That's not fair! Health is supposed to be our bailiwick! That's why we've got medi-cal missionaries!

Oh, but it is fair. Just like in the book of Job, God is turning Satan loose, and he won't miss a single opportunity. Settle down, the worst is yet to come, because the outcome of "the test" we're talking about is largely (if not entirely) pre-determined by whether or not church members have "become one with Christ."

What does that even mean?

Look at the final sentence of that last quotation. Which instruction do you suppose might not be "palatable" to those who fail to walk in the light? What could possibly leave a bad taste in the mouth? The obvious lead candidate is the Lord's instruction about "the self-denial and sacrifice demanded by the truth." [14] And so, "willing to be deceived," they fall for the counterfeit.

Did anyone really think they would be safe from Satan's counterfeits just by knowing dead people don't talk, and Sabbath isn't Sunday, and Jesus' feet won't touch the ground? Seriously? There's a lot more to finishing the work of the gospel than knowing the answers to a three-point quiz.

> The truth for this time, the third angel's message, is to be proclaimed with a loud voice—meaning with increasing power—as we approach the great final test. This test must come to the churches in connection with the true medical missionary work, a work that has the great Physician to dictate and preside in all it comprehends.

Really?! Medical missionary work.... There's a test over that?

Yes, but don't panic. Your salvation doesn't depend on perfect hydrotherapy technique, or knowing whether dandelion leaf tea can block spike protein bonding to the ACE2 receptor, or how to make a good vegan lasagna. [15] The test of medical missionary work has a lot more to do with self-denial and self-sacri-fice than with those kinds of specifics.

> True sympathy between man and his fellow man is to be the sign distinguishing those who love and fear God from those who are unmindful of His law. How great the sympathy that Christ expressed in coming to this world to give His life a sacrifice for a dying world. His religion led to the doing of genuine medical missionary work. He was a healing power. "I will have mercy, and not sacrifice," He said. This is the test that the great Author of truth used to distinguish between true religion and false. [16]

---

14. There's been so much focus of the accusation that God can't forgive, that we might totally miss the other side of that issue. Consider, for a moment, that self-sacrifice often comes in the form of a willing-ness to forgive someone who has wronged us. It's easy for the human heart to see our own "righteous anger" as something too valuable to sacrifice. But, consider: "He who possesses the Spirit of Christ will never be weary of forgiving." *Review and Herald*, May 7, 1895

15. But, again, you can find all that on the internet for free, so why not get up to speed?

16. E.G. White, "A Neglected Work," September 24, 1903; Manuscript 117, 1903

But the final test is supposed to be the Sabbath... or maybe it's the three angels. Whatever. Anyway, I know it's not health reform!

Indeed. The closing sentences of that "great final test" paragraph agree:

> The present truth for this time comprises the messages, the third angel's message succeeding the first and second. The presentation of this message with all it embraces is our work.[17]

No doubt about it, the Sabbath is the very heart of that third message, it's just that it "embraces" a lot more than we sometimes recognize. The Sabbath is a sign. It stands for something! Much like circumcision in the Old Testament, it is the sign of the covenant of sanctification.

> Speak also to the children of Israel, saying: "Surely My Sabbaths you shall keep, for it is a sign between Me and you throughout your generations, that you may know that I am the LORD who sanctifies you."[18]

> Moreover I also gave them My Sabbaths, to be a sign between them and Me, that they might know that I am the LORD who sanctifies them.[19]

The sanctification promised in the covenant includes as it's greatest privilege, the Lord's promise to transform our characters to be like His character. Which is why self-denial and self-sacrifice (the character of God that Jesus came to show us) is such a central issue. This is also the hidden temptation in those "works of apparent healing." Real medical missionary work *always* requires the sacrifice of time and effort, and often enough of food, clothing, and money. You can see how a "no fuss, no muss" miraculous imitation of "medical missionary work" would be both impressive and tempting.

> Those who distrust God and do not have faith in Him, but go to forbidden sources for relief, are under the condemnation of God. They are on the enemy's ground. The question is asked, Is it because there is not a God in Israel that ye go to inquire of the gods of Ekron? If pain and suffering in one are alleviated by a physician who does not walk and work in the fear of God, then the enemy works through that one to seduce another to have faith in his superior ability, and he may be relieved, and still another may find freedom from difficulties. But is there not a power behind the scenes at work to extol the abilities of the man who is living in transgression of the law of God? Is not the enemy laying his concealed snare to set the minds upon a wrong train of reasoning? Is it not his work to form links with those who love not and fear not God, with those who are in rebellion against Him? Thus Satan shall have power over many through the influence of a few who are full of misconception and who have proclaimed the virtue done to them through forbidden channels.

---

17. E.G. White, Letter to Brother and Sister S.N. Haskell, August 13, 1900; Letter 121, 1900.
18. Exodus 31:13
19. Ezekiel 20:12

It is harder to endure suffering than to obey a commandment. Sufferings are greater trials than actions. "Do something," the enemy says, "even if it is not the best thing. Get relief some way." Thus he tempted Christ. "If thou be the Son of God, command that these stones be made bread." Matthew 4:3. But Christ resisted him.

Satan is now working as he will continue to work. He will work in the same line and in many ways until his power is taken away. Those who begin now to place themselves in the hands of physicians who neither love nor fear God will encourage others to do the same thing that they have done. Is not the enemy in all this to remove the defense from the people of God? The Lord will have His people thoroughly tried and tested. If we cannot follow God by living faith, if we repair to those who have no connection with God, we are placing ourselves where Satan is trying to have us go and where he can use us. Thus he obtains control of the mind, then makes impressions on the mind, and others receive the impressions imparted by the first one deceived.[20]

We may think self-denial is a hard deal; that it's the unpleasant price we have to pay so we can walk on streets of gold and ride giraffes (or dolphins) when we get to heaven, but it's actually the best deal in the whole universe!

If any one has been laboring for anything else except the Lord's glory, he will be disappointed in receiving a reward. The reception of the penny by the laborers [in the parable of the workers hired to work in the vineyard] represents the character that God will give to those who follow Him.[21]

So the Sabbath is the sign of the covenant, which includes sanctification, which re-makes our characters to include self-denial and self-sacrifice, which are developed and tested by helping others, which is what we call medical missionary work, which the Bible talks about in Isaiah 58. And that's why—

We need the clear light of the Sun of Righteousness to shine upon us. This light is given to those who keep holy the Lord's Sabbath: but we can not keep this day holy unless we serve the Lord in the manner brought to view in the scripture: "Is not this the fast that I have chosen, to loose the bands of wickedness, to undo the heavy burdens, and to let the oppressed go free; and that ye break every yoke? Is it not to deal thy bread to the hungry, and that thou bring the poor that are cast out to thy house? when thou seest the naked, that thou cover him? and that thou hide not thyself from thine own flesh?" This is the work that rests upon every soul who accepts the service of Christ.[22]

And so God uses medical missionary work in two ways: first, as a tool to reach people who need the gospel, and, second, as an exercise to strengthen the faith of Christians. How? By taking up so much time, or food, or money, or whatever, that they don't have enough for their own needs… but then God provides for them, too. Remember the promise?

20. E.G. White, "Diary: January 1890," January 26; Manuscript 38, 1890
21. *Review and Herald*, July 10, 1894
22. *General Conference Bulletin*, May 31, 1909

God is able to make all grace abound toward you, that you, always having all sufficiency in all things, may have an abundance for every good work.[23]

It doesn't say God will give us everything we want. Nor does it say that He will give us everything we think we need. It just says he will give us everything we need to do "good works." For us to see that happen, to realize it's really true, is a big deal. A really big deal.

Why? Because God is still getting His people ready for the sealing and the time of Jacob's trouble.[24] Even at this point, there's need for the spotter to keep believers from being crushed by weights beyond their strength. So the training continues:

If there is a determination to rid yourself from everything that would separate you from God, you must have a clearer eyesight than you have now. It is not to understand all about faith: you may understand that, that does not do. It is to carry into the practice the self-denial that Christ has presented to you, that you may go here and there and somewhere else and be telling souls what they shall do to be saved.[25]

God's focus is the one thing that matters—a faith that's not just a theory; a faith that's strong; a faith that "works by love and purifies the soul."

Remember that the exercise of faith is the one means of preserving it.[26]

When it reaches that stage that God's people walk with Him in such confidence as [Hebrews 11] describes, the message will be attended by the refreshing showers of the latter rain, and the earth will be speedily lighted by His glory.[27]

There is, in this time period, an unavoidable element of confusion and chaos. We don't know all the particulars, but in the inspired writings there is a clear expectation of political, economic, social, and spiritual agitation. Most of the population will be focused on the increasingly difficult task of simply staying alive. Remember, it is about this time that "most of the rising generation will be swept off by death."[28] Will such a mass destruction of the "rising generation" be intentional on the part of the "established" generation? I hope not....

Significantly, this idea is not a "one off" sort of thing:

---

23. 2 Corinthians 9:8

24. Incidentally, you may wonder about the "great final test" in connection with medical missionary work coming before the test of Jacob's trouble and the avenging enemy. There's probably a half dozen ways to "reconcile" that "contradiction," but the easiest is simply that the "great final test" is the last one prior to the close of probation, the one which separates the sheep from the goats.

   Thanks to God's perfect judgment of "true faith," the testing experiences after the close of probation really serve as demonstrations rather than as any determinant of "saved vs. lost."

25. E.G. White, "Sermon: Thoughts on 2 Peter 1," May 28, 1907; Manuscript 189, 1907

26. E.G. White, Letter to Brother Ashley, August 4, 1904; Letter 355, 1904

27. *Bible Training School*, November 1, 1911

28. E.G. White, Letter to Brother and Sister Van Horn, 1878; Letter 51a, 1878. Quoted more fully on page 7.

Ere long we are to be brought into strait and trying places, and the many children brought into the world will in mercy be taken away before the time of trouble comes.[29]

That this "depopulation event" will affect believers as well as non-believers is clear, but we are also given this promise:

The Lord has often instructed me that many little ones are to be laid away before the time of trouble. We shall see our children again. We shall meet them and know them in the heavenly courts. Put your trust in the Lord, and be not afraid.[30]

But not everyone's attention is totally absorbed with the pressing immediate need; there are still the "thinking men and women." They may be a small percentage, but they're there, and God needs someone to reach them.

The present is a time of overwhelming interest to all living. Rulers and statesmen, men who occupy positions of trust and authority, thinking men and women of all classes, have their attention fixed upon the events taking place about us. They are watching the strained, restless relations that exist among the nations. They observe the intensity that is taking possession of every earthly element, and they recognize that something great and decisive is about to take place—that the world is on the verge of a stupendous crisis.[31]

The point is, the world's going to be even more of a mess than it is now, and God needs medical missionaries who can and will navigate that mess for the *demonstration* of the gospel. Sure, it's unpleasant; of course it's dangerous, but this is the last chance to save souls that will ever happen in all the universe for all eternity![32] The worse the mess, the better the chance that someone will be looking for something better. God needs workers who will show up for the job, no matter what else goes by the wayside. And the first thing to go by the wayside at that time, is probably a salary.

That's why the Lord has been inviting His people to get a taste of sacrifice before the tough times come.

The Lord desires His children to act in that self-denying, self-sacrificing way that will bring to us the satisfaction of having performed our duty well because it was duty. The only begotten Son of God gave Himself to an ignominious death on the cross, and should we complain at the sacrifices we are called upon to make?

---

29. E.G. White, "The Temple of God Must be Holy," October 30, 1899; Manuscript 152, 1899

30. E.G. White, Letter to Sister A.H. Robinson, November 27, 1899; Letter 196, 1899

31. *Education*, 179

32. This detail is not lost on those watching! "Angels of God who know the value of the great sacrifice made by the Son of God are amazed at the wide-spread indifference of the church who have had the light of the everlasting gospel.... The consequences are so fearful, the responsibilities involved so deep and wide, gladly would heavenly angels resign their places to you that they might take your place and discharge your God-given trust." E.G. White, Letter to A.T. Robinson, November 7, 1892; Letter 45, 1892

During my wakeful hours through the night season, I have been pleading with the Lord to guard our brethren against the tendency to promise to go here or there on the stipulation that they are to have a little higher wage. If they go in a spirit of self-sacrifice, trusting in Him, the Lord will grant sustaining power to mind and character, and success will be the result.

In the future, our work is to be carried forward in self-denial and self-sacrifice even beyond that which we have seen in past years. God desires us to commit our souls to Him, that He may work through us in manifold ways. I feel intensely over these matters. Brethren, let us walk in meekness and lowliness of mind, and put before our associates an example of self-sacrifice. If we do our part in faith, God will open ways before us now undreamed of.[33]

God's multi-tasking continues, and this willingness to sacrifice that He's trying to develop in us does more than just make our own faith stronger; it's exactly the demonstration that the "thinking men and women" of the world need to see.

If you work, making the Lord your dependence, be assured that the Lord always helps the humble, meek, and lowly. But you need the working of the Holy Spirit upon your own heart and mind, in order to know how to do Christian help work.

Pray much for those you are trying to help. Let them see that your dependence is upon a higher power, and you will win souls.[34]

"You will win souls!" But the key to that success is sacrificing till you don't have enough left to make it on your own without "a higher power."

It makes sense, really: the best way to show actual dependence on God is to keep going when there's nothing else to depend on! This is *not* a new idea, it's just a new demonstration:

He gives power to the weak, and to those who have no might He increases strength.[35]

I can do all things through Christ who strengthens me.[36]

And He said to me, "My grace is sufficient for you, for My strength is made perfect in weakness." Therefore most gladly I will rather boast in my infirmities, that the power of Christ may rest upon me. Therefore I take pleasure in infirmities, in reproaches, in needs, in persecutions, in distresses, for Christ's sake. For when I am weak, then I am strong.[37]

It's easy to think of "dependence" in terms of money, but there is at least one other arena in which this can play out. Paul mentions "persecutions," something many of us have had little experience with so far. "Dependence on God" in the face of persecution is a special challenge, and it, too, can display the reality of a "higher power."

---

33. E.G. White, "Interview Regarding Wages for Physicians and Surgeons," December 4, 1913; Manuscript 12, 1913

34. E.G. White, Letter to Brother Merrill, March 25, 1898; Letter 24, 1898

35. Isaiah 40:29

36. Philippians 4:13

37. 2 Corinthians 12:9–10

The evil done to us by another must remain unresented, unavenged, and the enemy is to be loved, because God loved him when he was His enemy.[38]

There is a beauty and force in the truth that nothing can make so apparent as opposition and persecution. When this is revealed, many will be converted to the truth.[39]

If you refrain from retaliating when you are provoked by others, you will surprise them. And if repeatedly you preserve your dignity under provocation, they will realize that you are in connection with a higher power.[40]

Adventists, especially, have no reason to be surprised at the Lord's leading them to absolute dependency. The classic dream came to Ellen White in 1868, but somehow we tend to remember the wagons and the horses, the shoes and the socks, and even the cords... but forget that, in the end, there's nothing *but* the cord to hold us up.

As the path grew more narrow, we decided that we could no longer go with safety on horseback, and we left the horses and went on foot, in single file, one following in the footsteps of another. At this point small cords were let down from the top of the pure white wall;[41] these we eagerly grasped, to aid us in keeping our balance upon the path. As we traveled, the cord moved along with us. The path finally became so narrow that we concluded that we could travel more safely without our shoes, so we slipped them from our feet and went on some distance without them. Soon it was decided that we could travel more safely without our stockings; these were removed, and we journeyed on with bare feet.

We then thought of those who had not accustomed themselves to privations and hardships. Where were such now? They were not in the company. At every change some were left behind, and those only remained who had accustomed themselves to endure hardships. The privations of the way only made these more eager to press on to the end.

Our danger of falling from the pathway increased. We pressed close to the white wall, yet could not place our feet fully upon the path, for it was too narrow. We then suspended nearly our whole weight upon the cords, exclaiming: "We have hold from above! We have hold from above!"... Much of the time we were compelled to suspend our whole weight upon the cords, which increased in size as we progressed.

At length we came to a large chasm, at which our path ended. There was nothing now to guide the feet, nothing upon which to rest them. Our whole reliance must be upon the cords, which had increased in size until they were as large as our bodies. Here

38. E.G. White, Letter to Brother and Sister Holland, November 10, 1892; Letter 16, 1892

39. E.G. White, "Revelation," April 27, 1896; Manuscript 15, 1896

40. E.G. White, "Lessons From the Sermon on the Mount," August 16, 1909; Manuscript 55, 1909

41. I find it interesting that the cords are distinctly said to be "let down" only *after* the wagons, luggage, and horses had been abandoned. I'm inclined to believe this means that the earliest stages of the journey were made with little or no indication of divine support or even encouragement. On the face of it, the whole exercise looks like a pretty rash endeavor. We'll see more of this idea in Chapters 37 and 38.

we were for a time thrown into perplexity and distress. We inquired in fearful whispers: "To what is the cord attached?" My husband was just before me. Large drops of sweat were falling from his brow, the veins in his neck and temples were increased to double their usual size, and suppressed, agonizing groans came from his lips. The sweat was dropping from my face, and I felt such anguish as I had never felt before. A fearful struggle was before us. Should we fail here, all the difficulties of our journey had been experienced for nought....

Should the cord break, we must perish. Again, in whispered anguish, the words were breathed: "What holds the cord?" For a moment we hesitated to venture. Then we exclaimed: "Our only hope is to trust wholly to the cord. It has been our dependence all the difficult way. It will not fail us now." Still we were hesitating and distressed. The words were then spoken: "God holds the cord. We need not fear." These words were then repeated by those behind us, accompanied with: "He will not fail us now. He has brought us thus far in safety."

My husband then swung himself over the fearful abyss... [and] I immediately followed. And, oh, what a sense of relief and gratitude to God we felt! I heard voices raised in triumphant praise to God. I was happy, perfectly happy.[42]

---

42. *Testimonies*, vol. 2, 595–597

CHAPTER 34

On Your Mark...

PERHAPS the most fundamental need, going into a race, is some knowledge of the course. You need to know where the race is going to start—the "mark" referred to in our chapter title—which direction you're supposed to go, and where the finish line is.

Due to the devil's efforts (primarily), and our own moral immaturity (secondarily), the race before us is more like an obstacle course than the headline-grabbing 100-meter competition. It would be nice to have a simple, straight, level track... but we don't, so understanding the course is more involved than it might first appear.

Given that we're talking about the final, decisive movements before the close of probation, it makes sense that the "point of the spear" needs to be aimed at the heart of the devil's accusations, and the Spirit of Prophecy evidence identifies that direction as toward the large cities.

> The burden of our cities has rested so heavily upon me that it has sometimes seemed that I should die. The work in the cities is the essential work for this time, and is now to be taken hold of in faith. When the cities are worked as God would have them, the result will be the setting in operation of a mighty movement, such as we have not yet witnessed.[1]

Don't miss the details! "Essential" means this is needed, and *nothing else is going to take its place.* That doesn't mean every believer is going to be called to a large city. There will still be a need for missionaries to the jungle and the desert and little villages near the arctic circle. That's all good! Carry on! But don't neglect the cities, because they are the spark plug for that "mighty movement."

Is "city work" *that* important? Really?

---

1. *Review and Herald*, November 17, 1910

The simple proof is the well known story of Ellen White's interaction with Elder A.G. Daniells, the General Conference president. Arthur White tells it well in "Chap. 18 - America's Cities—The Great Unworked Field" of *The Later Elmshaven Years*. Here are excerpts:

> Ellen White had a continuing burden for the great cities of America, cities that had no presence, or only a limited one, of the Adventist witness. She had laid the matter before church leaders assembled in Washington on June 11, 1909, just a few days after the close of the General Conference session. It was a most earnest appeal that she hoped would lead to unprecedented action in evangelizing the cities. A few months later she wrote of the experience, "Some of you did not understand the message that I bore, and may never understand it."

> Then in September, 1909, *Testimonies for the Church,* volume 9, carried a section titled "The Work in the Cities," with a strong appeal to ministers and laymen. "Behold the cities," she urged, "and their need of the gospel."....

> In an address given January 28 at the Pacific Union Conference session held at Mountain View, Ellen White referred to a conversation with Elder I.H. Evans, treasurer of the General Conference, a few days before, in which she placed before him "the great necessity of our people giving much careful consideration to the work that must be done in the great cities." She bemoaned the fact that in spite of the "needs of these cities" that "have been brought to the attention of our people over and over again," there were very few who seemed "willing to move forward along the lines indicated by our heavenly Instructor."

> "Something has been done," she acknowledged, but she urged, "God requires of His people a far greater work than anything that has been done in years past."...

A focal point of this discussion at the time was Ellen White's call for Elder W.W. Prescott to leave his position as editor of the *Review* and take up full time city evangelism. Elder White's account continues:

> She commented:

> "In studying this problem let us remember that the Lord sees not as man sees. He looks upon the terrible neglect of the cities.... It is not at all in the order of God that these cities should be left unwarned, unworked. It is the result of man's devising. There is a world to be saved."

> The brethren were stunned by her earnestness, and it was hard for them to grasp the gravity of the neglect of the big cities. A few days later, she reported: "Some did not take willingly to the idea of losing Brother Prescott, but I spoke plainly to them."....

> On January 3, 1910, Elder Daniells reported:

> "We are doing the very best we know how to carry out the instruction she [Ellen White] has sent us. Of course you know that we have limitations both as respects men and money. The question of working the cities in the East and South is a big one. We cannot do one half of what there is to be done, and what we would like to do along this line...."

"I have already written you that we have appropriated $11,000 above our regular appropriations to the work in these cities.... You must help us to get laborers, or we shall not be able to do but little more than we are now doing."

But all this seemed so paltry to Ellen White, seeing as she did the tremendous challenge. How could she stir the leaders of the church? How could she awaken them?

In correspondence passing between her and the president of the General Conference, the needs of the cities and work in the cities were frequently mentioned. Regardless of reports of steps being taken, which always encouraged her, the Lord continued to keep before her the need of larger plans and more earnest work. Writing on February 11, 1910, W.C. White told Elder Daniells:

"Mother's burden for the cities continues. It is pressed upon her mind night after night that we are not doing what we ought.... This morning Mother said to me that while our brethren have done a little here and there, they have not instituted that thoroughly organized work which must be carried forward if we shall give our cities a proper warning."...

"What can we do?" Ellen White asked again and again. "What can we do to persuade our brethren to go into the cities and give the warning message now, right now!"...

Elder Daniells, endeavoring to do what he thought was the best he could, arranged for a five-day meeting on city evangelism to be held in New York City, July 7–11.

Shortly after laying these plans, he was on the Pacific Coast and went to Elmshaven to report this, which he felt sure would cheer Ellen White's heart. She refused to see him! The messenger of the Lord refused to see the president of the General Conference, sending word to the effect that when the president of the General Conference was ready to carry out the work that needed to be done, then she would talk with him.

Arthur White knew Elder Daniells personally, of course. And—to his credit —he was not an author prone toward the sensational side of his story. He frankly admits that he "would perhaps hesitate to open up these matters... had not Elder Daniells himself on several occasions related this experience." And so it is only when he quotes Elder Daniells that we get the famous sound bite from the episode:

Finally I received a message in which she said, "When the president of the General Conference is converted, he will know what to do with the messages God has sent him."[2]

Shortly after Daniells' aborted visit to Elmshaven, Ellen White wrote him and Prescott:

Neither Elder Prescott nor Elder Daniells is prepared to direct the work of the General Conference; for in some things they have dishonored the Lord God of Israel. High, pure devotion to God is required of men placed in your position. Such a man was Daniel, who in his statesmanship maintained a clean and holy purpose. Such characters are needed now.

---

2. Arthur L. White, *Ellen G. White*, vol.6, "The Later Elmshaven Years," 219–224

I am to tell you that neither of you is prepared to discern with clear eyesight that which is needed now. You are in danger of voicing sentiments that will be misleading. We are living in the last days of this earth's history, and we need to have a burning desire to copy the life of Christ. The great work remaining now to be done awaits the efforts of consecrated, loyal men.

Some things were clearly opened before me during the last meeting I attended in Washington, D.C. But those who ought to have been the first to recognize the movings of the Holy Spirit were not sufficiently impressed to receive the light and to act in harmony with it. The work in the cities has not yet been carried forward as it should be.

Had the president of the General Conference been thoroughly aroused, he might have seen the situation. But he has not understood the message that God has given. I can no longer hold my peace. I have a message to come to all the people. We must awaken out of sleep.[3]

None of this is to denigrate Daniells or Prescott! They were better men than I, and accomplished more for the Lord's work than I. (Sadly, that's a pretty low bar, but it might be true of you, too.) But it does a lot to authenticate city evangelism as an important issue, one which could conceivably set in motion a mighty movement.

If we're on our "mark" at the beginning of this race, this is where our attention is going to be.

But... how is city evangelism going to start a mighty movement? It seems like a great idea, but how—in any realistic manner—could we ever expect it do that?

Here's one part of that puzzle, at the very least!

You are to go into these cities and begin work in a humble way. If we had faithfully followed from the first the instruction regarding city work, means would have come in for us to establish in these places schools and small sanitariums where we could treat the sick, and preach the gospel, and educate the people in Bible truth. We would have had means to sustain all the enterprises for missionary work that we could carry forward.[4]

Just so no one will miss the point, "means" means *money!* City work is intended to be the financial driver of all our missionary work! Indeed, it's no secret that the wealth of the world is concentrated in the cities, and—

There is a large work to be done here in the city of Washington that still remains undone. There is a large work to be done in the South and in the East; and our General Conference is to do its share in supplying the men that shall go out into these fields. And as men and women are brought into the truth in the cities, the means will begin to come in. As surely as honest souls will be converted, their means will be consecrated to the Lord's service, and we shall see an increase of our resources.[5]

3. E.G. White, Letter to A.G. Daniells and W.W. Prescott, June 15, 1910; Letter 58, 1910
4. *General Conference Bulletin*, June 4, 1909

I am greatly encouraged to believe that many persons not of our faith will help considerably by their means. The light given me is that in many places, especially in the great cities of America, help will be given by such persons.[6]

As we do this work we shall find that means will flow into our treasuries, and we shall have funds with which to carry on a still broader and more far-reaching work. Souls who have wealth will be brought into the truth and will give of their means to advance the work of God. I have been instructed that there is much means in the cities that are unworked. God has interested people there. Go to them; teach them as Christ taught; give them the truth. They will accept it. And as surely as honest souls will be converted, their means will be consecrated to the Lord's service, and we shall see an increase of resources.[7]

This is in the *Testimonies for the Church!* This isn't some secret that's been kept from us. The key is to "teach them as Christ taught." We just haven't done it yet. And the result?

Do you not know that unless you carry the truth to the cities, there will be a drying up of means?[8]

Money is important, but let's move on. We've seen this next quotation before, but it should have more of a kick now.

As Lucifer sees that we are making efforts to work the cities as if we meant to give the last message, his wrath will be aroused, and he will employ every device in his power to hinder the work.[9]

If *he* knows cities are a big deal, maybe we should clue in, too.

All of which brings us to the point of recognizing that there have been efforts made in big cities. They haven't been *entirely* ignored, but still... it seems like something's missing. If only God would tell us what it is....

News flash! He has!

By other churches the Seventh-day Adventist faith is regarded as a delusion. How will they ever know otherwise unless a spiritual work is done by Seventh-day Adventists in cities and among all nations? Then the other sects will see that they have made a mistake.

The world must have the light. Medical missionary work gives opportunity to communicate light and to present our faith to those of all classes and all grades of society.[10]

In our large cities, the medical missionary work must go hand in hand with the gospel ministry. It will open doors for the entrance of truth.[11]

---

5. E.G. White, "Talk: Proclaiming the Third Angel's Message in Cities at Home and Abroad," June 11, 1909; Manuscript 53, 1909

6. *Review and Herald*, September 30, 1902.

7. *Testimonies*, vol. 9, 100

8. *General Conference Bulletin*, May 24, 1909

9. E.G. White, Letter to G.W. Amadon, September 12, 1910; Letter 74, 1910

10. E.G. White, Letter to G.A. Irwin, W.W. Prescott, E.J. Waggoner, and A.T. Jones, February 21, 1899; Letter 36, 1899

11. E.G. White, "The Need of Aggressive Effort," November 14, 1901; Manuscript 117, 1901

Henceforth medical missionary work is to be carried forward with an earnestness with which it has never yet been carried. This work is the door through which the truth is to find entrance to the large cities.[12]

It is the Lord's purpose that His method of healing without drugs[13] shall be brought into prominence in every large city through our medical institutions. God invests with holy dignity those who go forth farther and still farther, in every place to which it is possible to obtain entrance. Satan will make the work as difficult as possible, but divine power will attend all truehearted workers. Guided by our heavenly Father's hand, let us go forward, improving every opportunity to extend the work of God.[14]

Notice, *someone doesn't like this idea:* "Satan will make the work as difficult as possible." Of course he will. Which is exactly why church members should be signing up in droves to make it happen! In fact, a slight variant of that last quotation begins with "Let many now ask, 'Lord, what wilt Thou have me to do?' It is the Lord's purpose that...."[15]

Still, medical missionary work poses a bit of a problem to many minds, for the simple reason that most of us aren't doctors. That's important. If you're not a doctor, you shouldn't be prescribing meds, or even performing surgery. If that's a temptation, just don't.

But how does that conflict with medical missionary work?

Ministers seem to have more calls to engage in medical missionary work than anyone other than health care professionals, and that has too often been a source of confusion. They're not doctors... how are they supposed to do medical missionary work? One particular statement from Ellen White has long depicted a time when the work of the ministry will certainly change, but why and how has been a source of confusion:

I wish to tell you that soon there will be no work done in ministerial lines but medical missionary work.[16]

What is this? Some weird restriction imposed by the heavy hand of government when religious liberty is all but lost? I think not. I tend to see it as the time when the minsters as a class adopt Christ's own method of labor. This is when they get it right! Indeed, they are encouraged repeatedly in this direction:

Let our ministers, who have gained an experience in preaching the word, learn how to give simple treatments and then labor intelligently as medical missionary evangelists.[17]

---

12. *Testimonies*, vol. 9, 167
13. In this connection, please recall the promise, the condition, the failure, and the fallout of reference 11 on page 68. Those are important points which deserve careful thought, though none of them changes God's final goal
14. *Testimonies*, vol. 9, 168
15. E.G. White, Letter to Brother and Sister D.H. Kress, July 18, 1905; Letter 203, 1905
16. *Evangelism*, 523
17. *Testimonies*, vol. 9, 172

Those who labor in our conferences as ministers should become acquainted with the work of ministering to the sick. No minister should be proud that he is ignorant where he should be wise. Medical missionary work connects men with his fellow men and with God.[18]

Actually, the encouragement to use "simple treatments"—something we might expect doctors, nurses, and other health care professionals to do on a regular basis—is also presented to gospel workers,[19] "workers for Christ,"[20] canvassers,[21] students,[22] and "God's people"[23] in general. There are probably more categories that could be found, but that's enough to support a simple thesis: Medical missionary work *isn't* for you—unless you happen to be a health care professional, minister, gospel worker, canvasser, student, or church member.

Oh... you don't know how to use simple treatments? There's a fix for that:

By reading and studying the various books and periodicals on the subject of health, learn to give treatment to the sick, and thus to do better work for the Master.[24]

Which is good, since that means everyone can get reorganized to help set that mighty movement into motion.

Oh... it looks like God already knew that.

We have come to a time when every member of the church should take hold of medical missionary work.[25]

A final thought here, as applicable in city work as anywhere else, and perhaps even more so, given the cities' devotion to fads and fashion. There is, often, a timidity about being seen as "weird." This is tricky, because there are definitely many categories of behavior—things like "stubborn," or "illogical," or "disrespectful"—that are definite turnoffs for most people. We should avoid those. But "weird," as in just different, isn't necessarily in that category. And yet we shy away from being different, and try to be "normal." This is not all good:

Preserve your brain power. Do not let any one come in with their false representations of how you must be like the world, and act like the world, and dress like the world, if you would have any influence in the world. You have the least influence when you do that way.[26]

18. E.G. White, "Diary: 'I am not able to sleep...'," April 19, 1901; Manuscript 33, 1901
19. *Counsels on Health*, 389
20. *Medical Ministry*, 320
21. *Counsels on Health*, 463
22. *Review and Herald*, September 9, 1902
23. *Welfare Ministry*, 127
24. E.G. White, Letter to Iowa Conference, August 28, 1902; Letter 136, 1902. Seriously, there's so much of this available for free on the internet that—for the vast majority—the credibility of "I don't know how," is down to zero. The reality is something more akin to "I never thought it was important." It's not good to be judgmental, so please remember that this covers a whole range from "I never really heard about it before," to "I thought God was over-reacting."
25. *Testimonies*, vol. 7, 62
26. E.G. White, "Thoughts on Revelation 22," May 22, 1907; Manuscript 188, 1907

CHAPTER 35

Get Set...

TWO of Paul's illustrations stand out as particularly vivid: the racer and the warrior. We're using the former in the chapter titles just now, but it's hard to avoid mixing the imagery. The last chapter—"On Your Mark"—dealt primarily with understanding that the race doesn't even really get started till God's church faces up to the need for evangelism in the large cities. All the large cities. World-wide. This chapter continues the race motif with the obvious next phrase as a title, but the content might go better with a soldierly theme. Oh well....

For now, the reader may think of "getting set" as something akin to a pre-mission intelligence briefing. There's stuff to know before you wander into the middle of a battle! This real-world truth is sometimes dismissed as unnecessary. The alternative suggested is to "study the true; never look at the counterfeit." We are often told that this is how the best of counterfeit detectives work. It is not.[1]

Familiarity with the truth is obviously important, and a too-constant focus on the devil is an unhealthy influence, but the idea of completely ignoring the false is patently misguided. Comments like these are too common to dismiss:

> As we near the time when principalities and powers and spiritual wickedness in high places will be fully brought into the warfare against the truth, when Satan's deceptive power will be so great that, if it were possible, he would deceive the very elect, our discernment must be sharpened by divine enlightenment, that we may not be ignorant of Satan's devices.[2]

---

1. See uscurrency.gov/educational-materials/download-materials or bankofcanada.ca/banknotes/audience-specific-resources/retailers-2/ for instance.
2. *Review and Herald*, December 4, 1900

The resources of the enemy are various, and we must not move like blind men or be ignorant of Satan's devices.[3]

There is nothing that the great deceiver fears so much as that we shall become acquainted with his devices[4]

We need wisdom and a better knowledge of Satan's devices, that he may not, right before our eyes, accomplish the ruin of precious souls.[5]

It is important and essential that all of Christ's followers understand Satan's devices and with a united front meet his attacks and vanquish him. They need to make continual efforts to press together even if it be at some sacrifice to themselves.[6]

The evils which have existed in all ages will continue to exist till the close of probation. We need to understand the cause of these evils, and the modes of Satan's attacks, that we may be able to resist them.[7]

There is the greatest necessity for us to know something of the working of the powers of darkness and of the iniquity that abounds, that we may feel the importance of rising up to the emergency.[8]

Satan's pretended homage to God has continued ever since his fall, and the eyes of all who love God must be kept open to discern the deception with which he, through human agencies, instills his evil principles into other minds.[9]

If we could always remember that Satan comes to us in disguise, his motives concealed, and he himself clad in garments of light, we would be on our guard, and would not fall a prey to his devices.... We should study the nature, character, and extent of this spiritual wickedness in high places, lest we become the dupes of the powers of darkness.[10]

Those who do not realize their danger because they do not watch, will pay, with the loss of their souls, the penalty of their presumption and their willful ignorance of Satan's devices.[11]

Surely that should be enough. Still, unless things have improved since 1909, the message has been a hard one to get across to those who need it:

There are few among those who claim to be Christians who realize how deceptive are the wiles of Satan, and are prepared to oppose them firmly.[12]

Despite that rather somber assessment, let's look at the terrain of this race, and the circumstances under which it is to be run. Some of these issues play out

---

3. E.G. White, "Counsel to Church Members in Switzerland," 1886; Manuscript 37, 1886

4. *Great Controversy*, 516

5. E.G. White, Letter to D.T. Bourdeau, 1887; Letter 39, 1887

6. *Testimonies*, vol. 3, 434

7. E.G. White, Letter to Brother and Sister Garmire, August 12, 1890; Letter 12, 1890

8. E.G. White, "Sermon: Morning Talk," October 22, 1894; Manuscript 42, 1894

9. E.G. White, Letter to Burr Corliss, April 14, 1896; Letter 15a, 1896

10. *Signs of the Times*, August 5, 1886

11. *Review and Herald*, April 25, 1907

12. E.G. White, Letter to D.A. Parsons, March 28, 1909; Letter 62, 1909

in both the church and the world, and some are unique to the church. God is trying to save souls in both camps, so it's no surprise to see an overlap of method.

We met the "thinking men and women" back on page 202, and we were told that they can be found in "all classes." Someone needs to help them. Fortunately, God is—though it's hard to see, sometimes. For starters, we should note the silver lining in all the worldly chaos. It does, at least, help this process along:

> Everything that causes us to see the weakness of humanity is in the Lord's purpose to help us to look to Him, and in no case put trust in man, or make flesh our arm.[13]

The reader will recognize this as just another on-going step in the process of uprooting the "earthliness" in our hearts. Since the problem persists through the close of probation,[14] it's no surprise that traces of it will crop up all along the way till it's eradicated. But that's hard to wrap our minds around, because we've grown up with a sense of respect for at least certain elements of worldly authority. To recognize that the Spirit of God is being withdrawn from even one's friendly next door neighbor, or the local police officer who has always been helpful and decent... that's hard.

And if it's hard for church members, imagine how scary it must be for someone raised as an atheist, say, who really has no hope for society beyond what humans can do. What are they supposed to think when they see this play out:

> Rulers of Kingdoms, presidents, nobles who are in high places, if they range under the banner of the prince of darkness, will learn their orders from him who created the rebellion in heaven, and who claims as his territory the fallen world. He does not bow in allegiance to the law of Jehovah, and all who are in rebellion are under his generalship, and will use their talent to maintain and strengthen the kingdoms of the prince of this world, and will practice evil according to the circumstances that will occur.[15]

If we had to use a political term to describe the Lord's approach to this worldly authority issue, it would probably be "populist" (though every political term is going to misrepresent God's government, which is reason enough for inspiration to go with "peculiar" instead). It seems that the "elite" society of earth doesn't impress Him much.

> Christ discarded kings and priests and rulers. From the men whom the world had favored, the men who had found their own enjoyment in fulsome flattery, He turned with gladness to a peculiar people, and showed which class was "blessed." That was a representation of what will be enacted at the judgment.[16]

13. E.G. White, Letter to P.B.W. Wessels, March 17, 1893; Letter 63, 1893

14. See discussion starting on page 131.

15. E.G. White, "Christ Our Strength," 1893; Manuscript 104, 1893

16. E.G. White, "The Judgment," December 16, 1897; Manuscript 137, 1897. Ellen White respected proper earthly authority, yet even in her day there was cause enough to regard *some* aspects with concern: "Nothing is more evidence of immoral character existing in our day than the majority of worldly kings, nobles, rulers, and legislators." E.G. White, "Diary: Corruption of the Cities and Unfaithful Shepherds,"

It's easy to *say* that there's nothing you can trust in the world, but most of us are actually strongly inclined (*conditioned?*) to believe what we're told, as long as we can be convinced that everybody else believes it. "The media," of course, excels at precisely that task of public persuasion, especially when the combination of corruption and record-breaking financial incentives is used to entice them. But God has a plan to disrupt that kind of mass control, and even expose it in the process. No surprise, He will use just the right ones to do the exposing! (Hint: *It's not us.*)

> In many ways Satan is revealing that he rules the world. He is influencing the hearts of men and corrupting their minds. Men in high places are giving evidence that their thoughts are evil continually. Many are seeking after riches and scruple not to add to their wealth through fraudulent transactions. The Lord is permitting these men to expose one another in their evil deeds. Some of their iniquitous practices are being laid open before the world, that thinking men who still have a desire in their hearts to be honest and just with their fellowmen may understand why God is beginning to send His judgments on the earth.[17]

Have you heard complaints about the "negativity" or "partisanship" of the news lately? "Thinking men and women" have been concerned with that for years. God hasn't given up on them, and His plan is working!

> The record of dishonesty and conniving and vileness that has resulted from the investigation into the cases of men holding official positions, and which has been opened before all through the courts, should certainly open blind eyes and lead us to inquire, Whom can we trust? Where can we find men of honor? As these evils are being revealed, even the worldling can see that corruption is filling the earth as it did in the time of Noah, and for which God had then to destroy the world by a flood. But instead of calling these men to repentance, the revelations are turning the office holders one against another, and they are exposing to the world every species of crime in the lives of judges and jurors and senators alike. Satan is at work to corrupt with his deceiving policies the rulers and the people. This work will be carried on from city to city until the guilt of the whole world will be manifest, and it will be plainly seen why God permits His judgments to fall on the earth. They will come because of the pride of heart, the falsehood, the dishonesty, the profanity that is manifest....
>
> God has designed that these revelations should be made, that those who read the accounts of them may understand that men's sins have reached unto heaven, and that the time is surely near when God will blot out iniquity from the earth.[18]

The only downside to using one corrupt "highly placed" sinner to expose another corrupt "highly placed" sinner is that there's no reason to expect that ei-

---

September 2, 1902; Manuscript 233, 1902

17. *Testimonies to Ministers*, 457

18. E.G. White, Letter to J.E. and Emma White, March 10, 1907; Letter 90, 1907

ther side—any side—will be giving the world a revelation of God's character. At best you'll get a perverted version of His justice urged against the "other side"—*"prosecute those criminals!"*—and a perverted version of His mercy for the *preferred* criminals! Ellen White, it turns out, had little hope in worldly "anti-corruption" efforts.

> ↘ Not one-hundredth part of the corruptions that exist are being made plain to the world. Little of the cruelty that is carried on is known. But some of the iniquity is being revealed that men may understand why God is sending His judgments on the earth.[19]

To accurately portray God's character is the work of the church, but with half of the virgins being foolish, or "not one in twenty of those who have a good standing with Seventh-day Adventists... living out the self-sacrificing principles of the word of God,"[20] or whatever the current percentages might actually be at the time,[21] you would be naive to believe in an Adventist version of infallibility. The cautions God has given in the past still apply!

If the warning "that we should no longer be children, tossed to and fro and carried about with every wind of doctrine, by the trickery of men, in the cunning craftiness of deceitful plotting,"[22] is important today, surely it will be more so then!

> It is written, "Prove all things: hold fast that which is good." Assumption is not worth a straw, for it can be made to favor one's own selfish ideas. To believe every spirit is to reach the place where we believe that nothing is trustworthy.[23]

> If we are to bear a part in this work to its close, we must recognize the fact that there are good things to come to the people of God in a way that we had not discerned and that there will be resistance from the very ones we least expected to engage in such a work.[24]

"Resistance" is an interesting word. Ellen White didn't say "apostasy" or "heresy." She specified "resistance." Which do you suppose is easier to identify? That question takes on importance when you see that the ability to distinguish really basic matters suffers under Satan's influence.

---

19. E.G. White, "In the Last Days," October 11, 1907; Manuscript 117, 1907

20. *Testimonies*, vol. 1, 632

21. Fortunately, we are dismissed from any responsibility for sorting out the wheat and tares, or the wise and foolish: "The parable of the ten virgins was given by Christ Himself, and every specification should be carefully studied. A time will come when the door will be shut. We are represented either by the wise or the foolish virgins. We cannot now distinguish, nor have we authority to say who are wise and who foolish. There are those who hold the truth in unrighteousness, and these appear just like the wise." E.G. White, "The Parable of the Ten Virgins," July 22, 1898; Manuscript 92a, 1898

22. Ephesians 4:14

23. E.G. White, Letter to Brother and Sister Hawkins, April 6, 1897; Letter 65, 1897

24. E.G. White, Letter to O.A. Olsen, September 1, 1892; Letter 19d, 1892

Those who have been long in the truth, yet who cannot distinguish between the pure principles of righteousness and the principles of evil, whose understanding in regard to justice, mercy, and the love of God is beclouded, should be relieved of responsibilities.[25]

Fortunately, God has a plan that deals with every aspect of the problem. The best part: if His people are wise enough to stay out of the troubles roiling the world, His plan will let them "keep their powder dry" to use only where it matters. But first He has to address the church's confused sense of mission, so—

God [will] sift His people; the chaff will be separated from the wheat. The tares are already binding in bundles to burn. There is to be, as we near the end, a revealing of true character. Those who have not the truth in the heart will reveal this, because they will not be sanctified through the truth.[26]

Before the great trouble shall come upon the world such as has never been since there was a nation, those who have faltered and who would ignorantly lead in unsafe paths will reveal this before the real vital test, the last proving, comes, so that whatsoever they may say will not be regarded as voicing the True Shepherd.... We have no time to lose in walking through clouds of doubt and uncertainty because of uncertain voices.[27]

One of the most critical areas in which "uncertain voices" have created "clouds of doubt and uncertainty" has been the minimizing of faith in the Spirit of Prophecy. This, too, will be addressed by the Lord, though this particular statement is worded ambiguously, so it's not clear if this will happen before the close of probation, or only in the final judgment. We can pray about this one.

Those who have been seeking to undermine the confidence of our people in the testimonies that God has given for their benefit, and in the leadings of Providence in our work, will some day be revealed as having acted a part similar to that acted by Judas....

There are today, among the professed people of God, some who are walking in the same path as did Judas. Unless they are converted, they will some day be numbered among the open enemies of God's work for this time.[28]

The question of which authority/authorities we acknowledge is central to the great controversy of the last days. In essence, the whole issue of the mark of the beast versus the seal of God is a question of authority. The world says, "You worship on Sunday or we'll kill you." And God says, "You worship on Sunday and I'll burn you." It's a choice every man, woman, and child will face one day.

The key to remember is that the higher authority can protect you from all lower authorities. Think: General vs. Sergeant. Which officer do you want standing next to you?

25. E.G. White, "Help to be Given to Our Schools," January 29, 1900; Manuscript 10, 1900
26. E.G. White, Letter to Brethren and Sisters in California, April 13, 1887; Letter 92, 1887
27. E.G. White, Letter to S.N. Haskell, August 22, 1892; Letter 13, 1892
28. E.G. White, Letter to J.A. Burden, November 25, 1908; Letter 332, 1908

And it shall come to pass in that day that the remnant of Israel, and such as have escaped of the house of Jacob, will never again depend on him who defeated them, but will depend on the LORD, the Holy One of Israel, in truth.[29]

Serious stuff... but it's a case of working through the pain to get to the gain. Eventually, things start to look up.

When the Sunday question is legislated to become a law, there will not be so great a danger of taking steps that are not of a character to receive the sanction of heaven, ... for the reason that the Lord gives light and knowledge just when it is most needed.[30]

That last quotation is a jump ahead, just to show that there's hope in the end, but the time period we're talking about is before the Sunday law. The next detail we need to look at is an important milepost in the progression of events. We'll start with a key specification given in the "mighty movement" statement that we saw back on page 206. Notice how the paragraph ends:

When the cities are worked as God would have them, the result will be the setting in operation of a mighty movement, such as we have not yet witnessed. May the Lord give wisdom to our brethren, that they may know how to carry forward the work in harmony with His will. With mighty power the cry is to be sounded in our large centers of population, "Behold, the Bridegroom cometh; go ye out to meet him."[31]

For many years I thought of that "mighty movement" as the loud cry, and it's certainly close to it. But there's an odd little twist to those final two sentences that adds detail that is both interesting and important. And it escaped my attention for decades.

The cause of my blindness was Adventist history! The problem is that the Bible verse she quotes is what Adventists know as the "midnight cry," and it was *"fulfilled"* back in 1844. Somehow I just subconsciously edited out any application of that parable to a future time. And yet Ellen White does it over and over again:

I am often referred to the parable of the ten virgins, five of whom were wise, and five foolish. This parable has been and will be fulfilled to the very letter, for it has a special application to this time, and, like the third angel's message, has been fulfilled and will continue to be present truth till the close of time.[32]

Prepare for the call, "Behold the Bridegroom cometh! Go ye out to meet Him."[33]

My mind was carried to the future, when the signal will be given. "Behold, the Bridegroom cometh; go ye out to meet him."[34]

---

29. Isaiah 10:20
30. E.G. White, "Counsel Regarding Matters Discussed at the 1889 General Conference," November 4, 1889; Manuscript 6, 1889
31. *Review and Herald*, November 17, 1910
32. *Review and Herald*, August 19, 1890
33. E.G. White, Letter to Brother and Sister R.A. Hart, March 1903; Letter 160, 1903
34. *Review and Herald*, February 11, 1896

The ten virgins are watching in the evening of this earth's history. All claim to be Christians. All have a call, a name, a lamp, and all claim to be doing God service. All apparently watch for his appearing. But five are wanting.[35]

Let no one put off the day of preparation, lest the call be made, "Go forth to meet the Bridegroom," and you be found as were the foolish virgins, with no oil in your vessels with your lamps.[36]

When the call shall come, "Behold, the Bridegroom cometh; go ye out to meet him," those who have not received the holy oil, who have not cherished the grace of Christ in their hearts, will find, like the foolish virgins, that they are not ready to meet their Lord.[37]

We cannot be ready to meet the Lord by waking up at the last minute, when the cry is heard, "Behold, the Bridegroom cometh," gathering up our lamps, from which the oil has burned away, and thinking then to have them replenished.[38]

Lest we lose sight of the connection of this future fulfillment and the medical missionary work to be done in the large cities, here are another couple examples that tie these ideas together:

Our cities are to be worked. To devote our efforts to other worthy enterprises, and leave unworked our cities, in which are large numbers of all nationalities, is not wise.... With mighty power the cry is again to be sounded in our large centers of population, "Behold the Bridegroom cometh; go ye out to meet Him."[39]

Medical missionaries are to go forth; workers in every line are to proclaim, "Behold, the Bridegroom cometh; go ye out to meet him."[40]

Each of these quotations places "the call" in the future, but that chronological factor seems almost incidental to Ellen White. Her emphasis is on the division between the wise and the foolish virgins. The risk of being found with no oil to meet the crisis is portrayed in a very solemn tone.

I seemed to have my mind carried to the future when the signal will be given announcing, "Behold, the Bridegroom cometh; go ye out to meet him." [Matt. 25:6.] But some had delayed to obtain the oil to replenish their lamps and too late they find that character, which is represented by the oil, is not transferable.[41]

Those who hide their light will soon lose all power to let it shine. They are represented by the foolish virgins; and when the crisis comes, and the last call is made, "Behold, the Bridegroom cometh; go ye out to meet him," they will find that while they have been mingling with the world, their light has gone out. They did not continue to

35. *Review and Herald*, October 31, 1899
36. *Youth's Instructor*, January 30, 1896
37. *Review and Herald*, February 3, 1903
38. *Signs of the Times*, August 6, 1894
39. E.G. White, "A Call to the Watchmen," August 8, 1910; Manuscript 13, 1910
40. *Review and Herald*, September 28, 1911
41. E.G. White, "Diary: November–December, 1895," November 30, 1895; Manuscript 61b, 1895

provide themselves with the oil of grace. The peace-and-safety cry hushed them to slumber, and made them careless in regard to their light. The ease-loving, world-loving professed Christians can not go in with the wise virgins to the marriage feast. When they solicit entrance, saying, "Lord, Lord, open unto us," the reply is made, "Verily I say unto you, I know you not.[42]

More than this, some of the "Bridegroom" quotations make it clear that, for the foolish virgins, this is the end of the line.

In reading this parable one cannot but pity the foolish virgins, and ask the question, Why is it that the wise did not divide their supply of oil? But as we make the spiritual application of the parable, we can see the reason. It is not possible for those who have faith and grace to divide their supply with those who have not.[43]

By failing to lift the cross you lose much in this life and everything in the future life. If you have decided to be towed along, as the ship is towed by the hardworking tug, you will find yourself in the condition of the foolish virgins, without oil in your vessel with your lamp. Prayers and exhortation, all the good advice in the world, cannot save you.[44]

The parable of the ten virgins is given to us that we may understand that there is an hour when the gates are closed.[45]

When the foolish virgins reached the banqueting hall, they received an unexpected denial. The master of the feast declared, "I know you not." They were left standing without, in the empty street, in the blackness of the night.[46]

All this takes on an especially ominous tone for Adventists because of statements like these:

But I must tell you that the church in her present state is represented by the ten virgins, five of whom were wise, and five foolish.[47] The foolish had lamps, but had no oil in their vessels with their lamps. Those represented by this class will die greater sinners than they were before they professed to believe the truth, because when they knew God, they worshiped Him not as God. Self, self, self, in all its perverted attributes, hardened the heart and closed the door against Jesus Christ, that He should not enter and abide with them.[48]

This is not a representation of open sinners, but of those who profess Christ, of the members of the church. They have no oil in their vessels with which to replenish their lamps....

42. *Review and Herald*, August 23, 1898
43. *Review and Herald*, September 17, 1895
44. E.G. White, Letter to Henry Wessels, April 5, 1899: Letter 66, 1899
45. E.G. White, Letter to S.N. Haskell, November 6, 1895; Letter 25, 1895
46. E.G. White, Letter to A.G. Daniells and W.W. Prescott, July 30, 1903; Letter 161, 1903
47. This 50/50 split is actually quite positive as compared to her frequent use of "not one in twenty" (e.g., *Testimonies*, vol. 1, 496, 505, 632; *General Conference Bulletin*, July 1, 1900) and "not one in one hundred" (e.g., *Testimonies*, vol. 8, 147; *Review and Herald*, September 3, 1889; Letter 121, 1898).
48. E.G. White, "The Lack of Spirituality in Our Churches," April 9, 1898; Manuscript 49, 1898

Great harm can be done by the open sinner who makes no profession of loving God and keeping His commandments. But this is not the class the parable represents. It represents those who claim to be children of God, but who do not practice it. These have not a burden for souls. They do not deny self. They do not lift the cross of Christ. They are seeking to have an enjoyable time with the world while claiming to be Christians.[49]

It's one thing to read about the evils and dangers of being unprepared, but even more arresting is Ellen White's depiction of the immediate change in the relationship between those who pass this test and those who do not.

The oil of grace cannot be lent by one to another, neither have the foolish virgins time to buy oil for themselves. The righteous are those who keep the commandments of God, and they will be forever separated from the disobedient and unrighteous who trampled underfoot the law of God. The pure ore and the dross will no longer commingle.[50]

"Behold, the Bridegroom cometh; go ye out to meet Him." Matthew 25:6. Lose no time now in rising and trimming your lamps. Lose no time in seeking perfect unity with one another. We must expect difficulties. Trials will come.[51]

Unity? Of course, that's what Jesus prayed for in John 17. But this is a selective unity, since the lines are drawn and there is to be no more "commingling" between pure ore and dross. We came to this point at the time of the alpha:

It is time that we stood upon a united platform. But we cannot unite with Dr. Kellogg until he stands where he can be a safe leader of the flock of God. Until he stands in this position, we have no right to sustain him.[52]

There can be no unity between truth and error. We can unite with those who have been led into deception only when they are converted.[53]

At some point, God's people will need to recognize that that ship has sailed (or, maybe, sunk).

This is no time for the messengers of God to stop to prop up those who know the truth, and who have every advantage. Let them go on to lift the standard and give the warning, "Behold, the Bridegroom cometh! Go ye out to meet him."[54]

And remember: this "close of probation verbiage" is all linked to the mighty movement that starts when the cities are worked as they should be. "Working the cities" is an obvious reference to evangelism. Souls are being saved, and money is coming into God's cause to be reinvested in more evangelism. That's got the earmarks of a "mighty movement." The church is on a roll!

49. E.G. White, "The Ten Virgins," October 19, 1898; Manuscript 144, 1898
50. *Testimonies to Ministers*, 235
51. *Testimonies*, vol. 8, 212
52. E.G. White, "Talk: The Foundation of Our Faith," May 18, 1904; Manuscript 46, 1904
53. E.G. White, Letter to J.E. White, March 15, 1905; Letter 121, 1905
54. E.G. White, Letter to Brother and Sister O.A. Olsen, September 1, 1895; Letter 64a, 1895

Well, maybe *half* the church. As in, ten virgins, five of whom have found themselves with no oil. And for them, the door is effectively shut long before they get there and knock. I'm no prophet, so you're entitled to your own opinion, but the closest thing I can find in the Spirit of Prophecy to explain all this, is this:

> Many who have known the truth have corrupted their way before God and departed from the faith. The broken ranks will be filled up by those represented by Christ as coming in at the eleventh hour. The time of God's destructive judgments is the time of mercy for those who have no opportunity to learn what is truth. Tenderly will the Lord look upon them. His heart of mercy is touched; His hand is still stretched out to save, while the door is closed to those who would not enter. Large numbers will be admitted who in these last days hear the truth for the first time.[55]

This statement has long been spoken of as the close of probation for Adventists, but in the setting of a future fulfillment of the parable of the ten virgins coming *before* the "loud cry" ever hits full volume, it appears more sudden and unexpected. Ellen White doesn't provide many details on this matter, so humility is in order lest we assert too strongly that which we can't prove to be true. This message of the Bridegroom's coming[56] isn't necessarily the same as the loud cry; and the loud cry isn't necessarily at exactly the same time as the latter rain... but there's enough evidence to say they are closely interrelated, and perhaps "sudden" is a good adjective for all of them.

> You are getting the coming of the Lord too far off. I saw the latter rain was coming as suddenly as the midnight cry, and with ten times the power.[57]

A note of caution just here. Do not think, "I'll wait until I see whole cities being destroyed, and then I'll really get serious about my religion." That would almost certainly be a fatal mistake. Why? Because that timing is backwards, and misses the window of opportunity. The wise virgins "understand the plan of the battle," and are working *with* God, not standing around watching to see what happens. And God has a very clear order of events:

---

55. E.G. White, Letter to Brother and Sister G.B. Starr, June 3, 1903; Letter 103, 1903. It's worth noting that the "eleventh hour" reference is drawn from yet another parable, the workers in the vineyard.

56. Interestingly, though Ellen White repeatedly speaks of a future application of this parable, she never uses the "midnight cry" label for future events. Perhaps as a means of maintaining a clear distinction between the two episodes, she exclusively uses "midnight cry" to apply to the events of 1844.

57. E.G. White, "Extract Regarding the Latter Rain," September 1852; Manuscript 4, 1852. Incidentally, the midnight cry of 1844 can be traced to a number of letters written by S.S. Snow and published in Millerite journals in the first half of 1844. His idea that the 2300 days would not end until the fall of 1844 was correct, but attracted little attention. That changed suddenly on the fifteenth of August, when he spoke at a Millerite camp meeting in Exeter, New Hampshire. From that date on, Snow's interpretation with its October 22 date for the end of the prophecy spread quickly and became the almost universally accepted view. That all happened in sixty-eight days.

The most solemn warning and the most awful threatening ever addressed to mortals is that contained in the third angel's message. The sin that calls down the wrath of God unmixed with mercy must be of the most heinous character. Is the world to be left in darkness as to the nature of this sin? Most assuredly not. God does not deal thus with His creatures. His wrath is never visited upon sins of ignorance. Before His judgments are brought upon the earth, the light in regard to this sin must be presented to the world, that man may know why these judgments are to be inflicted, and may have opportunity to escape them.[58]

The whole earth is to be lightened with the glory of the Lord as the waters cover the channels of the great deep. Prophecies are being fulfilled, and stormy times are before us. Old controversies which have apparently been hushed for a long time will be revived, and new controversies will spring up; new and old will commingle, and this will take place right early. The angels are holding the four winds, that they shall not blow, until the specified work of warning is given to the world; but the storm is gathering, the clouds are loading, ready to burst upon the world, and to many it will be as a thief in the night.[59]

The practical implication of this? The wise virgins will be swinging into action *before* life becomes completely unbearable on a widespread basis. They will not have the luxury of pointing to that level of chaos as a reason for their course of action.[60] In other words, they will look like fools.

But looks are often deceiving, and though the fate of the foolish virgins is effectively decided when the announcement is made, they will only recognize it when the door is shut, and they are "left standing without, in the empty street, in the blackness of the night."[61]

---

58. *Signs of the Times*, November 1, 1899
59. E.G. White, "The Crisis Imminent," February 18, 1892; Manuscript 27, 1892
60. The Spirit of Prophecy writings paint two quite distinct pictures of probation's close. In one set of statements, probation closes when life seems "normal," in a time of "peace and safety" (see *Desire of Ages*, 635, and *Great Controversy*, 338, for example), while the other set depicts a world in the grip of "God's destructive judgments." If "judgment begins at the house of God," it would appear that the time of decision for the church is the former, while those who "hear the truth for the first time" at the eleventh hour will be hurried along by the "ministry of controversy."
61. E.G. White, Letter to A.G. Daniells and W.W. Prescott, July 30, 1903; Letter 161, 1903. Quoted more fully on page 221.

The Eschatological Pivot Point—A Review

The closing of probation is a process that transpires over a period of time, not a "time's up" buzzer going off like the end of a basketball game. In it's opening phase, it occurs in what might appear to be "normal times":

> When life is going on in its unvarying round; when men are absorbed in pleasure, in business, in traffic, in money-making; when religious leaders are magnifying the world's progress and enlightenment, and the people are lulled in a false security—then, as the midnight thief steals within the unguarded dwelling, so shall sudden destruction come upon the careless and ungodly, "and they shall not escape."[62]

The trigger that most visibly marks the beginning of this process is God's final appeal to His people to join in the work of announcing the coming of the Bridegroom. Note the all-important qualifier in the first sentence, and remember that a failure to respond now, is fatal:

> When the cities are worked as God would have them, the result will be the setting in operation of a mighty movement, such as we have not yet witnessed. May the Lord give wisdom to our brethren, that they may know how to carry forward the work in harmony with His will. With mighty power the cry is to be sounded in our large centers of population, "Behold, the Bridegroom cometh; go ye out to meet him."[63]

When that cry begins to build, it shakes both the church[64] and the cities of the world. The virgins all awake, but some have oil (the Christ-like character produced through the ministry of the Spirit) which leads them to join in carrying the call to the world, and some do not. Those with no oil do not realize it yet, but there is nothing that can supply their lack. Try as they might, there is no escaping the eventual verdict, "Assuredly, I say to you, I do not know you."

But what does it mean to work the cities as God would have them?

> Henceforth medical missionary work is to be carried forward with an earnestness with which it has never yet been carried. This work is the door through which the truth is to find entrance to the large cities.[65]

Of course, doing things according to God's plan will not be well received in certain circles!

---

62. *Great Controversy*, 38

63. *Review and Herald*, November 17, 1910

64. "I asked the meaning of the shaking I had seen, and was shown that it would be caused by the straight testimony called forth by the counsel of the True Witness to the Laodiceans. This will have its effect upon the heart of the receiver, and will lead him to exalt the standard and pour forth the straight truth. Some will not bear this straight testimony. They will rise up against it, and this will cause a shaking among God's people." *Testimonies*, vol. 1, 181

65. *Testimonies*, vol. 9, 167

As Lucifer sees that we are making efforts to work the cities as if we meant to give the last message, his wrath will be aroused, and he will employ every device in his power to hinder the work.[66]

The "prince" of this world is an illegitimate usurper, but he still has ability enough to wreak havoc... when God allows it. But God doesn't allow what won't work out for good, so there's always a reason:[67]

We cannot with any safety give place to the enemy, for if we are found on the enemy's side, we will perish with the wicked in the plagues the Lord shall allow Satan to create in the earth against men and against beasts.[68]

The wrath of God[69] is preparing to come upon all the cities—not all at once but one after another. And if the terrible punishment in one city does not cause the inhabitants of other cities to be afraid and seek repentance, their time will come.... The destruction will begin in certain places, and the destruction of life will be sudden and but few will escape.[70]

As these disasters increase, they mark a second phase of probation's close. For the church, that work is done, but for the good-hearted, conscientious, God-fearing among the population, who have struggled through all that the devil could bring against them, fighting off his deceptions as best they could with nothing better to work with than perhaps a vague understanding of Scripture...[71] for them, the door is still open and they respond to the call, preparing hastily at the last moment to welcome the Bridegroom!

The time of God's destructive judgments is the time of mercy for those who have no opportunity to learn what is truth. Tenderly will the Lord look upon them. His heart of mercy is touched; His hand is still stretched out to save, while the door is closed to those who would not enter. Large numbers will be admitted who in these last days hear the truth for the first time.[72]

---

66. E.G. White, Letter to G.W. Amadon, September 12, 1910; Letter 74, 1910
67. Just imagine the frustration level that must have built up after six thousand years of trying to win at this game, but always losing!
68. E.G. White, Letter to M.J.Church, June 6, 1889; Letter 54, 1889
69. "I was shown that the judgments of God would not come directly out from the Lord upon them, but rather in this way: they place themselves beyond His protection. He warns, corrects, reproves, and points out the only path of safety; then, if those who have been the objects of His special care will follow their own course independent of the Spirit of God after repeated warnings, if they choose their own way, then He does not commission His angels to prevent Satan's decided attacks upon them. It is Satan's power that is at work at sea and on land bringing calamity and distress, sweeping off multitudes to make sure of his prey." E.G. White, Letter to Brother and Sister Uriah Smith, August 8, 1883; Letter 14, 1883
70. E.G. White, "Diary: Corruption of the Cities and Unfaithful Shepherds," September 2, 1902; Manuscript 233, 1902
71. Ask yourself, "Where would I be if I'd never heard of *The Great Controversy*?"
72. E.G. White, Letter to Brother and Sister G.B. Starr, June 3, 1903; Letter 103, 1903

CHAPTER 36

Go!

F ROM what we've seen so far, there's a mighty movement coming, and that's great, but it raises a few down-to-earth questions. The obvious starters are, How does it get started?[1] How does it grow? Who makes it happen? And what does it take to make it happen?

Truth be told, those questions are kind of ridiculous. Even a smattering of sacred history makes it all seem obvious.

How many people built the ark? How many people left Ur of the Chaldees, or led Israel out of Egypt? How many people stood up against the Midianites, or fought Goliath? How many stood on the plain of Dura, or announced the coming of the Lamb of God? How many nailed Ninety-five Theses on their local church door? How many started the "Millerite Movement"? How many started the Seventh-day Adventist Church?

True enough, those questions don't all have the same answer. But the range is one to three hundred, and only if you count Gideon's whole army! The lesson is clear: big things often start with a very small core group.

The Bible abounds with examples of one, or two, or a few, stepping out in faith before anyone else. Often, their courage inspired others to take a stand. Elijah, of course, failed to find even that much faith on Mt. Carmel, until *after* the fire from heaven. Though others finally stepped up to help him, all those with *pre*-pyro faith are now in heaven, and all those with *post*-pyro faith are dead.

The story of Jonathan and his armorbearer seems like a good case study. One faithful, fearless soldier came up with a plan. He shared it with a trusted com-

---

1. There is a section of Manuscript 67, 1910, titled "City Work. How Shall We Begin?" that should be studied in this regard. Unfortunately, I can't put *everything* into a single book!

rade, and together they committed their lives to God, asking for guidance. And then they just attacked a vastly superior force. How did *that* work? The back story is simply that Jonathan was "moved by a divine impulse."[2]

> There will be religious failures because men have not faith. When they look at the things that are seen, impossibilities present themselves, but God knows nothing of impossibilities. The great work of God will advance only by the push of faith.[3]

Saul—far from a wise and daring leader—"had been sitting in discontent and fear and trembling with his six hundred men under the pomegranate tree." But as "the noise that was in the host of the Philistines went on and increased... he began to think that the time had come for him to do something."[4] Saul was late to the action, so he tried to get out in front of a good thing and get a little credit for himself. That didn't work, but the power of his son's righteous example carried the day:

> Moreover the Hebrews who were with the Philistines before that time, who went up with them into the camp from the surrounding country, they also joined the Israelites who were with Saul and Jonathan. Likewise all the men of Israel who had hidden in the mountains of Ephraim, when they heard that the Philistines fled, they also followed hard after them in the battle. So the LORD saved Israel that day.[5]

It's hard to come up with a new idea. It's even harder to come up with a *good* new idea. But some people, at least, can *spot* a good idea when they run into it on the street. And when they do, they'll get on board.

> There is much knowledge among men, but to see the designs of heavenly wisdom in times of necessity, to see the simplicity of God's plan revealing His justice and goodness and love, and searching out the hearts of men—this many fail to do. His plan seems too wonderful for them to accept, and thus they fail to be benefited.[6]

OK, so it doesn't work with everyone... but *some* will get on board, if we just give them a chance and maybe some encouragement.

> Those in the churches should feel the burden of labor and the work, and ministers should encourage those that feel any burden in that direction unless there is something positive[7] in their life and in their character that makes it very objectionable. As soon as they begin to experience a desire to work, our finite minds must not pronounce upon it, and think that they must go through the minister's ordeal, all the way through, before they can be accepted as laborers. Let them go out. Let them test their power, their ability, and see what they will do, and not go to them and say, "You aren't a minister."...

---

2. *Patriarchs and Prophets*, 623

3. E.G. White, "The Building of the Lord's House," October 3, 1897; Manuscript 116, 1897

4. E.G. White, Letter to Brother and Sister, June 1, 1897; Letter 16, 1897

5. 1 Samuel 14:21–23

6. E.G. White, Letter to G.I. Butler, October 30, 1906; Letter 348, 1906

7. More of a synonym for "definite" than an antonym of "negative."

We must have more of a missionary spirit; we must be better missionaries, educated so that we shall acknowledge talent where it is. You say such a man has not had an education. So he has not. How big an education did the fishermen have? The Jews were surprised that they did not have more. They said, "These are unlearned and ignorant men." So they did not consider that they had an education, and yet they preached the Word of God with power.

It is not the education that is going to make men laborers. We want to get all the education that we can, but at the same time men who have no education are not to be restricted as though they were not fit to go until they had the education. If they are humble men, if they are God-fearing men, then the Lord can use them to go fishing. He will use men just as He used the fishermen, and if they have vitality and earnestness and devotion, the Lord will give them His power, His grace.

He will work with every one that will work, if they are devoted to Him, and, more than that, He will be to them the greatest Educator the world ever knew. He will take those men that will commit themselves to Him, and He will educate them. He will train them. He will fit them for the work. This is what we want.

We want our ministers to feel that they are under obligation to God to present individuals that shall go out and that shall work in different places to the very best of their ability. While they are under the ministers' watchcare, and while the ministers can give instruction and can fit them to go out, let them gather themselves right by their side, and not feel they are ignorant men. They can do more. They can do a great deal; they can open the Bible where they can, and teach the gospel. They need not stand in the desk.

But here is the very thing that needs prudence and carefulness. You say it will make us a lot of trouble. So it will, because some will go before they have any particular burden, and they will want to go. But is not that the very thing we will have to bear? Certainly it is. We have kept our hands too firmly to keep people back instead of urging them forward. It is some of the urging that is needed. Whether they are learned or can give an eloquent prayer or an eloquent speech, but one thing is essential—that they should be men that love and fear God and walk in humility before Him. And this is the only way we can let our light shine to the world.[8]

Knowledge is power, and to the degree that it bestows useful knowledge, education is a great thing. But it's not everything. God is looking for a demonstration of how Jesus would go about preaching, teaching, helping, and healing at the end of time. What's the best major for that? Or does it take a masters?

If those who know the truth fully realized the awful peril of their fellow men, they would have a burden to work for the Master. Going out into new fields, they would by the power of example lead others to unite with them.[9]

---

8. E.G. White, "Remarks Concerning Foreign Mission Work," November 12, 1896; Manuscript 75, 1896

9. E.G. White, Letter to Brethren and Sisters of the Iowa Conference, November 6, 1901; Letter 165, 1901

Move forward in hope, expressing gratitude, revealing the victory of faith in your own soul, and others will be influenced to follow the leadings of God. The light which God has given, He desires us to let shine to the world. It will be of no value unless it can be seen.[10]

When the Lord sees that you are faithful in doing what you can to relieve human misery, He will move upon others to provide means to care for those who need help.[11]

If we make a success, others will follow our example.[12]

Of all the efforts we've made to finish the work, perhaps the one great lack has been to actually just follow directions without worrying about ourselves in the process. The trick is to recognize that self-concern normally shows up as a desire for "support" of some kind other than (or, at the very least, in *addition to*) the support that God has promised to provide.

Imagine if Jonathan and his armorbearer, after thinking up the plan for a surprise attack on the Philistines, had given a sales pitch to the crowd under the pomegranate tree. How far would that have gone?

A military command structure is particularly resistant to innovative ideas arising from within the ranks. For obvious reasons, actually, and that's part of what makes this story so instructive. Carrying out an independent mission within the sphere of operations of an established command structure is how Jonathan found himself out of the loop on an order from the Commander-in-Chief. That order—despite being ignorant and misguided—almost cost him his life.

There are practical lessons in all this! Don't miss them! One of the most important is a simple piece of life-skill that has been distilled down to the phrase, "Expand into the vacuum."

The idea is, if you want to start something new, start somewhere new. Taking on an established command structure and trying to change it is almost certainly going to be resisted because it will likely mean something like firing a bunch of existing generals! It's odd, but they will often resist that without even considering your plan. Besides, just because you came up with a plan—even if it's a good plan—is not compelling evidence that those generals *ought* to be fired.

Instead, follow this inspired approach:

Christ says, "You go out, and teach the words that I have commanded you;" and He tells them to baptize those that shall be converted. They are to go. No one is to be appointed to stay right in one place. But as they feel the burden of the work of God upon them, they are to go out; they are not to go to places where every one knows just as much of the truth as they know. They are to go to places where men know not the truth.[13]

---

10. E.G. White, "A Worldwide Work," April 1, 1874; Manuscript 1, 1874

11. *Review and Herald*, January 15, 1895

12. E.G. White, Letter to J.H. Kellogg, August 28, 1895; Letter 42, 1895

13. E.G. White, "Sermon: Thoughts on Micah 6," May 19, 1904; Manuscript 164, 1904

We are not to give the call to those who have received the truth and understand it, to whom it has been repeated over and over again....

Christ came to save that which was lost, and He calls upon you to go forth to labor for those who know not the truth, instead of only sermonizing and doing a little work for the churches. You would then do fifty times as much in encouraging the churches and setting them a right example.[14]

We must bring the message before the people just as it is. The precious truth is to come to many who do not now know it. But how are we going to get it to them? Missionaries are to be in every city. Missionaries are to be all through our cities. We are not to delay to find out whether they can go or not. God says to go. He has given the very first charge that they are to go, and to warn those who are unwarned.[15]

The prohibitions that have bound about the labors of those who would go forth to warn the people in the cities of the soon-coming judgments should every one be removed. None are to be hindered from bearing the message of present truth to the world. Let the workers receive their directions from God. When the Holy Spirit impresses a believer to do a certain work for God, leave the matter with him and the Lord. I am instructed to say to you, Break every yoke that would prevent the message from going forth with power to the cities. This work of proclaiming the truth in the cities will take means, but it will also bring in means. A much greater work would have been done if men had not been so zealous to watch and hinder some who were seeking to obtain means from the people to carry forward the work of the Lord.

The Lord's mercy and love are misrepresented by a policy that would hinder the message of His grace from going to any part of the world. Is man to be a dictator to his fellow man? Is he to take the responsibility of saying, You shall not go to such a place? Let us rather say to those who desire to labor: It is your privilege to work for souls on every occasion and to make earnest request to God in their behalf.... Those upon whom the Spirit lays the burden of labor, and who are of good report in the church, encourage them to enter new fields. Let the work of the Lord go forward with power. Let the people be encouraged to prepare the way of the Lord and to make straight in the desert a highway for our God.[16]

As much as possible, "expand into the vacuum." This is particularly important for work carried on as an "individual effort." Copy Paul's example of working new fields. You may be entitled to raise funds wherever you want, but you'd be naive to think it won't cause ripples. Take a lesson from the high dive: a clean entry into the water that doesn't make a big splash gets more points.

But don't apply the same "rules" to larger, group efforts! There's a time and a place for a "Protest of the Princes"[17] approach, when the whole point is to make

14. E.G. White, "Talk: An Appeal to Our Ministers," April 15, 1901; Manuscript 149, 1901
15. E.G. White, "Discourse by Mrs. E.G. White at Pacific Union College," March 8, 1910; Manuscript 72, 1910
16. E.G. White, Letter to Officers of the General Conference, May 26, 1908; Letter 172, 1908
17. See Chapter 11 of *Great Controversy*.

a big splash! The "higher classes," and the "ruling classes" will never be warned if all of God's work is done "under the radar." But this is generally not the model for individual believers. (Martin Luther and a few others are exceptions here, that's why it's a "general rule," not an "invariable truth.")

The obvious downside to all this is the sparsity of support, which can easily result in suffering, self-denial, and self-sacrifice—none of which has much inherent appeal. We need a motivation that's strong enough to power through that.

> Those who receive Christ as a personal Saviour, choosing to be partakers of His suffering, to live His life of self-denial, to endure shame for His sake, will understand what it means to be a genuine medical missionary.[18]

How could they avoid it? After all, their work is going to be "identical with the work that Christ did."[19]

That's the kind of medical missionaries God needs. And once world conditions drive selfish souls out of the "ministry market,"[20] that's the only kind that will be around. Remember, we're talking now about the full-blown "mighty movement" which happens in a time of increasing chaos. Cities are taking a beating; there's probably some new pandemic spreading; believers have been scattered all over the globe; the general populace is mad about everything from politics, to the manipulation of the currency, to the tanking economy, to the WHO's sacrificing of "health care" to the profits of "Big Pharma."

What else can we put on that list? There are more than enough "conspiracy theories" to choose from, and though they can't *all* be correct, the public opinion of the powers-that-be will not be getting better any time soon. The Bible suggests, and the Spirit of Prophecy confirms, a coming swing, wherein the lower classes seek to even up what they see as a very lopsided score in terms of controlling world affairs.

> Come now, you rich, weep and howl for your miseries that are coming upon you! Your riches are corrupted, and your garments are moth-eaten. Your gold and silver are corroded, and their corrosion will be a witness against you and will eat your flesh like fire. You have heaped up treasure in the last days. Indeed the wages of the laborers who mowed your fields, which you kept back by fraud, cry out; and the cries of the reapers have reached the ears of the Lord of Sabaoth. You have lived on the earth in pleasure and luxury; you have fattened your hearts as in a day of slaughter. You have condemned, you have murdered the just; he does not resist you.[21]

---

18. *Testimonies*, vol. 8, 209
19. E.G. White, "Christ Our Example in Every Line of Work," October 27, 1902; Manuscript 130, 1902. Quoted more fully on page 81.
20. We'll be looking at this in Chapter 40.
21. James 5:1–6.

Without further information, it would be easy to see all this as happening at the second coming, since the next two verses read: "Therefore be patient, brethren, until the coming of the Lord. See [how] the farmer waits for the precious fruit of the earth, waiting patiently for it until it receives the early and latter rain. You also be patient. Establish your hearts, for the coming of the Lord is at hand."

But "further information" is why God invented the Spirit of Prophecy! We should not be blind to such matters.

> Unless we understand the importance of passing events, and make ready to stand in the great day of God, we shall be registered in the books of heaven as unfaithful stewards. The watchman is to know the time of the night.[22]

> The Lord is removing His restrictions from the earth, and soon there will be death and destruction, increasing crime, and cruel, evil working against the rich who have exalted themselves against the poor. Those who are without God's protection will find no safety in any place or position.[23]

It may come as a surprise, but it turns out God loves the bad guys, too.

> While Jesus ministered to all who came unto Him, He yearned to bless those who came not. While He drew the publicans, the heathen, and the Samaritans, He longed to reach the priests and teachers who were shut in by prejudice and tradition. He left untried no means by which they might be reached.[24]

With the rising tide of popular discontent and resentment against the "elites," God wants us to warn the rich people!

> The message of the apostle James, depicting the misery of the rich who have done wickedly, is to be repeated as a message of warning and appeal.[25]

God's servants have to navigate the same troubled waters, of course, but they have two advantages: for starters, at that point in earth's history there won't be any true followers who would qualify as "the rich," since they "desired to be taught," and God showed them "when to sell and how much to sell"[26] to support God's work. More importantly, they'll have a protection unknown to the world:

> The time has come, and this will be seen more and more plainly, when a faithful standard bearer for God, who ministers in word and doctrine, is far more secure than those who possess gold and silver.[27]

---

22. E.G. White, Letter to Friends of the Avondale School, December 20, 1896; Letter 60a, 1896

23. *Testimonies*, vol. 8, 49–50

24. *Desire of Ages*, 265

25. E.G. White, "Words of Instruction," September 17, 1909; Manuscript 61, 1909

26. *Early Writings*, 57

27. E.G. White, "Go, Work Today in My Vineyard," July 7, 1898; Manuscript 87, 1898

That kind of security will be important, since the odds of finding help in the traditional palaces of justice will be declining sharply:

> As we near the close of this earth's history, those who fear God and honor Him need hope for little justice. Rather they must expect injustice and oppression at the hand of those who regard neither God nor man.[28]

All this "social change" represents a major shift that will come, and is surely already in process. We should guard against the illusion that what we've seen for decades past, and what the world seems to be today, is actually stable. It is not, and great changes will be coming.

With a certain portion of both the general population and church members, there is an ingrained tendency to accept the world view of "respected authorities." It's easy to see why, since such sources have remained "respected" for many years, and there have been plenty of examples of "fringe" voices saying dumb things. Whether deserved or not, that "respectable status" has over time come to be very closely associated with the accumulation of staggering wealth.

In that light, it's prudent to note that there are dire predictions in the Spirit of Prophecy in regard to the course such "monied men" will take in the final days. This, too, will increasingly pose a test for those who have come to instinctively accept the "respected" version of events. Why "increasingly"? Because "the love of money," "the root of all evil" is an invasive plant that is spreading quickly into every field of human endeavor from which wealth can be extracted.

> The time is near when all these wicked inventions will come to an end. At the last the passion for obtaining means by fraud will increase.[29]

> Under the leadership of Satan there are men who today are doing all in their power to plunge the world into commercial strife.[30]

The old adage to "follow the money" is a valuable guide to those areas of the world economy most thoroughly corrupted.

Fortunately, though, we've been given good counsel on relating to "society":

> The students of God's Word will, in these last days, work away from the customs and appointments of the world's great counselors.... Only the wise virgins will be prepared, with oil in their vessels with their lamps, to go forth to meet the Bridegroom.[31]

> When we begin to work with parliaments, and with men holding high positions in governments, the enemy is roused to exert all his strength against us, and he will make the work hard. Do not let your work be known any more than is necessary; the best course to follow is that which will avoid opposition. The least said about the foolish errors of others,

---

28. E.G. White, "Ask, and Ye Shall Receive," July 22, 1898; Manuscript 93, 1898
29. E.G. White, "The Word of God Our Study Book," September 22, 1898; Manuscript 119, 1898
30. E.G. White, Letter to A.G. Daniells, October 27, 1910; Letter 114, 1910
31. E.G. White, Letter to W. Miller, 1898; Letter 109a, 1898

the better. Do not speak disrespectfully of ministers. Satan and all his hosts are working to make of none effect the law of God, and when we begin to work on controversial lines, he will lead men to believe that we do not regard their laws or obey their decrees. Believing this, they will make it as hard as possible for all who will not worship their idol Sunday.

We are not to reveal all our purposes and plans to men. Satan will take advantage of any indiscretion shown on this point. He does not work openly and above board. He works in an underhanded manner, and will continue to do so. Before the people are prepared for it, he leads men to set a powerful movement on foot by working on their minds....

From the light that has been given me, I see that we should fear lest rulers take their position against our work. Every opportunity to become acquainted with these men should be embraced; but we should do nothing that will produce anything like prejudice. It means a great deal to be as wise as serpents and as harmless as doves. We have so much determination in us that often we do things unguardedly and rashly. We must appear before these men as trying to help others, working on the lines of the Christian help work. As they see the good work we do in these lines, their prejudice, in a measure, will be removed; their hearts will be opened to the truth. Do not abruptly present the Sabbath; present Christ.[32]

Our danger does not arise from the opposition of the world; but it is found in the liability of our being in friendship with the world, and imitating the example of those who love not God or His truth.[33]

We need a mental shift.... We're used to an "acceptable" manner of "polite" presentation. That can be a plus. Genuine courtesy is always in style. But there will be times...

The disciples were not afraid to proclaim the truth. They expected that they would be persecuted. "Whom ye crucified." Why did they not keep that back? Because it was a testimony that they were to bear before the great men of the earth.[34]

In any case, we should certainly shun "a life of respectable conventionality, a life professedly Christian, but lacking His self-sacrifice, a life on which the verdict of Him who is truth must be, 'I know you not.'"[35]

Of course, whoever—like a modern Noah, Abraham, Moses, Gideon, David, John the Baptist, Martin Luther, or William Miller—is called of God to lead out, to pioneer some new, successful, and reproducible means of taking medical missionary work to the cities[36] clearly won't be in danger of living "a life of re-

---

32. E.G. White, "Interview Regarding the Religious Liberty Question," November 20, 1895; Manuscript 22, 1895

33. *Review and Herald*, February 5, 1895. Do note that there is no incompatibility between "trying to help others" and "lifting up Christ." That's what He did, remember?

34. *Review and Herald*, April 22, 1890

35. *Education*, 264

36. Mention must be made here of this still poorly comprehended counsel: "We are to be wise as serpents and harmless as doves in our efforts to secure country properties at a low figure, and from these outpost centers we are to work the cities." *Special Testimonies*, Series B, No. 14, 7

spectable conventionality." Such pioneers will be following in the footsteps of those who have worked to implement these counsels in the past, such as the remarkably successful "gospel-medical missionary evangelistic companies" led by J.H.N. Tindall starting in 1910.[37]

For the sake of clarity, let's state unequivocally that the Bible doctrines which have set Adventists apart from all other denominations are integral to any kind of "gospel-medical" work. There is no call for the church to provide (or even support) some sort of "non-denominational-ecumenical-social-gospel-humanitarianism"[38] that "loves" people enough to feed them, but not enough to warn them that their own selfishness will cost them eternity when the test of faith comes.

A new impetus is needed, led by those who aren't afraid of risk, but have the discipline to follow the leading of God to preserve them from the myriad pitfalls which will easily swallow up any effort not led and protected by Him. Combining old, well established truths with a new impetus can be tricky, though. What stays the same? What changes? And, perhaps most pragmatically, what could anyone do to grab the attention of a whole city of jaded, media-saturated, untrusting straphangers with more than enough to keep them busy just trying to pay bills?

Conveniently enough, we can find some guidance in this from the history of the beginning of the loud cry back in the 1890s, if we take in the whole picture. The challenge is that several decades of emphasis on "righteousness by faith" as a genuinely important theological issue have tended to strip other elements of the story from our thinking. One of these that we've already seen is the role of practical application; righteousness by faith always plays out in service to others. Call it medical missionary work or whatever you want, "righteousness by faith" without it is a deception.

But there is another overlooked element from back in the day: religious liberty. You may have heard that Jones and Waggoner faced opposition from some in positions of General Conference leadership. It's true, but that opposition wasn't all focused on the theology of righteousness by faith. Much of it had to do with religious liberty issues.

"It is God's design that our people should locate outside the cities, and from these outposts warn the cities." *Review and Herald*, April 14, 1903

"The cities are to be worked from outposts. Said the messenger of God, 'Shall not the cities be warned? Yes; not by God's people living in them.'" E.G. White, Letter to Brethren, September 20, 1902; Letter 182, 1902

37. Tindall's story can be found in my previous book, *d'Sozo*.

38. For Adventists to fund such organizations as United Way, or the Salvation Army, is at best a sad admission that we have neglected our duty to the point that the atheists or apostate Protestants provide a more efficient means of blessing the world than we can. They do some good things! Be thankful for that, but let the Lord's money go to His glory, not theirs.

We know that Brother Jones had been giving the message for this time—meat in due season for the starving flock of God. Those who do not allow prejudice to bar the heart against the heaven-sent message cannot but feel the spirit and force of the truth. Brother Jones has borne the message from church to church, and from state to state; and light and freedom and the outpouring of the Spirit of God have attended the Word, as events of a most startling nature in the fulfillment of prophecy show that the great crisis is rapidly approaching.

Brother Jones seeks to arouse the professed people of God from their death-like slumber to see the importance of giving the warning to the world. But he advances some ideas with which all do not agree, and instantly Brother Gage is aroused; he harnesses for the battle, and before the congregation in the tabernacle he takes his position in opposition to Brother Jones. Was this in the order of God? Did the Spirit of the Lord go from Brother Jones and inspire Brother Gage to do this work? Suppose that Brother Jones's statement concerning the formation of the image was premature; did the case demand such demonstrations? I answer, No, no; not if God had ever spoken to me.[39]

Notice that what got Jones in trouble was in relation to "events of a most startling nature in the fulfillment of prophecy," specifically, events that showed "that the great crisis is rapidly approaching." What was all this? Broadly speaking, it was the work of the National Reform Association, the primary force behind a very active push for Sunday sacredness legislation in the United States.

Was Jones "premature" in saying what he did about "the formation of the image"? Suppose he was, just for the sake of argument... but *stop the arguing!*

Jones was onto something, and the Lord was using the topic as a tool to "arouse the professed people of God from their death-like slumber." Sad to say, there's a need for the same work today, but the important point just now is that the same topic was also grabbing the attention of non-believers! Why? Well, largely because "events of a most startling nature" were playing out in real time. Anyone who could read a newspaper knew it!

What are the odds we could look around and see something similar today? I'd say the odds are good, right up there in the "Is the pope catholic?" range of probability. But... is it good for an evangelist to talk about *politics?*

When politics happens to be present truth... of course it is! Do note that the vast majority of politics is *not* present truth, and there is plenty of counsel to leave all that stuff for the world to fight over. But politics that impacts religious liberty? That has to do with freedom of conscience? That is threatening to "repudiate every principle of... Protestant and republican government, and... make provision for the propagation of papal falsehoods and delusions"?[40]

That kind of politics, in the daily headlines, is the *most present* of all present truth.

39. E.G. White, Letter to William Ings, January 9, 1893; Letter 77, 1893
40. *Testimonies*, vol. 5, 451

When the National Reformers began to urge measures to restrict religious liberty, our leading men should have been alive to the situation and should have labored earnestly to counteract these efforts. It is not in the order of God that light has been kept from our people—the very present truth which they needed for this time. Not all our ministers who are giving the third angel's message really understand what constitutes that message. The National Reform movement has been regarded by some as of so little importance that they have not thought it necessary to give much attention to it and have even felt that in so doing they would be giving time to questions distinct from the third angel's message. May the Lord forgive our brethren for thus interpreting the very message for this time.[41]

Let the watchmen now lift up their voice and give the message which is present truth for this time. Let us show the people where we are in prophetic history and seek to arouse the spirit of true Protestantism, awaking the world to a sense of the value of the privileges of religious liberty so long enjoyed.[42]

Notably, this last quotation speaks of "the people." That would be "the people of the world." That means evangelism, and it takes us right back to the work for the cities. This work needs the influence of the "medical," but is fatally incomplete without the "missionary." And the missionary message of the day is "Behold the Bridegroom cometh."

But what does that mean? And perhaps just as importantly, how are we supposed to get that message across to those tuned-out straphangers? After all, Old English isn't their native language. Fortunately, we've been given counsel on that, using the Big Apple as a stand-in for all such large cities:

New York will be worked; openings will be found in parts of the city in which there are no churches, where the truth will find standing room. There is a vast amount of work to be done in proclaiming the truth for this time to those who are dead in trespasses and sins. Most startling messages will be borne by men of God's appointment, messages of a character to warn the people, to arouse them. And while some will be provoked by the warning and led to resist light and evidence, we are to see from this that we are giving the testing message for this time.

Messages will be given out of the usual order. The judgments of God are in the land. While city missions must be established where colporteurs, Bible workers, and practical medical missionaries may be trained to reach certain classes, we must also have, in our cities, consecrated evangelists through whom a message is to be borne so decidedly as to startle the hearers.[43]

The idea of "startling" things keeps coming up! First we saw that the "mighty movement" would come at a time when "events of a most startling nature in

---

41. *Testimonies*, vol. 5, 714
42. *Testimonies*, vol. 5, 716
43. *Testimonies*, vol. 9, 137

the fulfillment of prophecy" were happening. Now we see that "most startling messages" are needed. Why? Because the goal is to "startle the hearers." It kind of makes sense, when you think of it.

How do you startle someone who's already been startled by the latest of an unending string of crazy events? Show them that it's prophesied in black and white.

Oh... you mean a prophecy seminar. We've done those... but not much happened.

OK. But take a look at the instructions one more time. See any other hot tips? Maybe here, for instance: "Messages will be given out of the usual order. The judgments of God are in the land."

I find that "out of the usual order" part intriguing. So, what's the usual order for a prophecy series? What's the topic on night one? Traditionally, Daniel Two, and for good reason, since the story of Nebuchadnezzar's dream and image is a great way to demonstrate the accuracy of Scripture. That's good and important, but maybe not the best approach for the *"cut to the chase, already"* mindset of the big cities.[44] Given that "the judgments of God are in the land," and that "startling events" have been doing the advertising for us already, and that the message of religious liberty is present truth... how about starting straight up with Revelation thirteen's beast from the earth? Get to the point, already! That cute little lamb is spitting fire now!

How's that supposed to work? What gets said when? I'd be foolish to pretend I could lay out some sort of master plan for all this,[45] but I do know how we'll figure it all out. It'll be done "by trying."

> I want to tell you, dear friends, we can do ten times more than we do.... Some may say, Sister White, what does this mean, "Go out into the highways and the byways?" How are we going to accomplish it? By trying. Go right to work, and as you begin to

---

44. "Know your audience" is always good advice. An interesting example of this played out in Adventist history when J.N. Loughborough and D.T. Bourdeau pioneered Adventist work in California. They had both previously worked in the famously frugal region of New England, where considerable care was required simply to keep their operations financially viable. In 1868, when they arrived in San Francisco, a letter from Ellen White was waiting for them. She wrote: "You cannot labor in California as you did in New England. Such strict economy would be considered 'pennywise' by the Californians. Things are managed there on a more liberal scale. You will have to meet them in the same liberal spirit."

    Rather than sell their smaller publications as they had previously, they simply gave them away. In return, they received donations worth far more. See J.N. Loughborough, *Miracles in My Life*, 72.

45. Delusions of a "full understanding" of coming events are best abandoned as rapidly as possible. "Human" is a pretty broad category, so I don't think any of us are exceptions here: "Let me tell you that the Lord will work in this last work in a manner very much out of the common order of things, and in a way that will be contrary to any human planning. There will be those among us who will always want to control the work of God, to dictate even what movements shall be made when the work goes forward under the direction of the angel who joins the third angel in the message to be given to the world. God will use ways and means by which it will be seen that He is taking the reins in His own hands. The workers will be surprised by the simple means that He will use to bring about and perfect His work of righteousness." *Testimonies to Ministers*, 299

try, you will feel the presence of angels right around you, and you will have the interpretation yourselves of what this means.[46]

One of the most daunting necessities of work in a big city environment is the need for money. It is a real need, but it is also something of a "giant in the land" sort of fearful excuse. In our fully monetized society, a lack of funds looms up as one of the most solid of undeniable realities. This is a carefully constructed and endlessly reinforced lie of the devil.

The work is many years behind, under the plea, "There is not means to open the cities." And there never will be means unless there is a decided change made.... Men in official positions need to wake up, to heed the words of God and go into cities. Physicians converted to the truth should unite with gospel ministers, and men who will not fail or become discouraged but work diligently, as Christ worked when He sent out His disciples. The very ways and means will come when men will follow the directions of the Lord Jesus.[47]

This kind of work will never look "normal." Imagine putting this in your startup business plan, and then applying for a bank loan:

Oh, that we might see the needs of these great cities as God sees them!... Can we expect the inhabitants of these cities to come to us and say, "If you will come to us and preach, we will help you to do thus and so"? They know nothing of our message. The Lord desires us to let our light so shine before men, that His Holy Spirit may communicate the truth to the honest in heart who are seeking after truth. As we do this work, we shall find that means will flow into our treasuries, and we shall have means with which to carry on a still broader and more far-reaching work. Shall we not advance in faith, just as if we had thousands of dollars? We do not have half faith enough. Let us act our part in warning these cities. The warning message must come to the people who are ready to perish, unwarned, unsaved. How can we delay?[48]

Business plans and hiring guidelines no doubt have a good purpose... but they may not be the final answer for every need in the Lord's work.

Men give the Lord but very little chance to work. They plan only in their line, in their way—not always in the best way, and according to the best methods. But Christ has done a vast amount of planning which men need to bring into their plans.[49]

Representations have been made to me, showing that the Lord will carry out His plans through a variety of ways and instruments. It is not alone the most talented, not alone those who hold high positions of trust, or are the most highly educated from a worldly point of view, whom the Lord uses to do His grand and holy work of soul-sav-

---

46. E.G. White, "Talk: Thoughts on First Peter 2," March 23, 1910; Manuscript 76, 1910

47. E.G. White, Letter to Dear Brother, March 8, 1909; Letter 189, 1909

48. E.G. White, "Proclaiming the Third Angel's Message in Cities at Home and Abroad," June 11, 1909; Manuscript 53, 1909

49. E.G. White, "A Message to the Church," November 8, 1891; Manuscript 84, 1891

ing. He will use simple means; He will use many who have had few advantages to help in carrying forward His work. He will, by the use of simple means, bring those who possess property and lands to a belief of the truth, and these will be influenced to become the Lord's helping hand in the advancement of His work.[50]

The very reason that the places [i.e., properties for schools] are secured to us by God is so that we may be out of the cities. There will be places where we cannot inhabit the cities. Our lives will be in danger if we do.

And this is why I have kept before you for years that the cities must be worked without delay....

Angels of God are watching. They will be all around you to help you and open the way before you. But if there is a hand stretched out to go to the cities to work, it is said, We have no means yet. Well, you must be ready, and go without means. But God does not intend that you shall go without means.[51] He intends that you shall open these cities and go very guardedly. If you do not, you will lose your lives before you know it.[52] It is no small work that is now resting upon us.

That which we might have done twenty or thirty years ago[53] will have to be done and carried forward in a very different manner than it could have been then. But do your best now. Do not delay....

You just go to work, and you see if you do not have ways open before you and if the hearts of the people are not moved. You tell them the simple story of the cross, and lay it right out before them that the salvation of their souls is hanging in the balance; and if you do this, the God of heaven will make the impression. He will do it....

"So then because thou art lukewarm, and neither cold nor hot, I will spue thee out of my mouth." It is because you feel no earnestness, no intensity. You do not realize that it is a case of life and death, and you know not how matters are breaking up in the cities. Why, there is the most awful condition in the cities! We hear the reports from one city and then from another. What are we to do? We have neglected the cities

---

50. E.G. White, Letter to D.A. Parsons, March 28, 1909; Letter 62, 1909. This is an obvious companion quotation to the "means to sustain all the enterprises for missionary work that we could carry forward" line of thought we looked at back on page 209.

51. This manuscript, a transcription of a talk Ellen White gave on the recently acquired property of Pacific Union College, does not appear to have ever been extensively edited or proofed for publication. One result of this is the lack of clarifying quotation marks in this passage about (1) the lack of money, (2) going without money, and (3) God not wanting the workers to go without money. The first comment clearly seems to represent some "administrator voice." But is the second comment from that same source, or is it Ellen White's statement of what needs to be done in faith, regardless? And is the third sentence intended to rule out #2, or an indication of the ideal? You may wish to read the manuscript in its entirety to help resolve such questions for yourself. It's a good read!

My guess is that "you must be ready, and go without means," is Ellen White's recommendation of what to do. Note that the spending of money is tempered by the "guardedly" comment in the next sentence. Also, compare this statement with the instruction on page 231: "We are not to delay to find out whether they can go or not. God says to go." That shorter quotation is taken from the same manuscript.

52. Worth noting: No one said this was going to be easy. It's just that it needs to be done anyway.

53. That would be something more like 130–140 years ago now.

so long that it will be harder for us to work them now; nevertheless, if those that are placed in positions of responsibility will even now wake up and repent and seek the Lord with all their hearts, the Lord will renew unto them His Spirit if they are whole-hearted in the matter, and He will give them the message just as He gave to us in the first messages that came. And I know how we worked all around us. Darkness was everywhere, but we had to urge our way....

Here is the work to be done on this land. Here is the work to be done in building. You need buildings. Why? Because the cities will be in such a condition that our people cannot live in them, and when I heard how much land there was in the possession of our people, I said, "Good." Now when conditions are such that it will be impossible for us to remain in the cities, we must raise everything we can to support ourselves, and then go out into the byways and into the highways to give the message. This is the very work we must do....

It is too late in the day, altogether too late, for great mansions, but what we do want is to make a thorough preparation, to be washed white and clean in the blood of the Lamb in the very simplicity of true godliness. Then you will see that you are in a position where you can have an influence upon others. But the world is growing worse and worse. It is becoming more and more impossible to get within reach of the people, because the wicked Satan himself is working to secure the world and the wicked, and to place his stamp upon all that it is possible for him to place it upon. You know whether he is doing this or not if you read the papers....

We do not want to make any mistake here and go on half-hearted, half-converted. Let us every one lay right hold upon the Holy Spirit of God, and we will know what it is. We enjoyed it at the very first when the message went forth, and we have enjoyed it many times since. But there is a sleepiness over our churches just as sure as you live, and we cannot afford to have it there. Let us awake.[54]

It will be a stretch, but God *will* have servants who will brave the challenge and push faith to greater degrees when it comes to medical missionary work in the cities. But to do so, he (or she)[55] will have to stare down the big question:

But someone will say, "Suppose I give away all that I have, and then become dependent on others. It would be said, 'That man was a fool to do as he did'; and what shall we do then?"

It's a whole new challenge in "first world" city evangelism. The population is as heathen as any traditional "mission field," but sophisticated, cynical, and often close to heartless. The risks are different: wild animals, deadly diseases, and hazardous travel are replaced with the ever-present pressure of financial catastrophe.

---

54. E.G. White, "Discourse by Mrs. E.G. White at Pacific Union College," March 8, 1910; Manuscript 72, 1910

55. There are actually only two options here, though you will hear otherwise from many sources. This issue, too, will present challenges, almost certainly rising to a life-threatening level at times.

If a missionary gets eaten by a big snake, or dies of Ebola, or goes down with a plane, it's a tragedy... but what a noble sacrifice! If your city mission project goes broke and you end up living in a pallet-wood shack under some freeway overpass, no one is going to call it noble. "It would be said, 'That man was a fool to do as he did'; and what shall we do then?"

Ellen White nailed it. But she wasn't done:

> That is not the way the Majesty of Heaven talked. He did not count the cost of saving sinners. He became a man of sorrows and acquainted with grief, and had not where to lay His head, that you might be saved. But we seem to think that if we make a little sacrifice, we have done a great deal, when we should say with David, "All things come of thee, and of thine own have we given thee."[56]

"We seem to think" a lot of crazy things! How about thinking of a way to fill the earth with the glory of God, and have a good time doing it?

> All day Jesus had been teaching and healing, telling the people that the way to be most happy is to seek to be a blessing to others, and that when men and women give themselves wholly to this work, the earth will be filled with the glory of God.[57]

Is God calling me? Is it my imagination? Will He bless my effort? Will I embarrass myself and the church? But... *if I don't go, who will?*

> God cannot display the knowledge of His will and the wonders of His grace among the unbelieving world unless He has witnesses scattered all over the earth. It is His plan that those who are partakers of this great salvation through Jesus Christ should be His missionaries, bodies of light throughout the world, to be as signs to the people, living epistles, known and read of all men, their faith and works testifying to the near approach of the coming Saviour and showing that they have not received the grace of God in vain.[58]

And for all those looking on... Is he just being stupid? Should I try to help him? Would I just be wasting my money? Do "simple remedies" really belong in "evangelism"? Is city work even worth the effort? Should I... maybe?... get involved *myself?*

OK, now. This is the point at which I can keep my promise from chapters ago. What? You've forgotten? Back on page 188 I mentioned that I had some more specific thoughts as to what the saints said that stirred up so much opposition from both the church and the world going into the "little time of trouble." The context of the situation as described in *Great Controversy* included "professed believers" who became "bitter enemies," "apostates," and "agents of Satan." And I am suggesting that we toss into that mix the unique phrase from the 1847 vision of the little time of trouble, "proclaiming the Sabbath more fully."

---

56. *Signs of the Times*, December 10, 1885
57. E.G. White, "Christ Stilling the Tempest," November 3, 1903; Manuscript 130, 1903
58. *Testimonies*, vol. 2, 631

Here's my thought (*not* explicit inspired instruction): The Sabbath has always been God's sign of sanctification, which is largely aimed at increasing the believer's faith. And the Sabbath has always done this by requiring the believer to set aside ("give up," from the perspective of the carnal heart) time that could be spent providing for personal needs (like food and shelter, in poverty) or personal pleasures (like any number of not-on-Sabbath activities, in affluence).

It's probably accurate to generalize and say that Sabbath observance usually did more to develop faith in the less affluent than in the more affluent, simply because trusting God to provide food is a bit more intense than trusting Him not to bore you too badly with nothing exciting to do. But what would "proclaiming the Sabbath more fully" be?

If "keeping the Sabbath" has been a matter of six days of labor and one of rest, perhaps "the Sabbath more fully" will look like a few people, then hundreds, then thousands, recognizing the call, "Behold the Bridegroom cometh," and actually going "out to meet Him" the same way Jesus responded to the message of John the Baptist:

> Tidings of the wilderness prophet and his wonderful announcement, spread throughout Galilee.... In Nazareth it was told in the carpenter shop that had been Joseph's, and One recognized the call. His time had come. Turning from His daily toil, He bade farewell to His mother, and followed in the steps of His countrymen who were flocking to the Jordan.[59]

On the face of it, it looks like Jesus voluntarily opted for a life of unemployed homelessness. He once famously described His financial situation as a step or two below foxes with holes and birds with nests.[60] What if a few people, then hundreds, then thousands did the same?[61]

It's odd, but suggesting how other people ought to spend their money turns out to be a really effective way to kick up a lively discussion. And, somewhere in that friendly conversation, there's a good chance that you might hear something akin to, "That man was a fool to do as he did."

The human race has produced a more than sufficient supply of "fools." But "the foolishness of God is wiser than men,"[62] and "God has chosen the foolish things of the world to put to shame the wise,"[63] so this matter of what is *genuinely* foolish and what is *truly* wise is a big deal. It's just that intentionally, knowingly,

---

59. *Desire of Ages*, 109
60. Luke 9:58
61. There will be variations, of course. While Jesus may have been homeless, He found shelter at times with those who weren't. Peter had a house where He was welcome, and the same was true of Mary, Martha, and Lazarus. It seems likely that there were more such relationships, since Luke 8:3 tells us that "many others... provided for Him from their substance." Paul worked as a tent-maker to cover his expenses, so we shouldn't jump to the conclusion that righteousness necessitates unemployment for everyone in every circumstance. Still, what if a few thousand individuals—with possible support from fellow saints—pushed that boundary?
62. 1 Corinthians 1:25
63. 1 Corinthians 1:27

walking away from the job that has supported you, or giving away the money you need for your own necessities... just seems irresponsible. A step too far. Not using what little common sense you may actually have. How could that be God's plan?

But slow down a bit. Everyone who believes *The Great Controversy* knows that the "saints" will come to the point of leaving jobs and homes. You don't show up for work when there's a bounty on your head! So walking away from a job or a house is not out of the question. In fact, it's simply a matter of timing.

How close to the close of probation do you want to be working for the profit of Corporate HQ? Or maybe you've been blessed by the Spirit of Prophecy's encouragement to learn practical trades that allow you to be self-employed. That's a great idea. But how close to the close of probation do you want to be working to pay off your thirty-year mortgage? Maybe cutting lose early, *before* the opportunity for evangelism disappears, isn't an all bad idea....

Is God calling for that level of radical faith? I sure can't answer that question for anyone else. To me, it's at least within the bounds of possibility. Voluntarily cutting off all normal means of support would certainly be a significant step toward letting people "see that your dependence is upon a higher power."[64]

Others may be inclined to consider other, more fiscally prudent, options.[65] That's great. That may be what God is calling them to do. But still, there's this:

> The poor widow gave her living to do the little that she did. She deprived herself of food in order to give those two mites to the cause she loved. And she did it in faith, believing that her heavenly Father would not overlook her great need. It was this unselfish spirit and childlike faith that won the Saviour's commendation.[66]

That's not exactly the same as my idea of what "proclaiming the Sabbath more fully" might look like, so I'm sure the friendly conversations will go on. My mental picture could be distorted, of course, but I am sure of this much—

---

64. E.G. White, Letter to Brother Merrill, March 25, 1898; Letter 24, 1898. Quoted more fully on page 203.

65. Here's an even wackier idea: What if the governments of earth (encouraged by the WEF) actually implemented the unbiblical practice of a "guaranteed basic income"? I class it as unbiblical because of 2 Thessalonians 3:10—"If anyone will not work, neither shall he eat." This Biblical prohibition does not apply, of course, to cases of legitimate need, but depending on a government policy to discriminate between legitimate need and plain old greed is a pipe dream.

   Still, that may be one way for the "wealth of the Gentiles" (Isaiah 60:5, 11) to support God's work at the very time His people are called to "Arise, shine; For your light has come! And the glory of the Lord is risen upon you." Isaiah 60:1. As much as I'd love to see the cash of corrupt governments, organizations, and individuals financing the loud cry, I must point out that Ellen White tells us clearly that much funding is to come from the freely bestowed offerings of *formerly* corrupt individuals who have been converted. You may recall that that is one of the predicted outcomes of working the large cities.

   As a side note, have you noticed the similarity between the composition of the World Economic Forum (Wikipedia lists "investors, business leaders, political leaders, economists, celebrities and journalists) and the "kings of the earth," "merchants," and "great men of the earth" mentioned in Revelation 18?

66. *Desire of Ages*, 615

At the eleventh hour, when the work grows harder and the people are more hardened, there will be a variety of talent brought in. These workers will prove faithful and receive their penny. Sacrificing men will step into the places made vacant by those who would not be fitted for a place in the heavenly temple.... If they will learn the lesson of walking humbly before God, if they will not seek to invent new plans, but will do that which the Lord has appointed them to do, they will be enabled to carry God's plan onward and upward without narrowing it.[67]

The "eleventh hour" is a busy time in God's work!

At the eleventh hour the Lord will gather a company out of the world, to serve Him. There will be a converted ministry. Those who have had privileges and opportunities to become intelligent in regard to the truth, and yet who continue to counterwork the work God would have accomplished, will be purged out, for God accepts the service of no man whose interest is divided. He accepts the whole heart, or none.[68]

I speak not my own words when I say that God's Spirit will pass by those who have had their day of test and opportunity, but who have not distinguished the voice of God or appreciated the movings of His Spirit. Then thousands in the eleventh hour will see and acknowledge the truth.... These conversions to truth will be made with a rapidity that will surprise the church, and God's name alone will be glorified.[69]

Many who are standing aloof from the Seventh-day Adventists are living more in accordance with the light they have received than are many Seventh-day Adventists. This may seem strange to you, but strange things will have to be demonstrated to show the foolishness of the wisdom of those who judge others who have not seen the light.[70]

The addition of "eleventh-hour workers" has got to be a good thing, but the question still remains as to who raises the cry, "Behold, the Bridegroom cometh," in the first large city?

A brave youth like David taking on Goliath? A gray-haired patriarch like Caleb, praying "Lord, give me this mountain where the giants live"?[71] A cleric like Luther, or maybe an established middle class farmer like Miller. Or some poor soul who really has nothing more to lose than the two mites she devotes to God's cause? Will the task be taken up by a life-long Adventist? Or one of the millions "who have not [yet] seen the light"?

67. E.G. White, Letter to Brother McCullagh, April 8, 1897; Letter 98a, 1897
68. E.G. White, "The Danger of Rejecting Light," May 19, 1898; Manuscript 64, 1898
69. E.G. White, Letter to O.A. Olsen, December 15, 1890; Letter 43, 1890
70. E.G. White, Letter to A.T. Jones, April 18, 1900; Letter 59, 1900
    Right here it should be noted that William Miller was certainly the spark plug for the "Millerite Movement," but not the only herald of the "Second Advent." We like Miller, because Adventism descended most directly from his work, and he was a respectable Baptist. But let's not forget Joseph Wolff (a Jew), Edward Irving, (Church of Scotland), and Manuel Lacunza (a Jesuit). Oh yeah... I almost forgot the little kids in Scandinavia! Wouldn't that be a comeuppance to the rest of us who were too "balanced" to act "irresponsibly"!
71. See Joshua 14:6–15.

Maybe it won't come from a novice... maybe someone with talent and experience from "former days" will step up to the plate in the time of greatest need. Maybe it won't be a "lone wolf"... maybe a small group will emerge from the scattered rubble of "the worst evil." Where are our doctors, our pastors, our evangelists? What if they got together and just went ahead?

And what if this person or group doesn't get it all perfect the first time? There's something about Ellen White's "By trying"[72] comment that makes me think there may be a learning curve involved. Will it look fanatical? Will it look fanatical when Satan crowds his own fanaticism into the picture? (Come on... you *know* he will.)

The questions are real, and to make matters worse, there are no pat answers. Mistakes *will* be made. People will feel called who are not called by God. Money will be lost, fanaticism will arise, and workers will be shamed.

And yet... and yet... the story of E.P. Daniels comes to mind.

---

72. See reference 46 on page 240.

CHAPTER 37

Four Inches Wide

TIME to stretch our imaginations, boys and girls. Remember the race metaphor we've been using? Let's cross that with another sport so that each runner's lane is only four inches wide. Oh, and it's also four feet off the ground. Welcome to the balance beam, but this time it's a lot longer than usual. In fact, it looks like it goes forever.

The overriding demand of the balance beam is that the athlete's center of gravity must stay in a narrowly defined vertical plane. Fail to do that, and the *"time to impact"* formula[1] takes over. It's hard... which makes it a pretty good illustration of the perennial challenge of the Christian life: keeping things in balance.

The case history of Elder E.P. Daniels[2] and those with whom he interacted is a tragic tale with almost too many lessons, illustrations, implications, and applications to keep track of, but the applicability of the account to the issues we've been covering is frighteningly pointed, so please stick this one out. Unlike many of the inspiring events of Adventist history, this is not a good bedtime story for little children, nor is it appropriate for someone who might be inclined toward emotion-based disillusionment. There's a reason it comes near the end of the book; hopefully, anyone who's had enough interest to read this far, will have enough maturity to deal with it.

Daniels was a talented but flawed pastor working in California. Ellen White acknowledged that "He is hasty; he feels strongly and acts impulsively."[3] And yet,

---

1. For those who care, that's $t = \sqrt{\frac{2d}{g}}$ where t = time in seconds, d = distance in meters (or feet), and g = the acceleration due to gravity, 9.8 meters (or 32 feet) per second per second.

2. For the record, E.P. Daniels was no relation to A.G. Daniells (note the additional "l"), the far more well known minister who served as General Conference president from 1901–1922.

3. E.G. White, Letter to J.H. Waggoner, November 4, 1885; Letter 10, 1885

in 1885 he led out in a notable revival in the Healdsburg church. There was a genuine—and impressive—turning to the Lord, with church members making needed confession and new converts accepting the truth. George Butler, then the General Conference president, said, "God did greatly bless them. There are many manifest tokens of this, it seems to me. I have not heard of a work for years that seemed to bear more evidences of God's work than this does in many respects."[4]

But the story's cast of characters includes several more people we need to meet. Chief among these is Elder J.H. Waggoner, a long-time editor and "Elder Statesman" of the denomination. Waggoner had seniority, credibility, and a moral problem that was not widely known. By today's more permissive standards, his emotional attachment to one Mrs. Chittenden might not raise eyebrows, but in the Lord's sight it was a serious matter.

Other key figures include J.N. Loughborough (another pioneer), Dr. E.J. Waggoner (J.H. Waggoner's son), and Elder A.T. Jones. These last two names are best remembered in connection with events of just a few years later. Other players in the drama were a Sister Baker (a member of the Healdsburg church who was regarded as "affected"—a euphemism for "mentally deficient"—even before she briefly believed she had received inspired instruction from God that she was to share with the church), Brother C.H. Jones (no relation to A.T. Jones, but a long-time manager in the nearby Pacific Press Publishing Company), and Professor Sidney Brownsberger (the president of the "Healdsburg School").

Because of the church's proximity to the school, students began attending the ongoing revival meetings in the church. It was a good and needed influence. Until it wasn't *all* good. Some elements of a critical spirit came into the meetings, directed primarily toward the Oakland church and conference leadership. Daniels at one point advised church members to not attend the conference camp meeting, which was coming soon, and objected to the collection of an offering in Sabbath School classes.

Word of these concerns found their way to conference leaders (chiefly J.H. Waggoner and J.N. Loughborough) in due time. They instructed Daniels to come to the camp meeting, which he did, though most of the church members and students at the school did not. At that time, a number of the more "senior" ministers mentioned above spent time with Elder Daniels, seeking to defuse the situation. The meetings were not particularly fruitful, other than that Daniels acquiesced to their strong request (some might say, "demand") to close out the revival meetings.

Letters from the time hint that a point of personal tension (possibly personal animosity) arose between Elder J.H. Waggoner and Elder Daniels during these consultations.

---

4. George Butler, letter to Ellen White, April 19, 1886

After camp meeting was over, a small group of conference leaders went to Healdsburg, but again anything resembling a heartfelt union proved elusive.[5]

Brother C.H. Jones' letters describing the conference leaders' efforts paint a calm, matter of fact picture. There's no hint of anything but a rational desire to prevent any sort of schism. It would be hard to find fault with their efforts as he portrays them.

Letters from local members, however, speak of a regrettable effort on the part of A.T. Jones to prove that Sister Baker's illusions of divine revelation were a direct result of Elder Daniels' preaching.[6] No one in the Healdsburg church had accepted her claims—which predated the revival, anyway—so this accusation seemed contrived and unfair to many. The common weakness of such claims is that they tend to backfire!

> The great burden of the Elders was to show that the meetings were fanatical and that Elder Daniels' preaching was the cause of it. I kept quiet that first evening, but the second evening I had considerable to say in the way of defending Brother Daniels and his work.[7]

As George Butler noted, the handling of the issue resulted in a—

> revulsion of feeling which was occasioned by the course of the Conference Committee in stopping the meetings, which by the way was Brother Waggoner's act especially it seems to me, and at the efforts they made to prove that all the work was nearly fanatical, these things all together produced feelings of decided unpleasantness in the hearts of some who had taken quite a prominent part in the work of [the revival].[8]

Ellen White would write:

> I find myself pondering the Healdsburg church and its revival and the condemnation of it with a sadness I cannot express by pen or voice....
>
> Elder Daniels might not be perfect in his plans, in his spirit, in some of his movements, but there should have been the most prayerful study how to cure the to-be-feared, existing evil without marring and wounding the work of God and endangering souls....

Note her call for balance: sure, there are problems, but take a measured approach that doesn't destroy the good along with the bad.

> I do not say that Elder Daniels has been right in all things. He has, without question, done and said many unwise things. But will you forbid him to work because there are mistakes and errors mingled with his work?...

---

5. C.H. Jones letters to W.C. White, October 12, 16, and November 17, 1885. Courtesy of the Ellen G. White Estate.
6. This is especially ironic in that A.T. Jones would unadvisedly endorse the "testimonies" of Anna Rice Phillips a few years later. A timely letter from Ellen White, who was in Australia at the time, helped him recover himself.
7. W.C. Grainger letter to Ellen White, October 9, 1885. Courtesy of the Ellen G. White Estate.
8. George I. Butler letter to Ellen White, April 19, 1886

Brethren, it is high time that revivals similar to the one that has stirred the church in Healdsburg should come to every Seventh-day Adventist church in our land, else the church will not be prepared to receive the latter rain....

Don't miss this point. A failure to receive the latter rain means a crop failure. Every time that happens, it prolongs the reign of sin and suffering for billions of people on earth, and for God Himself. Remember? This is the 99.999% of God's suffering due to sin that we too easily forget.[9] Dull scholars, indeed!

Although he may not reveal perfection in all things, although he may be hasty and impulsive, I see no reason to denounce him, discourage him, and stop his labors....

Why I dwell so much on this now is because there will be most remarkable movements of the Spirit of God in the churches, if we are the people of God. And my brethren may arise and in their sense of paring everything not done after their style, lay their hand upon God's working and forbid it.

That little word "if" deserves a lot more thought than it gets.

I know what I am talking about. Your management alarms me. I have no confidence in this kind of work you have been engaged in. You have placed matters in a miserable shape. Confusion has come into the church. A different course might have been taken by our brethren and saved all this bad result of reaction. There are always some who will be overzealous, who will follow impressions, who are never well and healthfully balanced, who are always first in the fire and then into the water. They are extremists, overdo everything they touch, and yet some of these are honest. These have precious qualities, and these are not to be misjudged and cast away as worthless.

Don't brush this compassion for wackos aside! It's the best hope any of us have for being saved!

How my brethren dared to take the position they have done in regard to the work at Healdsburg I cannot conjecture, only as that their discernment and wisdom have departed from them. If such a work comes to us, how dare we to pronounce against it because we see that the instrument is only a fallible, erring man?[10]

In many ways, it was a preview of the far more damaging events to come in 1888. Leaders, trying to maintain the integrity of the church they were called to protect, took "reasonable" measures to forcibly contain what they saw as a problem, and lost something vital in the process. They didn't see that—despite errors—there was a revival, a turning of hearts toward God. Their desire to "solve a problem" led them to adopt measures which savored of religious intolerance.

How did this happen? Why did this happen?

9. *Education*, 263. Quoted more fully on page 40.
10. E.G. White, Letter to W.C. White, November 17, 1885; Letter 35, 1885. In fairness to Willie White, it should be said that though this letter was written to him, he was not a part of the events in California.

Ellen White points to Elder J.H. Waggoner as the primary influence, and though it's probably impossible to prove, circumstantial evidence implies that his indiscretions played a more direct role than simply rendering him spiritually unfit to be leading God's church.[11]

> Elder Waggoner's prejudice came in, causing him to pass his judgment on the work, and others followed in its wake.

As might be expected from one who really *did* receive divine instruction, Ellen White was well aware of Elder Waggoner's involvement with Mrs. Chittenden. She had written very pointed letters to the man, and had agonized over his slow response. In her mind, his judgment while in that spiritual condition was nothing to respect.

> I tell you plainly, I have no confidence in Elder Waggoner's decisions or feelings. His son would naturally take his view of the case and seek to make his decisions appear true and righteous, because these decisions must be maintained.[12]

> From the letters written I have reason to judge a good work was begun in Healdsburg. Those who felt it was wrong, and condemned it, committed, I believe, one of the greatest errors. And now the condemnation has been made,... then there is a seizing hold of very little things to make good the decision that they made hastily and in an unwise manner. Thus I look at the matter.[13]

One measure of the opportunity lost is reflected in the reality that when God holds a revival, it's not the same as when we try. We probably can't explain how this works, but it's hard to deny:

> When Elder Daniels' meetings closed, there was an excellent interest among outsiders. Quite a number were converted, and no doubt many more would have embraced the truth if the meetings had been allowed to continue. A religious interest was awakened that seemed to affect the whole town. The Episcopal minister started revival meetings immediately after ours closed and gathered in forty-five, and the Methodists I understand reaped quite a harvest also.[14]

None of this is to say that Daniels' friends always behaved wisely. C.H. Jones complains of one such supporter who wrote "a very bitter letter to Elder Waggoner,... threatening him if he did not desist in his efforts to crush Elder Daniels, that they would tell things about him that would make him stop."[15]

---

11. It's worth noting that church standards in the "social decorum" category (Waggoner's weak point) are often viewed as fitting in among those "little things" that don't amount to much... except in God's sight.

12. E.G. White, Letter to J.H. Waggoner, J.N. Loughborough, A.T. Jones, and E.J. Waggoner, April 1886; Letter 76, 1886

13. E.G. White, Letter to W.C. White, November 17, 1885; Letter 35, 1885

14. WC Grainger letter to Ellen White, October 9, 1885. Courtesy of the Ellen G. White Estate.

15. C.H. Jones letter to W.C. White, October 16, 1885. Courtesy of the Ellen G. White Estate.

Jones may have known nothing that could be "told" to make Waggoner "stop," but someone seems to have had some such idea. In a similarly misguided manner, one who identified with the revival decided to start up "secret meetings," to which only "those that claimed to be in the light"[16] were admitted.

None of this was news, or new, to Ellen White. She'd had previous experience with the devil's efforts to corrupt the Lord's work.

> In regard to the revival meetings at Healdsburg, it surely bears fruit of being the work of God, but in every such revival Satan gains advantages by coming in through unconsecrated persons who have had little or no experience in a life of piety and godliness. These elements will press to the front and on such occasions will be the most forward, the most zealous and enthusiastic.

> The very ones who could not be trusted with any important religious interest would take any burden, shoulder any responsibility, as though they were men and women who had earned a reputation through a life of self-denial, of self-sacrifice and devotion, that they were capable of deciding important questions and leading the church....[17]

> Now I suppose these individuals were the very ones who were the most officious in the meetings in Healdsburg. From what I have been shown I would suppose that they were of that number that composed the private meetings, where only those who were wholly the Lord's met. I know what I am talking about, for these matters have been laid open before me several times; and yet I would say to my brethren and sisters in Healdsburg, I believe the Spirit of God has done a work for you.[18]

Challenges enough, and yet Ellen White consistently saw something of value. "Revival" often comes in unexpected ways, but it is at our peril that we fail to recognize and receive it.

> Let this work go forward everywhere. Let sins be confessed. Let iniquities be revealed. Let it extend far and near. This work will be done. Men may pronounce against it because it does not come in their exact line. Fanaticism will also come in as it always has done when God works. The net will gather in its meshes both bad and good, but who will dare to cast the whole thing overboard because all are not of the right kind of fish? I feel deeply over this matter. I do not doubt but that Elder Daniels has erred in some things, but has his error been of that character that it makes him unworthy of a place among God's people?[19]

Figuring out who's to blame in a situation actually is necessary, sometimes. But if that's all we do, we haven't accomplished much. What about helping someone? What about finding a way to correct mistakes and strengthen weak points?

---

16. William Ings letter to Ellen White, December 8, 1885. Courtesy of the Ellen G. White Estate.
17. For anyone seeking to "earn a reputation" as one "capable of deciding important questions and leading the church," please note that the proper approach includes "a life of self-denial, of self-sacrifice and devotion."
18. E.G. White, Letter to Brother and Sister Harmon, February 8, 1886; Letter 9, 1886
19. E.G. White, Letter to J.H. Waggoner, November 4, 1885; Letter 10, 1885

I have seen the harm done by our brethren's seeing something wrong in a man and then questioning or picking him to pieces and leaving no good thing in him, but just discarding him as a useless piece of timber, that I am most thoroughly distressed over this kind of management. Let the love of Jesus melt the iron out of your souls, and let sweet sympathy and compassion come in for those who show imperfections.[20]

I wish you could see what a delicate, dangerous matter it is to meddle with the work of God unless you have light from heaven to guide you in your decisions. I have not the confidence in Elder J.H. Waggoner's judgment in these matters that you have.... I fear you have grieved the Spirit of God. The fruits were good in the work at Healdsburg, but the spurious was brought in as well as the genuine. Then it needed men of discernment, of calm, well-balanced minds, to come in when there were peril and indiscretion, to have a molding influence upon the work. You could have done this. You had no moral right to stop the meetings and to stop Elder Daniels from going right forward with the work and making the very most of the interest started, to gather outsiders into the interest if possible.

I cannot sanction your course. I cannot see that while you were working to correct evils, as you might have done, that you should stop the work. If this is the way you manage when God sends good, be assured the revivals will be rare. When the Spirit of God comes, it will be called "fanaticism," as on the day of Pentecost.

Balance is hard. Correcting evil without killing the sinner is hard, even for God, as you may recall. It's really no surprise to find we need both a spotter and a strength coach in order to get this right. The good news is that God has a plan for that. The bad news? The tests will only get harder:

I wish to say some things in reference to the revival at Healdsburg.

I wish to say I am not in harmony with your treatment of this matter. That there were fanatical ones who pressed into that work I would not deny. But if you move in the future as you have done in this matter, you may be assured of one thing, you will condemn the work of the latter rain when it shall come. For you will see at that time far greater evidences of fanaticism.[21]

Condemn the latter rain... not because Satan's counterfeit is so theologically profound, but because self-denial and self-sacrifice are too "unpalatable" to tolerate in order to save an erring sinner.

There is an epilogue to the Healdsburg revival story: Elder Daniels, whose ability as a speaker had once truly been used by God, went on to aspire to "greatness" as an orator. With that focus, he polished his delivery technique until he gained considerable praise from misguided church members. Ellen White saw things differently, telling one of his strongest supporters, "If you

---

20. E.G. White, Letter to W.C. White, November 17, 1885; Letter 35, 1885
21. E.G. White, Letter to J.H. Waggoner, J.N. Loughborough, A.T. Jones, and E.J. Waggoner, April 1886; Letter 76, 1886

want a human influence mingled with mesmeric power in place of the divine, you can have it."[22]

Daniels' alliance with this gentleman soured after a time, and Daniels filed a lawsuit against him. He evidently talked about suing Ellen White, too, but dropped the idea. By the early 1890s, Daniels and his whole family, giving in to weaknesses for money, display, and a love of praise, left the church entirely.

Sadly, the revival in Healdsburg was a long, long time ago, and we are still here. It's safe to say that meaningful revivals have been rare....

Well, that was an interesting side trip!

In case you've forgotten, the whole E.P. Daniels saga was brought up simply as a cautionary tale to remember while imagining someone trying to take "city work" from its status as a "really good idea" to an accomplished reality. It has to happen, because that's what starts the "mighty movement." But Ellen White herself spoke of the questions, doubts, and concerns that will come with it:

> But someone will say, "Suppose I give away all that I have, and then become dependent on others. It would be said, 'That man was a fool to do as he did'; and what shall we do then?"[23]

Can you doubt that some church member will, one day, have the nerve to lay siege to a city for God... but try and fail? Perhaps he has faults. Perhaps he set off prematurely to serve the Lord in a role for which he was not well qualified. Perhaps he was lacking in twenty different ways. And now he's living under an overpass (metaphorically, at the very least) because he failed to overcome three of his deficiencies....

What are you going to do?

Can you protect the church and have pity on the erring, too?

Hey! He learned seventeen lessons that you may not know! Could you "restore such a one in a spirit of gentleness"?[24] Would you consider it a privilege to "bring to your house the poor who are cast out"?[25]

> Years ago I was shown that God's people would be tested upon this point of making homes for the homeless; that there would be many without homes in consequence of their believing the truth. Opposition and persecution would deprive believers of their homes, and it was the duty of those who had homes to open a wide door to those who had not. I have been shown more recently that God would specially test His professed people in reference to this matter.[26]

---

22. E.G. White, Letter to Brother Church, Brother Bell, and the Church in Fresno, February 21, 1890; Letter 38, 1890
23. *Signs of the Times*, December 10, 1885
24. Galatians 6:1
25. Isaiah 58:7
26. *Testimonies*, vol. 2, 27

Workers who may not seem to be the most talented,... because they do not bring self-importance into their work, will be enabled to do that which more talented workers fail to do. God is just as willing now as anciently to work through human effort and to accomplish great things through weak instrumentalities. We shall not gain the victory by numbers, but by entire surrender to Jesus.[27]

Remember, all this experimentation with "entire surrender" is happening in a time when it can truthfully be said that "your sons and your daughters shall prophesy, your old men shall dream dreams, your young men shall see visions."[28] Does anyone seriously think the devil will pass up the opportunity to inject "fanaticism" into that setting?

But how easy will it be to overreact to fanaticism? How easy will it be to "condemn the work of the latter rain"?

It is altogether easier to find fault and point out what they call mistakes than to stand shoulder to shoulder with those who carry the burdens. This always has been and always will be.[29]

Rather than finding fault, why not try this?

I ask you to read the whole of this thirty-fifth chapter of Isaiah, with the fifty-sixth chapter. When you are disappointed because of the spiritual lack you see in the churches and in individuals, read these promising words of inspiration. They are given for the encouragement of our churches, and are to be claimed in times of emergency.[30]

"Times of emergency" are coming. Getting ready is a great idea.[31]

I know that dead people don't talk, and Sabbath isn't Sunday, and Jesus' feet won't touch the ground....

Great. That's all important. Really, it is. But maybe now would be a good time to think as well about the immutable law of self-sacrificing love. It's such a simple idea. Not complicated, maybe not even four inches wide, but it does stretch off into eternity.

---

27. E.G. White, Letter to Brethren in the Southern Field, December 2, 1902; Letter 187, 1902
28. Joel 2:28
29. E.G. White, "Diary: January 1898," January 17, 1898; Manuscript 180, 1898
30. *Review and Herald*, May 6, 1909
31. The idea of "emergency preparedness" deserves a little clarification. Contrary to much that you might hear from the "Christian Prepper" movement, you shouldn't be shopping for an assault rifle and enough ammo for a small army. You probably knew that... but having just recommended "getting ready" for "times of emergency," it seems appropriate to offer this inspired advice:
    "In the name of the Lord I advise all His people to have trust in God and not begin now to prepare to find an easy position for any emergency in the future, but to let God prepare for the emergency. We have altogether too little faith." E.G. White, "Counsel Regarding Matters Discussed at the 1889 General Conference," November 4, 1889; Manuscript 6, 1889.
    I don't see any conflict between this statement and my recommendation, but if you do, go with the inspired piece.

CHAPTER 38

Hello, Mat

CONTINUING the balance beam imagery of the last chapter, consider that it takes an athlete only about 0.65 seconds to part company with the beam and make the acquaintance of the floor mat. It happens. Sometimes it happens a lot.

That being the case, it's a good idea to briefly consider a few common (and avoidable) ways to fall off the beam.

Perhaps the most obvious lesson to be learned is from the devil's effort to kill the midnight cry before it even got going in 1844. Unsurprisingly, his main attack was through a group of fanatics. Of course, this happened in 1844, which is just one of the reasons Ellen White wasn't the least bit surprised to see the same problem show up when there was a revival in Healdsburg forty-one years later. The devil uses the same tools over and over again, and it's worth knowing that.

We've looked at Healdsburg, now let's head on back to 1844 for an eyewitness account by James White:

> It was in the month of August, 1844, that the memorable Second-Advent camp-meeting was held at Exeter, N.H. This meeting was large.... [but some in attendance] were causing divisions,... urging upon the flock extreme views of entire consecration.... [claiming] to be wonderfully led by the Holy Spirit.... So wonderfully impressed to do this or that, and so directly taught by the Holy Spirit in relation to their entire duty, how could they err? The idea of mistakes on their part, in doctrine or in duty, was banished from them....
>
> Supposing themselves directly taught by the Holy Spirit, they were ready to reject the instructions and corrections of those who labored to help them. Such persons... labor under the terrible deception that all their impressions are from the Holy Spirit, and must at all hazards be promptly obeyed.... In no case could Satan strike the Ad-

vent cause so stunning a blow, and so completely cover it with reproach, as to lead on certain ones who bore the Advent name in the wild career of fanaticism....

[The fanatics taught] that Scriptural sanctification, purity and holiness, consisted chiefly in happy flights of feeling, and being led in the minutiae of the Christian life by impressions.... and with their false notions of entire consecration [i.e., total depen-dence on their impressions], they were in readiness for the torch of fanaticism. If Satan could control these, and bring reproach upon the Advent cause, and sadden the hearts of those he could not destroy, he would gain a victory that would cause wicked men and demons to triumph....

There was upon the Exeter camp-ground a tent from Watertown, Massachusetts, filled with fanatical persons.... At an early period in this meeting, they attracted much attention by the peculiar style in which they conducted their seasons of social worship in their tent. These were irregular, very lengthy, frequently extending into hours of intermission and rest, continuing nearly all night, and attended with great excite-ment, and noise of shouting and clapping of hands, and singular gestures and ex-ercises. Some shouted so loud and incessantly as to become hoarse, and silent, simply because they could no longer shout, while others literally blistered their hands striking them together.

[Because of the fanatics' influence,] a general gloom was coming over the meet-ing.... The wildfire was spreading, and how to stop it was the question. The people were told of the dangers of spiritual magnetism, and were warned to keep away from that tent. But this only caused a crowd of the curious, incautious, and those who claimed a right to investigate, and felt that they were responsible to no one, to gather round this tent. And it was evident that every hour some were being brought under this influence, several of whom were suffering impulse to ride over reason.

But when S.S. Snow[1] presented his understanding of the 2,300 days extend-ing to October 22 and "the midnight cry," the believers found solid ground for their feet once again and—

fanaticism, ultra holiness, unhappy divisions, and their results, melted away be-fore it like an early autumn frost before the rising sun.[2]

Certainly the Holy Spirit *is* given to guide God's people, but Jesus said He was to guide us into all *truth,* not into a mindless acceptance of every illogical impression that comes into our heads. It's clear that the Spirit *has* provided minute guidance on occasion when exactly that was needed, but He is not com-missioned to take the place of the mental powers God has given.

---

1. We've met Snow in passing: first on page 162, and again in a comment made in reference 57 on page 223. The story of his contribution to the Millerite movement is a good example of God's provision of "new light" just when it's needed. I'd love to include an account of all that, but this book is already too long.
2. James White, *Life Incidents,* 153–158, 120

> What human power can do, divine power is not summoned to do. God does not dispense with man's aid. He strengthens him, co-operating with him as he uses the powers and capabilities given him.[3]

> The Lord does not propose to perform for us either the willing or the doing. This is our proper work. As soon as we earnestly enter upon the work, God's grace is given to work in us to will and to do, but never as a substitute for our effort. Our souls are to be aroused to cooperate.[4]

This is another case of "As in the natural, so in the spiritual." Notice Ellen White's illustration:

> The farmer plows his land and sows the seed, but he cannot make the seed grow. He must depend upon God to do that which no human power can do. The Lord puts His own Spirit into the seed, causing it to spring into life.[5]

Well, that makes sense! But if the farmer follows some random (or demonic) impression to leave his corn seed on top of the ground, it won't be the Holy Spirit's fault when the crows eat it all.

It's not an easy task to write up objective rules to judge matters of someone else's individual guidance. What rule would have gotten it right when the Lord said, "Take now your son, your only son..."?[6] The challenge is that neither the side of "reason" nor the side of "faith" are cc'd or bcc'd when God speaks to an individual. That was a lesson Jesus taught to Peter, once upon a time.[7]

Given the universal pattern of any deceptive effort, we would assume that the "Watertown movement" began in a way that looked positive. More than likely, "good things" came from following those early impressions. But somehow the people were deceived and ended up in full blown fanaticism. How does that happen?

I'd be a fool to pretend I know all the possible answers to that question, but from what we've seen in this volume, at least one rational answer presents itself. Consider again these two statements that we've looked at previously:

> Satan can present a counterfeit so closely resembling the truth that it deceives those who are willing to be deceived, who desire to shun the self-denial and sacrifice demanded by the truth.[8]

OK... but how do we know they were shunning self-denial and sacrifice? In what way were they doing this? Again, it's likely that a myriad of answers may apply in a myriad of cases, but here's one that appears common:

---

3. *Desire of Ages*, 535
4. *Testimonies to Ministers*, 240
5. *Testimonies*, vol. 8, 326
6. Genesis 22:2
7. John 21:20–23
8. *Great Controversy*, 528

> Those who do not realize their danger because they do not watch, will pay, with the loss of their souls, the penalty of their presumption and their willful ignorance of Satan's devices.[9]

Human intelligence, human scholarship, human understanding are all great, but limited. A "theory of the truth" or a "theory of final events" will never save anyone. The decisive issues are deeper, down at the "self-denial and sacrifice demanded by the truth" level. But none of that makes understanding _expendable_ or _superfluous!_[10] We can "shun self-denial" by simply refusing to put in the effort to understand. It's called "willful ignorance," and it's enough to get some folks into the fanatical camp. So, don't be one of them. Even if "good things" are coming, cultivate the trait of self-distrust, and constantly compare every point with scripture. And not just the obvious "doctrinal" points. Consider the method—has God made a habit of communicating with His people in that manner? Consider the effect—are these impressions strengthening my understanding of God, or just relieving me of the need to really understand the situation?

We can take yet another look at both the possibility of "good things" and the "bad effects" that come from not using the minds God gave us. In 1911, a Mrs. Harris visited Ellen White, asking for counsel. Her husband had adopted the use of "the lot" to make business decisions. Well, actually, he was just flipping a coin or dropping a small card with "yes" on one side and "no" on the other. Anyway, his wife was concerned with this approach, even though "he has made successful land deals and has been able to turn thousands of dollars into the work."

"The work" mentioned here is the church, so that's obviously a good thing! The Lord is blessing!

Mrs. Harris goes on:

> In these deals he has sometimes been guided by the method above mentioned. His business affairs are assuming larger proportions, and greater sums of money are being involved.

Hallelujah! More money for the cause!

> If he continues to depend upon this method of guidance, I feel that his affairs may end disastrously at any time.

So who's right? Mr. Harris has made thousands for the Lord's work (and, likely, some for himself, too); Mrs. Harris is worried (but hasn't made any money for the church). How would the messenger of the Lord respond?

---

9. _Review and Herald_, April 25, 1907

10. A scholarly term for this logical trap is "Constructed Antithesis." The devil does this _a lot_. The idea is to take two complementary items and present them as opposed to each other. A classic example is, "Which is more important for your car, the gas or the oil?" Sure, you can say, "It must be the gas, because you can't go _anywhere_ without it." True enough, but if you have ambitions of driving more than twenty miles, you better have some oil, too.

Here is a course of action that if it appears all successful, will call in the talents of our people. The enemy of souls is very anxious to hinder the completion of the special work for this time by bringing in some erroneous transaction. He will bring it in under the garb of great liberality; and if those pursuing this course have apparent success for a time, others will follow. And the very truths that are testing our people for this time and which, if clearly understood, would cut off such a course of action, lose their force.

Interesting... but what might "the completion of the special work for this time" be? The three angel's messages, of course! Working with minds and hearts to "prepare a people"; "effecting transformations so amazing that Satan... stands viewing them as a fortress impregnable to his sophistries and delusions."[11] That doesn't happen when the mind is in neutral!

But if Satan brings it in "under the garb of great liberality"—if there's easy money to be made, and maybe even the church is getting some of it—"others will follow." Really? When the motive of heaven is service, we get distracted by the first fast buck that comes along? That's more than sad.

Still, for the sake of clarity, W.C. White asked:

Sister Harris says that Brother Harris always prays before he tosses up his coin. Would not that make some difference?

Ellen White's response: "Not a whit of difference."

The idea of flipping a coin, though, sounds really random, kind of irresponsible. But an impression from the Holy Spirit? That sounds "holy," at least by comparison. But the comparison we might make in our minds could use a little education. In this same interview concerning Mr. Harris and his coin flipping, Ellen White made a connection that probably came from both personal experience and from direct inspiration:

After the great disappointment of the Adventist people in 1844, we had all these things to contend with over and over again. Then I was raised up from a bed of sickness and sent to give a message of reproof for such fanaticism.

They used different methods. They would select a sign and then follow the course indicated by the sign. In one case they would not bury a child that had died, because they understood from the signs that they had set that the child was going to be raised from the dead.

They had so fully accepted their impressions as being revelations from the Lord that they were led by these impressions to do strange things. As a result, some of these people were arrested and put in prison.

When things go that far, most of us would say something was wrong—unless, of course, we had been led along step by step from the "good things are happening" stage. We are told that "by their fruits" we may know good trees

---

11. *General Conference Daily Bulletin*, February 27, 1893

from bad trees, but do we have to wait till someone gets arrested and put in prison? Not to mention that the "true believer" would likely interpret it as "persecution for righteousness' sake."

It turns out there are multiple categories of "fruit" to consider:

> God does not instruct us that we are to learn His will by any such way.
>
> Will it furnish us with experiences that will glorify God for us to decide what is His will by the dropping of a card or a coin and observing how it falls? No; no. Such tests as this will spoil the religious experience of the one who adopts them. Every one who depends upon such things for guidance needs to be reconverted.
>
> It is the Bible plan for a group of people to pray together and study His Word together for light, rather than that an individual shall follow his fancies supported by such methods. If the Lord is working for us, He does it in His own order. He does not step out of His order to adopt methods of such an earthly character.[12]

God's "own order" is also a fruit of the Spirit, and learning to depend on anything leaning another way is going to carry some risk. Will a person who "asks for a sign" be rejected by God? Well, Gideon wasn't. But there's also this thing called "progressive revelation," and we've got the benefit of a whole lot more revelation than he had. It seems likely that God is looking for a little of that "progress" to show up in our experience!

Does that mean that anyone in, say, the last hundred years, or twenty years, or five weeks, who has asked for a sign was out of line? (Here I speak for myself, so don't confuse this with inspired commentary.) I wouldn't say that. "Special" circumstances sometimes arise. We have all probably prayed for God's providence to "open and close doors." If there is no other way to determine His will, I'm sure He won't fault us for that. But when we begin to use "signs" or "impressions" as a shortcut to avoid study, or prayer, or any form of "self-denial and sacrifice demanded by the truth," we are flirting with the mat.

A final matter here which is applicable to almost every form of fanaticism: There is in any call to action a certain emphasis on individual responsibility. No one without a decent level of initiative and personal independence is going to be stepping forward in any conspicuous way. But that doesn't mean God wants His work to revert back to the "Wild, Wild West."

Imagine, for a moment, a "worst case scenario" in which every aspect of our current denominational organization just up and apostatized. Clearly, that would be a bad situation, even if only imaginary (though it did happen once, at the local conference level, when the "Holy Flesh" fanaticism hit in 1900). What to do?

---

12. E.G. White, "Mrs. E. G. White, 'Elmshaven,' Sanitarium, California," May 29, 1911; Manuscript 3, 1911. The sequence of the quotations from this manuscript has been rearranged to facilitate the flow of thought. I don't think it distorts anything, but "full disclosure" works best before being accused.

Is Judges 17:6 our model? "In those days there was no king in Israel; everyone did what was right in his own eyes." Interestingly—as if to underline the reality of the challenge—the exact words are repeated in Judges 21:25.

Is that the model we'll have to adopt under the pressures of the last days? Or, even, is that the ideal we should be aiming for?

Simple answers: "No" and "no."

> Satan well knows that success can only attend order and harmonious action. He well knows that everything connected with heaven is in perfect order, that subjection and thorough discipline mark the movements of the angelic host. It is his studied effort to lead professed Christians just as far from heaven's arrangement as he can; therefore he deceives even the professed people of God and makes them believe that order and discipline are enemies to spirituality, that the only safety for them is to let each pursue his own course, and to remain especially distinct from bodies of Christians who are united and are laboring to establish discipline and harmony of action. All the efforts made to establish order are considered dangerous, a restriction of rightful liberty, and hence are feared as popery. These deceived souls consider it a virtue to boast of their freedom to think and act independently. They will not take any man's say-so. They are amenable to no man. I was shown that it is Satan's special work to lead men to feel that it is in God's order for them to strike out for themselves and choose their own course, independent of their brethren....
>
> Has God changed from a God of order? No; He is the same in the present dispensation as in the former. Paul says: "God is not the author of confusion, but of peace." He is as particular now as then. And He designs that we should learn lessons of order and organization from the perfect order instituted in the days of Moses for the benefit of the children of Israel.[13]

Exactly what that will look like under increasing levels of duress, is not for me to say. But any spirit of "I'm the only one that counts" is clearly not an example of self-denial and self-sacrifice. Those Christ-like traits are the kind of criteria we should use when it comes to making policy decisions, whether we have a smoothly working organizational structure or not.

---

13. *Testimonies*, vol. 1, 650, 653

CHAPTER 39

Dangerous Wobbles

RANK fanaticism may be the surest way to get from the balance beam to the mat, but it's far from the only way. When Dr. Kellogg went from being "the greatest physician in our world," to being a purveyor of "the alpha of deadly heresies" back in the 1890s and early 1900s, "city work" was one of the major points of departure which got him off balance and eventually sent him crashing to the mat with his own brand of fanaticism.

Since we've seen a special importance in the work of city evangelism, especially in connection with the experience of the ten virgins and the loud cry, we'd be foolish to not pay attention to the lessons from back then.

One danger to which Kellogg fell prey still comes to us in the tension between God owning the soybeans on a thousand fields, and the less cheery reality of limited funds. First up is the question as to why funds should be limited at all. If we're doing God's will, isn't it God's bill?

Truly, it is. It's just that God's will includes a lot more than providing food and shelter to "the poor" who will be with us always. God's will takes in the fostering of intelligence, a willingness to see other parts of His work well funded, the need to differentiate and prioritize expenditures, and the constant need for us to remember our dependence on Him. Each of these matters is best addressed through a monetary policy which limits our available money supply. And so—no shock here—that's what God does.

With limited supply, decisions as to optimal allotment must be made. What is given away, is not necessarily immediately replaced. Sometimes, of course, it is. When pouring out vessels of oil, or dividing loaves and fishes, it has been known to happen. But such cases still tend to be exceptions. Nevertheless, the

Christian is expected to unhesitatingly provide assistance... sometimes. But not always. And therein lies a distinction to be maintained.

The Spirit of Prophecy has a great deal of counsel in this regard, but it's easy to miss the balance. The one ditch is selfishness in it's various forms, and the other ditch is full of all kinds of unwise—often foolishly sentimental—plans which damage either the objects of the benevolence or the cause of God.

The good news? In between the two ditches, there is still a road. We should look for it.

The more traditional and obvious error is the selfish ditch. The Bible is full of encouragement for God's people to do "good works," to help others, to "give" rather than "to receive."[1] We all know that selfishness is bad, but it's easy for "good Christians" to trick themselves into accepting Satan's principle of self-seeking, and think it's the right thing to do. How? By losing balance on the issue of stewardship.

> You may say you have been taken in and have bestowed your means upon those unworthy of your charity, and therefore have become discouraged in trying to help the needy. I present Jesus before you. He came to save fallen man, to bring salvation to His own nation; but they would not accept Him. They treated His mercy with insult and contempt, and at length they put to death Him who came for the purpose of giving them life. Did our Lord turn from the fallen race because of this? Though your efforts for good have been unsuccessful ninety-nine times, and you received only insult, reproach, and hate, yet if the one-hundredth time proves a success, and one soul is saved, oh, what a victory is achieved! One soul wrenched from Satan's grasp, one soul benefited, one soul encouraged. This will a thousand times repay you for all your efforts.[2]

No Christian should waste his Lord's goods, but defining "waste" without a clear view of eternity is a perilous effort. Getting past that barrier is a major step in a growing Christian experience.

> Read Isaiah 58, ye who claim to be children of the light. Especially do you read it again and again who have felt so reluctant to inconvenience yourselves by favoring the needy. You whose hearts and houses are too narrow to make a home for the homeless, read it; you who can see orphans and widows oppressed by the iron hand of poverty and bowed down by hardhearted worldlings, read it. Are you afraid that an influence will be introduced into your family that will cost you more labor, read it. Your fears may be groundless, and a blessing may come, known and realized by you every day. But if other-

---

1. After his conversion, Dr. Kellogg gave a series of sermons at the 1893 General Conference session where he stressed this point. You can find that story in my previous book, *d'Sozo*.

    And, if you're putting together a sermon encouraging Biblical generosity, here's a starter list of verses for you: Deuteronomy 15:7–14, 16:17, 24:15; Proverbs 11:24,25, 14:21, 22:9, 28:27; Isaiah 32:8, 58:7–11; Matthew 5:16, 26:10, 25:31–46; Mark 14:6; Acts 9:36; 2 Corinthians 9:8; Ephesians 2:10; Philippians 1:6; Colossians 1:10; 1 Timothy 5:10, 25, 6:18; 2 Timothy 2:21, 3:17; Titus 2:7, 14, 3:1, 8, 14; Hebrews 10:24, 13:21.

2. *Testimonies*, vol. 2, 31

wise, if extra labor is called for, you can draw upon One who has promised: "Then shall thy light break forth as the morning, and thine health shall spring forth speedily."

The reason why God's people are not more spiritually minded and have not more faith, I have been shown, is because they are narrowed up with selfishness. The prophet is addressing Sabbathkeepers, not sinners, not unbelievers, but those who make great pretensions to godliness. It is not the abundance of your meetings that God accepts. It is not the numerous prayers, but the rightdoing, doing the right thing and at the right time. It is to be less self-caring and more benevolent. Our souls must expand. Then God will make them like a watered garden, whose waters fail not.[3]

When it comes to veering off the road, selfishness is by far the more common ditch in which to land. But the other side of the road has made its mark on history, too. It's a big story, but we'll go with a severely condensed version for now. The first thing to note is that God's work is not quite as simple as just handing out cash:

How we can work to help all classes of people in the right way is a problem. There cannot be charity or benevolence exercised indiscriminately without doing positive harm to a large number.[4]

The challenge here is that "help" is only effective when it is properly matched with "need," and that varies quite a bit from case to case. Even when the individual thinks cash would be the most helpful thing, for "a large number," it may not be. Hmmm... what to do?

When you lay out money, consider, "Am I encouraging prodigality?" When you help the poor and wretched, consider, "Am I helping them, or hurting them?"[5]

It is not wise to give indiscriminately to every one who may solicit our aid, for we may thus encourage idleness, intemperance, and extravagance.[6]

The need to make sure our assistance is actually helpful is easy for some "naturally generous" folks to overlook. Indeed, it was largely this matter that Dr. Kellogg neglected as he slid into the ditch of his choice.

In the 1890s, Dr. Kellogg was opposed in different ways by church members —he would especially point to ministers—who didn't care for health reform, or who didn't care for medical missionary work, or who simply didn't care for Kellogg. Over time, the Doctor came to resent this, determined to ignore them, and set about making a name for himself through the constantly expanding "humanitarian" work in Chicago. These efforts were generous to a fault, but Dr. Kellogg was the best fund raiser in the denomination, and his stories grabbed

---

3. *Testimonies*, vol. 2, 35
4. E.G. White, "Diary: The Responsibility of Parents," 1910; Manuscript 91, 1910
5. E.G. White, Letter to J.H. Kellogg and Associates, January 6, 1899; Letter 4, 1899
6. E.G. White, "Our Duty in Ministering to the Poor," 1893; Manuscript 98, 1893

the most attention. Soon the Sanitarium and the growing work in Chicago had come to consume so much funding that there was nothing left over for foreign work. The church's mission was dying.

> The whole vineyard of the Lord has been robbed to carry on a work that is never-ending. It has consumed means that should have supplied the necessities of foreign fields. The means spent in Chicago would have given to new fields advantages for doing the very work that God has designated should be done. Look at the destitution that exists in portions of the field in foreign countries, and in contrast see the investment made in one great city.[7]

> I know that God would not have His money absorbed in Chicago as it now is. The money invested in this way consumes much time and labor. This is pleasing to Satan, for he knows that it will close the door against the support of missionaries in their work, and then the work of the gospel ministry will be held up to ridicule in comparison with the large work done in medical missionary lines.[8]

But money wasn't the only issue; the other great asset of the church is manpower. That, too, can be squandered:

> There is danger of loading down everyone with this class of work, because of the intensity with which it is carried on. This work has no limit; it can never be got through with, and it must be treated sensibly, as a part of the great whole.[9]

> But the Lord has not called Seventh-day Adventists to make this work a specialty. He would not have them, in this work, engross many workers or exhaust the treasury by erecting institutions for the care of outcasts, thus hindering the work of foreign missions. God calls for one hundred missionaries where there is now one. These are to go forth to foreign countries.[10]

> From the light God has given me, I know that the gospel message for this time is being largely turned aside, for work among the lowest class of people. This work is being made the all-absorbing work; but this is not in God's order. It is a never-ending work, and if it is carried on as it has been in the past, all the power of God's people will be required to counterbalance it, and the work of preparing a people to stand amid the perils of the last days will never be done.[11]

> We need a tender, compassionate, wise love, or we shall carry to extremes the work for those who have never felt the current of purity flowing through heart and brain. To spend all the means available for this class of persons is not wise, for it would take all the mental,

---

7. E.G. White, Letter to Kellogg, February 27, 1900; Letter 33, 1900. The "Workingman's Home," only one aspect of the overall Chicago City Mission, was a homeless shelter which provided room and board for up to four hundred men, primarily alcoholics.

8. E.G. White, Letter to J.H. Kellogg, July 2, 1900; Letter 92, 1900

9. E.G. White, Letter to J.H. Kellogg, January 5, 1899; Letter 3, 1899

10. E.G. White, Letter to Brother and Sister W.W. Prescott, February 17, 1900; Letter 28, 1900

11. E.G. White, "The Work for this Time," February 20, 1900; Manuscript 16, 1900

physical, and spiritual force of our workers. We are not required to do this for those whom we must watch as closely as we would watch a prisoner who seeks to escape.[12]

Worse than simply wasting effort, sending "young men and women" into the most corrupt part of Chicago was a recipe for trouble.

It is dangerous to set young men and young women at work among the abandoned classes. They are placed where they come in contact with every form of impurity, and Satan uses this opportunity to compass their ruin. Thus far more is lost than these workers save. Many of the efforts made for the abandoned result in the loss of the purity of the workers....

Medical missionary workers should be cleansed, refined, purified, and elevated. They should stand upon the platform of eternal truth. But I have been instructed that the truth has not been made to appear in its true bearing. The result that is worked out tends to corrupt minds; the sacred is not distinguished from the common.[13]

It is not safe to give young men and young women this class of work to do. The experiment would be a dear one. Thus those who could work in the highways would be disqualified for work of any kind.[14]

What about results? What and how much is gained? Are souls being converted? Are they strengthening God's work?

Many of those who are supposed to be rescued from the pit into which they have fallen cannot be relied upon as counselors, as those who can be trusted to engage in the sacred work done in these last days. The enemy is determined to mix error with truth. To do this, he uses the opportunity given him by the debased class for whom so much money is expended, whose appetites have been perverted through indulgence, whose souls have been abused, whose characters are misshapen and deformed, and whose habits and desires are grovelling, who think habitually upon evil.

Such ones can be transformed in character, but few ever are. Many make a superficial change in their habits and practices, and then suppose that they are Christians. They are received into church fellowship, but they are a great trouble and a great care. Through them Satan tries to sow in the church the seeds of jealousy, dishonesty, criticism, and accusing. Thus he tries to corrupt the other members of the church.

The same disposition that mastered the man from childhood, led him to break away from all restraint, and brought him into the place where he was found. He is reported to be rescued. But time shows that the work done for him did not make him a submissive child of God. Resentful feelings rise at every supposed slight. He cherishes bitterness, wrath, malice. By his words and spirit he shows that he has not been born again. His tendencies are downward, tending to sensuality. He is untrustworthy, unthankful, and unholy. Thus it is with all the debased who have not been soundly con-

---

12. E.G. White, "Words of Instruction Regarding the Medical Missionary Work," January 12, 1900; Manuscript 6, 1900

13. E.G. White, Letter to J.E and Emma White, July 13, 1900; Letter 162, 1900

14. E.G. White, "The Work for this Time," February 20, 1900; Manuscript 16, 1900

verted. Every one of these marred characters, untransformed, becomes an efficient worker for Satan, creating dissension and strife.[15]

Never allow inexperienced men—in the past a blot on God's fair creation—who have been rescued by medical missionary work, to make a tirade in their speeches against those who are ministering in word and doctrine. This has been done, and it will be done again, unless more solid, intelligent moves are made in the work.[16]

The ministers of God's appointment are more in the line of their God-given work than yourself and those you place on the stand at our large gatherings—men who will begin a tirade of the ministers—men who are undisciplined, uncouth, and unconverted. They are from the sloughs of Chicago and say after their drunken sprees, "I am saved."[17]

When it's all said and done, there is a certain amount of logic and good sense that needs to go into God's work.

There is not to be, in the use of God's money, a mercy for the shiftless class that would make mercy and compassion foolishness.[18]

Logic notwithstanding, if this sentimental concept of the work takes hold on minds, it is a hard spell to break. To point out the weaknesses and dangers of such an approach will invite a response of serious accusation!

While this class of work is magnified as it is now being magnified, and glowing descriptions which are not true are given of it, the counsel given to restrain it will be regarded as a resistance of the Spirit of God.[19]

Enough of the dreariness! There must be a bright side to all this medical missionary work. What is it *supposed* to look like?

In the working of the cause of God for this time the benevolent work should give special help to those who, through the presentation of truth at our camp meetings, are convicted and converted....

We must engage in the work of caring especially for those who have the moral courage to accept the truth, lose their situations [in the modern vernacular: "lose their jobs"] in consequence, and are refused work to earn means to support their families. There must be a fund to aid the worthy poor families who love God and keep His commandments. They are not to be left without help and forced to work on the Sabbath or starve because the means that God designed for His loyal people are diverted into channels that help the most unworthy and disobedient and the transgressors of His law....

Shall the poor among God's people be left without any provision being made for them? Shall it be made as hard as possible for them to obtain means to live?

---

15. E.G. White, Letter to J.H. Kellogg, December 12, 1899; Letter 215, 1899
16. E.G. White, "The Medical Missionary Work," May 10, 1899; Manuscript 177, 1899
17. E.G. White, "Diary: Warnings to Dr. Kellogg," 1899; Manuscript 199, 1899
18. E.G. White, "Diary: Warnings to Dr. Kellogg," 1899; Manuscript 199, 1899
19. E.G. White, "The Medical Missionary Work," May 10, 1899; Manuscript 177, 1899

God wants His loyal people to reveal to a sinful world that He has not left them to perish. Special pains is to be taken for this people who are cast out from their homes, and for the truth's sake are obliged to suffer.[20]

When our ministers, our canvassers, or our missionaries go forth to foreign fields, to engage in the work, and through privation lose their health, God expects every one of us to act as His human agencies, to take these men in, to receive them heartily. They must not receive the cruel idea that you will put them in some out-of-the-way place and draw from the little morsel of funds they have. What kind of reflections do you suppose will come to them?...

Ten thousand times more prosperity will rest upon the families and institutions who will work on these principles, and thus represent the character of Christ.[21]

Take note. Don't forget. That's a lot of prosperity!

It's also worth noting that some cases of need have a higher priority than others. Kellogg turned the whole list upside down, but there's no reason we should.

Those who are of the household of faith come first, not the depraved, polluted men who have destroyed themselves, filling soul and body with iniquity, as did the antediluvians, and as did the inhabitants of Sodom. Yet for these Dr. Kellogg has labored, while those with whom he should have linked up in perfect harmony he has treated as offensive.[22]

Among all whose needs demand our interest, the widow and the fatherless have the strongest claims upon our tender sympathy and care. "Pure and undefiled religion before God and the Father is this, to visit the fatherless and widows in their affliction, and to keep himself unspotted from the world."[23]

OK, who's next on the list?

The true medical missionary work is expressed in tender compassion to the Lord's poor, and in doing good to all the needy and suffering of the household of faith whose necessities in the providence of God come to our knowledge and require our notice. Every soul is under special tribute to God to notice with particular compassion God's worthy poor. Under no consideration are these to be passed by under the false pretense that charity makes provisions to reward the doers of evil who have ruined themselves through sinful indulgence, those who are not the friends of God.[24]

---

20. E.G. White, Letter to J.H. Kellogg, March 12, 1900; Letter 45, 1900. But what if you are the one suffering... and what if the church fails you? "Never need any one fear that observance of the true Sabbath will result in starvation. These promises [Isaiah 58] are a sufficient answer to all the excuses that man may invent for refusing to keep the Sabbath. Even if, after beginning to keep God's law, it seems impossible to support one's family, let every doubting soul realize that God has promised to care for those who obey His commandments. By keeping His law, we break the yoke of bondage, and live in freedom, delighting ourselves in the Lord." E.G. White, "Sermon: Cry aloud, spare not," August 30, 1902; Manuscript 116, 1902

21. E.G. White, Letter to Brother Sanderson, August 29, 1898; Letter 68, 1898

22. E.G. White, Letter to J.H. Kellogg, January 21, 1900; Letter 177, 1900

23. E.G. White, "Our Duty in Ministering to the Poor," 1893; Manuscript 98, 1893

24. E.G. White, "The Temperance Work," July 25, 1900; Manuscript 46, 1900

Any neglect on the part of those who claim to be followers of Christ, a failure to relieve the necessities of a brother or sister who is bearing the yoke of poverty and oppression, is registered in the books of heaven as shown to Christ in the person of His saints. What a reckoning the Lord will have with many, very many, who present the words of Christ to others but fail to manifest tender sympathy and regard for a brother in the faith who is less fortunate and successful than themselves.[25]

Jesus.... mingled with all classes of society that all might partake of the blessings He came to bestow. He was found in the synagogues and in the market places. He shared the social life of His countrymen, gladdening with His presence the households of all who invited Him. But He never urged His way uninvited. He was active to relieve every species of human misery that was brought to Him in faith for relief; but He did not bestow healing power indiscriminately where there was manifested an independence and selfish exclusiveness that would give no expression to their sorrows nor ask for the help so much needed. All who came unto Him in faith He was ready and willing to relieve.[26]

If one comes to your door and says he is hungry, do not turn him away empty. Give him something to eat, of such things as you have. You know not his circumstances, and it may be that his poverty is the result of misfortune.[27]

True beneficence means more than mere gifts. It means a liberal interest in the welfare of the various branches of God's work. It means to be a medical missionary of God's appointment. It means to teach the improvident the need of economy. There are thousands of the widows and the fatherless, the young and the aged, the afflicted and the crippled, who should be taught how to help themselves. Many, confined to their beds, are unable to work. But those who can work should be made to realize that if they do not work, they shall not be fed. Every one who is capable of eating a square meal is capable of working to pay for that meal. If made to pay for his food, he will appreciate the money-value of strength and time. Such beneficence carries with it valuable lessons. It not only ministers to the needs of the poor, but teaches them how to care for themselves.[28]

The conditions of inheriting eternal life are plainly stated by our Saviour in the most simple manner. The man who was wounded and robbed represents those who are subjects of our interest, sympathy, and charity. If we neglect the cases of the needy and the unfortunate that are brought under our notice, no matter who they may be, we have no assurance of eternal life; for we do not answer the claims that God has upon us.[29]

If no one ever came under your notice who needed your sympathy, your words of compassion and pity, then you would be guiltless before God for failing to exercise these precious gifts; but every follower of Christ will find opportunity to show Chris-

25. E.G. White, "Testimony Regarding Brother Buster," August 3, 1894; Manuscript 34, 1894
26. E.G. White, Letter to Brethren in Switzerland," August 29, 1878; Letter 2a, 1878
27. E.G. White, "Our Duty in Ministering to the Poor," 1893; Manuscript 98, 1893
28. E.G. White, "Unheeded Warnings I," November 27, 1901; Manuscript 156a, 1901
29. *Testimonies*, vol. 3, 524

tian kindness and love; and in so doing he will prove that he is a possessor of the religion of Jesus Christ.[30]

That's quite a list! Again, for emphasis since it seems this is an easy point to
lose sight of, there are some "controls" built in that should keep us from wasting all God's money and manpower.

> I use every penny I have in this helping work. But it makes a difference with me
> who I help, whether it is God's suffering poor who are keeping His commandments and
> lose their situations in consequence, or whether it is a blasphemer treading under foot
> the commandments of God....

> The Lord does not give into the hands of Sabbathkeepers the work of support-
> ing the disobedient and transgressors of His law, while the needy, suffering ones
> of God's people are left without provision because of wrong conceptions of duty.
> We are not called upon to make it a special business to reward the disobedient
> and transgressors of God's law who continue in sin, and who are educated to look
> for help to those who will sustain them. We shall find a rich blessing when we do
> our duty to the Lord's suffering, needy ones. We should not pass them by and re-
> ward the unholy and sinful.[31]

> Nothing can do greater insult to Jehovah and our Redeemer Jesus Christ who came
> to our world to live the law of God, than to assume the generous attitude that God's
> bounties are to be given alike to the most profligate, the most corrupt in soul, body,
> and spirit. This generosity should be exercised toward the worthy poor who have
> taken their position to obey God by becoming loyal to his commandments.[32]

But even with those boundaries, still, there's plenty to do! That being the
case, it makes sense to consider how best to meet these needs. Fortunately,
we've been given some light on that. Kellogg had it, too, but he didn't show
much interest in following it.

> Everywhere there is a tendency to substitute the work of organizations for individ-
> ual effort. Human wisdom tends to consolidation, to centralization, to the building up
> of great churches and institutions. Multitudes leave to institutions and organizations
> the work of benevolence; they excuse themselves from contact with the world, and
> their hearts grow cold. They become self-absorbed and unimpressible. Love for God
> and man dies out of the soul.

> Christ commits to His followers an individual work—a work that cannot be done
> by proxy. Ministry to the sick and the poor, the giving of the gospel to the lost, is not
> to be left to committees or organized charities. Individual responsibility, individual ef-
> fort, personal sacrifice, is the requirement of the gospel.[33]

---

30. *Review and Herald*, May 4, 1897
31. E.G. White, Letter to J.H. Kellogg, March 12, 1900; Letter 45, 1900
32. E.G. White, Letter to Brother and Sister S.N. Haskell, June 12, 1900; Letter 90, 1900
33. *Ministry of Healing*, 147

God has placed in our care the poor and the suffering, and these are to be cared for as Christ cared for them. The Lord would have this work done in the different churches, rather than that they should depend so largely upon institutions, for this will take out of the hands of the churches the very work God has appointed them to do. When fathers and mothers die, and leave their children unprovided for, the orphans should be cared for by the church. Open your hearts, you that have the love of God, and take them into your homes....

You are not to do this work by proxy. You are to give evidence to the world that you are Christlike. You are to practice self-denial and self-sacrifice....

By their indifference the churches of today are losing the most precious opportunities which it is their privilege to have. The burdens which they should bear they are placing upon some institution. If they would take up their God-given work, they would receive a knowledge of what practical godliness means.[34]

Do bear in mind that we've been looking at the guidelines for the benevolent, charitable work that is best done on an individual basis. This isn't to rule out institutions altogether, but the same principles kind of roll over to the larger setting:

It is that thirsting souls may be led to the living water that we plead for sanitariums, not expensive, mammoth sanitariums, but homelike institutions, in pleasant places.

Never, never build mammoth sanitariums. Let these institutions be small, and let there be more of them, that the work of winning souls to Christ may be accomplished.... The sick are to be reached, not by massive buildings, but by the establishment of many small sanitariums, which are to be as lights shining in a dark place.... By sanitarium work, properly conducted, the influence of true, pure religion will be extended to many souls.[35]

Building momentum in the right direction with this kind of work wasn't easy! Reading the history is tough, because every time someone started making headway, someone else would find a way to derail the whole effort. Ellen White's son, W.C. White, put it this way:

We seem to be in the midst of a very serious conflict, in which the people of God are endeavoring to establish many sanitariums according to His direction; and in which the enemy of our work is striving to defeat the Lord's purpose by leading the managers of sanitarium enterprises to locate in the large cities[36] and to build so largely in each principal center as to defeat the Lord's plan of erecting many sanitariums throughout the land.[37]

---

34. E.G. White, "Words of Instruction to Responsible Men," July 30, 1899; Manuscript 105, 1899

35. *Review and Herald*, February 2, 1905

36. A "city sanitarium" was never a good idea. "The same state of things exists today that existed before the flood, and the nearer we get to the large cities, the worse the evil is. My message Is, Do not build up sanitariums in the cities. The laws of the land will become more and more oppressive, as in the days of Noah." E.G. White, Letter to Brother and Sister Burden, December 15, 1902; Letter 201, 1902

37. W.C. White, Letter to Elder A.J. Read, July 3, 1902; WCW Letterbook 20, 59

In light of all this, it would be criminal to not mention that the Christian Help Band is the one variety of medical missionary work that Ellen White most heartily endorsed. I'm not aware of a single instance in which this kind of work was rebuked, reproved, discouraged, or even warned. Why would that be?

My guess: the Christian Help Bands were small—nine members, plus or minus a couple—local, and largely self-funded. There is an amazing increase in common sense when the decision maker is footing the bill. It just seems to work that way.

This largely comes from small groups' tendency to rely on a less-than-perfect, subjective process when deciding whom to help, how to help, and how much to help. It may be subjective, and it may be less than perfect, but it gives the individual worker the chance to see how each decision plays out. They can learn from the experience.

In a larger, more formal institutional setting, the tendency is to standardize decision making with professionally designed 13-point checklists (sometimes more, sometimes less) that can never fully capture the real circumstances. Plus, the decision maker may never have anything to do with the street-level implementation of the decision, and the one doing the work may have no input in the next decision. The tendency is for the work to become rote, maybe even mindless. That's no way to serve the Lord.

> Personal ministry is far more efficacious than preaching in the saving of souls. When God's people do personal work as He designs it to be done, the promises of Isaiah fifty-eight will be fulfilled to them. His righteousness will go before them; His glory will be their rereward.[38]

---

38. E.G. White, Letter to Brother and Sister D.H. Kress, April 28, 1902; Letter 68, 1902

CHAPTER 40

Cover Blown!

THE element of surprise is an invaluable asset for any military operation. Fortunately for us, Satan doesn't have a lot of it. *The Great Controversy* in particular and the Spirit of Prophecy in general is responsible for that. It's a great thing... but it raises some questions. The most obvious one is, Why doesn't Satan just change his plan?

If you knew, that your enemy knew, that you were planning to attack at dawn, wouldn't you at least consider moving it up to the night before? Of course you would, but maybe you don't have good night vision equipment. Maybe you'd lose too many soldiers and too many pieces of artillery and too many airborne assets. Maybe a night attack just isn't a good idea.

So how about advancing from the south instead of the northwest? That'll throw them off! Except for that whole swamp problem to the south. Getting all your men and vehicles through that? Nope, never gonna happen.

And so it goes. For all sorts of reasons, the original plan is the best plan, even without the element of surprise. That's the position Satan finds himself in; that's why he can't change his plan. The Lord put the best possible plan into print for everyone to read, and now Satan's stuck with it!

That's encouraging, but there's a corollary conclusion that goes along with it: God couldn't put any changeable details into the book. Why? Because Satan would change them, and we'd be preparing for an attack that is never going to come. That's why Ellen White said things like—

> The form of Satan's working will be changed as the circumstances change. He adjusts himself readily to circumstances.[1]

---

1. E.G. White, "Visit to Paris and Versailles, France," October 1886; Manuscript 75, 1886

Your letter [asking for details as to how the devil would attack the letter writer] is received, and I would be glad to satisfy your mind on every point, but that is not in my power. While I can speak to you in words of warning, you may ask many questions that it is not my duty or in my power to answer....

Should I specify the particular temptations, Satan would shift his operations and prepare some temptation you are not expecting.[2]

The light we have received upon the third angel's message is the true light. The mark of the beast is exactly what it has been proclaimed to be. Not all in regard to this matter is yet understood, nor will it be understood until the unrolling of the scroll; but a most solemn work is to be accomplished in our world. The Lord's command to His servants is: "Cry aloud, spare not, lift up thy voice like a trumpet, and show My people their transgression, and the house of Jacob their sins." Isaiah 58:1.[3]

That's why my story about President Harrison back on page 179 must be acknowledged as speculation. When the scroll is unrolled, it may play out that way. Or maybe not. Wouldn't it be great if Satan had worked on that idea for hundreds of years, and then had to scrap it because we were ready for his deception! Who knows? Not I; I'm not a prophet.

Among the more valuable pieces of cover-blowing advance warning that we've been given by one who *did* have the gift of prophecy is that there's something called the "omega of apostasy" coming at the end of time. Not a lot is specified about it directly. The basic information is found in three statements:

Be not deceived; many will depart from the faith, giving heed to seducing spirits and doctrines of devils. We have now before us the alpha of this danger. The omega will be of a most startling nature.[4]

In the book *Living Temple* there is presented the alpha of deadly heresies. The omega will follow, and will be received by those who are not willing to heed the warning God has given.[5]

Living Temple contains the alpha of these theories. The omega would follow in a little while. I tremble for our people.[6]

There's not much detail there, but still we've got a good outline of Satan's omega attack, for the simple reason that he launched it once before, but got stopped on the beach before penetrating to the heart of the Lord's work.[7] That

2. E.G. White, Letter to A.T. Jones, April 14, 1894; Letter 38, 1894
3. *Testimonies*, vol. 6, 17. Do note the linkage between the third angel's message, the mark of the beast, and Isaiah 58. It's a thing!
4. E.G. White, Letter to Our Leading Physicians, July 24, 1904; Letter 263, 1904
5. E.G. White, Letter to A.J. Reed, July 31, 1904; Letter 277, 1904
6. E.G. White, "Talk: The Foundation of Our Faith," May 18, 1904; Manuscript 46, 1904
7. I know, another mixaphor. My apologies if it bothers you.

was the "alpha of apostasy" back in Kellogg's day. There are lessons to learn from that episode.

The most detailed description Ellen White ever wrote of the omega, was actually about what the alpha would have grown into if it hadn't been stopped. It's kind of like saying, "This is a sprouted acorn; if it were full grown it would be an oak tree, but we pulled it up by the roots. When the next acorn grows up, it'll look like this one would have." The full account is well worth studying, but for now we'll skip to the very end of it.

> The founders of this system would go into the cities, and do a wonderful work. The Sabbath of course, would be lightly regarded, as also the God who created it. Nothing would be allowed to stand in the way of the new movement. The leaders would teach that virtue is better than vice, but God being removed, they would place their dependence on human power, which, without God, is worthless. Their foundation would be built on the sand, and storm and tempest would sweep away the structure.[8]

In the alpha, the attack started from misguided members of the church's medical force and spread to include a number of ministerial workers as well. With the omega, it may play out differently, though the inclusion of both medical and ministerial seems clear. The final downfall of the omega depicted above, comes during the "little time of trouble" as chaos increases. Remember, "populous cities" are being "reduced to ruin and desolation."[9] There will be "suffering ones, plenty of them."[10] It's in this setting that we find the omega, doing a "wonderful work" in the cities.

What kind of work will that be? Something similar to the professedly Christian, but sin-tolerating and third-angel's-message-ignoring kind of sentimental humanitarianism that Kellogg was running in Chicago back in the alpha. In other words, at exactly the same time that the Lord has medical missionary workers taking "this gospel" to all the world, the devil has his team doing their best to look like the real thing. It's a counterfeit. No surprise there.

But it doesn't last. It gets "swept away" by "storm and tempest" because that house is built on the sand. One storm, two houses; one stands, one falls. But... *Why? How?*

Because chaos produces shortages, and the day will come when there's not much left and the selfish heart has Lucifer's talking points stamped deep into its core: "I know what I want, and if I have to, I'll kill you in order to get it. I have to do that, since I can't trust God or anyone else to look after me."

8. *Selected Messages*, Book One, 205
9. *Great Controversy*, 589
10. E.G. White, Letter to Brother and Sister J.H. Kellogg, September 16, 1892; Letter 34, 1892. Quoted more fully on page 12.

And thus the cover story, the illusion of great charity, is destroyed by sinners' implacable hatred of the principle of God's government. So ingrained is this hatred, that even when it might serve their own master's cause, they cannot resist the pull of selfishness. It might be considered a case of "friendly fire," except that selfishness—under enough pressure—acknowledges no one as "friend."

In the end, the sinner's rebellion—like Satan's—knows no loyalty that could lead to self-sacrifice. Indeed, self-sacrifice itself is the enemy.

> It is this principle of self-sacrifice that [Satan's] kingdom is established to destroy, and he will war against it wherever manifested.[11]

That's what selfishness does. And with that, the whole hypocritical "humanitarian" operation is swept away, the counterfeit of love is unmasked, and anyone not already a confirmed citizen in full harmony with the evil kingdom gets one last chance to see the revelation of God's character in the lives of those living in obedience to His law.

Of course, those in the Lord's house face the same storm. Things are tight for them, too, but they have a promise they've learned to trust:

> God is able to make all grace abound toward you, that you, always having all sufficiency in all things, may have an abundance for every good work.[12]

It may not look like all they need; it may not be as much as they think they need; but still they trust. Maybe the Lord works a "loaves and fishes miracle" for them. Maybe not. Still, they trust. And their dependence on a higher power becomes more obvious by the hour, as does God's faithfulness in providing.

Imagine the witnessing opportunities! But time is limited, and the stakes are high.

> Calamities will come, calamities most awful, most unexpected; and these destructions will follow one after another. If there will be a heeding of the warnings that God has given, and if churches will repent, returning to their allegiance, then other cities may be spared for a time....
>
> The Lord will not suddenly cast off all transgressors or destroy entire nations, but He will punish cities and places where men have given themselves up to the possession of satanic agencies.[13]

Even though the great majority of the population is moving toward full support of the devil's plans to exterminate these people, there are yet a few "thinking men who still have a desire in their hearts to be honest and just with their fellowmen"[14] who are watching previously unimaginable events unfold around them. And these "criminals," these "Sunday-deniers," don't look like culprits.

---

11. *Desire of Ages*, 223

12. 2 Corinthians 9:8

13. E.G. White, "The Judgments of God," April 27, 1906; Manuscript 35, 1906

14. *Testimonies to Ministers*, 457. Quoted more fully on page 216.

They continue to serve others, though they should have nothing by now since they aren't allowed to buy or sell. They haven't died, they haven't caved, they haven't stopped serving. It's baffling, to the point that their own explanation of it all deserves consideration.... Could it be that God is with them? Could it be that they remain "honest and just" by His strength?

> Pray much for those you are trying to help. Let them see that your dependence is upon a higher power, and you will win souls.[15]

The saints are hanging in there; faith is growing; those "who would ignorantly lead in unsafe paths" have been revealed; "remedial missionary work" is confronting selfishness; confidence in "earthly support" is waning; the revelation of God's character through the lives of Christlike men and women is spreading; hearts are being won, though most reject the call to obey the eternal law of sacrifice. It's time to wrap up this operation. But Lucifer resists. He still has three accusations. Where can we find the final piece to this puzzle?

How about... Medo-Persia?

---

15. E.G. White, Letter to Brother Merrill, March 25, 1898; Letter 24, 1898. Quoted more fully on page 203.

CHAPTER 41

The Kings' Dilemma

ONCE again, the reader may be reassured that there is no typo in the chapter title. You are to be forgiven if you thought that "Kings-apostrophe" was supposed to be "King-apostrophe-s," but we're actually talking about two kings, both dealing with the same dilemma. It's rare that two circumstances should develop in such close parallel, but God has reasons for what went into the Bible, and like so many of the classic Old Testament "Bedtime Stories," the accounts of these two monarchs—and the people they loved—illustrate a far larger reality than is first apparent.

We'll take the stories in chronological order, rather than their placement in Scripture, so we start with Darius. The absolute ruler of Medo-Persia had a problem, and to make matters much worse, it was clearly, in part at least, his own fault. Having been conned into proclaiming a foolish royal decree crafted to appeal to his own sinful pride, he soon found himself saddled with the responsibility of executing his truest earthly friend and wisest political advisor.

Without the slightest sign of hesitance, Daniel had prayed to His God, and for this he must die. And, of course, it was impossible to change any law sealed with the King's signet. Try as he might, Darius found no avenue of relief. The law was immutable; to violate it would sacrifice the whole government of the Empire.

> The king... was greatly displeased with himself, and set his heart on Daniel to deliver him; and he labored till the going down of the sun to deliver him.

The despicable "governors and satraps" helpfully reminded Darius of the applicable statute: "Know, O king, that it is the law of the Medes and Persians that no decree or statute which the king establishes may be changed."[1]

---

1. Daniel 6:14–15

There was nothing that could prevent the infliction of the punishment, nor did Daniel himself fight the carrying out of the law. Indeed, he respectfully complied with the demands of (perverted) justice. Darius was stuck; with no other option, he threw his Chief-of-Staff to the lions... literally. It's just that the lions didn't perform as expected because God stepped in, sent His angel, performed a miracle, and saved the day—not to mention Daniel's life. The enemies who had plotted against Daniel and the King's best interest, were slain. End of story.

The prophet's life was spared by the angel, no doubt, but Daniel also credits it to the fact that he was innocent before God and had done no harm to the king. In short, spiritual realities trump physical ones.

But is it accurate to speak of "reality"—as in cause-and-effect—when it takes a full scale miracle to make things turn out right?

If the parallels to the plan of salvation haven't already occurred to you, they should now. There are minor misalignments, of course, but so many parallels that it's hard to miss the application to the larger picture. Like Darius, God found Himself faced with a complicated situation. Though *He* had not been deceived, the adversary had lied to Eve, and now the perfect, immutable, unchangeable, and eternal law of God decreed death. And so God sent the Angel of the Covenant to save humanity. In due time, Satan and all his host will die. End of story.

But the plot in the bigger story is substantially thicker than in the book of Daniel. Unlike Darius, the government of heaven was in jeopardy not only if the law were changed, but also if the King's justice displayed any partiality. Having the lions held back from Daniel, but not from his enemies, was no problem for Darius—impartiality not being an expected quality in ancient tyrant monarchs! But it posed a major issue for God. Being both "just" and the "justifier" of sinners was no easy challenge, and the lack of a convincing demonstration of His ability to accomplish that dual task left God and His government susceptible to Satan's charges. To this day, the very process of forgiveness stands accused of defilement. The altar of sacrifice, the cross, must itself be cleansed as the day of atonement comes to its close.

But there's another story! Some years after Daniel's night with the lions, our second king found himself in a similar situation. This time, the evil Haman persuades Ahasuerus to authorize the genocide of all the Jews in the kingdom. This doesn't seem like a problem, evidently, until it turns out that Esther is Jewish. Things go very badly for Haman, and he ends up on the gallows he had built for Mordecai. But in this episode, even the death of the enemy is not enough to solve the problem. The immutability of Medo-Persian statutory enactments still demands that the law be carried out.

And here's where it gets interesting: Esther appears before the king, putting her life at risk a second time. But of course he holds out the golden scepter and asks what she wants. She makes request:

> If it pleases the king, and if I have found favor in his sight and the thing seems right to the king and I am pleasing in his eyes, let it be written to revoke the letters devised by Haman, the son of Hammedatha the Agagite, which he wrote to annihilate the Jews who are in all the king's provinces.

That probably seemed like a great idea, but Ahasuerus would have gotten a better LSAT[2] score than his wife!

> You yourselves write a decree concerning the Jews, as you please, in the king's name, and seal it with the king's signet ring; for whatever is written in the king's name and sealed with the king's signet ring no one can revoke.[3]

The weakness of Esther's approach was the illegality of "revoking" any law duly appointed by the king. When Ahasuerus said "whatever is written in the king's name and sealed with the king's signet ring no one can revoke," it applied to both what had been done previously and what he was proposing they do next. In the end, the decree Mordecai wrote and sealed with the king's signet, did nothing to revoke the first law, it simply relied on a second law to accomplish the desired goal.

The immutability of the law remains intact, the honor of the government is maintained, and the innocent are not killed. Genius!

The only downside to this procedure is a tendency to make the government look, shall we say, a little *fickle*. After all, if you make a law that needs another law to essentially undo it, a casual observer might think that you were off the mark with the first one.[4]

That's the way it goes with arbitrary laws. Writing a law that conflicts with your own previous legislation is not a good look. With a reality-based law, on the other hand, having two laws in tension is just business as usual.

---

2. Law School Admission Test
3. Esther 8:5, 8
4. Politics is a tough business if what other people think actually matters to you. That's probably why the habits and policies of ancient monarchs tended to emphasize the "mon" as in "mono" role.

CHAPTER 42

The Two Laws

IN Adventist circles, any reference to "two laws" is generally going to focus on the distinction between the ten commandments and the ceremonial law. It's important to keep that distinction, because mixing up the two is just a bad idea all around.

This chapter, though, is headed down a different track. Our topic is a continuation from the last chapter about the tribulations of the two kings (though it might be noted that neither of *their* lives was put at risk). That unlikely scenario—an unchangeable law endangering someone they didn't really want to kill—showing up *twice* in scripture, is one of those things that makes you go "*hmmm...*".

Toss in the interesting detail about the two approaches to keeping God's people alive, and it's enough to make you think, "I wonder if that was repeated for the sake of emphasis? Maybe I ought to look at this."

By now, of course, any reader who's not blind or three days dead *knows* this book is going to argue for some significance in those stories.

Here's the thing: those kings with an unchangeable law that looks like it has bound their hands so they can't stop the execution of their friend or wife... that sounds a lot like God, with an unchangeable law that Satan flat out says makes it so God can't avoid executing the sinners He wants to save. The parallel is obvious.

Further, the distinction and sequence of "saved-by-miracle" and "saved-by-second-law" is another parallel that's obvious once you see it. Take a look:

For starters, we'll go back to the skate park illustration and the concern with gravity.[1] The mysterious attraction between two masses of matter doesn't depend on city council, legislature, parliament, president, or king. And none of

---

1. Bear in mind that gravity is serving here as an illustration, not as something equal to the law of heaven. The point is that gravity is as impossible for humans to change as the law of heaven is for God to change.

them could change it if they tried. The point is, God's law is just as certain and unchangeable. Lucifer claimed otherwise, but tried to cover all his bases by saying that *if* the law *couldn't* be changed, there could be no such thing as forgiveness. In all likelihood, he never managed to wrap his head around the idea of a sinner—even fallen angels!—being saved without changing the law.

> That wonderful Lucifer [and all the fallen angels]... had intelligence, the greatest intelligence. They did not lose their intelligence all at once. But they had not the power, the connection with God, the power of discernment, to understand that if they repented, they could be brought back again.[2]

Lacking the discernment of God's mercy because he had willfully severed his connection to God (and that "in the light of God's glory"), Lucifer didn't think *anyone* could be "brought back again." But he was wrong. Thanks to Christ's revelation of the Father's love, human beings *can* understand the idea of a God who loves even sinners. They may not understand every detail, they may even think that a lamb is enough to pay for their sin! But it's enough to allow faith to grow, and when it's full grown, it's the victory the overcomes the world.

But then there's Satan's mic drop[3] final argument: forgiveness must be *impossible* if the law can't be changed. How can you stop gravity? And, apparently, to the rest of the universe, it looked like Satan was winning the argument.[4]

God, however, has an answer to that impertinent gravity question: "Aerodynamics."

What?

Aerodynamics. That's how you deal with the downward pull of gravity. Planes fly without doing away with gravity. It happens all the time. Listen to your local airport radio traffic as long as you want—you'll never hear anything like this:

> *Tower, this is Flight 3589 ready for takeoff, runway two-seven-left. Requesting gravity cancellation at 1507 hours, and we'll be out of here.*

There is a law of sin and death—as real as gravity. But there is also a law of faith and the Spirit of life[5]—as real as aerodynamics. The key is faith. The "righteousness by faith" kind of faith. The "justification by faith," "faith of Je-

2. Ellen White, "Thoughts on Revelation 19," April 7, 1910; Manuscript 80, 1910
3. The term "mic drop" comes from the pathologically proud and wasteful (good microphones aren't cheap!) habit of hip-hop performers intentionally dropping the microphone to the floor at the end of a song. By extension, it's come to mean any presentation, argument, rebuttal, or witty come-back that ends the whole discussion due to its presumed unassailable brilliance.
4. "How shall the universe know that Lucifer is not a safe and just leader? To their eyes he appears right." E.G. White, Letter to Brother and Sister C.H. Jones, July 4, 1892; Letter 16a, 1892. Quoted more fully on page 20.
5. Romans 8:2

sus," simple "confidence in God" kind of faith. The faith Lucifer gave up... (all of which explains why "whatever is not from faith is sin"[6]).

That's the kind of faith that Jesus talked about when He said, "According to your faith, be it unto you."[7] And when blind men, and lepers, and women bowed down with infirmity, and paralytics let down through the ceiling were healed, they *weren't sick anymore.* The effects of their diseases—including diseases brought upon themselves by their own actions—were gone. Even the leper could rejoin family and society.

And when that faith is full grown, tested, and proved, it shows that God's people are *diasozo'ed*—made perfectly well, brought safely through the terrors of sin—and they can at last be grafted back into the family of the unfallen and loyal throughout the universe. We who were "aliens from the commonwealth," "strangers from the covenants of promise, having no hope and without God in the world," will be "brought near by the blood of Christ. For He Himself is our peace, who has made both one, and has broken down the middle wall of separation."[8]

> The plan of redemption is not merely an escape from the penalty of transgression, that we may be tolerated in heaven as a forgiven culprit, pardoned and released from prison, one who is barely tolerated, but not admitted to friendship and trust. We are not to be thus in heaven—merely admitted. Such a reception would be all that we deserve, but unsatisfying. We want to be taken back to confidence and love, not only to be rescued from the curse, but to be welcomed as accepted children, to be blessed of God. And we shall be amply satisfied. The sacrifice of Jesus Christ has made ample provisions for every repenting, believing soul. We are saved because God loves the purchase of the blood of Christ; and not only will He pardon the repenting, believing sinner, but He will take us back—not only barely permit us to come into heaven, but He, the Father, will wait at the very entrance to welcome us, to give us an abundant entrance to the mansions of the blessed.[9]

The only problem, of course, is that a welcome like that is simply not befitting of criminals and carriers of deadly pathogens. That "rescued from the curse" aspect has to be based on reality. We've seen this before, but it's one of those statements that we probably ought to read until we've memorized it by sheer brute force repetition!

> The atonement of Christ is not a mere skillful way to have our sins pardoned; it is a divine remedy for the cure of transgression and the restoration of spiritual health. It is the heaven-ordained means by which the righteousness of Christ may be not only upon us, but in our hearts and characters.[10]

---

6. Romans 14:23
7. Matthew 9:29
8. Ephesians 2:12–14
9. E.G. White, Letter to Uriah Smith, July 24, 1886; Letter 85, 1886
10. E.G. White, Letter to Sister, 1906; Letter 406, 1906

Once again, though, as we did back on page 105, we are forced to admit that this kind of healing is not common. We just don't see a great many examples of it in our day-to-day lives And that's where the significance of the two kings' stories comes in. Daniel—the first case—was saved by a miracle; Esther—the second case—was saved by means of another, equally royal, law.

No detail of scripture is mere happenstance. It is no coincidence that the Bible provides two pictures of a king, who in all other respects was as powerful and as free to do as he wished as anyone could be, but who is at the same time seemingly powerless to rescue a loved one from an immutable law. It is no random detail that the two stories occurred in the same order, and feature the same shift from "miraculous" to "cause-and-effect," as is required to fully vindicate God and His law from the devil's charge that it's all arbitrary—either an unjust mercy or a merciless justice. And don't overlook that the sanctuary service depicts this shift as complete only at the closing ceremony of the year.

Why is the full healing of spiritual disease so uncommon? Because we live in an environment almost devoid of the "vitamin" that is the only cure.

> The church is now as a vast hospital, filled with the spiritually sick, who need to be placed under the influence of the refining furnace,[11] until all dross is consumed.

> The future of the church depends on the efforts made by the members to understand the sinfulness of selfishness, and their willingness to take the remedy which will cure the disease from which they are suffering. Let a reformation take place, that those who accept the truth in the future shall not be contaminated by the corrupting influence of Satan.[12]

Examples of a faith that conquers selfishness, that will trust the Lord in everything, in every way, at all times, under any circumstance, are not everyday occurrences. Such a faith can only come from a profound appreciation of the character of the Father... and "this gospel" has yet to fill the earth with that knowledge of the glory of the LORD, as the waters cover the sea. We read Hebrews 11, but we live in a faithless world and a faith-challenged church. Never having seen the full power of faith, we remain categorically and experientially unprepared to make any such demonstration for anyone else's benefit.

And so God, in His mercy, declares those who possess even an immature-but-nonetheless-true faith, righteous, based on His knowledge of what faith *can* do.[13] And He "permits His people to be subjected to the fiery ordeal of tempta-

---

11. Even inspired analogies present some odd mixing of imagery. It's been a while since I last saw a "refining furnace" in a hospital ward. An autoclave, maybe?
12. E.G. White, "Diary: I had an interview with Brethren," August 14, 1901; Manuscript 108, 1901
13. This is an act of faith, too: "Christ would never have given His life for the human race if He had not faith in the souls for whom He died. He knew that a large number would respond to the love He had expressed for humanity. It is not every heart that responds, but every heart may and can, if it will, re-

tion"—the very temptations that too often defeat us—"not because He takes pleasure in their distress and affliction, but because this process is essential to their final victory."

We are yet some distance from that final victory, and so He never allows us to be tempted *too hard.* When the devil tries, Christ steps in as our "spotter," and saves our spiritual lives. For this He endures the scoffing, the cursing, the lying accusations of Lucifer. He bears, as well, with the continued uncertainty and scrutiny of even the unfallen universe, who continue to wait in hope that all the misery and horrors of sin will yet be outweighed by the glory of His people's final victory.

The Lord knows that the day is coming when He can not, "consistently with His own glory, shield them from temptation; for the very object of the trial is to prepare them to resist all the allurements of evil."[14]

He knows this. He's tried to tell us. But He also tried to tell His own disciples that they were "going up to Jerusalem, and all things that are written by the prophets concerning the Son of Man will be accomplished. For He will be delivered to the Gentiles and will be mocked and insulted and spit upon. They will scourge Him and kill Him. And the third day He will rise again."

Perhaps we share more of the disciples' dullness than we like to admit, and maybe there's a lesson for us in the sad reality that "they understood none of these things; this saying was hidden from them, and they did not know the things which were spoken."[15]

Will Christ's disciples of the end time walk as blindly into their great test as did the disciples at the time of the cross? I'm not a prophet... but we have been given a picture of a brighter alternative:

> Not with sorrow, but with rejoicing, should [Christ's followers] meet persecution. Each fiery trial is God's agent for their refining. Each is fitting them for their work as co-laborers with Him. Each conflict has its place in the great battle for righteousness, and each will add to the joy of their final triumph. Having this in view, the test of their faith and patience will be cheerfully accepted rather than dreaded and avoided. Anxious to fulfill their obligation to the world, fixing their desire upon the approval of God, His servants are to fulfill every duty, irrespective of the fear or the favor of men.[16]

Will the believers at the end of time "cheerfully accept" the trials intended to "prepare them to resist all the allurements of evil"? Or will they wander blindly into the final test? Inspiration seems to be silent on the topic, which

spond to that love that is without a parallel." E.G. White, Letter to Edson and Emma White, August 24, 1897; Letter 153a, 1897

14. *Great Controversy*, 528; Quoted more fully on page 85.
15. Luke 18:31–34
16. *Desire of Ages*, 306

usually means it's up to the believers themselves to choose. In either case, the Spirit of Prophecy does depict a change, a day when the faith of the living saints rises to a truly Biblical standard:

> When it reaches that stage that God's people walk with Him in such confidence as [Hebrews 11] describes, the message will be attended by the refreshing showers of the latter rain, and the earth will be speedily lighted by His glory.[17]

That glory will be impossible for the world to ignore. Like Jesus standing on the steps of the Temple with that little whip in His hands; before ever saying a single word, He had become the center of attention. That's what God wants to do with us.

> God is seeking to make His church the continued incarnation of Christ. The gospel ministers are the undershepherds; Christ is the divine Shepherd. The members of the church are the working agencies of the Lord. His church will stand out prominently. It is the Lord's body.[18]

There is yet another point of interest in the story of the kings. The satraps wanted Daniel dead, though they never said so explicitly, of course. Their law said, "Throw him to the lions." Now, admittedly, being thrown in with a bunch of hungry lions is often seen as a synonym for death. Functionally, it had always worked that way in the past, so it must have seemed like a safe bet.

Intent on seeing the law carried out, they never imagined that Daniel might come through unscathed. Nor could they have guessed that they would face the same danger themselves. We've seen this plot before in the parable of the two houses facing the same storm. The central issue is that a given challenge may be faced in different ways which produce spectacularly different results.

This basic picture is not uncommon in Scripture, though presented in various ways. We see another example of this with Nebuchadnezzar on the plain of Dura. He was mad enough that he wanted those three young men thoroughly dead. So he gave the command. And yet Shadrach, Meshach, and Abed-Nego walked unharmed in the fire that killed the soldiers who threw them in.

In both cases, the law was fulfilled. Daniel spent a night in the lions' den, and those who didn't get into the spirit of the music festival were tossed in the fire. The law was enforced, but the end result was a surprise to those who thought they knew how everything was supposed to work.

It's interesting that both the lion and the fire are symbols closely associated with Jesus, the Lion of the tribe of Judah, the One who will come in flaming fire to judge the world. Maybe that's just a coincidence, but nonetheless Scrip-

---

17. *Bible Training School*, November 1, 1911
18. E.G. White, Letter to Brother and Sister S.N. Haskell, August 13, 1900; Letter 121, 1900

ture often portrays this issue of diverging or unexpected outcomes in relation to encountering God.

Moses met with the Lord on the mountain while the people in the camp "trembled and stood afar off." The reality of their situation was such that they plead, "let not God speak with us, lest we die."[19]

In the dramatic portrayal of Christ's cleansing of the temple in *Desire of Ages*, this same contrast is seen:

> Overpowered with terror, the priests and rulers had fled from the temple court, and from the searching glance that read their hearts.... [After some time] slowly and thoughtfully, but with hate in their hearts, they returned to the temple. But what a change had taken place during their absence! When they fled, the poor remained behind; and these were now looking to Jesus, whose countenance expressed His love and sympathy. With tears in His eyes, He said to the trembling ones around Him: Fear not; I will deliver thee, and thou shalt glorify Me. For this cause came I into the world.
>
> The people pressed into Christ's presence with urgent, pitiful appeals: Master, bless me. His ear heard every cry. With pity exceeding that of a tender mother He bent over the suffering little ones. All received attention. Everyone was healed of whatever disease he had. The dumb opened their lips in praise; the blind beheld the face of their Restorer. The hearts of the sufferers were made glad.[20]

The different results came from the condition of the hearts. Where the law of sin and death reigned supreme, sin and death must be the result; where the law of faith and life held sway, blessing was available to all. Jesus made no arbitrary distinction. He would have healed the priests and rulers, too, if they been able to "discern" their need and His eagerness to supply it.

Of course, the same will be true in the last day, when—

> Our God shall come, and shall not keep silent; A fire shall devour before Him, and it shall be very tempestuous all around Him. He shall call to the heavens from above, and to the earth, that He may judge His people.[21]

For some, it is the worst of nightmares:

> The kings of the earth, the great men, the rich men, the commanders, the mighty men, every slave and every free man, hid themselves in the caves and in the rocks of the mountains, and said to the mountains and rocks, "Fall on us and hide us from the face of Him who sits on the throne and from the wrath of the Lamb! For the great day of His wrath has come, and who is able to stand?"[22]

For others, it is the culmination of all their fondest dreams!

---

19. Exodus 20:18–19
20. *Desire of Ages*, 162–163
21. Psalm 50:3–4
22. Revelation 6:15–17

It will be said in that day: "Behold, this is our God; We have waited for Him, and He will save us. This is the LORD; We have waited for Him; We will be glad and rejoice in His salvation."[23]

Malachi elaborates on this thought, first asking "Who can endure the day of His coming? And who can stand when He appears? For He is like a refiner's fire." This image of the refiner's fire is interesting. It resonates well with other portrayals we've seen of reality as opposed to assertion. The whole point of the fire is to make certain that what remains is pure. The dross is gone, only the precious metal remains.

The next verse offers no universal assurance, but it does open a door of hope when the prophet says that God—

> will sit as a refiner and a purifier of silver; He will purify the sons of Levi, and purge them as gold and silver, that they may offer to the LORD an offering in righteousness.

What's important is the purity of the metal, which is contrasted in the next verse with groups who are not pure, as determined by the judgment:

> "I will come near you for judgment; I will be a swift witness against sorcerers, against adulterers, against perjurers, against those who exploit wage earners and widows and orphans, and against those who turn away an alien—because they do not fear Me," says the LORD of hosts.

It's the final verse in the section, though, which might raise the most questions, for here the Lord gives the reason salvation is possible:

> For I am the LORD, I do not change; therefore you are not consumed, O sons of Jacob.[24]

It's odd. We might think that the "sons of Jacob" were "not consumed" because the Lord decided to be just a bit more tolerant of their mistakes. But the refiner's fire argues against that, and this makes it explicit: salvation comes through the unchanging reality of Who the Lord is. The difference between saved and lost is not found in God, it's found in the two groups themselves. It's not arbitrary, it's not fairy-dust; it's reality. And the law that spells out the difference between saved and lost doesn't *define* right and wrong; it's based on the *difference* between right and wrong. Misunderstanding that point, we are told, can easily lead to rebellion.[25] But it's reality, so don't ever count on it changing!

> The penalty of transgressing the law has fallen upon our Substitute and Surety, and for a time has been suspended, so that the guilty do not feel its weight; but the object of this suspension is not to teach us that its claims are over, its exactions set

---

23. Isaiah 25:9
24. Malachi 3:2–6
25. See reference 33 on page 33.

aside, but to attract us to holiness, to obedience. Nothing is changed except the manner of bringing men to obey the law. Obey its claims we must.[26]

We've spoken of the "reality" of the law. If we were to focus on that reality alone, it would present such an imposing sight that human courage would die without hope. This is the awe inspiring righteousness of God, the majesty of His glory, and the impossibility of achieving that in our own strength would rise up as a mountain before the believer... and then fall on us and grind our hopes, aspiration, pledges, promises, and intentions to powder.

"Reality" is a tough field to play on.

---

26. *Signs of the Times*, August 13, 1894

CHAPTER 43

Really?

WE closed the last chapter with the observation that "reality" is a tough field to play on. The present chapter title may be viewed as the incredulous reaction of any "Christian" whose concept of salvation has been formed according to either of the two prevailing schools of thought on the topic.

The most popular of these mental concepts is the "Jesus does it all" approach which seeks to simply "accept the merits of Christ" without the reality of the transformation that acceptance is said to produce in the life of the believer.

The currently out-of-style (but still largely practiced) second approach is the "creature merit" proposition which somehow imagines that our good works earn something... *anything*... toward salvation.

Since "reality" shatters both these delusions, fitting a non-arbitrary law of God into an arbitrary version of the Gospel is not going to be a good fit. It's like the new wine that bursts the old wineskins, and the more ingrained those arbitrary presuppositions are in our thinking, the more challenging it can be to wrap our heads around the truth of redemption. Of course, the devil has done his best to compound our natural dullness in this regard, so perhaps we should give credit where credit is due... and then we should shatter those delusions.

This chapter proposes to respond to the incredulous inquiry in its title by a simple change in the punctuation. The answer to the question is, "Really." Or, for those who prefer a more classical phrasing, "Verily, verily."

Perhaps this is unnecessary. Perhaps the previous chapters have made the case with enough clarity. Perhaps. But Ellen White struggled to make the point clear, and I doubt that my words can do better. And so, in support of this chapter's premise, and in support of all that has been said in prior chapters, let's look at two passages from Inspiration.[1] The first focuses on the fallacy of "creature merit," and the second, shorter, passage points to the reality of transformation.

Readers of a certain age may remember that in the later 1970s the pro-Desmond Ford element within the church championed this first manuscript as proof that Ellen White supported Ford's concept of "righteousness by faith" as purely "justification" and *never* "sanctification." Taken in isolation, certain passages from the manuscript might make that seem almost plausible.

> The danger has been presented to me again and again of entertaining, as a people, false ideas of justification by faith. I have been shown for years that Satan would work in a special manner to confuse the mind on this point. The law of God has been largely dwelt upon and has been presented to congregations, almost as destitute of the knowledge of Jesus Christ and His relation to the law as was the offering of Cain....
>
> There is not a point that needs to be dwelt upon more earnestly, repeated more frequently, or established more firmly in the minds of all than the impossibility of fallen man meriting anything by his own best good works. Salvation is through faith in Jesus Christ alone....
>
> Let the subject be made distinct and plain that it is not possible to effect anything in our standing before God or in the gift of God to us through creature merit....

This repudiation of creature merit is based on two simple truths: First, that anything good we might consider as "ours" came from God in the first place, and second, that even with good gifts in hand, we couldn't make a proper use of them without God's aid. The manuscript continues:

> If you would gather together everything that is good and holy and noble and lovely in man, and then present the subject to the angels of God as acting a part in the salvation of the human soul or in merit, the proposition would be rejected as treason....
>
> Many are struggling in their own finite strength to win salvation by good works. Jesus, they think, will do some of the saving; they must do the rest. They need to see by faith the righteousness of Christ as their only hope for time and for eternity.

Ford's position had a certain logic to it: if man can't do anything to earn salvation, then surely man doesn't have to do anything to receive salvation.

But "logic" is one of those human skills which needs to be verified by Inspiration before it is trusted as a safe guide. And this particular piece of wishful deduction doesn't even square up with the manuscript it was supposedly based on, let alone the full body of inspiration. Rejecting creature merit is right; ruling out the need for human obedience is simply rebellion. Juggling those two truths is hard for the human brain to do. But the manuscript continues:

---

1. As always, the reader is encouraged to consider the entirety of these sources. I've tried to catch the essence of the message in the excerpts chosen, but the "Reader's Digest" version is never quite as good as the full book.

God has given men faculties and capabilities. God works and cooperates with the gifts He has imparted to man, and man, by being a partaker of the divine nature and doing the work of Christ, may be an overcomer and win eternal life. The Lord does not propose to do the work He has given man powers to do. Man's part must be done. He must be a laborer together with God, yoking up with Christ, learning His meekness, His lowliness. God is the all-controlling power. He bestows the gifts; man receives them and acts with the power of the grace of Christ as a living agent....

Let this point be fully settled in every mind: If we accept Christ as a Redeemer, we must accept Him as a Ruler. We cannot have the assurance and perfect confiding trust in Christ as our Saviour until we acknowledge Him as our King and are obedient to His commandments. Thus we evidence our allegiance to God. We have then the genuine ring in our faith, for it is a working faith. It works by love.[2]

I like that word, "genuine." It's a word that references reality, and that's a big deal. The same word shows up in our second source, too:

A genuine work is to be wrought in every believer. Evil habits are to be overcome; wrong traits of character, inherited and cultivated, are to be conquered; besetting sins are to be abandoned; wrong feelings are to be purged away. Transformation of character is to be the testimony to the world of the indwelling love of Christ. When faith works by love and purifies the soul, a transformation will take place. No human being can do this great and important work for himself, nor can he do it for another. This is the work of Christ for all who will put themselves unreservedly into the hands of God.

That's what the "genuine" article looks like (a detail commonly ignored by those enamored of Dr. Ford's teaching). No room is given to "creature merit," but that certainly didn't negate the need for obedience. And if that's not clear enough, the next paragraph doubles down on both aspects:

The conversion of the human soul is of no little consequence. It is the greatest miracle performed by divine power. Actual results are to be reached through a belief in Christ as a personal Saviour. Purified by obedience to the law of God, sanctified by a perfect observance of His holy Sabbath, trusting, believing, patiently waiting, and earnestly working out our own salvation with fear and trembling, we shall learn that it is God that worketh in us to will and to do of His good pleasure.[3]

"Genuine." "Actual results." It's reality.

But it's also the "greatest miracle," so you can give up the idea of total understanding. Partial comprehension? Of course. Significant knowledge? Sure... with some serious study. Total understanding? Nope.

Why not? Hard-wired limitations in the machinery of human intelligence, I imagine. It's still true, and I suspect it will always be true, that "the secret

---

2. E.G. White, "Danger of False Ideas On Justification By Faith," 1890; Manuscript 36, 1890

3. E.G. White, "Words of Instruction Regarding the Medical Missionary Work," January 12, 1900; Manuscript 6, 1900

things belong to the LORD our God." So let's focus on "those things which are revealed" because they "belong to us and to our children forever."

But why stop there? Did you think that was the end of the verse? Surprise, it's not. There's another clause, and it tells us something important about *why* God has revealed any of this to us: "that we may do all the words of this law."[4]

What a great reason to study! So we can get rid of selfishness and learn to embrace the value of self-sacrifice. So we can put the whole "to give is to live" thing into continual practice.

Our pursuit of a Christlike character, our obedience to the simple laws of heaven (there are only two of them, after all), is what opens the way for God to perform that "greatest miracle performed by divine power." No creature merit, no indolent indifference. Just faith.[5] Simple confidence in God.

In fact, that manuscript on creature merit has another thought that fits in nicely right here. Right when we're stretching our minds, trying to grasp the truth that the whole plan of salvation is the biggest "natural remedy" in the universe; that neither justice nor justification is arbitrary. Right when we realize that the topic is likely bigger and more detailed than our puny brains can deal with; or perhaps some day in the near future when the Holy Spirit has made it plain that He is calling us to do something that others will regard as foolish, because millions of people are dying unwarned.... Any of those would be a good time to read this:

> How much do we believe from the heart? Draw nigh to God, and God will draw nigh to you. This means to be much with the Lord in prayer. When those who have educated themselves in skepticism and have cherished unbelief, weaving questioning doubts into their experience, are under conviction of the Spirit of God, they see it to be their personal duty to confess their unbelief. They open their hearts to accept the light sent them and throw themselves by faith over the line from sin to righteousness, from doubt to faith. They consecrate themselves unreservedly to God, to follow His light in the place of the sparks of their own kindling. As they maintain their consecration, they will see increased light, and the light will continue to grow brighter and brighter unto the perfect day.[6]

What a great promise! And it works. Really, it does.

---

4. Deuteronomy 29:29
5. For clarity's sake, it should be said that there is no merit in faith. It does not earn our salvation. It simply opens the door of our hearts to receive what God has offered.
6. E.G. White, "Danger of False Ideas On Justification By Faith," 1890; Manuscript 36, 1890

CHAPTER 44

How Can These Things Be?

THE question in the chapter title was famously asked by a highly educated, unusually talented, and honored member of the Sanhedrin. Jesus' response was a rebuke for his ignorance of truths so important. Typically—and vitally— that rebuke was delivered with such solemn dignity and earnest love that Nicodemus was not offended. That's a skill worth striving for, by the way.

What interests me in this account just now is Ellen White's description of Christ's comments on that occasion:

> In none of His subsequent discourses did He explain so fully, step by step, the work necessary to be done in the hearts of all who would inherit the kingdom of heaven.[1]

In the New King James Version, the entire account[2] takes up four hundred seventy words. Let that sink in, before I make it worse.

If we strip out John's introduction and explanatory stuff, Nicodemus' words, Christ's repetition of certain points, His own introductory words (the "Most assuredly, I say to you," and "Do not marvel" kind of thing), and His implied rebukes for Nicodemus' ignorance, the count drops to three hundred thirty-six. And that includes the one hundred one words in verses 18–21, which many "authorities" believe is John's summation of the story rather than Christ's own words.

I wouldn't want to be seen as quibbling with authorities, but whether the final figure is three hundred thirty-six or two hundred thirty-five, I think it will work for my purpose at the moment. Simply put, my purpose is to point out that Jesus wasn't that committed to fussing out every detail of what our theologian friends call soteriology. In her treatment of the story, Ellen White puts this into perspective:

---

1. *Desire of Ages*, 176
2. John 3:1–21

Nicodemus had come to the Lord thinking to enter into a discussion with Him, but Jesus laid bare the foundation principles of truth. He said to Nicodemus, It is not theoretical knowledge you need so much as spiritual regeneration. You need not to have your curiosity satisfied, but to have a new heart. You must receive a new life from above before you can appreciate heavenly things. Until this change takes place, making all things new, it will result in no saving good for you to discuss with Me My authority or My mission.[3]

In writing this, Ellen White implies that Jesus may well have said more to Nicodemus than that which we have represented by three hundred thirty-six English words. That seems likely enough. But still... this is His fullest "*step by step*" explanation of "the work necessary to be done in the hearts of all who would inherit the kingdom of heaven"?

Perhaps I will not be alone in saying that such a view of the passage is not intuitively obvious to me. Where is the "1, 2, 3"? Where's the *theology?*

At the moment, this is of personal importance to me. I thought I was done writing this book. Sure, the temptation to modify a word or two here or there always remains until the ink is on the paper (or the data bits are on somebody's "device," I suppose), but I had covered all I intended to cover.

And then what I assume is the "new theology" *du jour* began to divide a group of acquaintances whom I had previously perceived as a quite cohesive, like-minded set of individuals. It turns out that—for the moment—the key word is *individuals.* Their like-mindedness didn't extend quite as far as I thought.

It's no real comfort to find that the same issue is threatening the unity of the denomination, at least in North America, and who knows where else or what the future of the issue will bring. The whole thing is looking like a bad re-run. We've seen the Sanctuary Awakening Fellowship of the '60s, the Desmond Ford theology of the '70s (which in time more or less coalesced into "Good News Unlimited"). There were the Celebration Churches (left wing) and the "Lord Our Righteousness" movement[4] (hard right wing, I suppose) of the '90s, and the "emerging church" movement (brought to us courtesy of the Catholic mystics) but which didn't really take shape in Adventism until the birth of The One Project in 2011.[5] What else? Surely I'm missing something.[6]

---

3. *Desire of Ages*, 171
4. We met this group and its convict leader back on page 196.
5. This is a major element of my previous book, *Tremble*.
6. I might add feast keeping, lunar calendar, holy name, 2520, flat earth, and any number of conflicting positions loosely wrapped up as "anti-trinitarianism." To my thinking, these fit into a slightly different category, since they all make their claim to significance on the basis that this special practice or belief is *the secret key* to salvation. My greatest concern is that I have yet to see these ideas result in any discernible positive change in the character of the believers. There are, no doubt good and godly individuals in these groups, who demonstrate a respectable humility in relation to God's word, and display admirable self-denial and self-sacrifice. It's just that I've never seen these ideas actually *produce* those desirable qualities.

It's interesting to consider the Church's response to all the above. The SAF was vigorously opposed, until Desmond Ford convinced their key leadership to pull a stunning doctrinal 180° in the early '70s. For a time, that made Ford the giant killer of Adventism. But then his own issues surfaced, and the church divided into pro- and anti-Ford factions.[7] The bitter battles of the Ford era soured the church on "confrontational" measures, so most of the more recent movements have managed to glide along with very little formal opposition.

The Celebration Church movement died out (sort of) by the simple workings of the market economy. It turned out that an unending emphasis on freedom from responsibility wrapped over into the field of church finance, and they more or less simply went broke. Which is not to say that they didn't leave their mark on many congregations at a somewhat lessened intensity.

Basically the lesson learned is that it's easier to operate as a "movement within the movement" than it is to pay one's own expenses. How this might play out with the coming decline of the Baby Boomers is a question, since enough of them have been sufficiently attached to the church to be loyal in their financial support, but sufficiently uninformed that they have little to no idea what is going on at the college churches and One Project gatherings that they indirectly fund.

In a somewhat different vein, The 1888 Message Study Committee has carried on its work for the last few decades, earning respect for its revival of interest in the whole 1888/Loud Cry history, but occasionally raising concern with their own theological prescriptions. Over the decades, Wieland and Short's original thought of "corporate repentance" as the way to revive the latter rain gave way to "It's easier to be saved than it is to be lost," and more recently to the concept of a universal legal justification.

Currently, the "latest new thing" goes by the name Love Reality, and—superficially, at least—shows some similarity to recent 1888 Message Study Committee positions. Unlike that group, it has quickly attained a notoriety not afforded many recent Adventist sub-cultures, having been directly and by name identified as a source of concern by the General Conference president.

Right about here is where *I'd* like to ask, How can these things be?

How can God's church be beset by, and sometimes support, such a clutter of teachings? Are all these groups just random mutations of Adventism, waiting for ecological pressures to select the fittest to survive? Or is there a definable cause for this chaos, a weakness which might be addressed?

Though each of the "movements" mentioned has had its own distinctives, at their heart the common "felt need" that makes any of them seem important is the

---

7. Ford's views on justification and sanctification concerned many, but only when he attacked the significance of 1844 and the Sanctuary doctrine as a whole did he face a formal disciplinary inquiry.

question of "assurance." Understandably, the saints are interested in their eternal destinies, and "What must I do to be saved?" is not only a question of past ages.

Significantly, this is the question that Jesus explained more fully to Nicodemus than to anyone else. But if—when you read John 3:1–21—you don't see a clear "step by step" outline, then perhaps you can imagine how the topic has produced such a variety of creative (sometimes problematic) theological perspectives.

Before looking for those steps to salvation which Jesus explained to Nicodemus, let's get an idea of what we are looking for. What would we expect a step by step portrayal of salvation to look like? Would it have forty steps? That's a good Biblical number. Or maybe just ten, one for each of the commandments. Of course, all the law and the prophets hangs on just two great commandments... are we looking for just two steps?

> The plan of redemption is comprehensive. Its parts are few, and each part depends on each other, while all work together with the utmost simplicity and in entire harmony.[8]

How many steps can there be if there are only a few parts to the whole business? Doesn't sound like forty, or even ten, really. OK... with that in mind, let's look at what Jesus said to Nicodemus. I'll pull out just the parts of the passage that sound like requirements or conditions:

1. unless one is born again,[9] he cannot see the kingdom of God.
2. unless one is born of water and the Spirit,[10] he cannot enter the kingdom.
3. whoever believes in Him should not perish but have eternal life.
4. whoever believes in Him should not perish but have everlasting life.
5. He who believes in Him....

Being barred from the kingdom clearly makes items one and two important... but except for "water baptism," they seem beyond our control. When Ellen White expands on "born... of the Spirit," she plainly says that it is "by the Spirit of God." That's not something we can do by ourselves.

Filling out a full 60% of the list, "believes" certainly gets the most emphasis, so... is that it? *We're done?* Are we really left with "only believe"?

Almost. That's it on the "requirements" in this passage. Salvation is by faith, after all. But there's another detail or two worth contemplating. Like any serious effort to produce a product, this one has a way to see if it's working right, so verses 20 and 21 provide a "system check," or "quality control point": "everyone practicing evil hates the light and does not come to the light,... but he who does the truth comes to the light." Any "belief" that fails this test, just fails.

---

8. E.G. White, "The Pearl of Great Price," March 29, 1898; Manuscript 44, 1898
9. Worth noting that in *Desire of Ages*, Ellen White opted for the marginal reading, "born from above."
10. Identified in *Desire of Ages* as "water baptism and the renewing of the heart by the Spirit of God."

But if this is a product-oriented process, what's the product?

Faith. That thing Lucifer lost. That thing we are all given a measure of.[11] The faith that can grow from a tiny seed into a large tree. And faith is anchored right here in this passage with the most famous verse in the Bible—John 3:16, which is simply a description of Jesus' "whole purpose" in coming to earth. We've seen this before. He came to give us a knowledge of God's character so that we would believe Him—would have confidence in Him; would have faith in Him—when He says... *anything!*

That "anything" is the "Your word is truth" kind of thing, the "sanctify them by Your truth" kind of thing.[12] It's the "every word that proceeds from the mouth of God"[13] kind of thing. His Word is "light," and every bit of it is "truth."

But the process starts with being "born from above," and—for some folks—that's a concern. They read their Bible... they pray... they go to church and sing happy songs... and still they wonder when this whole "new birth" thing is supposed to happen. They don't feel that much different, and sometimes even the happiest of the happy singers[14] can act more like "your father the devil,"[15] than someone who has been "born from above." A paternity test might seem like just what's needed here, but they worry, "If this new birth thing doesn't work for them, will it work for me?" and "What would *my* paternity test show?"

That's a lot of serious uncertainty... wasn't the "step by step" description supposed to make this all clear and simple?

Where's the "step by step" that tells us how to be "born from above"?

{Long dramatic pause.}

It's hidden! The key is to recognize that "whoever believes in Him" *is already born again.* That "belief" is the marker of the new birth. It's already happened at that point. But how do we *get there?* That's where we need our step by step.

The answer is in the Bible story Jesus mentions in verse 14: "As Moses lifted up the serpent in the wilderness, even so must the Son of Man be lifted up."

Uhh... that sounds more like a step for Jesus to take, not for me.

Right. Have you noticed that most everything important here is what God is going to do or has already done *for* us? The "human part" of this whole thing seems kind of hard to track down. It's important, but it's so small it's not even mentioned directly in John 3. We find it in the book of Numbers!

11. Romans 12:3
12. John 17:17
13. Matthew 4:4
14. Apologies to musicians. It's just an illustration, and theologians, or health reformers, or Christian educators, or even pastors can fall victim to the same trap of thinking that their theology, or health care, or teaching, or pastoring is what shows that they are born from above.
15. John 8:44

Everyone who… looks at it, shall live.[16]

There it is! That's the first step! Just, "look."

That is a little cryptic, so let's fill out the idea. The "looking" here is simply cooperating with the whole purpose of Jesus' mission to earth. He came to show us the Father; He asks us to look at what He died to show us. It's through that revelation of the divine character that our faith is to grow.

How?

Probably any way you need. Let's say you're an emotional type, strongly influenced in that way. What more do you need than Jesus' willingness to *die for you*, to prove that you can trust Him? Or maybe you're more the intellectual sort, with a penchant for facts and accuracy. Check out the seventy weeks prophecy of Daniel 9 that precisely predicted the coming of the Messiah. That's why Jesus began His public ministry by saying, "The *time is fulfilled*, and the kingdom of God is at hand. Repent, and believe in the gospel."[17]

Not enough detail to be convincing? Check out the prophecy of Daniel 2. Who else do you know who's laid out the flow of empire hundreds of years in advance?

"Looking" at the truth about God is the corrective treatment for anyone who has ever questioned God's love or wisdom. It's the means to actually heal the self-inflicted damage humanity suffered through believing Satan's deception.

When God says, "Don't do A, B, or C," that's love. He's trying to keep us from walking off a very real, totally non-arbitrary cliff. To say nothing, would be heartless, at best.

When He says, "Look at the wisdom and love revealed through prophecy and the life of Christ," He's trying to inspire us with enough faith to listen when He says, "Don't do anything foolish all the way up to X, Y, or Z."

It comes down to this: We aren't safe (for ourselves or others) without His guidance, and even with His guidance, we aren't safe if we don't trust Him enough to follow it. That's the reality. And it's not arbitrary.

When Nicodemus asked "How can these things be?" Jesus' answer was, "Look." But when I used those words, I was lamenting the proliferation of divergent (if not actually heretical) "movements" within contemporary Adventism. Is there an answer to that? How *did* such a chaotic state of affairs come to be?

No doubt there's all sorts of history that might shed some light on the process, but we'll take a bigger picture approach, because it all stems from a very basic misunderstanding, one we looked at long ago:

---

16. Numbers 21:8
17. Mark 1:15

Right and wrong are not based upon God's moral government; God's moral government is based upon a distinction between right and wrong. The erroneous view which many have of this subject causes them to rebel against God's law of government as arbitrary.[18]

It's easy to see why. If God set up the "moral order" as it is—including punishment for moral shortcomings, and I don't like it, *who's to blame?* If it's only *His* definition of "wrong" that makes my pet sin a capital offense, *who's to blame?* If He's going to burn me up and cut me off for all eternity, just because *He* doesn't like what *I* like, *who's to blame?* Sounds arbitrary to me.

But it's not, because the law is based on right and wrong, not the other way around. "Right and wrong" *is* reality. Right is right because it preserves life, and wrong is wrong because it destroys life. Murder with an indulgence is still deadly.

But confusion here can produce a variety of results, not just rebellion. It can produce a lot of stress and conflict. Here's why, and how:

Every one of the "movements" mentioned a few pages back has been shaped by a split in church members' perception as to which is most important, "love" or "law."[19] Members who find themselves continually worried over their personal acceptance with God, naturally long for some sort of assurance.[20] No one who believes in "salvation" wants to be "lost." When they read that "perfect love casts out fear,"[21] who can blame them for desiring a life without fear?

But lacking any framework to see salvation as a real process with an underlying reality, it's not hard for them to be convinced that God's love must be more accommodating than they once believed. If the ground rules of Salvation are just whatever God wants, surely—unless He's a tyrant—He would be "reasonable."

"What I used to believe produced more fear than anything else... how could that be right?" The trouble is that once the process of accommodating human weakness begins, it's very hard to stop it!

Others aren't so prone to self-doubt or fearfulness, so they face a different quandary. With a firm belief in the immutability and perfection of the law (got *that* right), and a conviction that God's people must rise to the law's standard (give them another point), the question becomes, "What *is* obedience?"

They *want* to obey. They believe that by God's grace they should be able to obey. But what, exactly, does that mean? Which details are covered by the law? Let's take a long-time favorite category for an example: temperance.

---

18. E.G. White, "The Moral Law," February 1, 1896; Manuscript 79, 1896. Quoted previously on page 41.
19. Astute readers will recognize this as a "Constructed Antithesis," the logical fallacy mentioned in footnote 10 back on page 260.
20. This may not be your challenge in life, but don't scoff. A traumatic episode experienced by that person's mother during the third trimester of their gestation means they will be born with a low baseline cortisol level, resulting in a lifelong reduction in stress resilience. (Ellen White scores again on prenatal influences.)
21. 1 John 4:18

Well, that's easy. Booze and weed are out. Cross off tobacco. Meat's gone. Might as well scratch milk, eggs, and cheese. No fizzies. Late nights gotta go. Not much sugar.[22]

This particular list might go on happily for quite a while, but at some point it gets tricky: "*What? Iodized salt? That'll be two punches on your Temperance Card.*"

I'm all in favor of a healthy lifestyle. The more the merrier... until it reduces my effectiveness in God's work. And spending all my time worrying about *my* diet is not a good way to work for anyone *else's* salvation. Remember: "Of no talent [God] has given will He require a more strict account than of our time."[23]

But doesn't that approach make *me* the arbiter[24] of the question? Now *I'm* deciding what's worth my time and what's not, what's right and what's wrong. Even if I don't try to make those decisions for other people,[25] I've moved into a mindset that regards "God's law" much as did the ancient Jews:

> The rules in regard to purification were numberless. The period of a lifetime was scarcely sufficient for one to learn them all. The life of those who tried to observe the rabbinical requirements was one long struggle against ceremonial defilement, an endless round of washings and purifications. While the people were occupied with trifling distinctions, and observances which God had not required, their attention was turned away from the great principles of His law.[26]

> In the days of Christ the Sabbath had become so perverted that its observance reflected the character of selfish and arbitrary men rather than the character of the loving heavenly Father. The rabbis virtually represented God as giving laws which it was impossible for men to obey. They led the people to look upon God as a tyrant, and to think that the observance of the Sabbath, as He required it, made men hard-hearted and cruel. It was the work of Christ to clear away these misconceptions. Although the rabbis followed Him with merciless hostility, He did not even appear to conform to their requirements, but went straight forward, keeping the Sabbath according to the law of God.[27]

This process inevitably reduces the law of God to a poorly defined mess; focuses thought on "trifling distinctions"; portrays "the character of selfish and arbitrary men" (but blames it all on God); sets up a standard which is "impossible for men to obey"; and turns attention "away from the great principles" of God's law.

---

22. I actually mean no ridicule in any of this. For what it's worth, my wife and I are "limited-processed-foods, light-on-the-free-fats-and-refined-flours, grow-can-and-freeze-our-own-fruit-and-veggies, vegans," if that's a thing. We consider it a blessing that our circumstances allow this, but not everyone is so situated, for any number of reasons, both good and bad.

23. *Christ's Object Lessons*, 342

24. You're right. Same Latin root as arbitrary.

25. Allowing for individual freedom in making health decisions is a great idea, since concern that nutritional yeast is neurotoxic, or a few dozen other such topics, is far from universal. I repeat, this is not ridicule. Not everyone will care about this issue or that issue, but if it's making *you* sick, you *ought* to care!

26. *Desire of Ages*, 396

27. *Desire of Ages*, 283

We should follow Christ's example and "not even appear to conform."
Bam! Take that, you legalists!

OK, calm down. There's another detail to notice. Jesus also "went straight forward, keeping the Sabbath according to the law of God." He didn't do away with the law; He kept it. He just kept it according to "the light." That's an example we should follow, in every area of life.

But doesn't that put us right back at square one? The ten commandments are great, but "the right way" to keep them poses challenges. How do I find "*the right way*" to keep every detail of the law? Right now, all I want to know is how much spinach I can eat. After all, it does have oxalate in it.

We're back to this:

> Right and wrong are not based upon God's moral government; God's moral government is based upon a distinction between right and wrong. The erroneous view which many have of this subject causes them to rebel against God's law of government as arbitrary.[28]

God's law didn't create right and wrong any more than Newton created gravity. God's law and Newton's formula[29] both serve to describe their respective realities. Importantly, the law provides an understanding of the natural result of getting out of step with reality. The further out of step you get, the worse things are going to be. It's the formula, the law, that warns us that the result of falling four hundred feet is worse than it is for falling four feet. That's why the penalty for sin is proportionate to one's "deeds."

> I saw that some were quickly destroyed, while others suffered longer. They were punished according to the deeds done in the body. Some were many days consuming, and just as long as there was a portion of them unconsumed, all the sense of suffering remained.... After all those whom he had deceived had perished, Satan was still to live and suffer on much longer.[30]

---

28. E.G. White, "The Moral Law," February 1, 1896; Manuscript 79, 1896. Quoted previously on pages 41 and 302.
29. Again, only for those who care: $F = G\frac{m_1 m_2}{r^2}$
30. *Early Writings*, 294, 290. Two interesting—and I would say, interrelated—challenges present themselves in this statement: how to fit this picture into the Biblical understanding of the nature of man (since nerves and brain would certainly not be the last "unconsumed portion" of a physical body exposed to fire), and how to fit it into a non-arbitrary, non-coercive divine administration. I have my own ideas, built around "creature merit" and "consent," but they fall beyond the scope of this volume. You may well develop a more accurate understanding than my tentative efforts, but you'll need to incorporate the following:
   "The exercise of force is contrary to the principles of God's government." *Desire of Ages*, 22
   "God could have destroyed Satan and his sympathizers as easily as one can cast a pebble to the earth; but He did not do this. Rebellion was not to be overcome by force. Compelling power is found only under Satan's government." *Desire of Ages*, 759
   "Satan and all who have joined him in rebellion will be cut off. Sin and sinners will perish, root and branch... This is not an act of arbitrary power on the part of God. The rejecters of His mercy reap that which they have sown. God is the fountain of life; and when one chooses the service of sin, he separates from God, and thus cuts himself off from life. He is 'alienated from the life of God.' Christ says, 'All they

The longing for "assurance" and the desire for "specifics" both go adrift because they misunderstand the law.[31] The law does not consist of innumerable separate rulings ("reasonable" or otherwise) on everything from iodized salt to mass murder to spinach with oxalate.[32] The law requires love for God and man, and that calls for knowledge and the ability to serve each of them as best we can. For both knowledge and ability, we look to God, in faith.

The real issue is faith. Have you seen enough of God's character—infinite love, infinite wisdom, infinite power—to trust Him when He says... *whatever?* Can you rest in confidence that He'll help you with your iodized salt question?[33] Or that He'll lead you through the valley of the shadow of death when the world threatens your life? If so, you've been born again. Your salvation is secure, even if you have a lot to learn yet.

If you can't trust Him, *look some more.* Look at the revelation of the Father that Jesus gave. That's why He came; that's why He died. Keep looking until you can open your heart to accept the light He sent you and "throw yourself by faith over the line from sin to righteousness, from doubt to faith."[34]

If, like Nicodemus, you are "not so much impressed by the necessity of the new birth as by the manner of its accomplishment,"[35] and you're struggling to figure out the specifics because you honestly want to obey on every point, just know that the *universal* specifics are only two: Love God supremely and your neighbor as yourself.

---

that hate Me love death.' Ephesians 4:18; Proverbs 8:36." *Desire of Ages,* 764

"God does not stand toward the sinner as an executioner of the sentence against transgression; but He leaves the rejectors of His mercy to themselves, to reap that which they have sown. Every ray of light rejected, every warning despised or unheeded, every passion indulged, every transgression of the law of God, is a seed sown which yields its unfailing harvest." *Great Controversy,* 36

This is the ultimate reason "as in the natural, so in the spiritual" is so important!

31. Not to paint either party in the worst possible light, but one can see in these desires the roots of the dichotomy upon which the "man of sin" has built his success:

"The papacy.... is prepared for two classes of mankind, embracing nearly the whole world—those who would be saved by their merits, and those who would be saved in their sins. Here is the secret of its power." *Great Controversy,* 572

32. All we need now is a little lemon juice for that spinach and salt. Good stuff! I'll pass on the homicide.

33. But bear in mind that a lot of questions aren't important enough to require an answer. Don't lose your soul over something that God doesn't think is important, at least not for you, not right then.

34. See E.G. White, "Danger of False Ideas On Justification By Faith," 1890; Manuscript 36, 1890, quoted more fully on page 295. Note that this faith that "throws" the believer "over the line" is active! Endless sitting and looking—without the active element of faith—will only confirm the sinner in fatal inaction.

While physical objects may be measured in inches or centimeters for distance, or cubic inches or cc's for volume, such units are useless in measuring a *force.* The only way to measure a force is to put it to work and see what it accomplishes. Thermal force makes mercury expand; electrical force moves the dial on a voltmeter; a car's engine turns a dynamometer to measure horse power. Forces are always measured by the work they do, because that's the only way they can be measured. And faith is a force, so it's no surprise that "works" figure prominently in the judgment.

35. *Desire of Ages,* 173

The specifics given to fallen humanity are what we know as the Ten Commandments; feel free to preach and teach that they are applicable to all. Some moderation and good judgment are required even here, though, because it can not yet be said that everyone has had the same amount of "light." That's why "this gospel" needs to be "preached in all the world as a witness to all the nations"[36] by the "continued incarnation of Christ"[37] in His church. Until then, we need to be cautious that we don't provide another unneeded example of the "foolishness of the wisdom of those who judge others who have not seen the light."[38]

But what about the details? For yourself,[39] start with Inspiration but know that not every piece of counsel is applicable to you. If it says "eat less," but you're already losing weight... think again. If it says "take more time to relax," but you know you've been lazy in the past... think again.

Some of this will have to be learned "by trying. Go right to work, and as you begin to try, you will feel the presence of angels right around you, and you will"[40] learn what God wants you to do.

But I was hoping for something a little more solid, something I could sort of lock in place and plan on. That sounds kind of uncertain; I'd really like to eliminate that.

Right. I see. Eliminate uncertainty. That does sound good. But given that eliminating uncertainty is a major feature in exactly zero Bible stories (who would need faith then?), perhaps you should consider adjusting your expectations, instead. But if you really do want to obey God's law, here's a thought that you *can* mark down as rock solid, *zero uncertainty*:

---

36. Matthew 24:14. The function of taking "this gospel" to all the world was discussed on page 95.
37. E.G. White, Letter to Brother and Sister S.N. Haskell, August 13, 1900; Letter 121, 1900. Quoted more fully on page 288.
38. E.G. White, Letter to A.T. Jones, April 18, 1900; Letter 59, 1900. Quoted more fully on page 246.
    The tendency to judge prematurely is seemingly baked right in to fallen human nature. Why give up hope so quickly? During Ellen White's time in Europe, she wrote of professed Christians descended from the sturdier stock of former years:
    "The spirit that is now prevailing in these valleys to evade the truth is wonderful. Everything as far as doctrine and faith are concerned are exactly the reverse from the ancient Waldenses. What will awaken the people professing godliness to be firm for the truth and duty? Maybe persecution. The perils of the times may arouse in them the spirit of faithfulness and religious fervor and steadfastness to the faith. Certainly perils are before us; and if these perils of the last days will bring into exercise the power of piety and self-denial and cross-bearing, which has died out of their churches, we may see an army of faithful ones brought out of the Piedmont valleys and from the Alps mountains who show the graces of the Spirit of Christ as true followers of the true Shepherd." E.G. White, "Diary: April 1886," April 26, 1886; Manuscript 62, 1886 speaks of as "persecution," is a fine example of the ministry of controversy.
39. For others... best be cautious about defining the details for other people. You can counsel, you can share what you've found, but leave room for them to seek God's personal leading, to experiment, to move forward on their own faith that Christ will lead them.
40. E.G. White, "Talk: Thoughts on First Peter 2," March 23, 1910; Manuscript 76, 1910. Quoted more fully on page 240.

Those who endeavor to obey all the commandments of God will be opposed and derided. They can stand only in God. In order to endure the trial before them, they must understand the will of God as revealed in His word; they can honor Him only as they have a right conception of His character, government, and purposes, and act in accordance with them. None but those who have fortified the mind with the truths of the Bible will stand through the last great conflict.[41]

The key for both sides of this "love or law divide" is to recognize that there is no divide. God's love *always* acknowledges the universality and immutability of His law, and God's law is *nothing but* loving counsel intended to shield us from the drastic effects of getting crosswise to reality. We create problems when we focus on God as the "Law-giver" to the exclusion of God as the "Faith-giver." With an infinite range of possible circumstances, none of us will ever be lawyer enough to understand by ourselves every aspect of how to live out the principles of the law. We will always be looking in faith to the example and instruction of Christ. That's why faith is the basis of salvation, the means of healing, and the eternal preserver of health.

"Mercy and truth have met together; righteousness and peace have kissed."[42]

If only the saints could follow suit.

---

41. *Great Controversy*, 593. I find it concerning that "the truths of the Bible" spoken of here are often taken to be quite formulaic—Sabbath, state of the dead, etc. I rather suspect that God's "character, government, and purposes" deserve some of that attention. How else could we "act in accordance with them"?

   Lest it appear that this imposes a requirement so stringent that no one living with imperfect understanding of such matters could be saved, do note that the question here is not the believer's salvation, but his or her ability to "honor" God, and that this comment concerns those who are to live "through the last great conflict." The point is obvious: while the standard of "salvation" is and always has been "faith alone," there is a higher burden of proof required to completely refute Satan's final accusations against God and His government. While "what must I do to be saved?" remains a valid and important question, we are also justified in asking, "What can I do to help end the reign of sin on earth?"

42. Psalm 85:10

CHAPTER 45

It Is Done!

THE world is like a huge cliff, with thousands of people walking off the edge every hour. Those with ultralights, or hang gliders, or maybe even just a parachute, do OK. The others die. Aerodynamics is a wonderful thing. The equipment and lessons were offered free to all. Some trusted the One who made the offer; others were just too busy having fun, or making money, or hating those who had done them wrong. For whatever reason, they never believed God wanted their best good.

The difference between a controlled descent and falling like a rag doll provides a dramatic contrast, one that men and angels all need to understand.

> The good and evil actions of men are so under God's control that He accomplishes His purposes and wise counsels by making plain the contrast between righteousness and unrighteousness.[1]

Satan and his forces demonstrate the evil that comes from lack of faith; "the lives of Christlike men and women"[2] demonstrate what faith can do. One or the other of these two antagonistic principles will at last control each individual.

At the end of the day, the most important example of this is found in the experience of Jesus, because *both* of these statements are true:

> [On the cross] Christ felt much as sinners will feel when the vials of God's wrath shall be poured out upon them.[3]

> In His closing hours, while hanging on the cross, He experienced to the fullest extent what man must experience when striving against sin.[4]

---

1. E.G. White, "Diary: The Lord has appointed his work," February 21, 1901; Manuscript 14, 1901
2. *Testimonies*, vol. 9, 135. Quoted more fully on pages 101 and 114.
3. *Testimonies*, vol. 2, 210
4. *Youth's Instructor*, July 20, 1899

Christ gave us the pattern for "striving against sin" in the ultimate display of faith and self-sacrifice. This example, *as well as* the display of Divine love, was needed before He could proclaim, "It is finished." Both were tested in the storm that beat upon His house with the solid foundation.

> Upon the cross, Jesus was to gain the victory for [His followers]; that victory He desired them to accept as their own.[5]

The victory that Christ won, He has bequeathed to us. Not that we will be victorious in our own strength, but under His guidance, and with His blessing, it is our following in His footsteps that brings about the "great healing" of His people. We will be upheld as surely as was Jesus.

> The power that inflicted retributive justice upon man's Substitute and Surety was the power that sustained and upheld the suffering One under the tremendous weight of wrath that would have fallen upon a sinful world.[6]

Until that victory is secured, the Lord will judiciously use the "ministry of controversy"—up to and including a "time of trouble such as never was"—to bring about the healing of both body and spirit.

Only under such stress can full faith be called forth from His people. Only by showing the world that their "dependence is upon a higher power"[7] will they be able to win every soul possible. We instinctively draw back in fear from such dependence, but legions of trusting angels would "gladly... resign their places to you that they might take your place and discharge your God-given trust."[8]

And one day, after "this gospel" is fully portrayed to all the world; after faith rises to Hebrews 11 levels[9] and Christians have simple confidence in God in everything, in every way, at all times, under any circumstance; after the Sabbath is truly observed by living out Isaiah 58;[10] after the seal of God has proven to the entire universe the success of God's great "experiment on human hearts through the exhibition of His mercy and abundant grace";[11] after "every earthly support"[12] is surrendered; after all "earthliness"[13] is consumed; and the "complete fulfillment of the new-covenant promise"[14] is proven through "transformations so amazing that Satan... stands viewing them as a fortress impregnable to his sophistries and

---

5. *Desire of Ages*, 490
6. E.G. White, "The Sufferings of Christ," September 13, 1894; Manuscript 35, 1895
7. E.G. White, Letter to Brother Merrill, March 25, 1898; Letter 24, 1898. Quoted more fully on page 203.
8. E.G. White, Letter to A.T. Robinson, November 7, 1892; Letter 45, 1892. Quoted more fully on page 202.
9. See *Bible Training School*, November 1, 1911. Quoted on pages 201 and 288.
10. *General Conference Bulletin*, May 31, 1909. Quoted on page 200.
11. *General Conference Daily Bulletin*, February 27, 1893. Quoted more fully on page 16.
12. *Desire of Ages*, 121. Quoted more fully on page 91.
13. *Great Controversy*, 621. Quoted more fully on page 131.
14. *Great Controversy*, 485. Quoted more fully on page 89.

delusions," and even "cherubim and seraphim... look on with astonishment and joy"[15]—*then* the sick will be healthy and the sinner will be forgiven and the Great Medical Missionary Himself will at last joyously pronounce them "perfectly well" and welcome them (plus all who had true faith, even if they didn't fully understand "this gospel") into the family of the unfallen.

The law has not changed. Sinners have been healed. God did not lie. At long last, the universe hears, "It is done!"

In the end, those who trusted God to supply their needs, who refused to "divorce the medical missionary work from the gospel ministry"[16] because they saw the need of taking up "a work identical with the work that Christ did,"[17] find that God is faithful. There never was any need for them to abandon service for others in order to take up the far-too-heavy burden of caring for themselves. Lucifer was wrong. God's provision was enough, more than enough, to meet even the challenge of the last days.

> John sees "them that had gotten the victory over the beast and over his image, and over his mark and over the number of his name, stand on the sea of glass, having the harps of God." And he says, "They sang the song of Moses, the servant of God, and the song of the Lamb." This is the same company mentioned by Isaiah, to whom it was promised that they should ride on the high places of the earth, and be fed with the heritage of Jacob their father.[18]

It's the medical missionaries of Isaiah 58 who get the victory over the beast. It's the medical missionaries who honor the Sabbath. It's the parents who understand the importance of "the choice and preparation of the home"; the youth who recognize that "true education is a missionary training"; the conscientious stewards of their God-given health who avoid "stimulants and narcotics," "extremes in diet," and even "flesh as food," who will live through whatever *Disease X* the combined forces of demons and human corruption throw at the world. It's the believers who put in the effort to learn how to serve "in the sickroom" who understand that there's no contradiction between "prayer for the sick" and "the use of remedies," who come to understand that a life "in contact with nature" is a huge step forward in the work of "mind cure"—these are the ones who will be in position to benefit those suffering ones caught in earth's final wave of illness. And it is those who understand the value of both serving "the helpless poor" and carrying on a "ministry to the rich" who will welcome the converts with the wealth to fund the loud cry.

---

15. *General Conference Daily Bulletin*, February 27, 1893. Quoted more fully on page 16.

16. E.G. White, "Come Out and Be Separate," November 1905; Manuscript 21, 1906. Quoted more fully on page 50.

17. E.G. White, "Christ Our Example in Every Line of Work," October 27, 1902; Manuscript 130, 1902; Quoted more fully on page 81.

18. E.G. White, "A Warning for This Time," 1900; Manuscript 48, 1900

And the Lord has blessed us with a full chapter on each of those topics. You can find them all in a single book.[19]

So that's my case, and now perhaps you will agree with me that Ellen White's masterpiece, *The Ministry of Healing*, is the pattern we need to follow in order to successfully finish the work of taking the three angels' messages to "every nation, tribe, tongue, and people" and meet the challenges outlined in her more famous book, *The Great Controversy.*

Both are necessary, for the combined goal is *Diasozo*—"made perfectly well, *and* brought safely through."

And yet... and yet... there is incredible danger in simple agreement. Pretend for the moment that every word of this book is perfectly true. Surely then I would be right, and you should agree with me. Then we would both be right, and we could walk and talk with God daily, delighted that we have learned His ways. Like "a nation that did righteousness, and did not forsake the ordinance of their God."[20]

> There are many who, unless they humble their hearts before the Lord, will be surprised and disappointed when the cry is heard: "Behold, the Bridegroom cometh." Matthew 25:6. They have the theory of the truth, but they have no oil in their vessels with their lamps. Our faith at this time must not stop with an assent to, or belief in, the theory of the third angel's message. We must have the oil of the grace of Christ that will feed the lamp and cause the light of life to shine forth, showing the way to those who are in darkness.[21]

If we do nothing to help others—even if we "afflict our souls" and "bow down our heads like a bulrush"[22]—there will be no revelation of the Father's character. The world will be no better off, and the loud cry will be no nearer completion. The cities will see no mighty movement, the funds will dry up, we will all die, and the Lord will continue the long delayed process of "preparing a people." He is, if nothing else, patient.

> When men begin to weave in the human threads to compose the pattern of the web, the Lord is in no hurry. He waits until men shall lay down their own human inventions and will accept the Lord's way and the Lord's will.[23]

Understanding the truth is no replacement for doing His will. So, please, find an armor bearer or two and attack the Philistines. Inspire and challenge others' zeal with the clear evidence of divinely supported success. Seek God's instruction before taking up His mission, but remember the divine ideal of a "speedy prepa-

---

19. Each of the phrases set off by quotation marks is a chapter title in *Ministry of Healing*. And I never even got to "Help in Daily Living" and the endlessly applicable "In Contact with Others."

20. Isaiah 58:2

21. *Testimonies*, vol. 9, 155

22. Isaiah 58:5

23. E.G. White, Letter to Brother and Sister J.A. Burden, July 29, 1901; Letter 181, 1901

ration for work."[24] Be mindful of fanaticism, knowing that it will come, but that it will never be reason enough to ignore God's call. Shake the gates of hell in a big city or two, and don't be bashful in sharing how you did it. There are plenty of others looking for the best ways to meet that challenge.

The role that God's people are called to play in earth's final days is what Ellen White described as "justification by faith."

> It is the work of God in laying the glory of man in the dust, and doing for man that which it is not in his power to do for himself.[25]

Perhaps the only thing "man" *can* do is to choose faith or demand the right to choose his own way. Sadly, that second option always ends in death.

But the exercise of faith—accomplished through no power or riches or wisdom or strength or honor or glory or blessing of man[26]—sets in motion all the events and accomplishments that end the great controversy. Though the work of salvation will amaze the universe forever, its mysteries will never again leave the slightest of doubts as to the character of God:

> In the light of the Saviour's life, the hearts of all, even from the Creator to the prince of darkness, are revealed. Satan has represented God as selfish and oppressive, as claiming all, and giving nothing, as requiring the service of His creatures for His own glory, and making no sacrifice for their good. But the gift of Christ reveals the Father's heart. It testifies that the thoughts of God toward us are "thoughts of peace, and not of evil." Jeremiah 29:11. It declares that while God's hatred of sin is as strong as death, His love for the sinner is stronger than death. Having undertaken our redemption, He will spare nothing, however dear, which is necessary to the completion of His work. No truth essential to our salvation is withheld, no miracle of mercy is neglected, no divine agency is left unemployed. Favor is heaped upon favor, gift upon gift. The whole treasury of heaven is open to those He seeks to save. Having collected the riches of the universe, and laid open the resources of infinite power, He gives them all into the hands of Christ, and says, "All these are for man. Use these gifts to convince him that there is no love greater than Mine in earth or heaven. His greatest happiness will be found in loving Me."
>
> At the cross of Calvary, love and selfishness stood face to face. Here was their crowning manifestation. Christ had lived only to comfort and bless, and in putting Him to death, Satan manifested the malignity of his hatred against God. He made it evident that the real purpose of his rebellion was to dethrone God, and to destroy Him through whom the love of God was shown.
>
> By the life and the death of Christ, the thoughts of men also are brought to view. From the manger to the cross, the life of Jesus was a call to self-surrender, and to fellow-

---

24. Chapter 58 of *Counsels to Parents, Teachers, and Students*, and chapter 44 of *Fundamentals of Christian Education* both bear this title. The content is similar, but not identical… so read both!
25. *Testimonies to Ministers*, 456
26. There are good reasons all those attributes are ascribed to God in Revelation 5:12.

ship in suffering. It unveiled the purposes of men. Jesus came with the truth of heaven, and all who were listening to the voice of the Holy Spirit were drawn to Him. The worshipers of self belonged to Satan's kingdom. In their attitude toward Christ, all would show on which side they stood. And thus everyone passes judgment on himself.

In the day of final judgment, every lost soul will understand the nature of his own rejection of truth. The cross will be presented, and its real bearing will be seen by every mind that has been blinded by transgression. Before the vision of Calvary with its mysterious Victim, sinners will stand condemned. Every lying excuse will be swept away. Human apostasy will appear in its heinous character. Men will see what their choice has been. Every question of truth and error in the long-standing controversy will then have been made plain. In the judgment of the universe, God will stand clear of blame for the existence or continuance of evil. It will be demonstrated that the divine decrees are not accessory to sin. There was no defect in God's government, no cause for disaffection. When the thoughts of all hearts shall be revealed, both the loyal and the rebellious will unite in declaring, "Just and true are Thy ways, Thou King of saints. Who shall not fear Thee, O Lord, and glorify Thy name?... for Thy judgments are made manifest." Revelation 15:3, 4.[27]

Remember that "to give is to live," that self-denial and self-sacrifice are prized by heaven, and are to be cultivated on earth. More than any other time, this is so now, for the soil of earth is depleted of holiness, and the weeds of sin are more rampant than ever. While happiness has always been the natural result of blessing others, it has been a long, hard slog to get God's people within striking distance of refuting Satan's claims. Nevertheless, Christ has assured us that "the way to be most happy is to seek to be a blessing to others, and that when men and women give themselves wholly to this work, the earth will be filled with the glory of God."[28]

"Wholly to this work" is a tall order, but it's not complicated. It just means that Christ's "whole purpose" is our whole purpose. Few of us—perhaps none of us—are fully there, yet. But God's plan for the healing of souls long absorbed in chasing the devil's rabbit of self-interest, is moving forward. Our Substitute is our Spotter, never allowing the weight of temptation to kill us. And He is also our Surety, providing in His own life the demonstration and guarantee that human beings can be brought back into His image. The challenge is before us.

Now we, Christ's purchased possession, must become soldiers of His cross, and conquer in our own behalf, on our own account, through the power and wisdom given us from above. The influence of the cross of Calvary is to vanquish every earthly and spiritual evil power; and we need to know the plan of the battle, that we may work in harmony with Christ.[29]

The "plan of the battle" is simple of, course, but foreign to the unconverted heart:

---

27. *Desire of Ages*, 57–58
28. E.G. White, "Christ Stilling the Tempest," November 3, 1903; Manuscript 130, 1903
29. *Review and Herald*, September 29, 1891. Quoted more fully on page 75.

It is our privilege to lay hold of the divine nature and say, Lord, you promised it. We ask thee to give us a spirit of self-denial and self-sacrifice.[30]

The tests today may be "little things," but those who are faithful in that which is least will be rewarded with far greater challenges. When one's life is on the line, it will be the memory of God's faithfulness in those little tests that provides courage for the big ones. And they'll be here, soon enough.

Kneeling to drink, and punching at the air, won't make the cut. Gideon started with thirty-two thousand soldiers, but routed the Midianites with only three hundred.[31] But don't worry. There's room for you in God's army! There are nearly five hundred times as many openings today![32]

PS: To those who actually read the whole book from front to back.... Congratulations! And thank-you! It's a long haul, I know. In a world "educated" by four-minute YouTube videos, reading any book is a rarity. And so I offer the following suggestion with much trepidation: You might want to read it again!

Way back in the Introduction, we looked at Ellen White's explanation that it is the "relation that... ideas have to one another that gives them value." There are many heavily interrelated ideas in the material we've covered.[33] When reading through the first time, the mind is occupied with connecting each new link in the chain as you go along. A second reading—after one has gained some familiarity with the further end of the chain—gives opportunity to see a multitude of "minor" relationships that couldn't be dwelt upon in the text, since they would make no sense to first-time readers.

So... I simply offer the suggestion, knowing that there is more to be seen than is possible with a once-over read. And yet, perhaps it is not necessary. After all, seeing that the Lord is right, that the law is not arbitrary, that healing does not violate justice, that spiritual fairy dust has no place in the plan of salvation... once you've seen that picture, you can't unsee it.

After that, spotting it in the Bible and Spirit of Prophecy is like looking for water in the ocean. Try reading the first chapter of Desire of Ages, for starters (but don't stop there; the next eighty-six chapters are loaded, too).

God bless,
Dave Fiedler

---

30. *General Conference Bulletin*, May 17, 1909

31. For those obsessed with measurement, that's 0.9375%, which makes Ellen White's "not one in a hundred" comment look pretty realistic.

32. You can do the math on this one! And, no, I don't think it's vital to know whether it's literal or symbolic.

33. In case you wondered, this is footnote number 1,105, and while a minority admittedly deal with trivia, the great majority cite some piece of Inspired wisdom.

Made in the USA
Columbia, SC
16 September 2024

41833205R00176